PROBLEMS IN FOCUS SERIES

Each volume in the 'Problems in Focus' series is designed to make available to students important new work on key historical problems and periods that they encounter in their courses. Each volume is devoted to a central topic or theme, and the most important aspects of this are dealt with by specially commissioned essays from scholars in the relevant field. The editorial Introduction reviews the problem or period as a whole, and each essay provides an assessment of the particular aspect, pointing out the areas of development and controversy, and indicating where conclusions can be drawn or where further work is necessary. An annotated bibliography serves as a guide for further reading.

TITLES IN PRINT

The Wars of the Roses
    edited by A. J. Pollard
The Reign of Henry VIII
    edited by Diarmaid MacCulloch
The Mid-Tudor Polity c. 1540–1560
    edited by Jennifer Loach and Robert Tittler
The Reign of Elizabeth I
    edited by Christopher Haigh
The British Problem, c. 1534–1707
    edited by Brendan Bradshaw and John Morrill
The Early Stuart Church, 1603–1642
    edited by Kenneth Fincham
Culture and Politics in Early Stuart England
    edited by Kevin Sharpe and Peter Lake
The Origins of the English Civil War
    edited by Conrad Russell
Reactions to the English Civil War 1642–1649
    edited by John Morrill
The Reigns of Charles II and James VII & II
    edited by Lionel K. J. Glassey

Series Standing Order

If you would like to receive future titles in this series as they are published, you
can make use of our standing order facility. To place a standing order please
contact your bookseller or, in case of difficulty, write to us at the address below
with your name and address and the name of the series. Please state with which
title you wish to begin your standing order. (If you live outside the United
Kingdom we may not have the rights for your area, in which case we will
forward your order to the publisher concerned.)

Customer Services Department, Macmillan Distribution Ltd
Houndmills, Basingstoke, Hampshire RG21 6XS, England

The Reigns of Charles II and James VII & II

EDITED BY
LIONEL K. J. GLASSEY

First published 1997 by
MACMILLAN PRESS LTD
Houndmills, Basingstoke, Hampshire RG21 6XS
and London
Companies and representatives
throughout the world

ISBN 0–333–62500–5 hardcover
ISBN 0–333–62501–3 paperback

A catalogue record for this book is available from the British Library.

This book is printed on paper suitable for recycling and made from fully
managed and sustained forest sources.

10   9   8   7   6   5   4   3   2   1
06   05   04   03   02   01   00   99   98   97

Typeset by EXPO Holdings, Malaysia

Printed in Hong Kong

Published in the United States of America 1997 by
ST. MARTIN'S PRESS, INC.,
Scholarly and Reference Division
175 Fifth Avenue, New York, N.Y. 10010

ISBN 0–312–16508–0 (cloth)

Contents

Preface

The completion of this book has taken longer than it should have done, and the fault is entirely mine. I should like to thank all the contributors for the prompt production of their essays, and to apologize to them for the tardy delivery of my own. I should also like to thank Vanessa Graham and Simon Winder of Macmillan; the former for suggesting the project and for offering much early encouragement, and the latter for his patience and understanding as the later stages were bedevilled by delay. I am grateful, too, to Patricia Ferguson, Barbara Beggs, Chris Fildes and Beverley Lynn for their much-appreciated secretarial help.

It proved oddly difficult to find a title for the collection which had not been used before and which reflected the intentions of the contributors. In the end I settled, perhaps rather dimly, for the names of two monarchs. Speaking as someone who teaches in a School of History and Archaeology containing a Department of Scottish History, I make no apology for including King James's Scottish numeral. I hope, however, that the social historians who are the authors of Chapters 7, 8 and 9 will forgive the implication that periods of history are bounded by the restoration and deposition of kings.

University of Glasgow   LIONEL K. J. GLASSEY

vi

1. Introduction

LIONEL K. J. GLASSEY

Henry Fairfax, D. D., Dean of Norwich, died aged sixty-eight in May 1702 and was buried in the south aisle of the nave of Norwich Cathedral. His monument represents him as deposited in the midst of a small stone library, although during his lifetime he had been described by a hostile critic as a man who never looked into a book and was 'good for nothing but his pipe and his pot'.[1] A long Latin inscription refers to his defence of religion as one of the deprived fellows of Magdalen College in Oxford during King James's reign. It also mentions the circumstance that he was a nephew of the victorious Parliamentarian general at Naseby, Sir Thomas Fairfax, who had been (so the inscription goes) 'a wise man whether one contemplates his actions or his counsels'. These laudatory references to the Captain-General of the New Model Army and a rebel who had defeated his King, Charles I, in battle, gave great offence in early eighteenth-century Norwich. An order was given to scrape the words 'Naseby' and 'wise' off the marble on which they were inscribed. A visitor to the south aisle of Norwich Cathedral today can still see the gaps in the Latin text where a Parliamentarian hero had once been celebrated.

I

This anecdote, dating from thirteen years after the end of the period covered by this collection of essays, is perhaps faintly absurd. It is here related because it illustrates, in lapidary fashion, a theme of great importance which runs through all the following chapters. This is the enduring legacy of the Civil War of the 1640s, still evidently capable of arousing strong passions sixty years later. The war had not been a romantic affair. It had been fought, at least in some areas, with great brutality, and it had led to much human suffering and much material destruction.[2] Every man and

1

3

woman who lived through the reigns of Charles II and James VII & II, and had reached the age of, say, fifty in 1689, would have had some personal memory either of actual violence or of the insecurity and fear of their childhood or adolescent experience. While the war continued, no-one could tell how long it would last. After it seemed to have ended in England in 1646, it was renewed in 1648 and again in 1651, and campaigns continued intermittently in Scotland and Ireland through the late 1640s into the 1650s.

When the war had finally ground to a halt, the succession of republican, theocratic and military regimes which followed the execution of the King in 1649 broke down one after the other. Oliver Cromwell's Protectorate gave some promise of permanence, but it did not long survive his death in September 1658. A year after Cromwell's death, a workable political settlement capable of providing peace and stability seemed further off than ever as the commanders of regiments of the army sparred with each other. Society never quite disintegrated; local government, economic life and the administration of the law continued after a fashion. It has been argued that 'anarchy' is too strong a word to apply to conditions in the British Isles in the winter of 1659–60, except perhaps for the last weeks of December 1659.[3] To those who lived through that winter, however, 'anarchy' cannot have seemed very far away.

It is too simple to say that the Restoration in the spring of 1660 was welcomed because it offered a return from all this insecurity to normality. The reasons for the Restoration of the Stuart monarchy, and the motives of those who accomplished it, were complex. One kind of normality, certainly, was the presence on the throne of the legitimate heir of Charles I. But how was the political, social, economic and religious 'normality', over which Charles II would preside, to be defined? There could be no return to the 1630s, as though the intervening period had never been. Those who accepted the Restoration in May 1660 were far from united in their expectations. Some believed that the Restoration offered the best opportunity of achieving the ideological and religious aspirations which had led them to draw the sword against Charles I in 1642. Charles II, they thought, would have learnt wisdom from the mistakes of his father and would be willing to make concessions, as indeed seemed to be promised in the manifesto, the Declaration of Breda, that he issued as a basis for his return. Some believed that the Restoration of Charles II provided a

chance for revenge against those who were perceived to have
started the war, carried it on and profited from it. Some had a
more mundane objective in view: to recover, or to retain, the land
or office or local power that they had lost, or acquired, during
and after the war.

There were those, too, who did not welcome the Restoration
at all. Many men and women had clutched at a vision of a
promised land at some point during the previous two decades: a
virtuous republic of free citizens; a godly Puritan commonwealth; a community of neighbourhoods released from the
oppression of kings, bishops and landlords. These utopias had
been successively snatched away from those who had been
captivated by them. There was still room for hope that the
opportunity to re-enter them might yet recur. In Chapter 2,
Mark Goldie makes it clear that much intellectual debate after
1660 had its origins in the 1640s and 1650s and turned on the
attempt to reassert, or to refute, ideologies and principles that
had been advanced during the conflicts of the middle of the
century.

The task of Charles II and his advisers in 1660 was not so much
to restore 'normality' as to find some method of encompassing
the different hopes of those who had acquiesced in the revival of
the Stuart monarchy in some harmonious settlement that all
could accept. At the same time, it was necessary to try to reconcile
those who were still clinging to the ideal of a commonwealth
without a king; or, if this turned out not to be possible, at least to
limit the power of republicans and radicals to do damage. The
process was often summed up in the phrase 'healing and settling'.
The preamble to the Act of Indemnity and Oblivion passed by the
Convention in 1660 proclaimed the King's 'hearty and pious
desire ... to bury all seeds of future discords and remembrance of
the former, as well in his own breast as in the breasts of his subjects one towards another'. A later clause in the Act made it a civil
offence, for which damages were recoverable, to reproach any
person in a manner 'tending to revive the late differences or the
occasion thereof'.[4] To owners of property, and especially of
landed property, this appeal to reconciliation was attractive.
'Future discords' were not, of course, avoided. However, as James
M. Rosenheim shows in Chapter 7, the common interests of
landowners as landowners were becoming at least as powerful a
determinant of their attitudes and behaviour as their differences
in politics and religion.

II

The fear of a renewed civil war, and a desire to prevent this threat from becoming reality, were uppermost in the minds of many of the subjects of Charles II and James VII & II throughout the period covered in this book. References to the memory of 1640 (when the Long Parliament had met), 1641 (when the Long Parliament ran out of control, Strafford was executed and Ireland had blown up in rebellion) or 1642 (when the fighting had begun in England) abound in parliamentary debates, in private letters and in the pamphlet literature of the late 1670s and early 1680s. Clearly, such recollections had powerful resonances. When in December 1678 it was proposed to impeach the King's minister Danby, the report 'gave infinite distraction and disquiet ... as if we were perfectly at 1641 with the case of the Lord Strafford in view and all the train of consequences that attended'.[5] 'Remember 1641', said Sir George Downing to the House of Commons in the same month, when a suggestion was made to receive part of the revenue in the Chamber of the City of London rather than in the Exchequer.[6] In October 1688, the Prince of Orange's *Declaration*, printed in Holland and distributed in large quantities before and after his arrival in November, drew its readers' attention to 'that Cruel and Bloody Massacre which fell out in [Ireland] in the Year 1641'.[7]

Earlier, in the first weeks of 1680, the presentation to the King of petitions requesting that the Parliament elected in the late summer of 1679 be allowed to meet reminded many, including the King, of events forty years before. Charles told Henry Mildmay, aged sixty and a former colonel of horse in the Parliamentarian army, who presented a petition from the county of Essex, that he 'remembred 40 and 41. Mildmay insolently reply'd "And I remember 59 and 60"'.[8] When Parliament eventually did meet in the autumn of 1680, the debates on the Exclusion Bill to eliminate the Duke of York from the succession to the throne revealed a consciousness on the part of many MPs that civil war was close. Some MPs may have been making debating points to alarm the House and embarrass their opponents, but others appear to have been genuinely frightened that no solution to the problem of a Catholic heir to the throne, other than civil war, was possible. In particular, speaker after speaker in the debate on 2 November 1680 leading up to the resolution to bring in the Bill implied that there would be a civil war whether the Bill was passed or not. If it passed, the

Duke would fight for his inheritance. If it did not pass, there would be a Catholic King and an attempt to root out the heresy of Protestantism – in other words, a civil war. The Duke's exclusion in England would still leave him King of Scotland, and war between the two countries would result. War in the British Isles would give Louis XIV the opportunity to join in.[9] The arguments employed in this debate reflected those in circulation outside the House of Commons and merged into a wider fear that civil war would result from the spread of 'Popery and arbitrary government'. J. D. Davies points out in Chapter 10 that a belief was current in Europe in the 1680s that the British Isles were once again on the verge of civil war, and that this was to weaken Britain's role in European diplomacy in the critical period leading up to the outbreak of the War of the League of Augsburg.

In 1688, the forebodings of the period of the Exclusion Crisis were realized when the Prince of Orange landed at Torbay and the King went to Salisbury to command his army against the invader. A civil war with an international dimension seemed actually to have started. Local insurrections in the North of England were reminiscent of what had happened in 1642. 'The war is prosperously begun', one Secretary of State wrote to the other from Salisbury.[10] His optimism was misplaced, but a battle on Salisbury Plain was expected, and surprise was expressed when the news of such a battle failed to arrive.[11] A naval action was anticipated also. It is well known that the English Admiral, the Earl of Dartmouth, failed to intercept the Dutch fleet on its passage through the Channel in the first days of November; what is less familiar is that he pursued the Dutch round the south coast with orders to engage. On 19 November he was within sight of the Dutch transports at anchor, before a second 'Protestant wind' dispersed his own fleet and damaged it beyond the possibility of further activity until the spring.[12]

During October, November and December 1688, one phrase, or some variant of it, recurs over and over again in public pronouncements and private letters: 'the effusion of blood'. Invariably, the context was that bloodshed must be avoided if at all possible. The prayer for peace and unity authorized for use in October in the face of the planned Dutch invasion beseeched the Almighty 'to prevent the Effusion of Christian Blood in our Land'.[13] A petition of peers to the King in mid-November requested him to summon a free Parliament 'to prevent the shedding of blood'.[14] At the same time, the nobility and gentry of

York petitioned the King to use such means as seemed to be appropriate 'for preventing the effusion of Christian blood'. A little later, after James's flight from London on the night of 10–11 December, the gentry of Lancashire put themselves under the protection of the Prince of Orange who was, they declared, endeavouring to rescue the nation from Popery and slavery 'with as little effusion as possible of Christian blood'.[15] The Earl of Bath assured the Prince of Orange that Plymouth had been secured 'without any effusion of blood'.[16] Princess Anne, on leaving Whitehall secretly, left behind a letter to her stepmother, the Queen, in which she wrote 'I ... hope all things may be composed without more bloodshed'.[17] The committee of peers, meeting first at the Guildhall, then at Whitehall, in the emergency conditions after James's flight, ordered Lord Feversham to withdraw his forces from the Prince's route to London to forestall 'the effusion of blood'. Feversham responded by disbanding James's army altogether 'to hinder the misfortune of the effusion of blood'. At the same time, William explained his decision to go direct to London, abandoning his plan to pass through Oxford, as dictated by his desire 'to prevent the effusion of blood'; and Lord Dartmouth, still in command of the fleet which was now at Spithead, began to dismiss Catholic officers 'to prevent the effusion of blood'.[18] The phrase had clearly become formulaic, but the frequency with which it was used reveals a genuine concern to avoid a civil war and a repetition of the experience of the 1640s.

Notwithstanding the urgent emphasis on the avoidance of 'the effusion of blood', a civil war did break out, although in England it was rapidly stifled. Even in England, the Revolution was not wholly bloodless. The estimates of men killed in skirmishes between the two armies at Wincanton and Reading vary, but the total figure may have been about fifty.[19] Plenty of blood was shed in Scotland and Ireland, as Ronald Hutton emphasizes in Chapter 4. In Scotland, the Duke of Gordon did not surrender Edinburgh Castle until 14 June 1689, and during the period when the Scottish Convention was debating the offer of the Scottish crown to William his garrison intermittently fired on the city, with results reported, rather strangely, as 'several Persons killed, tho not many'. Meanwhile, Viscount Dundee required to be defeated in a military campaign, that of Killiecrankie, which was not complete until the late summer of 1689.[20] In Ireland, a full-scale war between organized armies followed the Revolution and lasted

until 1691. In one battle alone, Aughrim in July 1691, the killed
and wounded on both sides amounted to 9000 men.[21]

III

If it is possible to identify any one reason why the memory of
the Civil War and the fear of its renewal so much influenced the
mentalité of the period, that reason would have to be religion.
Forms of worship, structures of church government, attitudes to
those of a different persuasion, the theology of Christian belief,
the development of the perennial conflict of Catholicism and
Protestantism in Europe – these, as John Spurr makes clear in
Chapter 5, were matters of grave concern to persons in all classes
of society. Moreover, as Peter Borsay observes in Chapter 8, a different kind of vulnerability, especially among town dwellers, was
engendered by the threat of plague and fire. These natural
calamities also had a religious dimension: either might be interpreted as a providential visitation punishing sin; and fire could
be, and often was, ascribed to incendiaries of a different religious
persuasion.

In the 1660s the principal fear was that Puritanism would
revive. By the late 1670s Catholicism had become more prominent as a potential danger. Protestantism was on the defensive, or
in retreat, all over Europe. Catholicism was the religion professed
by the heir to the throne, by the Queen, by more than one of the
King's mistresses and by Louis XIV. Underneath this visible
surface, the Treaty of Dover, the French subsidies and Charles's
own private views on religion (which found expression only when
a Catholic priest was admitted to him on his death-bed) might
have given some substance to the indistinct apprehensions of
Charles's subjects if they had known about them. King James was
later to tell Sir John Reresby that a conference of Jesuits described
by Titus Oates had indeed taken place on the day that Oates had
specified, but not at the White Horse Tavern as Oates had
thought. It had been held at, of all places, St James's Palace itself,
where the then Duke of York had resided; 'if that had been
understood by Oats', said the King, 'he would have made ill worke
for me.'[22]

The 'Popish Plot' of 1678, with all its excesses, can be
interpreted as the reflection of a perfectly genuine 'popular
ideology'.[23] Titus Oates articulated a set of ill-informed,

propaganda-influenced, but deeply felt concepts, incorporating what were essentially folk-memories of the reign of Mary Tudor, the plots of Mary Queen of Scots, the Armada and Guy Fawkes, plus the more recent memory of the Irish Rebellion of 1641. Tim Harris illuminates in Chapter 6 the mechanics of the process by which Oates's message was disseminated, so that a powerful and uncontrollable surge of anti-Catholic 'public opinion' emerged which dictated the course of politics over a period of two or three years.

This is, of course, emphatically not to say that the charges of Oates and his fellow-perjurers against individual Catholics were true, or even half true. Oates was a professional informer. It is surprising that neither the King nor any of the surviving Privy Councillors in 1678 seem to have remembered Oates's earlier appearance before the Council in 1675, when he had tried unsuccessfully to incriminate a member of the Hastings corporation, with whom he had evidently quarrelled, on charges of speaking irreverent, scandalous and opprobrious words.[24] This earlier discouragement may have persuaded Oates, if only subconsciously, that to achieve results in his chosen career some element of religious prejudice had to be built into his accusations.

Having said this, it should also be emphasized that religion was not the all-important feature of the Revolution of 1688. King James was not overthrown in the winter of 1688–9 only because he was a Catholic, and for no other reason. Contemporaries had bracketed together 'Popery and arbitrary government' as a shorthand encapsulation of their distrust of the Duke of York during the Exclusion debate, and when James eventually came to the throne it was 'arbitrary government' at least as much as 'Popery' that aroused resentment. The appearance of the Duke of Monmouth as an alternative Protestant claimant in the summer of 1685 had attracted little response from the property-owning classes. It was James's management of his powers in politics and government that caused alarm. The assertion of obsolescent royal prerogatives such as the dispensing and suspending powers; the employment of Catholics in high office notwithstanding the 1673 Test Act; the changes in the law courts among the judges and at the universities; the expansion of the army; the insult to the country gentry implied in their dismissal from the commissions of the peace and the militia; the remodelling of the corporations; the temporary imprisonment of the Seven Bishops (not so much their trial, in which they were of course acquitted); the strong-arm methods of seeking to secure the election of a packed, pre-engaged Parliament: these were among the main grounds for complaint against James. The fact that he was a Catholic King exacerbated these complaints, but did not create the conditions in which his replacement by William was possible.

Moreover, James's deposition was an unexpected development which few anticipated and which James himself only made possible by his escape to France. The initial purpose of many who joined in the early stages of the Revolution was to assist the inscrutable William in bringing James to see reason in his conduct of domestic affairs, not to overthrow him altogether. The Revolution in England has something of the character of a counter-revolution. The objective was not necessarily to remove a Catholic King from the throne. It was to persuade a Catholic King to subordinate his private convictions to the duties of Protestant kingship in the hope of a return to stable monarchical government.

Admittedly, the Revolution in Scotland was different. The Scottish Convention did not deem James to have 'abdicated' by his flight. He was declared to have 'forefaulted' the Scottish crown because he had broken 'the knoune lawes, statutes and freedomes of this realme'.[25] The word 'forefaulted' had been reached with some difficulty, and the decision to use it was significant.[26] The Scottish Revolution did not aim at a return to a former stability imperilled by James's aberrations. It aimed at persuading a new King to agree to reform and change; not only reform in the management of the Scottish Parliament, but also, and especially, change in the organization of church government. Religion was more to the fore in Scotland than in England in 1688–9, and the rapid creation of a Presbyterian Church of Scotland in the immediate aftermath of the change of monarchs was to be a permanent legacy of the Revolution.

IV

The vulnerable, fragile character of a society which remembered one Civil War and feared another, and the tensions injected into politics by religion, should not obscure another aspect of the history of the British Isles in the period covered by this book. As Chapter 8 by Peter Borsay and Chapter 9 by J. M. Ellis both demonstrate – albeit with important qualifications – the national

economy, local society, and metropolitan and provincial culture
were all in a phase of expansion. This expansion clearly had a
potential for dynamic growth in the future. Ronald Hutton
confirms in Chapter 4 that similar trends are apparent in
Scotland and Ireland. Many parts of the British Isles were wealthier in the late 1680s than they had been in the early 1660s, and
this wealth was diffused further down the population.

In some respects not covered in this book, there were signs of
change and development which were to lead to the emergence of
a more intellectually sophisticated society in the eighteenth
century. A belief in the malevolent power of witchcraft was still
apparent in the 1680s, but it was already being actively discouraged by at any rate some of the more enlightened judges of
Charles's reign.[27] Philosophical enquiry was still overwhelmingly
dominated by Christian belief, but it was beginning to incorporate
a debate about the significance of the discoveries of organized
science. Sir Isaac Newton, Robert Boyle, John Flamsteed and
Edmond Halley were joined in their different spheres by statisti-
cians and political economists such as Sir William Petty and
Gregory King. Medicine and schoolteaching were in the early
stages of the process which saw the doctor and the pedagogue
established as members of 'professions' by the middle of the eighteenth century.[28] The period conventionally described as 'the
Restoration' saw considerable, if not always wholly respectable,
achievements in literature, where Andrew Marvell and John
Dryden were accompanied by a host of lesser but talented and
original figures.

Space does not permit a more full consideration of these
aspects of the period; it would require another collection of essays
to do justice to them. It is important to remember, however, that
while politics and religion were among the main preoccupations
of many of those who lived through the reigns of Charles II and
James VII & II, they were not the only ones. The 'prevention of
the effusion of blood' was one concern; the maintenance and
extension of the modest prosperity described by J. M. Ellis in
Chapter 9 was another. 'It was very strange', wrote Sir John
Reresby about the reception in Yorkshire of the news that William
of Orange was preparing to invade, '... that neither the gentry
nor common people seemed much afeard or concerned at it,
saying, The Prince comes only to mentain the Protestant religion;
he wil doe England noe harm.'[29] By 'only to maintain the
Protestant religion' is meant that this was the sole purpose of the

Prince's expedition, not that his purpose was unimportant. Even so, the impression of indifference that Reresby records, and his sense of the strangeness of it, is revealing. Perhaps, after all, the Restoration of 1660 and the Revolution of 1688 are inappropriate boundary markers for the organic evolution of British society.

2. Restoration Political Thought

MARK GOLDIE

I

In 1661, the Speaker of the House of Commons, Sir Edward Turnor, likened England after the execution of Charles I to the five-day anarchy permitted among the ancient Persians so that they might appreciate kingly rule. 'The forms and species of government are various', he explained, 'monarchical, aristocratical, and democratical: but the first is certainly the best, as being the nearest to divinity itself'.[1] As these remarks suggest, civil war and regicide made a generation of gentlemen more, not less, willing to endorse the doctrines that sovereignty lay in the crown and that rebellion was never justified. It now seemed incontrovertible that the crown's supremacy was the foundation of the gentry's own authority. 'There can be nothing', wrote Thomas Hobbes, 'more instructive towards loyalty and justice than will be the memory, while it lasts, of that war'.[2]

During the Civil War the Long Parliament's defenders had deployed, with increasing self-confidence, the arsenal of anti-absolutist arguments developed by Scottish Calvinist and French Huguenot radicals in the late sixteenth century. They asserted that the source of political authority lay in the community, and that the king was an officer of the state, answerable to the people. The community, incorporated in parliament, might legitimately coerce a tyrannical ruler to defend its rights. The premise was populist, the conclusion revolutionary. In 1649 the Rump Parliament declared that 'the people are, under God, the original of all just power' and 'the Commons of England, in Parliament assembled ... have the supreme power in this nation'.[3]

The legislation of the early 1660s, as the Earl of Clarendon put it, 'pulled up all those principles of sedition and rebellion by the roots'.[4] Several statutes provided explicit affirmations of political doctrine, among them the Regicide, Militia, Treason,

12

Corporation and Triennial Acts. They declared that the period of the 'late usurped governments' had seen 'many evil and rebellious principles ... distilled into the minds of the people', which must now be 'prevented'. Parliament's war was not a legitimate resistance but a 'barbarous rebellion' bred by 'fanatic rage'. The attempt to enforce regular parliaments was a 'derogation of his majesty's just rights and prerogative inherent to the imperial crown'. The crucial pronouncement was that 'neither the peers of this realm, nor the commons, nor both together in Parliament, or out of Parliament, nor the people collectively or representatively, nor any other persons whatsoever, ever had, hath, or ought to have, any coercive power over the persons of the kings of this realm'.[5]

The Cavalier Parliament instituted an oath embodying these abjurations, which was added to the existing oaths of Allegiance and Supremacy. Office-holders and clergymen were required to swear that 'it is not lawful upon any pretence whatsoever to take arms against the king, and that I do abhor that traitorous position of taking arms by his authority against his person or against those that are commissioned by him'. In 1665 yet another oath was devised, although not generally imposed: 'I will not at any time endeavour any alteration either in church or state'.[6]

The next element in the disciplining of doctrine was the condemnation of dangerous texts. In 1660 a proclamation ordered the burning of two defences of the regicide, John Milton's *Defence of the People of England* (1650) and John Goodwin's *The Obstructors of Justice* (1649). In Scotland, George Buchanan's *Rights of the Kingdom of Scotland* (1579) and Samuel Rutherford's defence of the Covenanters' war, *Lex Rex* (1644), were denounced.[7] The chief republican theorist of the Interregnum, James Harrington, author of *Oceana* (1656), was jailed. Sir Henry Vane was executed in 1662 after audaciously 'acknowledging no supreme power in England but a Parliament'. He was, said Charles II, 'too dangerous a man to let live'.[8] In 1663, the tract *Mene Tekel* claimed that Scripture 'doth not forbid a private person to resist ... a cruel and tyrannous governor'. The printer was hanged, disembowelled and quartered.[9]

Throughout the Restoration, censorship and sedition laws made it difficult to disseminate radical ideas. In 1677 John Starkey was prevented from republishing Nathaniel Bacon's *Historical Discourse of the Uniformity of Government* (1647) and its *Continuation* (1651), because they argued for the elective and contractual origins of kingship.[10] In 1681 Shakespeare's *Richard II* – about a King deposed

– was banned.[11] In 1686, Dr Henry Edes of Chichester was convicted of high misdemeanour for recommending, during dinner conversation, Philip Hunton's *Treatise of Monarchy* (1643), one of the Long Parliament's principal theoretical defences.[12]

II

During the Restoration era, the cult of kingship flourished as never before. It drew upon a diversity of rhetorical and cultural resources, and was expressed in drama, poetry, sermons, prayers, treatises, and the visual and plastic arts. We can identify at least six types of monarchical idiom.

First, the Augustan. The deployment of Greek and Roman models came naturally to people steeped in classical learning. The 'commonwealthmen' had drawn inspiration from the virtues of the Roman republic, the writings of Cicero, Livy and Plutarch, and the examples of Cato and Brutus. Royalists, by contrast, extolled the Emperor Augustus, and the courtly encomia written by Horace and Virgil. Augustus represented stability in the wake of civil war, martial glory, and refined arts and manners. Charles II's coinage depicted him wearing the imperial laurel wreath; his statues which today stand at Chelsea Hospital and in Edinburgh have him garbed in imperial dress; and his contemporary biography was called *Augustus Anglicus* (1686). John Dryden's *Astraea Redux* (1660) closes with the acclamation:

> Oh Happy Age! Oh times like those alone
> By Fate reserv'd for Great Augustus Throne!
> When the joint growth of Armes and Arts foreshew
> The World a Monarch, and that Monarch You.[13]

Second, the Platonic. Medieval writers assimilated earthly rule to a cosmology which described God's government of the universe. The ultimate source was Plato's *Timaeus*. The divine principles of unity and harmony were said to be reproduced at each level of creation, in the macrocosm of the heavens and the microcosm of the sublunary spheres. This idea in early modern thought has been characterized as the 'great chain of being' and as the 'political theory of order'. God was monarch of creation, the lion the king of the jungle, the head the ruler of the body, and the monarch the head of the body politic. To unhinge these correspondences was to violate cosmic harmony. In his *Discourse Concerning Supreme*

Power (1680), Sir John Monson wrote, 'God is a God of order ... his providence upholds all according to the same model by setting a kind of hierarchy and regiment amongst all the several societies of the creatures'. Thus, for example, 'bees, which of all others maintain a most perfect polity of monarchical government amongst them ... are the best emblems of good subjects'.[14]

Third, the Davidic. The Bible, of course, matched the classics as a pre-eminent cultural resource. Typological explications of the Scriptures were commonplace: people and events in the Old Testament were identified as prophetically foreshadowing the Christian era. What God ordained for his Chosen People was prescriptive for modern times. Dozens of sermons dwelt on 2 Samuel, Chapters 19–22, and compared Charles II with King David. In his *Parallela* (1660), Simon Ford declared that David's return after Absalom's rebellion seemed 'verbatim ... a chronicle of these times'. In Dryden's great Tory poem, *Absalom and Achitophel* (1681), Charles is the 'Godlike David', whom 'the sober part of Israel' proclaim their 'Lawful Lord'.[15]

Fourth, the cultic. Charles I was accorded saintly status, and several new churches, such as that at Tunbridge Wells, were dedicated to Charles the Martyr. The anniversary of his execution, 30 January, was appointed a day of remembrance, and, together with 29 May (Charles II's accession day) and 5 November (Gunpowder Plot day), was included in the Prayer Book. Sermons on Charles the Martyr were vehicles for inculcating the new political orthodoxies. They dwelt upon the sacredness of majesty, the damnableness of rebellion and the duty of obedience. Charles I's *Eikon Basilike* (1649) was a bestseller: its frontispiece showed the pious King holding a crown of thorns and bathed by divine rays. Royalist images of kingship drew upon both the awesome majesty of God the Father and the patient suffering of God the Son.[16]

Fifth, the miraculous. Charles II revived the ancient practice of 'touching for the King's Evil', the royal healing power said to cure scrofula. He touched 100 000 or so people during his reign. Parish authorities signed certificates of candidates for touching and sometimes paid the travel expenses of the poor. The ritual, and the disease's pathology, were explained by the royal surgeon John Browne in his *Charisma Basilicon* (1684). He included a poem:

The Healing Virtue of the Royal Hand,
(Next to our King, the Glory of the Land)
Which Heaven on our Monarchs does bestow,

To make the Vain, Conceited Rabble know
That Pow'r and Government, from Heaven flow.[17]

Sixth, the feudal. The crown's feudal rights, the residuum of which were abolished in 1641, were not revived after 1660, but a handful of writers tried to revive a feudal case for monarchy. In his *Tenenda non tollenda* (1660), Fabian Philipps argued that feudal tenures were the sinews of stable kingship and that their abolition was a terrible mistake. All landed proprietors ought to have a direct bond of homage to the king; in a freeholding society no obligations would extend beyond the contractual.[18]

None of these discourses and practices, however, was integral to the dominant style of royalist political theory that developed in the second half of Charles II's reign. It is important to stress, for example, that the 'royal touch' played no part in the theoretical defence of absolute monarchy, and it is mistaken to suppose that the formal doctrine of the Divine Right of Kings was 'mystical' or 'magical'. It was, as we shall see, starkly juristic, and no less rationalist than its rivals.

It is also the case that few of these manifestations of royalism necessarily entailed prescriptions about the actual distribution of power within the English polity. Except for a handful of republicans, politicians of every stripe abhorred the regicide and applauded the principle of monarchy. What type of monarchy remained an open question. Some courtiers urged the king to augment his power in more substantive ways. The Duke of Newcastle's *Advice* (c. 1659) was powerfully influenced by Machiavelli. Newcastle ponders, like his mentor, whether it is best for kings to be loved or feared, and he devises a set of maxims of state. He advises that the power of arms and money is essential: 'Without an army in your own hands, you are but a king upon the courtesy of others'. The king must also be vigilant against urban élites, for 'every corporation is a petty free state against monarchy'. He should also be careful to discipline preaching and the universities, or 'philosophical book men will raise rebellions'. The creation of peers should be limited; parliaments should not be prolonged; the press should be censored.[19] In the early years of the Restoration these ambitions were only partly achieved, but by the time that the Earl of Orrery, in his *Treatise of the Art of War* (1677), urged Charles II to professionalize his army, many had come to feel that the character of the regime was in process of drastic alteration.

III

Practically all of the Restoration era's systematic political theorizing belongs to the decade between 1675 and 1685. Before that, the Cavalier–Presbyterian consensus that made the King's return possible still obtained. After that, fear of 'Popery and arbitrary government' generated a Whig sensibility, while fear of 'Presbyterian fanaticism' generated Tory sentiment. Many individuals would veer from one allegiance to the other, but the ideological fissure was real enough.

The term 'Whig' is distracting: it was not coined until 1679 and was never the exclusive party tag. Contemporaries talked of the 'Presbyterian party'. They meant those whose ideals were anchored in the attempts during the 1640s to force Charles I to a negotiated settlement in which significant authority would be transferred to Parliament. These aims were embodied in the Newcastle and Isle of Wight treaties (1646–8). Such projects were revived in 1660, but swept aside in Charles II's hurried restoration. In a crucial sense, the 'Whig movement' was the revival of the Presbyterian ambition to entrench 'mixed monarchy'. Henry Foulis, an aggressively Cavalier divine, devoted much of his indictment of Presbyterians, his *History of the Wicked Plots* (1662), to proving that they were guilty of seeking a conditional restoration. He was glad that the Restoration settlement had not 'chained up his majesty to some Newcastle or Isle of Wight like conditions'. His book was to be popular among Tories.[20]

In 1675 the King's chief minister, the Earl of Danby, attempted to impose the 'no alteration' oath of 1665 upon members of Parliament, and was fiercely resisted by the Earl of Shaftesbury. In 1675–7 Parliament was prorogued for fifteen months, provoking demands that the principle of regular parliaments be upheld. By the close of 1678 fears of a standing army, a 'pensioner' or bribed Parliament, and Popish counsels at court were added to the opposition's tally.[21]

The year 1675 marked a turning-point. Tories such as Roger North deeply regretted the failure of 'Danby's Test', regarding it as essential for suppressing 'the old republican principle that power is in the people'.[22] On Shaftesbury's part, there appeared a tract entitled *A Letter from a Person of Quality*, sometimes attributed to his assistant John Locke. It may be regarded as the manifesto of the embryonic Whig cause. It opens with the unequivocal assertion that 'there has now for divers years, a design been carried on, to change the lawful government of England into an absolute tyranny'. Danby's oath was part of a design to 'declare us first into another government more absolute' and then 'make us swear to it'. The 'high episcopal man and the old Cavalier' would engross to themselves 'all the power and office of the kingdom'. The 'first step' was the Corporation Act and 'the next step' the Militia Act, their doctrinal apparatus swept into statute by 'the humour of the age, like a strong tide'. Now 'priest and prince' were to be 'worshipped together as divine in the same temple'.[23] Shaftesbury's *Two Speeches* (1675) was no less forthright. 'My principle is, that the king is king by law, and by the same law that the poor man enjoys his cottage', and that if the king should govern 'by an army, without his parliament, 'tis a government I own not, am not obliged to'. The Earl singled out for attack the Anglican hierarchy, for systematically encouraging the notion 'that monarchy is of divine right'.[24] Shaftesbury's party had no doubt that the political theory of absolutism had become state doctrine.

Among modern historians the concept of absolutism poses difficulties, especially in the English context. Both the fabric of government – the constraints on military, fiscal and statutory power – and the intentions of individual monarchs – the languor of Charles II – inhibit its application. As we have seen, in 1660 the political élite was willing to pay an ideological price to prevent popular insurrection, and some advisers had urged Charles to seize greater power. None the less, we ought to distinguish practical from theoretical ambition, for it is clear that absolutism achieved greater perfection in the ideological than in the governmental sphere. There is a further inhibition: no absolutist theorist denied the role of parliament or the rule of law. We shall need to discover how such a position was coherent. The main aim of the Tory ideologists was not substantially to alter the English polity, but to offer the most persuasive theory to explain existing constitutional arrangements, and thereby to provide the crown and the Anglican–Royalist élite with the trump cards.

IV

When, in his *Two Treatises of Government* (1689), John Locke assaulted Tory political thought, he singled out the 'false principles' of Sir Robert Filmer. It is Filmer who stands – alongside King James VI & I – as the best known exponent of absolutist theory in

Stuart England.[25] Filmer's fame was posthumous. He died in 1653, having published several tracts on behalf of the Cavalier cause during the Civil War, most notably *The Freeholder's Grand Inquest* (1648). However, his chief work, *Patriarcha, or the Natural Power of Kings* (*c.* 1628?), remained in manuscript until 1680, when Archbishop Sancroft arranged for its publication to bolster the Tory cause. Filmer threw down two gauntlets. He claimed that absolute monarchy was ordained by the law of nature, exemplified at the Creation in Adam's rights as husband, father, property owner and king; and he argued that an investigation of medieval English history revealed that parliament was subordinate to the crown. Filmer's patriarchal and constitutional theses were central to Tory absolutism.

Filmer put the case starkly and comprehensively – but he was scarcely a lone voice. In the decade of Tory absolutism several treatises made their mark, notably William Falkner's *Christian Loyalty* (1679), Thomas Goddard's *Plato's Demon* (1684), George Hickes's *Discourse of the Sovereign Power* (1682), Nathaniel Johnston's *Excellency of Monarchical Government* (1686), John Nalson's *Common Interest of King and People* (1678), William Sherlock's *The Case of Resistance* (1684), Edmund Bohun's *Defence of Sir Robert Filmer* (1684) and, in Scotland, Sir George Mackenzie's *Jus Regium* (1684). Their ideas were remarkably homogeneous, and they were echoed in hundreds of sermons and pamphlets. Their principles were also strikingly continuous with two earlier crescendos of absolutist theorizing: the first decade of the century, when James I and his defenders argued against his Scottish Calvinist and Continental Catholic detractors, such as George Buchanan and Cardinal Robert Bellarmine; and the 1640s, when Charles I's polemicists wrote against the Parliamentarians.[26]

We can encapsulate the Tory case by examining one example: a manuscript tract, written by Francis Turner, Master of St John's College, Cambridge, future Bishop of Ely, and a key figure in court circles.[27] Written in 1677, it was provoked by the passages in Shaftesbury's *Two Speeches* cited earlier. Turner's tract is headed 'Whether the royal power and sovereignty of kings be immediately from God only, and neither from the pope, or people, nor from the laws of the countries where they are kings'. His uncompromising answer is that 'monarchy is of divine right' and that 'England is an absolute monarchy'.[28]

Turner's first move was to claim that 'supreme power (wherever it be) is, and of necessity must be, absolute'. This is the essence of the doctrine of sovereignty: the idea that in any given state there must be an ultimate source of law and arbitration. Such sovereignty is absolute in the sense that there can be no appeal beyond it: for if there were a further person or body to whom appeal could be made, then *that* person or body would be the true sovereign. Absolute sovereignty can thus be said to be an analytical entailment of statehood. This concept is a fundamental legacy of early modern political thought, and offered the most difficult challenge to parliamentarian and Whig theories of constitutionalism and resistance, many of which were evasive on the topic of sovereignty. We chiefly associate it with the French theorist, Jean Bodin, whose *Six Books of the Commonwealth* (1576) was written amid the chaos of the French religious wars, and with Thomas Hobbes, whose *Leviathan* (1651) was written against the backdrop of the English Civil War. Both were profound influences on Tory thought, although Turner preferred to quote Arniseaus, a German follower of Bodin, and Grotius, a Dutch precursor of Hobbes.[29]

It does not follow from their doctrine that sovereignty must lie in a single person, the king. Turner's parenthesis – supreme power '(wherever it be)' – concedes this point. Hobbes was careful to say that sovereignty could lie in 'a monarch or an assembly', and his account is less a defence of the immutable rights of the House of Stuart than of obedience to *de facto* power. When published in 1651, *Leviathan*, to the consternation of legitimists, read like a plea to accept the Commonwealth. Sovereignty, although it could not be divided or shared, could be held by a corporate body. Parliament, although a multiplicity of people, was a corporate body, and spoke with one voice when acting as the sovereign legislature. The recognition of this point meant that the idea of sovereignty remained crucial in political thought long after the era of personal monarchy, for the effect of the Revolution of 1688 was to place sovereignty in crown-in-parliament.[30] None the less, despite Turner's concession, it was not until after 1688 that Tory theorists accepted that sovereignty lay in crown-in-parliament.

Accordingly, it was incumbent upon them to demonstrate that absolute sovereignty ought to lie personally in a monarch. Turner's next move was to show that pure monarchy was ordained by God. It was conventional to follow the Greeks and Romans in distinguishing three possible modes of government: monarchy, aristocracy and democracy – rule by one, by the few and by the many. Plainly, there were in history examples of aristocracies and democracies, but Turner asserts that these were 'political aberrations and deviations'. In the pristine beginnings of the world, during the first 1656 years after the Creation, down to the Flood, only monarchies existed. Thereafter, God's Chosen People continued to be ruled by monarchs. Turner thought that one of the most dangerous allegations made by Civil War writers was that for 400 years Israel was not a monarchy.[31]

The archetype of all monarchy was Adam's rule. He was 'monarch of the world', and his government began with his 'dominion over his wife'. Monarchy was the natural form of government, for it was a species of fatherhood. Fathers were of 'political and natural' kinds. Here Turner voiced the commonplaces of contemporary catechisms, which explained the Fifth Commandment in terms of 'political, spiritual, domestical, and natural' fathers: princes, priests, masters of servants and blood fathers. Turner's argument is familiar from Filmer, but marks a fundamental divergence between Hobbes and the mainstream of Tory thought. Hobbes grounds absolute government in the consent of the people, and he imagines an original state of nature of free, ungoverned agents. It is fear of the brutish state of nature that persuades people to accept civil sovereignty. This thought appalled most royalists: absolute authority based on popular consent seemed like a house built on sand, and its premise a blasphemous neglect of scriptural history. Filmer remarked, 'I consent with [Hobbes] about the rights of exercising government, but I cannot agree to his means of acquiring it'. He opened *Patriarcha* by denouncing those royalists who had foolishly built their theories upon 'the natural liberty and equality of mankind'. The Hobbesian type of argument was occasionally heard in the Restoration: it is contained in Dudley Digges's *Unlawfulness of Subjects taking up Arms* (1644), reprinted in 1662, 1664 and 1679. However, most Tories followed Filmer's patriarchal line, and completely rejected the idea of a covenanted absolutism.[32]

Their rejection of the notion that 'man was born free' was categorical: we are not born free, because we are born into families, and hence into subjection, and it has been so since the dawn of time. Tories thought the contrary notion a recent, and supremely dangerous, innovation. It was devised to license the deposition of kings, and it made way for rebellion and anarchy. They attributed its prominence to the teachings of Counter-Reformation Catholics, who wished to diminish the authority of earthly rulers in order to exalt the pope's dominion. The teachings of Bellarmine, Mariana and others were brought home to English audiences in the European debate over King James I's Oath of Allegiance of 1606, which followed the Catholic attempt to assassinate the King in the previous year. Restoration Tories were steeped in the writings of that generation. It led them to treat all radical doctrines about popular and parliamentary rights as being at root 'Papistical' and 'Jesuitical'. They talked of the 'king-killing doctrine of the Jesuits'. They claimed that English Puritans inherited their teaching from Catholics. These charges remind us that the Divine Right of Kings was as much an anti-Catholic as an anti-Puritan and anti-Whig doctrine. Turner says that his treatise is against 'the pretences of the pope or people'. The claim that the Whigs were peddling Popish doctrines was not as outlandish as it seems. In 1681 a book by Robert Parsons, an Elizabethan Catholic radical, was reprinted, perfectly tuned for the Whig cause. For the Tories, therefore, patriarchalism was the authentic political dogma of true Protestants.[33]

Turner augments his biblical patriarchalism with prudential arguments from the ancient Greeks. Monarchy was prescribed not only by God but also by Aristotle. In his *Nicomachean Ethics*, Aristotle pronounced that monarchy is 'best'.[34] This was typical of the royalists' highly selective reading of the classics.

It remained to prove that England was a pure monarchy. This was not obvious, for the chief contention of Parliamentarians and Whigs was that England was a 'mixed monarchy'. That is to say, it combined elements of all three of the classical modes of government, and thus, by a harmonious balance of forms, reaped the advantages of all of them. Monarchy was represented in the king, aristocracy in the House of Lords, and democracy in the House of Commons: power was shared between them, and no element could act alone. The Tories energetically repudiated this notion of 'polyarchy'. Turner called it 'a simple contradiction'. Monarchy cannot be mixed: if mixed, it is not monarchy, but something else under the guise of monarchy – as in Poland or Venice, where the king or doge is a figurehead in an aristocratic polity. Hobbes contemptuously called the idea 'mixarchy', and Filmer entitled one of his pamphlets *The Anarchy of a Limited or Mixed Monarchy* (1648).[35]

Unfortunately, the doctrine of mixed monarchy had achieved its most telling formulation by, of all people, King Charles I. His *Answer to the Nineteen Propositions* (1642) was issued in a moment of concessiveness just prior to the Civil War. It expressed the idea with succinct cogency:

> There being three kinds of government among men, absolute monarchy, aristocracy and democracy, and all these having their particular conveniences and inconveniences, the experience and wisdom of your ancestors hath so moulded this out of a mixture of these as to give to this kingdom (so far as human prudence can provide) the conveniences of all three, without the inconveniences of any one, as long as the balance hangs even between the three estates ...[36]

Yet, far from marking a decisive capitulation, the *Answer* was repeatedly disowned by Restoration royalists. It was, Turner wrote, 'a manifest mistake', founded on a confusion about the 'three estates'. The classical ideal of the mixed polity could only be grafted on to the English constitution by equating the three feudal estates with the three classical modes. But that involves a confusion – indeed a dishonest sleight of hand – for the three estates were *not* king, lords and commons, but lords spiritual, lords temporal and commons. Scores of Acts of Parliament, as well as medieval treatises, could be cited which referrred to the king *and* the three estates. Turner charged that William Prynne, one of the chief defenders of Parliament in the Civil War, had 'falsified the records'. This sleight of hand involved a doubly damnable demotion: of the king, to being merely one among co-equal estates, and of the church, to being not an estate at all. That the king was *above* the estates in parliament could be clinched by noting his acknowledged constitutional powers over parliament. He had the right of veto over legislation, so that it was his will that gave life and force to the law. And he had the right to summon and dismiss parliament when he chose. The king, therefore, had 'none co-ordinate or equal to him'.[37]

The supremacy of the king could further be demonstrated by exploring the origins of parliament and the common law. It was a contemporary commonplace that precedence was prescriptive: that the antiquity of an institution lent it legitimacy. Whether crown or parliament was the more ancient institution became a critical question. Filmer argued that parliament was a relatively modern institution, being no older than the feudal Middle Ages, and that in its original form it was an extension of the king's council. It was not, therefore, a body which sprang from the community at large, nor was its antiquity so venerable as to be lost in

the mists of time. In particular, parliament grew out of arrangements that followed William I's conquest of the English people.
Turner echoed Filmer in insisting that what had occurred in 1066
was a conquest which had resulted in a complete transformation of
the polity. Similarly, the notion that the common law – the law of
the community as expressed in the courts – could be traced back
indefinitely, and that its antiquity preceded the English monarchy,
was a 'wild assertion, without any just proof'.[38] These ideas would
achieve fullest expression in the work of the Tory historian, Robert
Brady, in his *Full and Clear Answer* (1681) and *Introduction to the Old
English History* (1684), where he showed that medieval kings
decided who to summon to parliament, that knights and burgesses
were only intermittently summoned, and that these commoners
did not at first assemble in a separate House.[39]

Having established where supremacy lay, Turner's final task was
to show that subjects had an inviolable duty of obedience to their
rulers, and that a right of armed resistance against kings was cate-
gorically forbidden by God. His chief proof-text was Romans
13:1–2: 'Let every soul be subject unto the higher powers. For
there is no power but of God: the powers that be are ordained of
God ... they that resist shall receive to themselves damnation.'
Countless sermons took this as their text. It is ubiquitous in
Christian political writing, whether as a text to be swallowed
whole, or to be finessed and qualified. The republican Algernon
Sidney made the characteristic Whig move of referring to verses
3–4, which pronounced that rulers are 'the minister of God to
thee for good', and so, by implication, rulers who were wrong-
doers were not those to whom St Paul demands obedience. But
Tories drew no such distinction: kings, whether tyrants or not,
must never be resisted. They came to believe that this amounted
to a formal doctrine of the Church of England. Before his execution in 1685, the rebel Duke of Monmouth pronounced 'I die a
Protestant of the Church of England', but the divines who
attended him – Turner was one of them – urged, 'My Lord, if you
be of the Church of England, you must acknowledge the doctrine
of non-resistance to be true'.[40]

V

A juristic theory of sovereignty, a natural law theory of patriarchalism, a scriptural doctrine of non-resistance and an historical

theory about parliament – these provided the foundations of Tory absolutism. The strident defence of these claims provoked Whigs to charge that Tories were sycophantic connivers in the growth of Stuart despotism. Yet Tories denied that theirs was a theory of arbitrary power. They insisted that they were friends of the rule of law and of parliaments. Integral to Tory absolutism was a series of mitigations, which took the rough edges off their central planks.

Despite Whig ridicule, patriarchalism did not entail that the claims of the House of Stuart depended upon proving direct hereditary descent from Adam. In principle it could be shown, for few denied that Genesis was true history, and until at least the 1630s such genealogies were drawn up. Yet the hereditary principle played less of a role in Tory divine right teaching than is generally thought, although the Exclusion Crisis did enhance it. Tories recognized that monarchies could be elective, could be acquired by conquest (the *jus gladii*), and that rules of inheritance differed widely – in France the Salic Law excluded women. Turner argued that there is a crucial distinction to be drawn between the authority of the crown and the mode of acquiring it. 'Authority and dominion' come from God, but human agency may designate the person who is to hold it. Election, conquest, donation and inheritance are merely modes of acquisition. Turner suggested parallel examples. A wife chooses who shall be her husband, but the husband's authority does not derive from her consent. A town chooses a mayor, but the mayor's authority comes from a higher power. The cardinals elect the pope, but papal authority is said to be God-given. Accordingly, there was ample scope in Tory thinking for consent in the conduct of human affairs, but understood as a mode of designation and not of authorization. The clinching argument that sovereign authority must be God-given was that rulers had the right of capital punishment. Since the Commandment enjoins, 'Thou shalt not kill', the right to take life could not have been transferred by the consent of the people, for it was not a right that the people had to give.[41]

The next mitigation lay in the doctrine of non-resistance. It did not follow from Tory doctrine that subjects should blindly submit to any royal command. People did not abandon their duty to make moral judgements about the rightness of what princes and magistrates demand. They were not obliged to obey a command to do something which was *malum in se*, wrong in itself – wrong by the laws of God and nature.[42] Tories drew a distinction between active and passive 'obedience': active obedience to godly commands, but passive *resistance* to ungodly commands. They contrasted Romans 13 with Acts 5:29: 'We ought to obey God rather than men'. Subjects might remonstrate with princes, protest their grievances and refuse to obey ungodly commands, but if they were persecuted for their recalcitrance, they must suffer and not rebel. Absolutists were fond of quoting the early Christian Fathers, who had advised patient suffering under the persecutions of heathen emperors. They pointed out that St Paul's Epistle to the Romans was written in the time of the brutal Emperor Nero.

Unquestionably, kings who flouted natural and divine law could be called tyrants. But absolute monarchy should not be equated with tyranny or despotism, although Whigs increasingly failed to tell the difference. Tyranny, Tories insisted, should be defined not in terms of types of government, but of moral rectitude: *all* modes of polity, including aristocracies and democracies, could become despotical, and did so when they no longer pursued the public good and the moral law. The Interregnum, they claimed, saw a real tyranny: of swordsmen, sectaries and the monstrous multitude.

These notions had a number of important consequences. The Divine Right of Kings was never a licence for royal immorality. It is sometimes said that the preaching of that doctrine was naive in the face of Charles II's sexual promiscuity. That misses the point. His God-given sovereignty inhered in the kingly office, not in his personal character. This principle had a vital consequence when the reign of a Catholic king was in prospect. Turner noted this by remarking that Israel was once well governed by Cyrus the gentile: 'Cyrus (though a pagan prince ...) was *unctus domini* ... the Lord's Anointed'.[43] Thus the future James II had a perfect right to inherit the throne. All human beings, including princes, were sinners, and some were superstitious idolaters, but this did not disbar them from exercising earthly rule. Restoration divines were quite prepared to attack the King's moral and theological failings. They were ready to defend the Church of England and to oppose royal inclinations towards the toleration of Papists and Protestant Dissenters. They insisted that they retained a right of judgement and reproof, as interpreters of the Scriptures and guiders of conscience.

This led to a further consequence. Tories were ready, when necessary, to engage in what would now be called 'civil disobedi-

ence'. They did so most dramatically in the reign of James II.
Their sermons raucously denounced the King's religion; when
the King demanded they accept Catholics in the universities, they
refused; when the King required them to read the Declaration of
Indulgence from the pulpits, they refused. The action of the
Seven Bishops, whom James put on trial for sedition in 1688, was
no breach of non-resistance, for they did not take up the sword.
When James stormed at them that this was the 'standard of rebellion', they replied that, although they were 'ready to die at your
feet', they had 'two duties to perform, to God as well as your
majesty'.[44]

A third mitigation of absolutist doctrine vindicated the role of
laws and parliaments. 'Far be it from me', wrote Turner, 'to say or
think that the government of this nation is arbitrary or that the
rights and liberties of the subjects depend upon the sole will of
our sovereign'. Indeed, 'the power of our kings is limited (without
any prejudice to its being absolute)'. That English kingship was
both absolute and limited was a standard Tory paradox. How
could it be so? Turner begins with the analogy of God's government of the universe, for God is both absolute and self-limiting.
God's omnipotent will is guided by his reasonableness: he does
not act arbitrarily or whimsically, but by the light of reason. He
cannot lie, for his rectitude is as intrinsic to his nature as his
omnipotence. He has written the laws of nature in the hearts of
mankind, and he abides by the immutabilities of the natural
order which he created. He also limits himself by the promises
that he has made to mankind. The government of earthly kingdoms should follow this divine pattern. Absolute will gives force to
the laws, but that will ought to be guided by reason. A king should
govern wisely as well as forcefully, and should seek wisdom
through counsel. That is the role of courtiers, ministers, divines
and parliaments. The single human intellect is deficient: wisdom
is best found in the collective wisdom of the community, or at
least of its educated élite. In Tory philosophy, parliament was not
a counterbalance to the crown – the mechanical analogy was misleading – it was the embodiment of the community's counsel,
lending wisdom to the sovereign will. It was a matter of ethics, not
physics: constitutions do not balance rival interests – they seek
righteous rule. Such constitutionalism must always be conditioned
by a grasp of the fact that wise counsel is not law until the sovereign makes it so, for law requires command, promulgation and
punitive sanction.

Turner went on to argue that kings were limited by 'their grants, promises, and coronation oath'. The English have a rich legacy of public laws because earlier monarchs, like God, had made promises and concessions. In their coronation oaths kings solemnly undertook to uphold the promises of their predecessors. The royal legislative will was, like divine law, channelled through ordinary and regular courses. Every parliamentary statute was a self-limitation by the crown. In the same way, custom and common law were allowed by the king, as a wise self-limitation; although, again, common law had no force without the king's sanction. This principle of *concessio* generated extensive liberties; but, consistent with the principle of sovereignty, it was important that such liberties should be understood as royal franchises and not as the inherent rights of the people.[45]

Taken together, this system of mitigations in Tory absolutist doctrine produced two fundamental ideas: that England's monarchy was absolute *and* limited – although not mixed – and that absolute rule was not the same as arbitrary rule. In all these respects, Tory absolutists diverged fundamentally from Hobbes. Nothing shocked them so much as Hobbes's apparent insistence that moral judgement must be given over to the sovereign's hands, that the sovereign was the sole teacher of right and wrong, and that accordingly 'tyranny' was only a word for monarchy mis-liked. Hobbes seemed to place all his weight on will and command, on the passions and the interests, and none at all on what the Aristotelian tradition called 'right reason'. Sir Philip Warwick complained that 'Mr Hobbes makes the passions and not the moral virtues the foundation of government'.[46]

The philosophy which Francis Turner privately adumbrated in 1677 provided the mainstay of Tory thinking during the Exclusion Crisis. It achieved its most prominent public impri-matur in 1683 when the University of Oxford issued its *Judgement and Decree* 'against certain pernicious books and damnable doc-trines, destructive to the sacred persons of princes', and con-signed to a bonfire the books of the authors it damned. The first five of the 27 propositions which it anathematized were: 'All civil authority is derived originally from the people'; 'There is a mutual compact ... between a prince and his subjects'; 'That if lawful governors become tyrants ... they forfeit the right they had unto their government'; 'The sovereignty of England is in the three estates, viz. king, lords, and commons. The king has but a co-ordinate power and may be overrruled by the other two'; and

'Birthright and proximity of blood give no title to rule'. Among the authors condemned, and which 'we interdict all members of the university from ... reading', were Buchanan, Bellarmine, Parsons, Hunton, Milton, Rutherford and Hobbes.[47]

VI

In turning to the Whig response to this aggressive restatement of the absolutist position, we first need to recall that the republication of Filmer's works was pivotal. His patriarchal thesis provoked one body of Whig writing, and his feudal thesis another. The three best known Whig treatises belong to the first category: John Locke's *Two Treatises of Government* (written *c.* 1680–3 and published in 1689), Algernon Sidney's *Discourses Concerning Government* (written in 1681–3 and published in 1698) and James Tyrrell's *Patriarcha non Monarcha* (published in 1681). To the government, these works were treasonable: in 1683 Sidney was executed, partly on the evidence of his manuscript, and Locke fled to Holland.

Locke's book belongs in the canon of classic works of political philosophy that are constantly studied today.[48] More than 80 editions have been published. Modern interpretations of it are awkwardly poised between academic disciplines. In historical eyes, it recapitulated the Calvinist theory of revolution, developed during the Reformation in such books as Philippe du Mornay's *Defence of Liberty against Tyrants* (1579) and Buchanan's *Right of the Kingdom in Scotland* (1579).[49] In the eyes of political scientists, it is judged to have enunciated the foundations of modern liberalism. Certainly Locke's immediate polemical needs were richly productive of insights of wider theoretical bearing, especially in his defence of the right of private property.

Locke takes Filmer's doctrine to be paradigmatic of Tory absolutism. He attacks him because 'the pulpit, of late years, publicly owned his doctrine, and made it the current divinity of the times'. He is thus refuting 'a generation of men'. He denies that Divine Right is an ancient theory, and turns the Tory account of the history of political thought on its head. That absolute monarchy is 'sacred and divine' is a novelty of 'this latter age'. If Filmer's cohorts can be refuted, then 'governments must be left again to the old way of being made by contrivance'.[50]

The First Treatise is a minute dissection of Filmer's arguments. Locke's chief strategy is to deny that familial obligations are prescriptive for civil society. Paternal and political power have different spheres and purposes, and the authority of the magistrate is simply not the same as that of a father, husband or master. We have obligations of honour and gratitude to parents, but political subjection is quite different and must have another origin.

Accordingly, in the Second Treatise, Locke is able to assert that our natural state, prior to government, is one of freedom and equality. Regardless of the historical record (the Book of Genesis), this is a state that we *are* naturally in, in the sense of it being the human condition, if we were to subtract the constraints of government. (Locke does, however, add, from his reading of travel literature, the anthropological claim that many primitive societies do in fact exist in a pre-political state.) By natural freedom Locke does not mean licence to do whatever we desire, for we are still bound by divine and moral law. And by natural equality he does not mean a levelling of property or social status, but equality of rights.[51]

The state of nature is an unstable condition, especially when the 'industrious and rational' generate property and become prey to the greedy and lazy. In order to avoid a state of war, people combine together to form civil society. Government's chief purpose, therefore, is the protection of 'life, liberty and estate'. Political society is created by an act of consent – the social contract – and the only foundation for legitimate political rule is the voluntary consent of citizens. Again, the historical record need not be relevant. Governments come about in many ways – through conquest, usurpation and patriarchy – but they have no legitimate authority until the people consent to them.[52]

Government, for Locke, is a trust from the people – its powers are delegated to it. If it breaches its trust, by acting despotically, power reverts to the people. When governments become tyrannical they may be said to declare war on their citizens. Government is then judged to be dissolved, and the community may act in self-defence: the people may resist, by force of arms if necessary.[53]

When Locke described tyranny, he came closest to narrating Charles II's conduct. Government is dissolved, he says, when the prince hinders the legislature from meeting, when the 'ways of election' are corrupted, when property is invaded, and when a prince submits to a foreign power. Not all his meanings are obvious: for example, the invasion of property *may* refer to the sequestration of money and goods from Protestant Dissenters caught worshipping illegally. Nor can we be sure how much Locke revised his text for publication in 1689, although his reference to a 'prince [who] abandons his government' surely refers to James II's flight in 1688.[54]

We can identify two key moves that Locke makes which are designed to counter the most forceful of absolutist claims. First, he holds that in the state of nature we may all exact retribution against those who breach the law of nature, even by punishing with death. He has in mind the rival claim that since people have no right to kill others, they cannot be said to transfer such a right to a ruler. Locke believes we do have such a right, and do transfer it. Crucially, it is a right that we recover under tyranny, for we exert that right against the tyrant himself. We execute him as a malefactor.[55]

Second, Locke resolves an intractable difficulty posed by theories of mixed monarchy in the face of absolutist discussion of sovereignty. He recognizes that it is hopeless to speak of each element in a mixed monarchy having the right to restrain another by force. This was how Civil War authors tried to argue when asserting Parliament's right against the King. This either left confused the question of where supremacy lay, or it led to a near-republican demotion of the King, which Parliamentarians were reluctant to assert; above all, it confused the ordinary business of constitutional restraint with the circumstances of the violent breakdown of government. In the latter circumstances, Locke claims, the constitution is dissolved: power reverts not to parliament but to the community. Hence a revolutionary 'parliament' – such as the Convention that met in January 1689 – is in fact a constituent assembly of citizens who may 'erect a new form [of government] ... as they think good'. These are the last words of the Second Treatise.[56] This feature of Locke's argument is markedly radical. Whereas most earlier texts of Calvinist resistance placed the right of resistance in the hands of the 'lesser magistrates' – the estates in parliament or the nobility – Locke permits any individual to exact vengeance against the tyrant, on behalf of the community. This is a licence for tyrannicide. At the same time, Locke is careful to deny that he is creating 'a ferment for frequent rebellion', and his defence of private property implies a denial that he is reviving the social levelling of the Civil War era. His must be a doctrine safe for Whig gentlemen. He distances himself from such populist rebels as Spartacus and Jack Cade, and even from Cromwell.[57]

Filmer's patriarchal theory provoked the Whig texts that are best known today, but contemporary Whigs thought that his historical claims about the origins of parliament – which we saw echoed in Francis Turner's and Robert Brady's tracts – were no less urgently in need of refutation. William Petyt's *Antient Right of the Commons of England Asserted* (1680), William Atwood's *Jani Anglorum Facies Nova* (1680) and John Somers's *Brief History of the Succession* (1680) encapsulate Whig legal–historical orthodoxies, which can be summed up in the term 'immemorialism'. English liberties and parliamentary rights were said to have existed since before records began. In so far as they had an ultimate source, they were traced to the 'Gothick polity' of the German tribes beyond the Roman Empire, whose communitarian virtues, as against Roman imperial vices, were extolled in Tacitus' *Germania* (AD 98). To the Whigs, the Saxon antiquity of parliament and the common law was fundamental dogma. The 'witenagemote' and 'mickelgemote' were ancestors of modern parliaments. The year 1066 marked no discontinuity, no conquest, and each successive reign, each coronation oath, saw the confirmation of Edward the Confessor's summation of Saxon laws. That Magna Charta was a fundamental declaration of English liberties was a Whig piety impervious to Brady's demonstration that it was in fact a limited demand by noblemen for a relaxation of their feudal military obligations. The Whig myth of continuity had no room for feudal interruptions. The whole immemorialist idiom tended to be static in its historical approach, but the idea of an Ancient Constitution, endlessly preserved and renewed, was too important to abandon, whatever the plausibility of Tory historiography. It left a muddle in Whig thought for, as the Marquis of Halifax acutely observed, it is not possible to maintain both that Magna Charta is inviolable and that parliamentary statute is supreme.[58]

John Somers's tract applied Ancient Constitutionalism to the exigencies of the Exclusion Crisis. He argued that in Saxon times kings were elected and subject to 'parliamentary agreement and limitation'. Parliaments ever since had exercised their right to control the succession and discipline wayward monarchs. Edward II, he noted, was formally deposed, and at his successor's coronation the Archbishop of Canterbury preached on the theme of '*vox populi, vox dei*' – the voice of the people is the voice of God.[59]

It is often said that Locke was silent on these matters. It is true that the *Two Treatises* argues from reason and nature rather than history and law. Yet it is clear that he endorsed a conventional doctrine of mixed monarchy. A revolutionary convention might erect 'a new form' but it would be prudent to erect 'the old form ... in new hands'. He took for granted a parliament of monarch, aristocrats and commoners, and a community of landed gentlemen. He recommended Ancient Constitutionalist texts: Nathaniel Bacon's, mentioned earlier, and John Sadler's *Rights of the Kingdom* (1649, 1682). He helped draft *The Fundamental Constitutions of Carolina* (1669), which provided for an aristocratic government by eight Lords Proprietors and a hereditary nobility of 'landgraves' and 'caciques', a system 'agreeable unto the monarchy ... and that we may avoid erecting a numerous democracy'. Locke was no democrat, no republican, no Leveller.[60]

In the eighteenth century, Algernon Sidney had as elevated a status as Locke in the Whig pantheon. His martyrdom guaranteed that, but so too did his *Discourses*, which succeeded in providing both a compendium of conventional Whig sentiment, and a vicious republican assault on kingship. Sidney had served the Republic of 1649, had deplored Cromwell's Protectorate as kingship in masquerade, and had denounced the corruption, venality and oppression of Charles II's regime in his (unpublished) *Court Maxims* (1664–5).[61] Readers of the *Discourses* could find elements of every variety of Whig discourse: natural law consensualism – 'man is naturally free' and 'all just magistratical power is from the people'; the familiar Latin constitutionalist tags – *salus populi est lex suprema* (the safety of the people is the supreme law), the king is *major singulus* but *universis minor* (greater than any subject, but less than the community); the shibboleths of Ancient Constitutionalism – Saxon elective kingship, Tacitus, the witenagemote, Magna Charta and the nullity of the Conquest; traditional applause for mixed government – 'the best governments of the world have been composed of monarchy, aristocracy and democracy' – and a corresponding deprecation of pure democracy as well as pure monarchy.[62]

However, a tone of increasing militancy insinuates itself into the text. The call to arms against tyrants is categorical: 'Why should they not be deposed if they become enemies to the people?'. In the passage read out at his trial, he talks of the people's 'revenge' and 'deliverance'.[63] Above all, Sidney advocates a republic. To be sure, mixed government must have a monarchical element, but its exemplars are the presidential executives of ancient and modern republics: the consuls and 'dictators' of

Rome, the judges of Israel, the doges of Venice. His heroes include Cincinnatus; his enemies Augustus; his models Sparta, Rome, Venice, the Netherlands, Florence before the Medici, and the Swiss cantons.[64] At first sight, his republic is aristocratic: 'the nobility ... was the principal support of the ancient regular monarchy'. He stresses, with Calvin, that the Hebrews were governed aristocratically by the Sanhedrin of seventy. Sidney was conscious of his own ancestry among the Protestant aristocracy: his great uncle, Sir Philip Sidney, died fighting to help the Dutch republic overthrow its Spanish Catholic overlords. Here, however, is a clue to a more populist strain of republicanism. Sidney's republic is not pacific but militant: 'the best government is [that] which best provides for war'. And the foundation of war is a nation in arms. The original referent of 'nobility', he explains, was the armed freeman: the Greek citizen, the Roman *vir*, the knight, the hidalgo, the gentleman. To bear arms is the mark of the free man, the source of civic nobility. Sidney's was a vision that would profoundly influence the makers of the American republic a century later.[65]

The signal influence on Sidney's 'classical republicanism' was Machiavelli's *Discourses* (*c*. 1516), which extolled ancient Rome through a commentary on Livy. That influence was also manifest in Henry Neville's *Plato Redivivus* (1681), a dialogue between a Venetian nobleman and an English gentleman. Neville's doge-like king of England would be stripped of his powers over foreign affairs, the army, the revenue and the appointment of officers of state. Neville was especially interested in analysing the modern English polity along lines laid down in Harrington's *Oceana*. Harrington had suggested that political power was naturally proportional to the ownership of property. As the landed wealth of the monarch and old aristocracy declined and that of the gentry increased, the power of the crown became more precarious: its downfall in the Civil War seemed inevitable. The royal revival after 1660 was, for Neville, chimerical, for it no longer had natural foundations. England was a gentry commonwealth, with the shadow of kingship.[66]

The ideological collision of the 1680s was to be resolved in the very different political climate which emerged after the Revolution of 1688. In 1694 Halifax pronounced that 'the forms of government to which England must be subjected are either absolute monarchy, a commonwealth, or a mixed monarchy, as it is now' and 'which will most probably prevail and continue'.[67] As he correctly saw, the Revolution was as fatal to republican as to absolutist aspirations. What succeeded was 'mixed monarchy', a doctrine so ingrained that it survives today to hybridize and complicate a polity which aspires to be democratic.

3. Politics, Finance and Government

LIONEL K. J. GLASSEY

One familiar view of the Restoration was well expressed by John Evelyn:

> This day [29 May 1660] came in his Majestie *Charles* the 2d to London after a sad, & long Exile ... The wayes straw'd with flowers, the bells ringing, the streetes hung with Tapissry, fountaines running with wine ... Trumpets, musick & myriads of people flocking ... I stood in the strand, & beheld it, & blessed God: And all this without one drop of bloud.[1]

Evelyn may well have rubbed shoulders with the Covent Garden barber, Thomas Rugg, who recorded that, 'beeinge in the Strond', he listened to 'such shouting as the oldest man alive never heard the like ... all things [done] that might express joy'.[2] Thomas Lamplugh, a future Archbishop of York, also witnessed the King's entry into London. 'Never was any Prince so welcome to his people', he told his friends, adding that there had been 'such acclama[ti]ons as I want words to expresse'.[3] North of the border, Edinburgh had rejoiced at the proclamation of Charles II a fortnight earlier. John Nicoll, a lawyer, described in his diary the sound of bells, trumpets and drums, with toasts 'breking numberis of glasses', and much 'dancing about the fyres, and using all uther takins of joy for the advancement and preference of thair native King to his croun and native inheritance'.[4]

I   The Restoration

The immediate mood of the Restoration was one of euphoria and relief. But this mood was neither universal nor lasting. The Republicans and Cromwellians of the 1650s did not abandon hope of a revival of their fortunes after 1660. There was a long sequence of plots and conspiracies through the whole period from the Restoration to the Revolution of 1688. Six episodes, not including the Prince of Orange's invasion in November 1688, amounted to armed insurrections: Venner's rising in January 1661; the combined revolts in Yorkshire, Westmorland and Durham in October 1663; the Pentland rising in November 1666, culminating in the battle at Rullion Green; the Covenanters' rebellion in May–June 1679, culminating in the battle at Bothwell Bridge; the Earl of Argyll's rebellion in May–June 1685; and the rebellion by the Duke of Monmouth in June–July 1685 culminating in the battle of Sedgemoor. An outbreak of lawlessness among the native Irish in Leitrim, Roscommon and Longford, 'Nangle's rising', in the early summer of 1666, might be regarded as a seventh; and the Dublin Plot of March–April 1663 came very close to making an eighth. Both the King and the Duke of York were the putative targets of genuine assassination conspiracies. An attempt to kidnap and assassinate the Duke of Ormonde was made in 1670. The Archbishop of St Andrews actually was assassinated in 1679. Before 1688 these demonstrations of hostility to the Stuart regime were often badly led, uncoordinated and ill-organized, but they needed to be taken seriously. Consequently, so far from the tranquillity and stability promised by the festivities attending the Restoration, the prevailing atmosphere of the years after 1660 was one of vulnerability and insecurity.[5]

Republicanism, then, was not somehow 'switched off' at the Restoration; nor was Puritanism. Both were driven underground, but both could resurface unexpectedly and with explosive effect. Algernon Sidney, that roundest of round heads, offered his uncompromising principles to the electors of Amersham in 1679 and 1681, and received a majority of votes although he was twice unseated on petition. He was executed in 1683 for carelessly leaving a manuscript in which these principles were expressed lying about at a time when the Rye House Plot suspects were being rounded up. Richard Rumbold, captured after Argyll's rebellion, had been a private soldier, then a lieutenant, in Oliver Cromwell's own regiment.[6] His words at his execution, frequently quoted by historians of the Levellers, echoed the radical Army sentiments of 1647: 'he said, he did not believe that God had made the greater part of mankind with saddles on their backs, and bridles in their mouths, and some few booted and spurred to ride the rest'.[7] Edmund Ludlow, possibly the last surviving regicide, reappeared briefly in London shortly after the Revolution of 1688, after spending the years since 1660 in exile in Switzerland. He seems to have been under the impression that the Revolution represented a revival of the political and constitutional aspirations of the Rump from forty years earlier.[8] The activities after 1660, however eccentric, ineffectual or unsuccessful, of veterans from the 1640s such as Sidney, Rumbold and Ludlow indicate that the Restoration was not the inauguration of a new age of moderation in politics and religion. Rather, they provided the justification for a conviction that the extremism of an earlier period was now to be firmly discouraged, to forestall the possibility that it might revive.

Another feature of the Restoration is a certain continuity between the Interregnum years and the reign of Charles II, evident in quite a different sense. Many of those active in Restoration politics were men who had served Cromwell in the 1650s. Charles II could not afford to disregard their experience. Some, like General Monck, had facilitated the Restoration and required to be rewarded – in Monck's case, with the dukedom of Albemarle. Some were indispensable because of their up-to-date knowledge of some branch of government. An example was Sir George Downing, a Harvard graduate and a former chaplain in the New Model Army, who was an expert on Anglo-Dutch commercial relations and a fertile source of suggestions for financial expedients. Some, like Sir Anthony Ashley Cooper, later to be Earl of Shaftesbury, were ambitious and thick-skinned, and were able to exploit their talents as natural survivors, even if (like Cooper), they had sat in Barebone's Parliament and in Cromwell's 'Other House'.[9] At a lower level, men like Samuel Pepys began their careers in government service in the 1650s and simply carried on into the 1660s.

In the localities, too, there was more continuity in office-holding and in the conduct of local administration through the Restoration than might have been supposed. The Restoration was, of course, accompanied by an upheaval in office-holding, as country gentlemen and wealthy townsmen who had been proscribed in the 1650s for their Royalist sympathies resumed their natural place in local society at the expense of the more intractable adherents of the Rump or of the Protectorate. Detailed studies of particular communities do indicate, however, that in many places a number of individuals survived from the 1650s into the 1660s in positions of local authority. Cheshire, Hampshire, Sussex, Devon, Norfolk and Glamorgan are examples of counties in which changes in the commission of the peace in the early 1660s were undoubtedly extensive but less than completely comprehensive.[10] The element of continuity was particularly strong at the level of office-holding below that at which gentry families were involved. In Devon, for example, hundred bailiffs and head constables did not change significantly.[11] The towns were subjected to a more rigorous scrutiny in 1662–3, when the commissioners appointed by the Corporation Act purged municipal government of those deemed to be politically suspect, but even in the towns the extent of the changes varied. In some places, it was hard to find suitable replacements for those dismissed; in others, the cycle of annual elections meant that the purges were temporary and the men disgraced in the aftermath of the Restoration were once again serving as aldermen or mayors after a few years.[12] 'Continuity' in politics and government is a concept that is hard to measure, but in general there seems to be a good case for the view that the Restoration of 1660 was less of a clean break with the immediate past than its most enthusiastic supporters might ideally have wished.

The concept of a clear-cut 'Restoration Settlement', incorporating a sharp divide between the years before and the years after 1660, has similarly been subjected to reinterpretation. There was, of course, a conscious attempt at, and shortly after, the Restoration to establish new ground-rules for the remainder of Charles II's reign in the areas of religion, finance and government. There was, equally, a desire to resolve intractable problems arising from the extensive transfers of land from royalists to their victorious opponents in the 1640s and 1650s. These were all important issues that could not be resolved quickly by a set of snap decisions. Ronald Hutton has suggested that, rather than one 'Restoration Settlement', there were two.[13] The first was a somewhat hesitant attempt to reconcile conflicting aspirations in a spirit of 'healing and settling' in 1660. The Act of Indemnity and Oblivion, passed in August 1660, reflected this impulse towards moderation in that only 33 persons were excepted from it, and even this was more than the King had originally wanted. The first settlement was undermined in the winter of 1660–1 by a combination of circumstances. The publicity given to the shadowy 'White Plot' of cashiered army officers and to the more visible Fifth Monarchist insurrection led by Venner in London in January 1661 indicated that 'healing and settling' was misconceived as far as the more extreme radicals were concerned.[14] Despite some misleading early

results, the general election in March–April 1661 produced a
more militantly Anglican, royalist House of Commons than had
been expected.[15] Clarendon, the minister most closely associated
with the moderate programme of 1660, was embarrassed by the
revelation that he had inadvertently become the King's uncle-in-
law through the clandestine marriage of his daughter Anne to the
Duke of York, and he temporarily lost influence at court.[16] As a
consequence of these developments, the second 'Restoration
Settlement' of 1661–2 proved to be more aggressive. The Militia
Act, the Treason Act, the Corporation Act, the Licensing Act, the
Act of Uniformity, the reversal of Strafford's attainder and the
execution of Sir Harry Vane all represented a shift towards an
uncompromising royalist policy which the King himself, whose
instincts were for moderation, found impossible to resist. A third
settlement might additionally be discerned in the parliamentary
session in the spring of 1664 when, in response to the radical
plots and planned insurrections in the North of England revealed
in the autumn of 1663, the 1641 Triennial Act was repealed and
replaced by a new and ineffectual Triennial Act, and the
Conventicle Act intensified the persecution of Dissenters.

This division of the settlement into successive phases, when
external pressures and changing circumstances operated on
policy-making, is very persuasive. It helps to elucidate episodes
which have long puzzled historians, most notably the vicissitudes,
and the eventual failure, of the attempt by the King and his advisers to arrive at an acceptable compromise on the religious issue.
Intelligent contemporaries did not conceive of a single, clearly
defined solution to all the quarrels, conflicts and dislocations of
the years since 1642. The Restoration provided in many of its
aspects a muddled, *ad hoc* settlement, worked out along pragmatic
rather than preconceived lines. This was especially the case with
regard to one issue, perhaps less important to the contemporary
mind than religion, but still of fundamental significance to the
political and constitutional development of the Stuart regime for
the future: namely, finance.

II   The financial settlement

Of all the more important aspects of the Restoration Settlement,
it was perhaps the settlement of finance that reflected the least
continuity with the period before 1642. It was plain that the

financial system of the early Stuart kings was defunct. In 1660 even the most nostalgic veteran of Charles I's regime could summon little enthusiasm for the return of purveyance, wardships or ship money. The Interregnum regimes had introduced methods of raising revenue, and techniques of managing it, that offered obvious attractions to the restored monarchy. Moreover, the financial arrangements for the new regime required to be worked out in conjunction with Parliament. The condemnation of unparliamentary taxation in the Petition of Right of 1628 now had statutory sanction; it had been incorporated in the Act Abolishing Ship Money of 1641.[17] The Declaration of Breda had, furthermore, concluded with a statement to the effect that the arrears of pay of General Monck's soldiers would be satisfied by parliamentary statute.[18] The King could, and did, revive the administrative institutions of the financial system – the Treasury, the Exchequer, the Household and so on – by appointing new officials without reference to Parliament. However, by far the greater part of the money that was to flow through these institutions had to be sanctioned by Parliament. This raises an obvious question, which has often been asked, but which cannot easily be resolved because opposed but equally plausible answers can be made to it. Did Parliament – more specifically, the House of Commons – contrive, either by accident or design, to limit the King's political independence, and to guarantee its own continued existence, frequent meeting and influence in policy formulation, by restricting the revenue available to the King?

The financial settlement itself, immensely complicated in detail, can readily be summarized in outline.[19] In 1660 Charles II faced a mountain of obligations which required to be met as a matter of political urgency. An army of more than 60 000 men and a fleet of more than a hundred ships, together costing approximately £100 000 a month, had to be paid off. The arrears of pay of the soldiers and sailors, and large debts on equipment and naval stores, had to be discharged. These arrears and debts combined to make a sum of rather more than £1 100 000. The undischarged debts of Charles I, the obligations incurred by Charles II in exile, and the legitimate debts owed to the creditors of the Rump and the Protectorate governments, together totted up to a further sum of between £900 000 and £1 000 000. The Convention of 1660 and the first session of the Cavalier Parliament (which extended over two meetings to May 1662) made a number of grants of direct taxation apparently conceived as a once-for-all award to Charles to enable him to meet these enormous sums and to begin his reign with a clean sheet. This was, of course, impossible. The money raised by the poll tax of 1660 and the assessments of 1660–2 could not be collected quickly, or concentrated in the Exchequer in a form that made rapid disbursement feasible. Even so, the taxpayers, who had already borne heavy burdens in the 1650s, knew what these sums were for and approved of their purpose. There is little evidence of resistance. The most pressing priority, the disbanding of the regiments of the New Model Army, was nearly complete by the beginning of 1661. Although Charles never shook off the accumulated debts, arrears and interest repayments that he incurred at the start of his reign, the initial grants were sufficiently generous, despite the shortfall between what was ideally required and what was paid, to avoid political disaster.

There remained the issue of what revenue Parliament was to make available to the King as the unusual conditions of the transition from Interregnum to Restoration receded into the past and his reign settled into normality. This permanent settlement was to be crucial to the financial and indeed to much of the political history of the remainder of the reigns of Charles II and his brother down to the Revolution. Unfortunately, the making of one centrally important decision is obscured in a fog of mystery because of the limited contemporary evidence relating to the inner workings of the Convention. This decision, embodied in the report of a Commons committee for 'settling the revenue' submitted in the late summer of 1660, was that the King should receive 'for his constant yearly support' £1 200 000 *per annum*. He was to be granted a permanent ordinary revenue which, in conjunction with the surviving hereditary sources of income (like the crown lands), would make up that sum.[20] The figure of £1 200 000 may have been arrived at after a calculation of Charles I's income and expenditure in the later 1630s, with some allowance for inflation.[21] It echoes, approximately, the sums of £1 300 000 offered to Oliver Cromwell by the First and Second Protectorate Parliaments in, respectively, the Constitutional Bill of 1654–5 and the Humble Petition and Advice of 1657, though the Convention in 1660 cannot have envisaged that Charles II's military expenditure would remotely correspond to that of the late Lord Protector.[22] However the sum was arrived at, it seems to have been accepted without much discussion. To make up this ordinary revenue, Parliament granted: to the crown in perpetuity, half of the Commonwealth excise (this was regarded as a permanent compensation for the

extinction of the feudal revenues, especially those arising from
the Court of Wards); and to Charles II for his life, the customs,
assessed on a new Book of Rates, and the other half of the excise.
When it became clear, in the summer of 1661, that these revenues
together amounted to less than £1 200 000 – in fact, to £865 000 –
a new tax, the hearth tax, was granted to the crown in perpetuity.
So far from seeking to keep the Stuart monarchy in an impoverished condition to win political and constitutional advantage for
Parliament, the House of Commons appears to have conceived
this settlement to have been an adequate one for normal conditions. Not everybody thought that the revenue was enough.
Downing observed, as early as August 1661, that the King needed
£1 500 000 or £1 600 000 *per annum* if he was to resist the trading
competition of the Dutch and avoid 'begging of his Parliaments
even for his ordinary subsistence'.[23]

Whether the sum of £1 200 000 was regarded as too much or
too little, and whether or not it was arrived at after precise calculation, the circumstance that it was pitched upon at all raises an
interesting point: if, as has already been suggested, the financial
system of Charles I was defunct, there was still in 1660 some residual trace of the theory that had underlain it. The King was still
expected to 'live of[f] his own'. His 'own', his ordinary revenue,
should be sufficient to enable him to maintain routine executive
government, including embassies to foreign nations, the course
of justice in the law courts, and a dignified though not extravagant household. It should not be necessary for him to resort to
expedients that were only dubiously lawful, or to place undue
burdens upon his subjects. If he needed more for special purposes, such as the defence of the realm in emergencies, or the
sort of aggressive commercial and naval competition with the
Dutch that Downing envisaged, then Parliament would grant
additional supply if it thought fit to do so, and as indeed it was
already doing in 1660–1 to pay off the soldiers of the New Model
Army.

It is commonly said that this financial settlement worked badly
in practice, and that its deficiencies stored up great difficulties for
Charles, which led to many of the embarrassments that encumbered the political developments of his reign. In the short term
this is unquestionably true. Charles's ordinary revenue from the
customs, the excise and the hearth tax was not to reach an
average annual yield of £1 200 000 at any point in the 1660s and
1670s,[24] and his total income needed to be periodically reinforced

from other sources. Some of these other sources were politically unexceptionable. Charles's marriage to Catherine of Braganza brought him a Portuguese dowry, although this was to some extent offset by the acquisition, as part of this dowry, of Tangier, which was expensive to garrison and which involved England in costly conflicts with North African pirates. War with the Dutch in 1665–7 and again in 1672–4 was undertaken partly in the hope that the success of the Rump in capturing quantities of lucrative Dutch prizes in its earlier war in 1652–4 might be repeated. The King might also draw on the capital value of his assets. In 1670–1 a sale of fee farm rents – annual fees paid by those to whom former crown lands had been alienated – brought in large sums, but inevitably diminished future income. Other non-parliamentary means of supplementing the King's income aroused suspicion or resentment in the Commons, or had to be kept hidden from view. Dunkirk, acquired in 1658, was sold to France in 1662. In the 1670s, Lord Treasurer Danby seems to have devised some method of supplementing the King's English income from Irish sources, although the amounts raised by this practice have remained elusively unquantifiable. Most notoriously, the King's willingness to agree to the clandestine part of the Treaty of Dover in 1670, committing him to the re-establishment of the Catholic religion in the British Isles, brought him irregular and intermittent subsidies from Louis XIV for the remainder of his reign.

Not only was Charles obliged to make up the shortfall in his income by recourse to these additional sources of money; he found that the House of Commons was less than whole-heartedly willing to respond to appeals for financial reinforcement. It is true that the Dutch war in the mid-1660s produced large grants, mostly in the form of 'assessments'; that is, direct taxes on property awarded over a term of months. The price of this in the political context was a chorus of accusations of waste and corruption in the management of these sums from the representatives of resentful taxpayers in the House of Commons. Their attitudes were expressed by Brome Whorwood, the country gentleman MP who sat for the city of Oxford, who remarked to his fellow-members in 1666, 'When we have raised the King's supply we may go home like fools, as we came'. The House resolved, significantly, to pass over these words in silence despite their insulting character.[25] Such criticisms mounted to a crescendo in 1667 as the Dutch fleet attacked the ships laid up in the Medway and the war drew to its ignominious close. Thereafter, the

Commons required to be managed with care if it was to be persuaded to make extraordinary grants, and these grants tended to be, more frequently than had been the case in the past, temporary extensions of indirect taxes for a period of years, rather than direct taxes. Clifford achieved a modest success in the session of 1670–1 by extracting additional excise duties, a stamp tax (the 'law duty') and a 'new model' subsidy. Danby contrived to convince a grudging House of Commons in 1677–8 that the King's preparations for war against France required extraordinary supply in the form of an extension of the additional excise and wine duties granted in 1670–1, a poll tax and two assessments. This backfired when it became clear that the war with France was not to take place after all, and the three 'Exclusion' Parliaments produced no extraordinary grants apart from an assessment designed to pay off the unnecessary troops in the spring of 1679.

So far, the view that the financial settlement of the Restoration worked badly in practice seems to be confirmed. Through the 1660s, Charles's debts mounted, expenditure consistently exceeded income and the large sums provided by Parliament were soaked up by the Dutch war. The Plague in 1665 and the Great Fire of London in 1666 both dislocated trade, on which the customs revenue depended. Nor did the situation improve in the 1670s. The subsidy and other extraordinary taxes granted in 1670–1, plus the sale of fee farm rents at about the same time, did not stave off the Stop of the Exchequer at the beginning of 1672. The Stop of the Exchequer was an operation by which the King extinguished a large part of his floating debt by unilaterally cancelling the payment of interest to his creditors among the bankers in order to release funds required for the third Dutch war. It achieved this objective at the cost of alienating the monied interest in the City, destroying credit and creating a legacy of compensatory repayments, annuities and interest charges that was to persist through the Revolution and ultimately into Queen Anne's reign nearly forty years later.[26] The last extraordinary grant of Charles's reign was made for an earmarked purpose by a hostile House of Commons in the spring of 1679, and by the winter of 1679–80 the general financial situation seemed bleak. Sir Charles Lyttelton, a serving soldier waiting for his arrears, wrote gloomily '... 'tis allmost miraculous the government does yet subsist ...'.[27] Charles's floating debt was again at the level it had reached just before the Stop of the Exchequer. The additional excise duties granted in the early 1670s were due shortly to expire. Customs

receipts were thought to be faltering, partly because Dutch commercial competition had revived after the Treaty of Nijmegen
restored peacetime conditions in Europe, and partly because
trade with France had been prohibited following a balance-of-pay-
ments scare in 1678. At hardly any point since 1660–1 could the
financial situation, as conditioned by the Restoration financial settlement, be said to have been satisfactory, and contemporaries saw
little prospect of future improvement.

There is, however, another side to this argument. Even if it is
granted that the financial settlement of the early 1660s had not
worked particularly well, it is hard to see how either Parliament or
the King's ministers could have done better in the hectic conditions of 1660–1 when considerations other than finance – notably
religion – loomed large in everybody's mind. Contemporary techniques of calculating revenue yield, of estimating and accounting
for income and expenditure and of drawing up balance sheets,
were unsophisticated. 'Parliaments', remarked Clarendon sagely
(and with hindsight), 'do seldom make their Computations right,
but reckon what They give to be much more than is ever received,
and what They are to pay to be as much less than in Truth They
owe.'[28] What is perhaps surprising is the accuracy of the
Convention's perception of the King's expenditure as likely to be
about £1 200 000. In the event, Charles's crude average annual
expenditure for ordinary purposes over the whole of his reign has
been calculated as between £1 100 000 and £1 250 000.[29]
Admittedly, rigorous economies and retrenchments had to be
made from time to time at the instigation of successive finance
ministers, notably by Clifford in 1668, by Danby in 1676, and especially by Rochester in a sustained burst from 1679 to the end of
the reign. These economies included such undesirable features
as the suspension of pensions and salaries, thus building up
arrears which would eventually have to be satisfied. Even so, it
seems fair to conclude that in 1660–1 Parliament had made at
least an adequate, and possibly a generous, financial provision for
the King's ordinary needs. With reasonable care and frugality, his
revenue could be made sufficient. The considered conclusion of
the late Douglas Chandaman, the historian whose highly technical elucidation of Restoration finance has been regarded as
authoritative since it was published in 1975, is, simply, that
Charles II was more extravagant than he should have been.
Exchequer disbursements to the spending departments connected with the King's pleasures – the Household, the Wardrobe,

the Privy Purse, the Chamber – tended to rise in reckless fashion when Charles felt himself, often on no particularly good grounds, to be solvent.[30] Had Charles been more prudent and economical, he could have managed perfectly well, as indeed he did towards the end of his reign in the early 1680s, when he was compelled by a sustained political crisis to recognize that a more conscientious frugality was not merely desirable, but necessary.

This verdict on Charles's extravagance might be thought to be a little severe. It is easy to forget that Charles entered into his inheritance with an enormous backlog of intangible obligations to gratify. Royalists who had ruined themselves in the service of his father, who had encumbered their estates with debt or lost them altogether, whose fathers or brothers had been killed in the battles of the Civil War, whose houses had been besieged, burnt or occupied by enemies and who had perhaps endured years of exile, were clamouring for the King's attention in 1660 and the years immediately following, and Charles would have earned a reputation for insensitive ingratitude, with damaging political consequences, if for reasons of parsimony he had overlooked their claims on his generosity. To some extent, he actually did earn such a reputation. Expense incurred in relieving distressed Cavaliers by means of pensions, gifts or grants of land was one thing; quite another, and more notorious both in contemporary estimation and in historical folk-memory, was Charles's extravagance with regard to his mistresses. Any precise calculation of how much Charles spent on his mistresses would be difficult if not impossible. Two of them, Lady Castlemaine and the Duchess of Portsmouth, were rapacious by any standards, although the statements that the Duchess cost the nation £40 000 a year, and £136 668 in 1681 alone, are almost certainly exaggerated.[31] One estimate among Danby's papers suggests that she received £55 198 over a period of three years from 1676 to 1679, and that the King's payments to the Duchess and to Nell Gwyn together over the same period totalled £71 240.[32] These sums are not small, but they are not as outrageous as contemporaries seem to have assumed. Charles's illegitimate children were probably more expensive than his mistresses, since they had to be educated and equipped with a household commensurate with their rank over a period of as much as twenty years. Ormonde remarked in 1683 that the King might be out of debt in twelve months were it not for the insatiable demands of his children and their mothers.[33] It is, however, unlikely that the total amount of Charles's expenditure on mistresses and children significantly affected the overall financial complexion of his reign. And Charles was not markedly lavish with regard to another traditional royal expense, ostentatious building. His one excess in this direction was his new palace, designed by Sir Christopher Wren, at Winchester. This was planned at the very end of his reign, when Charles might reasonably have thought that he could afford it, and in any case the building works, which had cost less than £50 000, were abandoned when he died.[34]

Any judgement on whether or not Charles was 'extravagant' must inevitably be subjective. It is appropriate at this point to pose another, quite different, question about the financial settlement of the Restoration. Can a case be made, if one takes a longer perspective which incorporates the 1680s and James's reign as well as the 1660s and 1670s, for the view that Parliament, so far from being deliberately niggardly with the intention of deriving political and constitutional advantage for itself, was so generous to the Stuart monarchy in 1660–1 that it inadvertently created conditions in which the crown might eventually become financially independent?

The two mainstays of the ordinary revenue were the customs and the excise, both of which were linked in their yield to commercial prosperity. This naturally caused difficulties at times of economic stagnation or crisis, as in the years of war, plague and fire in the mid-1660s. However, the development of what turned out to be a sustained trade boom – indistinctly apparent in the late 1660s and early 1670s, gathering strength as England withdrew from the Franco-Dutch war in 1674, only briefly interrupted by the prohibition on French trade from 1678 to 1681, and in full swing all through the 1680s until the Revolution – transformed the royal finances.

Associated with this commercial prosperity are a number of other considerations which are relevant in the context of government finance. In the first place, tax farming – that is, the system by which (to put it simply) the right to collect a tax is leased to a consortium of financiers in return for a lump sum conveniently available to the government – had some advantages, but also one notable disadvantage, namely a reduced yield. Direct collection by salaried government officials was slower, but more easily supervised and ultimately more efficient. The customs began to be directly collected in 1671, and the excise and the hearth tax in 1683. The significance of this was considerable, not only for finance but indirectly for politics. The number of lucrative jobs in tax collecting at the ministers' disposal expanded at a time at which the possibilities of exploiting the resources of government patronage to manage the House of Commons were beginning to be appreciated by hard-headed politicians such as Clifford, Arlington and Danby.

Second, the growth of commercial prosperity and the rise in the customs and excise yield coincided with the period of retrenchment at court in the early 1680s. The King, wrote Roger North,

> grew more sensible of the niceties of state government, than he had been before, especially relating to the Treasury. He found that to be his sheet-anchor; for the Parliament would not always be in a giving humour; and the less, if he could not subsist without their help; for that animated his enemies, by giving hopes that his necessities would, at length, reduce him to the state of *carte blanche.*[35]

During the last years of his reign, Charles's total net income exceeded his expenditure fairly comfortably, even without parliamentary grants. This would have been the case even without Louis XIV's French subsidies, renewed from 1681 but an additional bonus rather than an essential condition of the circumstances that made it possible for Charles to ignore the 1664 Triennial Act in 1684 and to survive without any meeting of Parliament at all for the last four years of his reign.

A third consideration takes us into James's reign. When Parliament did eventually meet, it did so in unusual circumstances. The 1685 Parliament, summoned by James within weeks of his succession to the throne, met in a somewhat artificial atmosphere of gratitude and enthusiasm for the stability and prosperity provided by the Stuart monarchy since the upheavals of the Popish Plot, but also at a time at which that prosperity seemed to be threatened by nothing less than a new civil war, irresponsibly provoked by the Earl of Argyll and the Duke of Monmouth. Their rebellions in the West of Scotland and the West of England began, respectively, just before and just after Parliament met for its first session on 19 May. Professor Chandaman is at pains to point out that this Parliament was not the obsequious – indeed, servile – body of opportunist time-servers of Whig legend.[36] Its financial provisions were designed to provide James with precisely the same revenues as his brother, plus a modest increment in the shape of additional customs duties for eight years to rectify the damage done to the navy by Charles II's economies and a further supplement in the shape of additional customs and excise duties for five years to defray the cost of suppressing Monmouth's rebellion. A further grant of supply, voted by the Commons but lost in the prorogation of November 1685, may represent some further evidence of 'servility'; but it is hard to deny that the result was that James VII & II was by some distance the most solvent of the Stuart monarchs of the seventeenth century. His net income – with only the most negligible of French subsidies – climbed towards £2 000 000 *per annum*. When he planned to summon a Parliament in 1688–9, it was because he wanted a statutory confirmation of his Declaration of Indulgence and the repeal of the Test Act, not because he wanted money.

This is, of course, a less than complete picture of government finance in the 1680s. James's finances were indeed healthy; he did manage to reduce the burden of royal debt; he could, with care, have avoided another meeting of Parliament at least until 1693, when the additional duties granted in 1685 would have expired. However, he alarmed his subjects for reasons connected only indirectly, but still significantly, with finance. James's resources were exploited to expand his army, as well as to revive the fighting strength of his navy. His purpose in spending something over £600 000 *per annum* on his land forces, compared to the expenditure of less than £300 000 *per annum* for this purpose at the end of Charles II's reign,[37] was naturally questioned even by many of those who were otherwise content to see the crown's finances in a flourishing condition. Moreover, the international situation had been growing steadily more dangerous during James's reign, and the long-awaited European war finally broke out in September 1688 with the French invasion of the Rhineland. This was before William's expedition to England set sail, when the crown was still apparently secure on James's head. Had James remained on the throne, it is unlikely that he could have avoided involvement in the War of the League of Augsburg; and, if he had joined in, his expenditure would presumably again have mounted beyond the resources of his net income. William III's crude average annual expenditure through his reign – including the peacetime years after 1697 – amounted to somewhere in the region of £5 300 000. James's ministers would have been required to perform miracles of electioneering and management to secure a House of Commons willing to fund expenditure on this scale without insisting on the abandonment of James's programme in the area of religion.

This takes us into the realm of hypothesis. To return to James's reign, it seems to have been the case that finance was not a particularly serious issue in the development of the crisis that led to the Revolution. Some attempt was made to accuse James of constitutional impropriety because, in the first weeks of his reign, his officers continued to collect those taxes which had technically expired with his brother. It was unwise of James to authorize the collection and payment of taxation by proclamation, thus giving, as Roger North lucidly put it, 'a direct handle to his majesty's enemies to say, that his majesty, at the very entrance upon his government, levied money of the subject without act of parliament'.[38] This episode lay behind the reiteration in the Declaration of Rights of the principle that unparliamentary taxation levied by an exercise of the prerogative was illegal.[39] But James had lost no time in summoning a Parliament at the start of his reign, the merchants themselves requested that the customs should continue to be collected (to avoid a situation in which unscrupulous traders might undersell those who had paid the duties just before Charles's death), and the 1685 Parliament, in the event, retrospectively validated James's action without much apparent protest. Thereafter, James's financial circumstances continued to prosper. The Revolution of 1688 begins to look like that rare phenomenon: a political revolution with no discernible background in the financial difficulties of the regime overthrown by it.

III   The conduct of government

The old palace of Whitehall, extending from the Thames across the modern Whitehall to the Horse Guards and St James's Park, was the principal residence of both Charles II and James VII & II during their reigns. This enormous group of buildings was in many ways a symbol of royal government in the last four decades of the seventeenth century. It lay between the City of London to the north-east and the Houses of Parliament at Westminster to the south, within easy walking distance of both, but part of neither. It housed the Kings, their mistresses, their household, several of their ministers and some government offices, including those of the Privy Council. Foreign ambassadors were received in the Banqueting House. The Admiralty was accommodated within the palace when the Duke of York was Lord High Admiral in the 1660s. There were chapels, theatres, tennis courts and bowling greens. The palace had never been envisaged as an architectural whole. It had accumulated over time with several piecemeal rebuildings, and it was thought to contain more than two thousand rooms, some of which flooded when the tides on the Thames were exceptionally high.[40] After the Revolution, William, who preferred Kensington, rarely used Whitehall. When the old palace burned down in 1698, the conflagration marked the end of a long and by then obsolete tradition of English government in which the monarch, the court, the ministers and the administration had been obscurely conceived in terms of a single physical location. Had the new palace at Winchester been completed after Charles's death, this tradition might, perhaps, have survived.[41]

Whitehall had originally been acquired by the crown from Cardinal Wolsey. Its use as a focus of the court by Charles and James, and its disappearance less than ten years after the Revolution of 1688, might well suggest that the character of Restoration government rather looked back to the Tudors, than forward to the Hanoverians. In some ways, this impression would be correct. For example, it is relevant to ask who composed 'the government' at any given moment in the reigns of Charles II and James VII & II. The sequence of 'Clarendon's ministry' from 1660 to 1667, 'the Cabal' from 1667 to 1673 and 'Danby's ministry' from 1673 to 1679 is familiar as a convenient method of partitioning the years from 1660 to 1679 into manageable segments. It can be challenged on the grounds that it is by no means clear that contemporaries thought in terms of a 'ministry' led by a single politician, or by a group of politicians, in the sense that became familiar in the eighteenth century.

There is no doubt that Clarendon enjoyed great prestige in the early 1660s, and that he was deemed to be the King's leading minister by virtue of his age and experience. Other politicians in high office were regarded as his allies and associates, most notably the elderly and ineffectual Earl of Southampton. However, it is easy to be misled by Clarendon's own magisterial account of his years in office, written during his old age in exile, into supposing that he exercised more influence than in fact he did. Clarendon had long periods of inactivity because of ill health, especially from December 1662 to March 1663 and again in the autumn of 1665. Some of the policies with which he was associated were failures. He could not secure a moderate religious settlement, and the phrase 'Clarendon Code' attached to the repressive legislation of the Cavalier Parliament was (as has long been recognized) a misnomer. He was opposed to war with the Dutch in 1664, yet war broke out. He disapproved of Downing's ingenious scheme of 1665 for mobilizing government credit through negotiable Treasury orders to be repaid in sequence, yet Downing's policy was adopted. He disliked the Irish Cattle Bill in 1666, yet it passed with the backing of prominent courtiers hostile to Clarendon's ally Ormonde in 1667.[42] His opponents on these issues were as often as not his fellow-ministers. If Clarendon was, in any sense that means anything, a 'chief minister', he was not a very successful one.

There was no sense at all in which the 'Cabal' was 'a ministry'. The circumstance that five more or less prominent politicians (Lord Clifford, Lord Arlington, the Duke of Buckingham, Lord Ashley and the Duke of Lauderdale) had names or titles the initial letters of which formed the word 'cabal' was an accident to which attention was drawn at the time, and the nickname stuck. It meant very little in practical terms. The complex world of court politics in the late 1660s and early 1670s defies easy classification. If any one minister was predominant, it was Arlington, whose reputation on the historical stock exchange has risen while that of Clarendon has fallen.[43] The King himself has a claim to be regarded as his own 'first minister' during the years when he pursued an unofficial foreign policy, that of the Secret Treaty of Dover, alongside a public one of friendship with the Dutch. The initiatives which led in 1672 to the Declaration of Indulgence in the area of religion, and the war with the Dutch in the area of foreign policy, also began with the King.

With the emergence of Danby in 1673, we are in a political world which does approximate a little more closely to that of the eighteenth century. Danby held office, not as Lord Chancellor like Clarendon, nor as Secretary of State like Arlington, but as Lord Treasurer – a post which, transmuted into that of First Lord of the Treasury, was that which successful eighteenth-century prime ministers were to occupy. Danby appreciated, more clearly than Clarendon, that continuity in government was likely to be achieved through the mobilization of the patronage powers available to a minister who controlled the royal finances. His political memoranda indicate that he recognized the importance of planning ahead for parliamentary sessions by attracting uncommitted MPs by inducements in the form either of office or money. He had consistent policy objectives and a group of allies on whom he

could rely, such as Henry Coventry and Sir Joseph Williamson, the
two Secretaries of State, or Lord Finch, the Lord Chancellor. Even
so, Danby did not preside over a united administration. He could
never be sure that his efforts to sustain the King's government
would not be undermined by the King himself, or by other ministers who might strike out an independent line. He had little in
common, for example, with the ex-Presbyterian Lord Privy Seal,
the Earl of Anglesey, or with Arlington, who retained influence in
the household office of Lord Chamberlain after his retirement as
Secretary of State, while Sir Robert Carr, the Chancellor of the
Duchy of Lancaster, was an active enemy.

Carr, a second-rank politician, supplies a good illustration of one
reason why it is difficult to speak of a 'ministry' before the
Revolution of 1688. His office was not a particularly prominent one
(despite the presence of its holder in twentieth-century cabinets),
but he had a patent to hold it for his life and he could not easily be
sacked from it.[44] It was difficult, although not absolutely impossible, to get rid of office-holders who conceived themselves to
possess their offices as a form of property.[45] The Duke of Ormonde
was not prepared to retire as Lord Steward of the Household
in the winter of 1678–9 unless he received a compensation of
£15 000.[46] The atmosphere in which court and ministerial appointments were made is well illustrated by a contemporary newsletter:

> Capt. Bridges ... has bought Mr Godolphin's place of Bed
> Chamber-man, Mr Godolphin has bought Mr Hide's place of
> Master of the Robes, and a Contract has beene on foote
> betweene Mr Secretary Coventry, And the said Mr Hide about
> the Secretaryship [of State], But it seemes his Majesty cannot
> bee without Mr Coventryes service at this Conjuncture, & so a
> Stopp is put to the businesse.[47]

When, in January 1681, the Earl of Sunderland was dismissed as
Secretary of State after voting for Exclusion, his wife thought it
unusual and indeed improper that he was not to receive financial
compensation for the loss of his office.[48] In short, it was sometimes difficult to secure the appointment or dismissal of ministers
without some reference to reasons other than their competence,
political reliability or loyalty. In these circumstances it was hard to
envisage a 'ministry' as a closely knit team of like-minded men.

There was, therefore, an archaic flavour about the ministerial
politics of the Restoration years. Towards the end of Charles's
reign, however, an innovation is discernible which, perhaps

superficially, foreshadowed a more permanent development after the Revolution. Contemporaries began to refer to a small group of active ministers as 'the King's Cabinet Council' or, more laconically, as 'the Cabinet'. This was connected only indirectly with the scheme associated with Sir William Temple for streamlining the Privy Council. Although adopted in April 1679, this in the event proved to be only a short-lived expedient of no permanent significance. Earlier than this, in August 1678, a newsletter reported that 'his Majestie in the Cabinet Councell' had decided that troops should be transported to Flanders.[49] In April 1679, Henry Coventry remarked that the Earl of Essex was not only a Commissioner of the Treasury but also 'of the Cabinet Council' and 'in very good grace'.[50] A few days later, at the time of the unexpected remodelling of the Privy Council, it was hinted that Privy Council reform would render unnecessary a Cabinet 'of such model as hath been before'.[51] By late 1682, the notion of 'membership' of the Cabinet was hardening. 'I finde', wrote one observer, 'my Lord Sunderland soe fully restor'd to favour that his station is a Cabbinet Councellor, as well as a Privy one'.[52] It was rumoured the following January that even household officials as prominent as Arlington, who was still Lord Chamberlain, had been refused admission to the King's bedchamber, although the Duke of Ormonde was allowed in, not in his capacity as Lord Steward, 'but as he is one of the Ministers, *i.e.* I suppose of the Cabinet'.[53]

There was nothing new in the concept of an inner ring of influential ministers. The Privy Council had been divided into committees since the Restoration, with a reform of nomenclature and membership in 1668 preceding that of 1679. Ministers holding 'offices of business' who sat on most or all of these committees naturally tended to supply a hard core to the direction and implementation of the King's policies. However, the term 'Cabinet' to describe this hard core, although sanctioned by contemporary usage from the late 1670s, means very little. It is not clear how often the 'Cabinet' met, whether it did so at prescribed times, what business was discussed, whether ministers were expected to attend unless unavoidably prevented, or whether gatecrashers, such as Arlington in 1683, were invariably excluded. The Cabinet in this loose informal sense continued in James's reign, when the term was also sometimes applied to a separate clique of Catholic advisers. Reresby mentioned that the King summoned a Cabinet meeting at short notice for the morning of

the day upon which he fled from London in December 1688.[54]
The real starting point for the continuous history of the Cabinet,
and for its organic development over time is, however, usually
thought to have come after the Revolution, in the early years of
William's reign. Before then, the phrase 'Cabinet Council', like
that of 'Premier Minister d'estat' which was applied to Danby in
1679,[55] retains a somewhat shadowy quality, and had yet to
acquire any precise definition.[56]

  The conduct of government, and the composition of governments, thus combined elements inherited from the past, innovations thought worth retaining from the Interregnum, and
concepts, as yet imperfectly realized, that were to develop
significantly in the future. James displayed more reforming
energy than Charles during his short reign; he wanted to get rid
of the anomalous Duchy of Lancaster,[57] to rationalize the administration of the American colonies[58] and to reduce the size and, if
possible, the expense of the Household.[59] Unlike Charles, James
seems to have consciously aimed at efficient, cost-effective government. Neither monarch fully appreciated that the smooth func-
tioning of government, and especially the implementation of
governmental or religious change involving legislation, depended
more and more on the co-operation of Parliament, secured if
necessary by 'management'.

IV   Politics and political management

The principal issues in politics in the reign of Charles II were religion, foreign policy and finance. For most contemporaries, religion outweighed the other two, but all three were linked. There
was a religious dimension to foreign policy, as France emerged in
the 1660s as the most formidable and aggressive Catholic power
in Europe. There was a financial dimension to foreign policy,
since money had to be found to pay for war or preparations for
war. When all three came to the fore simultaneously, the result
was a full-scale political crisis, as in 1672 when the Stop of
the Exchequer (2 January), the Declaration of Indulgence
(15 March) and the outbreak of the third Dutch War (17 March)
followed each other over a period of a few weeks. Other points of
contention surfaced from time to time, notably the regulation of
trade (especially Irish trade) in the 1660s, or constitutional
questions relating to the duration of parliaments and the royal

power of adjourning or proroguing them in the 1670s. In James VII & II's reign, finance was temporarily in abeyance, but a new issue related indirectly to finance emerged; namely, the size and disposition of the army.

Perhaps the main focus of political debate on these topics was the court. Small groups of active politicians lobbied for and against the adoption and implementation of specific religious policies, strategies in foreign affairs or techniques of financial management. Senior ministers enjoying influence with the King advanced arguments for, or sought to rebut arguments against, a particular course of action, in the Privy Council or in one of its committees, or in private audience with the King. At this level, politics was still rooted in court faction, as had been the case at least for the preceding one hundred years. Good examples of the operation of personal ambition in the insulated atmosphere of court politics can be identified in the Earl of Bristol's attempt to seize the initiative in government in 1663, and Clarendon's resistance to Bristol's pretensions; or in the Duke of Buckingham's maverick interventions in affairs in 1667–8 and again in 1678, when on both occasions he was rumoured by surprised courtiers to be high in the King's favour.[60]

If Whitehall was one arena of policy formation and political activity, Westminster provided an alternative stage for discussion which no ambitious politician could afford to ignore. All who were active at the higher levels of court politics either possessed, or aspired to, a seat in the House of Lords. The House of Commons, irrespective of its role in granting taxation, provided both an opportunity for a man of business to make a reputation for himself as a faithful exponent of royal policy, and an indication of the likely attitudes and opinions of the responsible classes of society outside the world of the court. Both Houses together validated policy through legislation. It was still not impossible for a policy initiative to circumvent Parliament, as the Declarations of Indulgence of 1672 and 1687 demonstrated, or for Parliament to be kept in ignorance of the real character of royal policy, as was the case after the Secret Treaty of Dover. These were not examples which inspired much confidence, however, and the weight of experience and information gained by the parliamentary classes in the 1640s and 1650s, combined with the respect for traditional institutions expressed by ministers such as Clarendon, ensured that Parliament was regarded after 1660 as a feature of the political process not lightly to be overlooked.

This introduces an aspect of the political history of the period from the Restoration to the Revolution which has attracted much attention from historians. How was Parliament to be managed? A number of politicians, notably Arlington, Clifford and Danby, were groping towards the realization that the King's government might be more strong and successful if it could consistently rely on a majority of votes in both Houses of Parliament than would be the case if it could not. Conversely, those opposed to some aspect or another of royal policy recognized the advantages of combining together a group of MPs on some more solid foundation than simply congruity of opinion. The point at issue here, and the subject of much recent historical debate, is whether or not the first steps in the direction of organizing votes in Parliament amounted to the early origins of party politics.

A political party is not easy to define. It is more than a group of like-minded people acting together, or a faction inspired by allegiance to one prominent individual in the hope of reward. A fully developed political party will have an ideology; that is, a body of general principles covering a number of aspects of politics and government. It will have a programme; that is, a set of pragmatic proposals for implementing its general principles. It will have an organization, at several different levels: a headquarters at the centre, local offshoots in the constituencies to win elections, a management team in both Houses of Parliament to win divisions once Parliament has been elected. It will have a leader or leaders, who may perhaps be challenged by rivals, but who at any given moment are recognized to be at the head of the party. A final characteristic of a political party is that it should have some continuity over time; it must hold together in the face of difficulties, and if its leaders die or retire, new ones should come forward to transmit the ideology and the programme forward to the next generation. It should be emphasized that this no doubt elementary and over-simplified definition is of a political party in an advanced form. The several characteristics emerge at different speeds and with different emphases when parties are in an embryonic stage. No-one now supposes, as some nineteenth-century historians did, that the use by contemporaries of the terms 'Whig' and 'Tory' in the last few years of Charles II's reign means that politics suddenly began to be conducted by forerunners in full-bottomed wigs of Gladstone and Disraeli. What can be said is that a concept of the possibilities of political organization along party lines began to develop, and to be acted upon, in the reign of

Charles II, even if this fell some way short of party politics or a party system in the sense that can be discerned a generation later in the reign of Queen Anne.

In the early years after the Restoration, this concept was as yet rudimentary, but it can be traced.[61] Andrew Marvell, the poet and MP for Hull, wrote six lines in his 1667 satire *Last Instructions to a Painter* which have often been quoted as evidence for an early, conscious distinction between a Court and a Country party in the House of Commons:

> Draw next a Pair of Tables op'ning, then
> The *House of Commons* clatt'ring like the Men.
> Describe the *Court* and *Country*, both set right,
> On opposite points, the black against the white.
> Those having lost the Nation at *Trick track*,
> These now advent'ring how to win it back.

The next two lines are revealing in that Marvell suggested that the outcome of parliamentary activity depended on fortuitous and unpredictable accident:

> The Dice betwixt them must the Fate divide,
> As Chance does still in Multitudes decide.

However, Marvell went on to qualify this with a reference to the partiality of Sir Edward Turnor, the Speaker from 1661 to 1671:

> But here the *Court* does its advantage know,
> For the Cheat *Turnor* for them both must throw.[62]

Marvell's description of a House of Commons containing, if not divided between, two 'parties' – which, however, were not so organized that votes could be calculated in advance – corresponds to other contemporary perceptions of parliamentary politics in the 1660s.

Clarendon's account of his somewhat old-fashioned methods of pulling together a 'Court party' is well-known. Clarendon disliked what he called 'great and notorious Meetings and Cabals in Parliament', and he preferred a more discreet system of 'management' by ex-Cavaliers of his own generation with a regional base, such as Sir Hugh Pollard from Devon or Sir Job Charlton from the Welsh border counties. His concept of parliamentary management was sufficiently nebulous for him to allow a back-bench country gentleman, Sir Robert Paston, to make the first proposal of the all-important grant of supply for the Dutch war in November 1664.

He clearly regarded the attempts by Sir Henry Bennet (later
Arlington) and by younger men such as William Coventry and
Thomas Clifford to mobilize a more organized Court party bound
together by links of obligation and office with grave misgivings.[63]
During the 'Cabal' years after Clarendon's fall, it was Clifford who
emerged as the principal coordinator of a Court party in the
House of Commons. This could not be a very coherent party
because, as has already been suggested, it was not altogether clear
who composed the King's government or what government policy
actually was. Even so, Clifford, who was in the Commons until his
elevation to the peerage in 1672, won over some influential, formerly hostile MPs, and contrived from the front bench to manage
a relatively harmonious session in 1670–1.[64] Danby carried
Clifford's techniques a stage further in the mid-1670s, by concen-
trating on attracting the votes of the run-of-the-mill MPs; 'he reckoned', wrote Burnet thirty years later 'that the greater number was
the surer game'.[65] These successive Court parties of Clarendon,
Arlington, Clifford and Danby undoubtedly had an existence in
the minds of contemporaries, but they do not fit the definition of
party in the fully developed sense inasmuch as they do not meet
the test of continuity over time. The fall of Clarendon in 1667, the
partial retirement of Arlington in 1674, the enforced resignation
of Clifford in 1673 and the disgrace of Danby in 1679 broke up
their respective followings.

The 'Country party' was equally prone to disruption from shifting allegiances and changing circumstances. A number of MPs
consistently criticized the ministers of the 1660s and 1670s and
opposed the policies pursued by them – such as John Vaughan
and Sir Thomas Littleton during the Clarendon years, or William
Lord Cavendish (who, as the son of a peer, sat in the Commons)
and Henry Powle during the Danby regime – but there was no
obvious method of organizing an 'opposition party' that would
not have aroused potentially damaging memories of 1640–1.
There were, however, some straws in the wind. Sir Thomas Meres
referred in the Commons in 1673 to members 'of this side of that
House, and that side', as though the seating arrangements had
come to manifest a significant distinction. His words were
described as 'not parliamentary'.[66] By the mid- to late 1670s, it was
possible for a minister, like Danby, or an opposition politician,
like Shaftesbury, to compile, or to commission, lists of the
members of both Houses and to mark the majority of names with
some indication of their likely attitudes. Danby and his allies

Sir Joseph Williamson and Sir Richard Wiseman drew up a number of lists of actual and potential supporters and of likely opponents.[67] These lists contain some puzzling attributions and incongruities, but it is the fact that they were compiled at all that is significant. Politicians were thinking in terms of counting heads.

During the summer of 1678, and the autumn and winter which followed, the issues of foreign policy, finance and religion again came to the forefront to the point of crisis. The preparations to join in the Franco-Dutch war were more advanced than is sometimes supposed. Troops were shipped to the Low Countries, and were engaged under Monmouth and Ossory (Ormonde's son) in the last action of the war at Mons in August 1678 as a truce was concluded.[68] The subsequent revelation that the King and Danby had used these preparations as a cover for extracting supply from Parliament and a subsidy from Louis XIV, without intending a serious commitment to war, was to lead to Danby's loss of office and fall from power early in 1679. Meanwhile, the King still had to find the money to pay, or disband, the troops raised for a war he had, it appeared, not proposed to fight. The religious issue was, of course, the Popish Plot. This was revealed by Christopher Kirkby and Israel Tonge in August 1678, sensationally elaborated by Titus Oates in September, and given spectacular publicity by the discovery of the body of Sir Edmund Berry Godfrey in October.

This combination was to produce Danby's incarceration in the Tower, three general elections in two years, the most stormy parliamentary sessions since the Restoration, and a sequence of kaleidoscopic shifts both in the ministerial politics of the court and in the alignments of members of both Houses of Parliament. The words 'Whig' and 'Tory' began to be used – the latter some time after the former – to describe attitudes and opinions. Both had become fairly familiar by about the end of 1682. It is not surprising that commentators who looked back on these events from the standpoint of the reigns of William and Anne and the Hanoverian succession saw the origins of their own divisions in the midst of this troubled period. Writing at the end of William's reign, James Welwood observed that

> The Discovery of the *Popish Plot* had great and various Effects upon the Nation ... it gave the Rise to, at least settled that unhappy distinction of Whig and Tory among the People of *England,* that has since occasion'd so many Mischiefs.[69]

Gilbert Burnet and Roger North, from their different standpoints, agreed that party divisions began in the latter part of Charles II's reign.[70] Lord Cowper, explaining British politics to the newly succeeded George I in 1714, wrote

> [Two] parties began to form themselves and give names to each other about the time the Bill of Exclusion was set on foot, in the reign of Charles II.

He noted, but discounted, the theory that the parties had really originated in the Civil War, before continuing

> This contest [over the Exclusion Bills] was also managed by a paper war; wherein they who were for excluding the Duke of York were by their adversaries in division called Whigs; and the others, who struggled to secure the crown to him, were called Tories.[71]

Later, by the early nineteenth century, Charles James Fox and Lord John Russell took it for granted that the system of politics with which they were familiar had emerged in the late 1670s and early 1680s.[72]

These hindsight views are, of course, not evidence to sustain the proposition that the parties of the early 1680s were indeed parties in the developed sense defined above. The Whigs possessed an ideology and a programme: to resist the growth of what they called 'Popery and arbitrary government'; to define more closely the limits of monarchical power; and to enact legislation in order to achieve these objectives. The Tories possessed at least an ideology: to defend the Stuart monarchy and the Church of England against a revival of what they believed to be republicanism and rebellion. Over time, the Tories also developed a programme: to assist the King in eliminating the Whigs from office at court, in London municipal politics and in the provinces.

These ideologies were not entirely straightforward, and may perhaps be interpreted in different ways. It has been suggested that the Exclusion Bill was not so prominent a feature of the Whig programme as has usually been thought, but was rather only one of a number of possible strategies for preserving the nation from 'Popish tyranny'.[73] The early Whigs were less concerned with Exclusion, which provided for a hypothetical future danger from a Catholic succession, than with the more immediate danger from Charles himself, a King who had resorted to deceit to improve his revenue and expand his army, and who was suspiciously sceptical about the Popish Plot. Similarly, the Tories were not just blind upholders of prerogative. They argued that Exclusion was unnecessary. If James were ever to ascend the throne, he would still be bound by the law. He would not be able to apply the principle *cuius regio eius religio* ('the ruler determines his country's religion') to a nation in which parliamentary approval would be needed to repeal the Reformation and Elizabethan statutes which guaranteed the Protestant Church.[74] These and other subtleties of party ideology were elaborated in what Cowper called the 'paper war' which followed the lapse of the Licensing Act in 1679.

Granted an ideology and a programme, there remain two very pertinent questions: Who were the 'party leaders'? What is the evidence for party organisation? Shaftesbury, for long regarded as the founder of the Whig party and its first head, may have been 'one of the Whig leaders', but he was never 'the Whig leader' in undisputed control of a party whose members without exception regarded him as such.[75] As for the Tories, no one politician has ever been clearly regarded as 'the Tory leader'. Possibilities might include the finance minister Rochester, the ageing grandee Ormonde, or Sir Leoline Jenkins, the Court party's front-bench spokesman in the Commons in the session of 1680–1; but none of these would have been likely to have claimed the distinction for themselves or to have been regarded as possessing it by others. A case might be made for the King himself, with the Duke of York, after 1681. Another circumstance that has clouded the identification of 'party leaders' is that many politicians changed sides. Halifax had been an associate of the opposition peers in the mid-1670s, but was active in opposing Exclusion in November 1680. Notwithstanding an alleged remark that anyone who was neither a Whig nor a Tory was a rascal, Halifax is chiefly remembered for defining a non-party position in politics, that of 'trimming', which he conceived to be the stabilization of politics by support for the weaker side until the 'ship of state' is again balanced and upright.[76] Essex had been in high office in the 1670s, but he ended his life in the Tower, accused of complicity in the Rye House Plot. Sunderland voted for Exclusion while Secretary of State, lost office, but was back in favour by 1682. If politicians as prominent as Halifax, Essex and Sunderland cannot clearly be classified as adherents of either party, then they can hardly be regarded as party leaders.[77]

The evidence for party organization has similarly been called into question. The Green Ribbon Club at the King's Head Tavern in

Chancery Lane, once regarded as the Whig party headquarters, was as much a convivial as a political organization. It met intermittently and did not count Shaftesbury among its members.[78] Local initiatives and activity in the constituencies at election times were not coordinated by any central planning for which much evidence survives. Likewise, the tactics of debate in the two Houses of Parliament cannot readily be shown to have been managed with significantly more sophistication than had been the case in earlier periods.

This case has been trenchantly argued in a spirit of revisionism which has greatly enlivened the historiography of the period. It has not, however, won complete acceptance.[79] A number of points may tentatively be suggested on the opposite side. Ministerial politics, the competition between 'ins' and 'outs' at court, did not necessarily correspond to the politics of ideology in the pamphlet press, in London or provincial municipal politics, or in Parliament. Even in Anne's reign, when the parties were more coherent, there were several politicians, such as Godolphin, Marlborough or Robert Harley, who were unclassifiable, or classifiable only at the risk of over-simplification, as Whig or Tory. The difficulty of attaching labels to men like Halifax, Essex or Sunderland in the earlier period does not really matter. Sir William Temple's intricate inside account of ministerial politics in 1679–80, written apparently in February 1681, does not mention Whigs or Tories. The motivation of (for example) Essex is described by Temple simply as a desire to resume his former office of Lord-Lieutenant of Ireland at the expense of Ormonde. The impression that Temple's memoir produces is of faction politics, the competition for office of ambitious men from which Temple clearly was anxious to distance himself. Yet Temple also described the nation as 'divided into two strong factions with the greatest Heats and Animosities, and ready to break out into Violence ... The Heads on both Sides desiring it', and he refers to 'both Parties who could agree in nothing else' and 'Lord Shaftesbury and his Party'. Temple's picture is of aspirants for office and power who were locked into a world of court intrigue at Whitehall, yet who were simultaneously conscious of, and eager to exploit, the tumult of conflicting opinion in the nation outside.[80] This is not incompatible with a concept of 'party' in parliamentary and electoral politics, even if 'party leadership' was erratic and fluctuating.

The evidence for organization in the mobilization of opinion, in the management of elections and in the coordination of voting

in both Houses of Parliament is elusive, but it is not entirely
absent. The distribution of mass petitions for signature and their
subsequent presentation implies some measure of organization,
as does the orchestration of pope-burning processions, anniversary demonstrations and other manifestations of street theatre.[81]
The Green Ribbon Club, if not a party headquarters, was
nevertheless active in the distribution of printed propaganda, in
the countryside as well as in London.[82] The unsuccessful attempt
to purge the county benches of pro-court JPs during the short
period during which Shaftesbury and his allies were included in
the Privy Council, and the more successful and competent purges
of Exclusionists in 1680 and again in 1681 following the dissolution of the Oxford Parliament, indicate a recognition that party
allegiance extended into the countryside.[83] The loaves and fishes
of local power were to be enjoyed by men of loyalty and withheld
from men of faction. Voting patterns in the House of Lords can
be measured by a number of surviving lists covering the period
from the autumn of 1678 to the end of the 1680–1 session. These
suggest that about half of the lay peers who voted took a consistent line on what might hypothetically be called either the 'Whig'
or opposition side, or the 'Tory' or court side. The proportion
was higher, about three-quarters, when the issue was specifically to
do with religion. The division in November 1678 on whether to
add the declaration against transubstantiation to the oaths to be
required by the parliamentary Test Act, and the vote in December
1680 on the Catholic peer Lord Stafford's guilt or innocence of
complicity in the plot, were of this type.[84] This is not proof of the
existence of a party organization in the Lords but, if there was
some form of management behind the scenes, this is approximately the pattern one would expect. The level of organization in
the House of Commons is obscure, and it is not easy to discern
any very sophisticated degree of mobilization of MPs along party
lines. Even so, it has been suggested that small groups of MPs who
spoke frequently, who were elected to numerous committees and
who evidently commanded the attention of the House, constituted 'steering groups'. These influenced other members in a
fashion which, if not 'party leadership', can be described as
marking a stage in the transition from 'faction' to 'party'.[85]

In the constituencies themselves, an impression derived from
the letters and papers of some of those involved in municipal and
parliamentary elections is of a whole-hearted, almost boisterous
commitment to adversarial politics. For example, Viscount

Yarmouth (the former Sir Robert Paston) was the leader of a Court caucus in Norfolk who interested himself in Norwich, Great Yarmouth, Thetford and King's Lynn as well as the county. He sent out circular letters, organized meetings of his supporters in Norwich inns, coordinated their activities, and arranged for the witnesses in petitions about disputed elections to travel to London for the hearings. He and his friends attributed the same degree of organization (interpreted as knavish cunning) to their opponents. 'All persons', wrote one of his agents after a vigorous city election in Norwich, 'that have ever dealt with this phanatick crew have found them so full of tricks of dishonesty that they had great need to have their friends true and firm'. When, in July 1679, Yarmouth decided that he might better serve the King's interest if he was promoted in the peerage, he was created Earl of Yarmouth less than a fortnight later.[86]

Norfolk local politics may well have possessed a quality of vehemence that was unusual in other places. Even so, there is plenty of evidence that opinion, votes and concerted campaigns were being organized, and that the level of sophistication in this organization was increasing, during the general elections of 1679–81. Sometimes this resulted from a clash of strong and energetic personalities, as in Cheshire where Henry Booth conducted a vigorous effort on behalf of Exclusion in the elections to the Oxford Parliament. Sometimes the care devoted to electoral politics emerged out of traditional local rivalries which only gradually identified themselves with the divisions in national affairs. It would, admittedly, be hard to find much evidence for the national coordination of these local initiatives from London, and such evidence as there is defies easy interpretation. When Shaftesbury was consulted about the choice of candidates for the Buckinghamshire constituencies in January 1679, it seems only to have been the result of a chance meeting.[87] But many constituencies, singly or in groups, experienced an intensification of consciously organized political activity in the conditions of the early 1680s. So did a number of towns, as they engaged in an internal competition for municipal power. London, in particular, became an arena for a most intense struggle for the prizes, first of the office of Sheriff, then of the office of Lord Mayor, in the summer and autumn of 1682. One side was habitually referred to as 'Whig', and the other was occasionally described as 'Tory' but more often, by those sympathetic to it, as the 'loyal', 'moderate' or 'honest' party. 'The Whigges resolve with might & maine to oppose Mr North's being sheriffe', wrote Lord Longford, a keen observer, in June 1682; in August he referred to 'the Whiggish party (I meane those that are violent)' and 'the moderate party'; by October, 'it is Evident the Whigs make out their numbers by the raskallity & meanest of the People, the other partye being chiefly made up of the substantiallest & ablest Cittizens'.[88] These labels were attached to active and organized groups in the wards and livery companies of the City.[89] By the following January, the Duke of Ormonde, well into his seventies but alert to the political slang of the new generation, wrote, 'We are now come under the three denominations of Toryes, Whigs and Trimmers ...The language of the last is moderation, unity & Peace, joyning with the Whigs in their care of Relligion & property, & with the Torys for Monarchy & a just & legal prerogative'.[90]

The Whigs and Tories discussed by Ormonde early in 1683 possessed ideologies and programmes, and, perhaps more debatably, leaders and organization. Whether they possessed the further criterion of continuity is problematic. The names persisted into the eighteenth century and were still familiar, after much change and discontinuity, in the nineteenth. This means little in the context of the 1680s, when party divisions were regarded as regrettable and it was not anticipated that they would survive. When, for example, an opposition developed with surprising speed in the second session of the 1685 Parliament after an harmonious first session, no-one thought of it as a revived 'Whig' party. Sir John Reresby recorded that 'severall of [the King's] servants and officers of the army that were of the Hous devided against him'.[91] It was an expression of the disquiet of the men of loyalty at the King's policies. Little evidence for the concerted mobilization of MPs survives, even though the Court party was losing divisions within a week of the King's speech at the opening of the session.

The interval between parliamentary sessions from November 1685 to January 1689 enhanced the obsolescence of the party names, and inhibited their revival. Some former Whigs, attracted by the prospect of toleration for Dissenters or by the chance to recover local influence, attached themselves to James's bandwagon in 1687–8.[92] Many former Tories, purged from local office and alarmed at the King's assault on the Church of England, began to wonder if an unequivocal commitment to the Stuart monarchy was, after all, the wisest course to follow. Even the Duke of Ormonde, that archetype of old Cavalier loyalty, is alleged to have expressed doubts in the last year of his long life:

The old Duke of Ormond[e] who dy'd Some month [*sic*] before the Revolution in 1688 knew of that design, & told Dean Jones that he wou'd neither draw his Sword agst King James nor by G-d for him. He was not us'd to swear but then he was heartily disgusted at that King's proceedings.[93]

The clandestine conspiracy that culminated in the Revolution in the winter of 1688–9 was conducted by men who might have taken opposite sides in politics in the early 1680s but who were now prepared to sink their differences and co-operate in a joint venture to bring James to his senses. For example, the Earl of Derby, a moderate courtier, and Henry Booth, now Lord Delamer and one of the most vehement of spokesmen for Exclusion, together planned a rising on behalf of the Prince of Orange on the Lancashire/Cheshire border in November 1688. Conversely, men who had formerly been allies now found themselves on opposite sides, as when the Earl of Danby and Sir Henry Goodricke placed Sir John Reresby under house arrest at York when he refused to abandon his loyalty to the King.[94]

It would be easy to conclude, from the disintegration of Whig organization and leadership in the aftermath of the Rye House Plot in 1683, and the dislocation of Tory ideology in the Revolution, that the origins of the Whig and Tory parties of the eighteenth century cannot be found in the political crisis of the early 1680s. The parties of Anne's reign had reshaped ideologies, changed programmes, different leaders and revamped organizations. Above all, there had been a break in continuity in the mid-1680s, between the period when the names 'Whig' and 'Tory' were first used and the period late in William's reign when they came back into fashion. Even so, the body of opinions and attitudes that were labelled 'Whig' and 'Tory' in the early 1680s survived. They naturally changed in response to the circumstances and conditions of the 1690s and early 1700s, but there remained a concept of a group of Whig views at odds with a group of Tory views which was never quite extinguished. There was even some continuity of personnel. Men such as Thomas Wharton and Lord Cavendish (later the first Duke of Devonshire) on the Whig side, and Sir Christopher Musgrave and the Earls of Nottingham and Rochester on the Tory side, spanned the transition from the late 1670s into Anne's reign. Wharton never lost his sense of a conflict between Whigs and Tories, even at times when that conflict might have seemed to be most in abeyance. His famous anonymous letter, written on Christmas Day 1689 and reproaching King William for abandoning the principles of the Revolution, concludes with the passage

> This [a proposal to settle a large revenue on Princess Anne, to make her independent of William] was laboured by the Torrys and high church men, and carried for you [that is, defeated] by the honest old Whig interest; so that, Sir, you have clear demonstration, which is the stronger; and we hope you will no longer delay espousing the honester part of the nation.[95]

The early 1680s did not perhaps witness the establishment of two semi-permanent organizations which were genuinely parties and which enjoyed a continuous existence into the Hanoverian period. What can be discerned in the latter part of Charles II's reign is a developing perception on the part of contemporaries of the opportunities offered by a more intensive organization of political activity, in urban and constituency politics as well as in Parliament. These opportunities were to be grasped after the Revolution in an environment of annual parliamentary sessions, often devoted for long periods to technical financial issues. A new cohort of politicians in the early 1690s, exemplified by Robert Harley, attended regularly and spoke frequently. They mastered and exploited procedure, and developed a strong sense of tactics.[96] Here, perhaps, was the soil from which party politics in the full sense sprang; but it is surely not too fanciful to suggest that some preliminary spadework had been undertaken by the previous generation.

V   The later Stuart monarchy

The Prince of Orange's entry into London on 18 December 1688 was very different from that of Charles II on 29 May 1660:

> It happened to be a very rainy day. And yet great numbers came to see him. But, after they had stood long in the wet, he disappointed them: for he, who neither loved shews nor shoutings, went through the park. And even this trifle helped to set people's spirits on edge.[97]

The style of monarchy of William II of Scotland and III of England was different from that of either of his two immediate predecessors. William was not necessarily a more 'modern' King.

He led armies in battle, he chose and dismissed his own ministers, he conducted his own foreign policy and he vetoed bills
which had passed the Commons and the Lords. The political and
constitutional powers of the crown were to remain considerable
until the early nineteenth century, when the combination of
George III's ill-health and George IV's indolence initiated the
process by which the monarchy was to become essentially orna-
mental. To set against this, William dropped the practice of
attending debates in the Lords, as both Charles and James had
done. He was forced to accept a financial settlement which
reduced the freedom of action of the crown. He spent months of
each year abroad, on campaign or, after 1697, on visits to his
Dutch palace at Het Loo.

Inevitably, William was less familiar with the political routines of
the three kingdoms the crowns of which he wore than Charles
and James had been. He felt, he told Halifax in February 1689,
'like a King in a play'.[98] This sense of unreality must have been
shared by many of William's new subjects. The norms of political
behaviour and constitutional practice were shattered by the
Revolution, no less than by the Civil War and its aftermath forty
years earlier. Some welcomed this uncomfortable fact. Others
looked forward to the prospect, by no means improbable, of a
second Restoration. In the spring of 1689, the conviction was
gradually forcing itself upon the nation that, whatever lay in the
future, the Restoration of the Stuart monarchy in 1660 had ultimately proved a failure.

4. The Triple-crowned Islands

RONALD HUTTON

During the past few years there has been much excitement, and some self-congratulation, among English historians over the redis-covery of what has been termed 'the British dimension' to England's story. By this is usually meant the manner in which the realms of Ireland, Scotland and England reacted with each other during the early modern period and helped to shape the develop-ment of each other. More rarely, it involves an acknowledgement by an English scholar that the histories of the other two nations might be worth studying in their own right. These developments are undoubtedly both important and praiseworthy, restoring ele-ments to the story of Tudor and Stuart England, in particular, without which it was at times gravely distorted. None the less, there is a danger that too much self-satisfaction over what has occurred may lead to other distortions and insensitivities. For one thing, there is a problem of language. The archipelago concerned consists of two main islands, the larger being Britain and the smaller Ireland. The term 'British', therefore, can only correctly apply to the larger island, and to stretch it to cover the latter involves a geographical error coupled with a potential political statement. The same difficulty applies to the wider name of 'British Isles'. It is, of course, rendered almost insoluble because of the lack of an alternative, and 'British' remains the simplest shorthand for the peoples, and characteristics, of the whole archi-pelago. Only inhabitants of the larger island, however, seem to employ it with a complete lack of any sense that something rather delicate is involved. This situation is compounded, with the same insouciance, by English historians who casually put together Scotland and Ireland in the same category of a 'British problem' or 'British question', as though those two nations had a great deal in common. In reality their differences were much greater than their similarities, each had at least as much in common with England as each other, and to consider them together involves an

Anglocentricity as crass as that which the recent change of perspective has been intended to remove. That is the problem, and the irony, which underlies the writing of this chapter.

I

The principal thing which the two smaller kingdoms had in common, of course, was the need to reckon with the might of the largest, and this was never displayed more dramatically than in 1649–53, when English armies conquered Scotland and Ireland simultaneously. For the latter, it was to be the second of three successive occasions upon which English rule was imposed upon the island. It was none the less the most traumatic, coming as it did at the end of the most destructive conflict which the land has ever known, *an cogadh do chriochnaigh Eire*, 'the war that finished Ireland'. For the Scots, the experience was unique. Their whole national identity had been built upon a tradition of successful resistance to the English and of allegiance to an unbroken line of kings claimed to stretch much further into the past than that of England. Now, within two years, the traditional enemy had seized the whole country and abolished its monarchy. Its national Church, or Kirk, the other symbol of its independence, was stripped of its control over Scottish religion. Furthermore, the English republicans reformed these other realms with a radicalism which they had scrupled to bring to their own. The Scottish nobility, already partly ruined by civil war, lost their social and legal power. In Ireland more than half the total land mass changed hands, the proportion owned by Roman Catholics being reduced from 59 per cent to less than 9 per cent,[1] while many Protestant royalists were dispossessed. This vast collection of estates was distributed among English settlers, who formed a new ruling élite together with existing Protestant gentry who had supported the victors. The medieval English settlers of Ireland, who had mostly remained Catholic, were thrust from power and wealth along with the surviving Gaelic chiefs. The Parliaments of Scotland and Ireland were abolished, and those nations represented instead in a new imperial assembly at Westminster, by a heavily outnumbered set of seats occupied mostly by Englishmen. Throughout the latter half of the Interregnum, the conquered realms remained passive, their destinies at the disposal of political events in England. When the republic imploded, and the English

Parliament of 1660 proclaimed the restoration of the monarchy, the foreign vice upon both countries was suddenly released, to leave each in a very different situation. The withdrawal of the English automatically returned the traditional Scottish ruling class to power. Ireland, by contrast, was left in the hands of the new body of landowners, protected against those whom they had dispossessed by a standing army.

Despite the difference in contexts, the Restoration settlements in all three countries did have strong similarities, for in each one the ruling élite seized the initiative from the King and worked the newly reconstituted national assemblies to secure itself. In England the Convention Parliament of 1660 allowed cathedral clergy and bishops back into the Church, while the succeeding, 'Cavalier', Parliament restored to them their old powers, pushed more radical Protestants out of the established clergy and the town councils, and denied the Crown any discretionary right to allow some back. In Ireland, a Convention of English settlers likewise decided to restore bishops to its Church immediately, with toleration of moderate Protestant groups who wished to worship outside it: a policy intended to reunite all followers of the reformed faith. The government in Dublin, however, showed irritation when the King tried to restrain it from persecuting Protestants whom it did not consider to be moderate.[2] Its annoyance was considerably greater when tussling with the monarch over the issue of the Irish Catholics. Many of the latter had given loyal service to Charles II and his father, and the great expropriation of their land had been the work of an illegal regime; to undo it, however, would not only alienate the new Irish ruling class but also most public opinion in Britain. As the bulk of Ireland's Catholics had risen in rebellion while Charles I was still in effective control of Britain, it could be argued that they would have been dispossessed even had the monarchy not fallen. The new King's immediate remedy was to restore those who had served him most faithfully and to promise the same to all others who had not taken part in rebellion, provided that land was found to compensate those who now possessed their estates. Before the end of 1660, it was already obvious that very little could be found, and in 1662 Charles was persuaded to agree to an Act of Settlement by a new Irish Parliament which freed slightly more land for compensation but in most cases confirmed the new owners. The persuasion consisted partly of the inducement of an apparently generous financial settlement, and partly of evidence that more Catholics had been rebels against the Crown than the King had supposed.[3] In the same fashion, the Protestant settlers blocked moves to ameliorate the condition of Catholics who had owned no land and merely wanted freedom to practise their religion in public. The King was persuaded to give up plans to allow the followers of Rome into towns and to accord their priests a right to carry out their duties without molestation. The best that they could obtain, in April 1662, was an understanding that they could worship safely if they did so with the utmost discretion.[4] By the end of that year Irish Catholics in general, and former landowners in particular, had gained small satisfaction from the restoration of their nation's Crown and Parliament.

In England and Ireland episcopacy had been abolished by revolutionary governments, apparently against the inclination of most Protestants in those realms. In Scotland, by contrast, the bishops had been removed several years earlier, by a national movement which had enjoyed overwhelming popularity. Their offence had been to take the part of royal agents in a campaign to strengthen the Crown and to Anglicize the Kirk. The establishment of Presbyterianism was initially a matter of patriotic pride, and at the Restoration Charles II showed no inclination to reverse it. He knew well enough that the majority of Scottish ministers had been fervently loyal to the monarchy in the 1640s and 1650s, and was concerned only to punish some who had not been. In 1660, therefore, he promised the maintenance of the Kirk 'settled by law'. He and the churchmen both reckoned without the altered feelings of the traditional Scottish ruling class, which had not forgiven that Kirk for conniving in the exclusion of many of them from power in the 1640s. To the bulk of nobles and lairds, episcopacy now seemed to provide a potentially invaluable weapon for the defence of hierarchy in both society and religion. In early 1661, Charles and his advisers in London were taken completely by surprise as a Scottish Parliament cleared the way for a restoration of the old ecclesiastial government. The final decision on the matter was tactfully left to the King, who postponed one. His ministers in Scotland now did their utmost to convince him that public opinion was overwhelmingly in favour. In August Charles gave way, and then tried both to appoint the leading Presbyterian clergy as bishops and to ensure safety for those who now wished to worship outside the Kirk. Once again he was thwarted, as many of the most respected ministers resigned their livings and the government in Edinburgh set about an escalating persecution of those who continued to preach. By the end of 1662 a novel and serious problem of religious non-conformity had been created in the northern kingdom.[5]

In one further major respect, the Restoration settlements of all three kingdoms had a basic similarity. In each, the national assemblies undertook an overhaul of a royal financial system which had been seriously out of date by the early Stuart period. In England the Convention Parliament abolished the old feudal dues of the Crown and substituted an excise on beer and cider, to which the Cavalier Parliament added a hearth tax. The Scottish Parliament of 1661 copied the excise and increased the customs rates, while the Irish equivalent did both those things and copied the English hearth tax.[6] In every case the political nations concerned were convinced that they had raised the regular income of their Crown to an unprecedentedly high level, from secure sources. In every one they were rapidly proved wrong, as the shortfall from the new systems left them incapable of covering yearly expenditure. In this, as in the different religious settlements, the groups who dominated the three representative bodies had provided a legacy of difficulty for the King, his successor and their various ministers. It remains now to see how these were addressed in Scotland and Ireland. Hitherto, as stressed, the experiences of the three nations had possessed much in common. From now on they were to diverge, save in the single respect that each was to be divided and insecure.

II

After 1660 Scotland was once again a wholly independent kingdom, and the bloody events of the past twenty-five years had left both Scots and English anxious to avoid interference in each other's affairs as far as possible. Unhappily, the relationship between the two realms was still problematic, and its focus was altering. After the catastrophe which each had met in trying to impose its religion on the other, both now seemed content that their churches and laws should differ to some degree. Economic difficulties, however, were starting to produce stresses almost as great as those of ideology had done. The new English Navigation Acts shut Scots out of trade with the growing English colonies, even while competition and tariff barriers were constricting the traditional Scottish overseas markets in the Netherlands and

France. This disadvantage was made much clearer to the Scots by the two major wars waged by Charles II in the 1660s and 1670s. Both were against the Dutch, traditionally major trading partners of the Scots and commercial rivals of the English. Both were concerned with English economic interests, and yet the Union of the Crowns meant that Scotland was automatically brought into them. The Scots were thus compelled to make sacrifices for a struggle which brought them no benefit at all. In this predicament, they had three theoretical courses of action open to provide a remedy. One was to control the monarch and so cause him to accord a higher priority to Scottish interests. As Charles II and James II both saw themselves primarily as Englishmen, this was out of the question. So was the second solution, to secede from the Union, which was made impossible both by the lack of an alternative ruler and the certainty of all-out war with England and Ireland if it were attempted. The third was to negotiate a closer relationship with the English which would permit some opening to the Scots in England's trading system. This was actually attempted in 1668–70, but rebuffed as the English Parliament could see no compensatory reward in the process. All that Restoration England required of Scotland was that it caused no trouble, an attitude close to that of the monarch who asked for it to be quiet, obedient and cheap to run. The religious settlement and the Dutch wars meant that even this would be difficult to achieve. As a result the Scottish politicians competing for access to power, and to the riches which it conferred, had to indulge in endless manipulation and misrepresentation at the royal court and alternate conciliation and repression at home. It is no wonder that they have gone down in history with an unpleasant reputation.

At the Restoration, Charles was careful to construct a government in Scotland, as in England, which mixed together leaders of all the parties of the past decades except republicans. At the head of the new regime the King installed his favourite Scotsman, John, Earl of Middleton, a black-haired, red-faced, hook-nosed soldier who had served him faithfully all through the years of exile. Middleton's combination of political shrewdness and boozy affability made him a popular leader, but he was also right for the moment. While in exile he had undergone a personal conversation to Anglicanism, and this made him the more ready to combine with the majority of the Scottish political nation to bring back bishops into the Kirk. This process also enabled him and his allies to push out of the government those members who found the change unacceptable. His position had two enduring weaknesses. One was that the reform of the Kirk created a much greater proportion of non-conformity than he and his cronies had expected, and which only stiffened as they tried desperately to repress it. The other was that he lacked a trusted supporter at the side of the King. That crucial position was occupied by his namesake John, Earl of Lauderdale, red-haired, coarse-featured, uncouth, and more than Middleton's equal in ruthlessness and cunning. Lauderdale's natural rapport with Charles, whom he had known for twelve years, was compounded by an alliance with the King's most trusted English adviser, Sir Edward Hyde. As a result he landed the post of Secretary of State, which involved residing near the King's person. The power of this position did not enable him to prevent the restoration of episcopacy in Scotland, which he strenuously opposed. It was, however, enough to save him in 1663, when Middleton attempted to eliminate him at last by having him excluded from office by Act of Parliament. Lauderdale was able to convince Charles that this was but one of many occasions upon which his enemy had exceeded his authority and attempted to coerce his monarch, and the dark-haired Earl lost his post instead.[7]

Lauderdale's way was now open to make himself the most powerful man in Scotland, and this he proceeded to do and to maintain the position for sixteen years. During the 1660s he generally operated as one of a triumvirate, making sure that he was the one who stayed by the King's side most of the time while his two allies enforced their policies upon the Scots. He also made sure that he dropped first one and then another of his existing partners at regular intervals and substituted different allies. It was a process that gradually increased the number of former friends with grudges against him, but also ensured that he always had a queue of prospective partners eager for the rewards of co-operation with the King's all-powerful favourite. Thus from 1663 to 1664 Lauderdale worked with the Earls of Glencairn and Rothes, from 1664 to 1666 with Rothes and Archbishop Sharp of St Andrews, and from 1666 to 1671 with the Earl of Tweeddale and Sir Robert Murray. During the 1670s he was far more the dominant partner in his relationships, and his allies operated very obviously as his agents: they included the Earls of Kincardine, Atholl, Argyll and Moray, and also his own brother Charles. With the exception of the mediocre Charles, he made sure that he cast off and replaced these men in turn every few years. Throughout, he observed certain other rules of behaviour. One was to refer all the actions of the Scottish government to the King for prior approval and to assure him that their main end was always the increase of royal power. Another was to shut off from Charles, as far as possible, all channels of communication with Scotland except those which he himself controlled, and to ensure that whenever he himself was in his native land he had a trusted supporter by the King's ear. A third, naturally enough, was to guarantee that the information which Charles received about his northern realm was always processed to produce an impression favourable to the great Earl (soon promoted to a Duke), whom men called 'John Red'.[8]

Lauderdale's principal problem, of course, was that Scotland was a troubled land and that its greatest trouble lay in the religious division which Middleton had bequeathed to him. Having opposed it at first, he found himself compelled to uphold it in order to make himself acceptable to the bulk of the Scottish social élite. Indeed, there was initially a danger that he would be over-shadowed by men prepared to harass non-conformity with more diligence. His allies Rothes and Sharp both enforced the new penal laws with enthusiasm, and in 1665 the most hawkish of the Scottish prelates, Alexander Burnet, Archbishop of Glasgow, broke through the cordon around the King. With the help of Edward Hyde, Burnet secured a royal audience and persuaded Charles that even more severity was needed. When a rebellion known as the Pentland Rising occurred in 1666, it seemed as if his arguments were fully vindicated. Lauderdale, however, brilliantly turned the event to his advantage by convincing the King that the rising had itself been provoked by excessive brutality. Rothes and Sharp were disgraced, Burnet sacked, and a policy instituted of comprehending the moderate Presbyterian ministers while toughening the law against conventicles, or religious meetings outside the Kirk. This policy continued into the 1670s, with more dissenting ministers being comprehended and even harsher laws passed against the others, including the death penalty for addressing an open-air meeting. All this effort did nothing to prevent an increase in conventicles and a proportionate one in government severity, culminating in the harrying of selected areas by Highland troops in 1678.[9] By then, symbolically, Archbishop Burnet had been reinstated at Glasgow as Lauderdale's ally.

What brought down 'John Red' was, ultimately, the collapse of the English government at the opening of the Exclusion Crisis. This caused his enemies to go to England in a body and complain to the King, allying with the politicians whom the Crisis had brought to the leadership of the English Parliaments. While Charles hesitated, the Scottish Presbyterians were emboldened to rebel again, in 1679, with enough force to take Glasgow before they were defeated at Bothwell Bridge. These events persuaded Charles both to legalize conventicles in private houses and to give Lauderdale honourable retirement. He was replaced as effective viceroy of Scotland, however, not by any of the fallen Duke's clients or enemies but with the King's own brother James, Duke of York, sent north to get him out of England until the Exclusion Crisis was resolved. The presence of a prince, after thirty years of royal absenteeism, was a tremendous boost to national morale, symbolized by the rebuilding of Holyrood Palace. James was rewarded with a clear declaration of his right to the succession. The same Parliament which made this, unhappily, also tried to safeguard the Episcopalian Kirk with a new oath imposed upon all clergy and officers of state. It was at once so stringent and so clumsily worded that it caused a new exodus of ministers from the Kirk and the flight into exile of one of the most important nobles, the Earl of Argyll. When James returned triumphantly to England in 1682, he left behind him the complete ruin of the policies of comprehension and toleration, and a yet more savage persecution of Dissenters under way.

The royal Duke had, indeed, taken little personal part in these developments. They had been the work of a combination between the bishops and a new gang of politicians who had come to power, known by their subsequent titles as Earl of Aberdeen, Duke of Queensberry, Duke of Perth and Earl of Melfort. The spectacle of their relationship reminds one of a Roman gladiatorial arena. What brought them together at the opening of the 1680s was the desire to gain office and to ruin Lauderdale's remaining protégés. This done, the last three turned upon Aberdeen in 1684, using the position of Melfort, resident at the royal court, to undermine him. With Aberdeen gone, Perth and Melfort (who were cousins) used the same trick, two years later, to remove Queensberry. They then proceeded to run Scotland between them for two years, the one in Edinburgh and the other in London, using Lauderdale's methods of feeding information to the monarch.

By then the monarch had changed, James having succeeded in 1685, with his proclamation in Scotland followed by a bloody rite of passage in which Argyll returned, rebelled, and was defeated and beheaded. The punishment of his supporters in the Highlands was matched by the continuing brutal harrying of dissent in the Lowlands. James, however, unlike his brother, had a policy of his own to enforce upon Scotland. It was the monomania which governed his approach to all three of his realms: to improve the position of his fellow Roman Catholics. When he made this clear, in 1686, Perth and Melfort promptly secured their own power by converting to his religion, but proved completely incapable of persuading a Parliament to endorse any measure for Catholic relief, even when the King promised free trade with England. Instead, during 1687 James used theoretical powers over the Kirk confirmed to the Crown during Lauderdale's rule, and proclaimed freedom of worship first to Catholics and then to Protestant non-conformists. The Scottish political nation faced the reality that the royal authority had seemed since the Interregnum to be a principal guarantee of national independence: they could hardly resist it. The new measures still kept the Kirk episcopalian, even if a disestablished Presbyterian church could now be organized beside it. Scotland's Catholics were too few to represent either a menace to their compatriots or an object of great attention from the King. As a result, the land slipped into political limbo, the social and religious élite remained quiet, persecution ended, James's attention was diverted elsewhere, and Perth and Melfort busily made money; until the change of regimes in England altered everything.[10]

III

Despite the points of similarity drawn out earlier, the contrast between Scotland and Ireland in these years must be obvious. Not only did the latter have an alien Protestant ruling class perched uneasily on top of a mainly Catholic population, but it had the status both of an independent kingdom and of a colony. Irish land and offices were part of the English spoils system, to be granted by the sovereign to reward English subjects at will, while no Bill could be offered by the government in Dublin to an Irish Parliament until it had first been vetted by the regime in London. Irish Protestants had therefore almost as much reason to fear the machinations of politicians across the water as they had those of the dispossessed Catholic landowners: indeed, the two were connected, for the latter still regarded royal favour as their best means to restitution. In this situation, Charles II and James II were hardly ideal monarchs. The former suffered from an endemic carelessness with paperwork and administrative detail (a real problem for a kingdom which he ran by post) and a sporadic desire to do something more to help the followers of Rome. The second was himself a Catholic by conversion.

Charles opened his rule over Ireland by confirming in power the Protestants whom he found in charge of it, making two of them Earls of Mountrath and Orrery respectively. These and a third of their group were made Lords Justices to run the land, and it was they who negotiated the settlement of it outlined above. By the end of 1661 the King felt secure enough to replace them with the greatest of all Anglo-Irish royalists, James 'the White', Duke of Ormonde, who had run Ireland for Charles I and adhered faithfully to his son in exile. He crossed over as Lord-Lieutenant in mid-1662 and almost immediately found himself involved in the problems of implementing the Act of Settlement. It had turned out that many more Catholics qualified for restoration under it than the Protestants had expected, and Ormonde became caught between a Parliament determined to narrow the qualifications and a King intent upon stopping this. To make matters worse, the shortfall on revenue was so bad that the army was going unpaid. Breakdown was averted because Ormonde and Orrery joined forces to soothe the MPs, the English government borrowed money for the soldiers, and long discussions between the Privy Councils of the two nations, and the Catholics, produced an Explanatory Act of the land settlement in 1665. This directed all purchasers of confiscated property to relinquish a third of their estates to compensate those who had to return their property to Catholics. As a result, the latter had succeeded by 1670 in owning 22 per cent of the island. Large numbers of those entitled to restitution, especially those of native blood, were left dispossessed, and the Protestant ascendancy was assured. The best that could be said of the situation was that for the time being the Protestants, the King and the most influential Catholics were all pacified.

These achievements were largely the result of co-operation between the old royalist Ormonde and the former Cromwellian Orrery, and in 1668 they quarrelled. To a great extent this was inevitable. Both were able soldiers and administrators, and politicians of unusual cunning, but there the resemblance ended. Orrery was the younger son of a brilliant *parvenu* family, and

Ormonde the head of Ireland's oldest and most powerful noble dynasty. The Earl was a former Royalist who had defected to the republic and then back again; he was fiercely ambitious, brimmed over with ideas and loved to parade his intelligence. The Duke cultivated a relaxed atmosphere of genteel dilettantism, and was immoveably loyal to the house of Stuart and the Episcopalian Church. Sooner or later the instinctual resentment between the two men was bound to surface. It happened when Orrery became convinced that the continuing deficit in the Irish revenue was worsened by mismanagement, and he went to court to complain to Charles. In countering the charges, Ormonde was handicapped by his genuine inaptitude for finance, the high-handed way in which he treated the King, and the fact that his enemies in England, such as the Duke of Buckingham, were now in favour at court. After an inquiry, Charles saved his face by formally recalling him to a position of honour in England and replacing him successively with two men not associated with either him or his opponents: Lord Robartes and Lord Berkeley. Neither lasted long, the former making himself obnoxious to everybody and the latter repeating Ormonde's mistake of making an enemy of Orrery, while adding a further one of financial corruption. Throughout this period policy remained more or less consistent, save that in 1671–2 Charles attempted some slight further measures to relieve Catholics. This was the period in which he used his prerogative to accord them private worship in England, and in which both his brother James and his Lord Treasurer, Clifford, had converted to Rome and were seeking advantages for their co-religionists. In these circumstances, it is remarkable how little he did in Ireland, consisting of protection for priests who denied that the pope could depose kings, the appointment of a commission of English politicians (none sympathetic to Catholics) to review the land settlement, the commissioning of a few Catholic JPs, and the re-admission of the followers of Rome to corporate towns. The main result of this policy was to disturb Protestants in both kingdoms, and in 1673 the Cavalier Parliament forced the King to withdraw his concessions in both.[11]

By then, Ireland had a new Lord-Lieutenant of real weight, appointed in 1672. He was Arthur, Earl of Essex, a young man from a notable English royalist family, chosen for his intelligence, honesty, vigour and independence from any court faction. For five years he proceeded to govern the land with considerable success, until felled by two weaknesses. The first was that patrician

contempt for court intrigue which had been one of his recommen-
dations, and which prevented him from bothering to keep agents
permanently around the King, as Lauderdale did. The second was
the perennial problem of the public revenue, the rock upon which
successive Irish administrations struck. In 1671 Charles had
decided that the fiscal system had to be entrusted to an expert
instead of to one of the grandees eligible to lead the government.
He allowed himself to be persuaded that Richard, Viscount
Ranelagh, was one: a smooth-talking young Irish Protestant adven-
turer who offered the King a bribe of £48 000 for the contract.
Adroit Ranelagh certainly was, for he solved the problem of the
army's arrears by forcing its soldiers to take lump sums far smaller
than those owed to them. An expansion in trade then raised the
royal income at last, allowing the nimble Viscount to balance the
books, slip the King regular payments for his Privy Purse and
pocket the remainder, to the eventual total of about £100 000. In
1677 Essex effectively signed the order for his own dismissal by
demanding an inquiry into the public accounts: Charles, who had
been implicated in the shady dealings with them, rapidly declared
that his Lord-Lieutenant was being honourably recalled as part of
a policy of rotating people in top offices.[12]

At this point the King played safe and re-appointed old
Ormonde, with the understanding that he would not interfere
with Ranelagh. The Duke ran his nation for the next seven years,
aided by a number of strokes of luck. One was the outbreak of
the Exclusion Crisis in England, making Charles only too happy
to leave his western realm in trustworthy hands without much
intervention. Among the royal servants brought down by the crisis
was Ranelagh, who became the object of so much criticism and
speculation in England that the King found it necessary to retire
him with a golden handshake to keep his mouth shut. Ormonde
thus regained control of the finances, and in the same period
death removed a number of his old opponents, such as Orrery.
He was careful, likewise, to keep friends and relations around the
King to provide a good report of all his actions. Thus his position
only weakened when the crisis in England was completely over
and the royal advisers felt sufficiently secure to meddle elsewhere.
This came in 1684, from a group centred upon the royal Duke
James and the Hyde family, who had traditionally been his
strongest supporters. At this stage the government in Dublin had
never been doing better, with royal commissions tidying up both
the finances and problems in the land settlement. The only

obvious remaining problem was the state of the army, which indeed needed reform. Ormonde agreed with this, but he did not concur with a worry which affected both the royal brothers, that too many of the officers were old Cromwellians whose loyalty might not be counted upon in a crisis. Just before his death, Charles had decided to replace the old man with one of the Hydes, and to have this officer corps remodelled.[13]

As soon as James succeeded, this work acquired a new emphasis: to install officers who were not merely trustworthy but Catholic. Nevertheless, in Ireland his policy of Catholic emancipation was tempered by initial caution. Not only had he benefited personally from the land settlement but he harboured an English distrust of the natives. We have (at second hand) a remark of his that the true division in Ireland lay not between the religions but the races.[14] In the gap between the two lay the dispossessed medieval English settlers, distrusted by Protestants as Catholics but regarded by the King as Englishmen,[15] and these produced a politician of first-rate ability. He was Richard Talbot, an individual who, like Lauderdale, combined physical coarseness with mental brilliance. Associated with James since before the Restoration, he had never hitherto achieved high office because of his religion and the persistence with which he lobbied at each opportunity for the interests of his community, the dispossessed 'Old English' gentry of Ireland. In 1685 he was made Earl of Tyrconnel and sent to reform the Irish army. He had every intention of remodelling the officer corps to put in as many 'Old English' as possible, but he was at first hampered by the King's wish to enact Catholic emancipation in England with the aid of the Anglican royalists. Accordingly, James replaced Ormonde with one of the Hyde brothers, the Earl of Clarendon, while the other, the Earl of Rochester, became his chief minister at London. This was an axis potentially as powerful as that which Perth and Melfort had made between London and Edinburgh, and as staunch Protestants the Hydes were unlikely to undermine the ascendancy of their faith in Ireland.

Their fatal weakness, of course, was precisely that they *were* staunch Protestants. Whereas the Scottish cousins had converted to secure their position, Rochester and Clarendon refused to support James's campaign to give Catholics office, and so fell from power in 1686. Tyrconnel had adroitly allied with their enemy at court, the Earl of Sunderland, but his main advantage lay in his own prowess in managing the King. Again and again he would outrun his powers in Ireland, trying to calm Protestant fears with lies and obfuscations. As soon as he made things too hot for him there, he would bolt for court and convince James that he was acting only to help fellow Catholics of proven devotion to the Crown. Then he would return with enhanced powers and repeat the process. In this fashion he had made 60 per cent of the army Catholic by September 1686, and the proportion had been pushed to 90 per cent two years later, most of the officers being 'Old English'. In January 1687 he replaced Clarendon at the head of the government, with more restricted powers, and flagrantly ignored the curbs on him to hand over most of the civil government to Catholics, from Privy Councillors and judges down to justices and town councillors. By the end of the year James had given up any attempt to restrain him and was happy to let him create a safe haven for Catholics if any disaster befell them in Britain. As that disaster occurred, with the landing of William of Orange, Tyrconnel was preparing to pack an Irish Parliament which would force the Protestant settlers to return much more of the lands seized from Catholics who had not been implicated in rebellion. Instead, he found himself offering James his haven, much sooner than expected, with England united against him, an Irish army much more inexperienced and undisciplined than that which he had replaced, and bridgeheads in the north held by furious Protestants. It was a recipe for disaster.[16]

IV

So, if this is how policy was made and executed, what was the quality of life that resulted? It should be stressed now that the history of Scotland and Ireland during the time of the restored monarchy is one of remarkable success, if measured by bread alone. The population of Ireland increased from a probable 1.7 million in 1672 to about 2.2 million in 1687, at a time when that of England was static or falling. At the same time prices of produce fell, proving that the greater number of people were not pressing upon resources. The value of exports rose from £402 389 in 1665 to £570 343 in 1685. When the Parliament in England banned the importation of Irish cattle in order to help domestic farmers, butter and wool exports from Ireland swelled instead, finding new markets in Europe as well as in Britain. The condition of ordinary people remained poor, but was still above subsistence level. The wealthier were helped considerably by rising rents and falling interest rates.[17] The growing prosperity of the landed and mercantile élite helped to create a market for consumer goods and for literature and entertainment, causing one sour commentator in 1682 to portray the land as given over to vanity and extravagance.[18] Yet the period was also a notable one for the culture of the natives. Although the lords who had patronized poets had almost all gone, some of those poets were able to continue schools of their own, such as that at Blarney which had been founded by the MacCarthy chiefs and was now run by Tadhgó Duinnin. In the work of masters such as Dáibhidh ó Bruadair, Gaelic poetry made some of its finest achievements during these years.[19]

In Scotland, likewise, prices fell and output grew. The difficulties in foreign trade were to some extent compensated for, by the growth of internal commerce based on the exchange of the new surplus produce. Lowland grain was taken into the uplands and bartered for part of a swelling trade in Highland and Galloway livestock, which spilled over profitably into England. A native sugar industry was established with state encouragement.[20] The new profits and contacts furnished by the cattle trade helped the slow process of assimilating Highland chiefs to the culture of the Lowlands, while Gaelic bards of the traditional sort, such as Iain Mhor, produced poetry as good as any preserved from their predecessors.[21]

A combination of material well-being and spiritual wretchedness is, however, as true of collective as of individual mentalities. It was the first Scotsman known to history, Calgacus the Pict, who articulated this sentiment when (at least according to Tacitus) he accused the Romans of having 'made a desert and called it peace'. Ó Bruadair certainly agreed with it, characterizing the reign of Charles II as 'the sum of the purgatory of the men of Ireland'.[22] The bitterness of his sort of Irish, of defeat and dispossession, was matched by the insecurity of the Protestant landowners, afraid at once of rebellion and of a legal *coup d'état* engineered at the royal court. Some of the rise in population during the Restoration period was accounted for by Catholics returning from exile, many of them former landowners who haunted the vicinity of their forfeited estates hoping for a change of luck.[23] Some became 'tories' or bandits, such as the swashbuckling Redmond O'Hanlon in Ulster, Dudley Costello in Connacht, or the three Brennans in Leinster, who once broke into Ormonde's huge castle at Kilkenny and stole some of his plate. Their raids caused considerable local disorder.[24]

Until the last two years of the reign of James II, the Catholic three-quarters of the population continued to worship covertly and in continual fear of persecution. During the time of the 'Popish Plot' scare, it had to put up with the spectacle of its Archbishop of Dublin dying in prison and its Archbishop of Armagh, Oliver Plunket, hanged, drawn and quartered in London. Charles had been quite aware of Plunket's innocence, but wanted to use the witnesses against him to convict (on equally specious grounds) one of his own enemies in England.[25] Of the minority who adhered to Protestant beliefs, almost two-thirds frequented dissenting conventicles,[26] subject to periods of proscription and harassment.[27] In this situation the established Protestant Church remained too weak and too lazy to occupy the land conquered for it. There was virtually no missionary work in this period, and the countryside remained full of ruined churches, allotted to ministers who never troubled to visit them.[28] This was the squalid reality within the undoubted truth that during this period Ireland was the most peaceful of the three kingdoms.

The most troubled, by contrast, was Scotland, and recent work has achieved a consensus that this was almost wholly the fault of the government.[29] The crudity with which episcopacy had been reimposed at the Restoration caused about a third of the established ministry to leave the Kirk. Replacements – let alone of sufficient calibre – were hard to come by. If a majority of landowners wanted the bishops back, that still left a sizeable minority, plus thousands of commoners, who did not, and they were dangerously concentrated in the southern half of the country, and especially in the south-west. In Galloway, for example, seven-eighths of the clergy had been deprived, and that was where the most stubborn conventicles subsequently arose and both risings began. It is clear, in retrospect, that the government's periods of coercion actually stiffened resistance, that the dioceses which had the most intolerant prelates produced the most non-conformity, and that the two dissenter rebellions were provoked largely by the excesses of royal officers. The period's third rising, of Argyll, was the work of a noble who had been hounded into exile by political rivals, employing an oath which even those who framed it admitted did not make a lot of sense. The culmination of the process, from 1680 to 1686, was what has gone down in Scottish historical memory as the 'killing times', the most severe period of religious persecution in the nation's history. On one level, it was a tragi-comedy in which the government passed more and more Draconian laws to deal with one sect of extremists, the Cameronians, who had declared open war but who could not muster more force than a single Irish tory band. In 1684 the Privy Council decreed summary execution for all who refused to abjure their principles. It is certainly true that the Cameronians could be described as fanatics using terrorist methods, but they had themselves been provoked by almost twenty years of persecution of Presbyterian meetings. Their proclamations, representing no more than a tiny fraction of non-conformists, provided men such as Archbishop Burnet with an excuse to turn also upon the peaceful and politically loyal majority.[30]

Parallel errors were committed in the Highlands. An objective study of the region during this period reveals both that it was not especially violent compared with the rest of the nation and that the old traditions of raiding were in decline. The only regular scene of disorder was Lochaber, the result of an administrative anomaly which made peace-keeping there difficult, and it seems plain that excellent results were achieved on the occasions when the government employed the chiefs collectively to impose order, within a regular structure of rights and duties. These occasions were, however, very few. Instead, the men in power in Edinburgh generally preferred two other courses. One was to use Highland feuding as an excuse (together with conventicles) to call for taxes to keep up a regular army. The other was to reward chiefs who were political allies at the expense of their local rivals. Thus, first Lauderdale allowed the Earl of Argyll to seize three islands from the Macleans in the 1670s, and then James, while in Scotland, used portions of Argyll's forfeited estate to build up a personal following among neighbouring clans such as the Camerons. The rivalries thus fostered were to bear bitter fruit in the next generation; as was the notion, encouraged by the central government, that the Highlands were a place of peculiar savagery, best controlled by external intervention and proportionately atrocious punishments.[31]

It is important not to exaggerate. The 'killing times' gained their prominence in Scottish national mythology because they provided the martyrology for what subsequently became the established Kirk. The total death-toll among dissenters in the period was about a hundred by judicial or summary execution and three to five hundred on battlefields.[32] Both figures are exceeded by the single blood-letting when Monmouth's Rebellion was crushed in England. Robert Wodrow's famous account of the two Presbyterian women drowned tied to stakes at Wigtown in 1685 must be set against the fate of perhaps a thousand other Scotswomen in that century, burned at stakes for the alleged crime of witchcraft. Indeed, in both Scotland and Ireland, the years in question represented a lull between two terrible periods of bloodshed. In Scotland they divided the wars of Montrose and the Cromwellian conquest from those of the Jacobites. In Ireland they separated the conflict in which perhaps a third of the population perished from that in which thousands of bodies would rot unburied at 'Aughrim of the slaughter'. In both realms they were, as has been stressed, a time of considerable prosperity.

For all that, the abiding impression is one of sordid, low-level religious persecution, punctuated by the occasional atrocity, and universal political insecurity amid which crooks, adventurers and informers made profits. That this situation was created must be ascribed largely to the political élites who made the Restoration settlements. That it was maintained, and culminated in yet more violence, must be held against their sovereigns. In the last analysis, the failure of the restored monarchy in the triple-crowned islands was not a matter of fortune, nor even a problem of 'multiple kingdoms', but the fault of the men who wore the crowns.

5. Religion in Restoration England

JOHN SPURR

'Notwithstanding that our civil wars are through the mercy of God ended,' lamented a Nonconformist in 1668, 'yet our religious jars and rents are not healed'.[1] Healing England's religious wounds was not as easy as bringing the monarchy back, but everyone knew that it was essential: religious differences had led the country into civil war once and might easily do so again. But how was religious harmony to be regained? The answer that sprang to many, if not most, minds was to impose religious uniformity on the nation. Since religion was the foundation of all government, justice and virtue, it was clear that there should only be one religion in one state: 'uniformity is the cement of both Christian and civil society'.[2] Others, however, objected 'that the requiring of greater uniformity in opinion and practice in the things of religion, than the church of God is capable of, is no means of union, peace or concord, but a most effectual and certain means of division, separation, strife and contention'.[3] Unity would emerge by recognizing and permitting diversity of religious belief and practice. So religious unity might be restored either through uniformity or through a regulated diversity. Few of the English had as yet considered a third option, which was to remove these questions from the political arena altogether, and treat religion as a purely private matter. This unwillingness to separate religion and politics reflects the contemporary assumption that religious unity is 'the chiefest pillar that upholdeth human society, and obedience to supreme authority'.[4] For all our stereotypes of life under the 'merry monarch', Restoration England was not a society which wanted to turn its back on religion. Religion was valued for itself and for its contribution to the moral health of the community. This did not, of course, mean that the subjects of Charles II were willing to accept religion on the same terms as their forbears: like every other age, the Restoration sought to shape its religion in its own likeness.

I

Charles II was restored to the throne on the understanding of a 'liberty to tender consciences' which would help to 'compose' the 'animosities' resulting from 'several opinions in religion'. Various religious parties might expect to benefit from the return of the monarchy: the royalist Episcopalians or Anglicans, as we can anachronistically call them; the Presbyterians, former Puritans who had refused to go along with the regicide but still sought a national church purged of over-bearing bishops; and the Independents, a loose grouping of congregationalists who had often been eager republicans and Cromwellians. Some concessions were also possible for the Baptists, but were unlikely to be extended to the minor sects, such as the Fifth Monarchists or Muggletonians, or to the nation-wide Quaker movement which had begun to spread terror among the gentry in the later 1650s. For the first year of Charles's rule, the signs were all of political compromise and a generous religious settlement. It seemed likely that a broad-based national church administered by bishops in tandem with their clergy would emerge from the negotiations. But then the scene shifted dramatically. The settlement as imposed by the 1662 Act of Uniformity and the revised Book of Common Prayer was narrow and uncompromising: all those who wished to serve as ministers of the church had to have episcopal ordination; there was to be strict uniformity to the Prayer Book; and the religious and political affiliations of the past had to be renounced. There is no adequate single explanation for the nature of the religious settlement. Clearly the breakdown of negotiations between Presbyterians and Episcopalians at the Savoy Conference and the new Parliament elected in 1661 are important factors. One influential suggestion that a small group of Laudian bishops shaped the religious settlement and foisted it upon the nation is no longer regarded as convincing. There was, after all, widespread and spontaneous enthusiasm for the restoration of a familiar church, clergy and worship among the gentry of the counties. This enthusiasm needed channelling if it was to have political effect, and here the churchmen did play a significant part: Gilbert Sheldon, Bishop of London and from 1663 Archbishop of Canterbury, and a small group of Anglican MPs in the Cavalier Parliament did much to promote the interests of the zealous Episcopalians. But the eventual religious settlement was the work of many hands, and we should acknowledge that its legislative form was the product of parliamentary horse-trading rather than the church's theological self-definition.

The Act of Uniformity set out the terms for those who wished to be clergymen of the Church of England and it outlawed other religious denominations. A number of clergy who would in principle have continued to serve a national church refused to serve the church as it was defined in 1662. These ministers were 'ejected' from their parishes on the fateful 24 August, St Bartholomew's Day, 1662. In total, 1760 English clergy were forced to leave their parishes between 1660 and 1663, along with another 120 clergy in Wales and around 200 lecturers, university dons and schoolmasters. At least 171 of the 1760 are known to have later conformed to the church. The Uniformity Act thus laid down the principal religious distinction of Restoration society by creating the two legal categories of conformist and Nonconformist, or Anglican and Dissenter, and this distinction was further elaborated by a series of discriminatory laws passed against Protestant Dissenters.[5]

Some of this legislation was designed to keep political power in reliable hands: thus the Corporation Act of 1661 was used to restrict local government to conforming Anglicans. But other legislation, such as the 1661 Quaker Act, aimed to suppress religious dissidents and their meetings. In 1664, MPs frightened by a botched rising in Yorkshire passed a Bill proposed by Sheldon's confidantes against 'seditious sectaries and other disloyal persons'. This Conventicle Act forbade meetings or 'conventicles' of five or more 'under colour or pretence of any exercise of religion'. The 1665 Oxford Parliament passed the Five Mile Act, banning Nonconformist ministers from living within that distance of any city or town or of any parish of which they had been an incumbent, unless they took the 'Oxford Oath' abhorring armed opposition to the King and disavowing any future attempt to alter the government of the church or state. The first Conventicle Act expired in 1668 and was succeeded by an improved permanent version in 1670, which increased penalties for ministers and decreased them for congregations, and made convictions easier.

The target of all this legislation, the Dissenting community, was not a large group. Figures can be misleading since many Nonconformists also attended church, but Dissenters were probably somewhere between 4 per cent and 10 per cent of the population. They tended to be concentrated in specific areas – often where Dissenting clergy had gathered, or in towns such as Exeter, Norwich or London which offered some shelter from persecution. Bristol, for example, was home to a Presbyterian, two Independent and three Baptist congregations, and a Quaker meeting. Although there were Dissenters from every walk of life, Dissent became identified with the urban classes, with merchants, artisans and textile workers. The persecution of Dissent waxed and waned according to political priorities and the zeal of local magistrates. The Somerset Quaker John Whiting counted seven great persecutions of the Quakers, while the Bristol Baptist congregation counted eight. Dissenters and their ministers suffered harassment, fines – which were often levied by distraint, the seizure and forcible sale of their household goods – and imprisonment. The harshness of imprisonment, which always carried a risk of illness or even death from gaol fever, was unpredictable: Isaac Pennington, the Quaker leader, suffered six spells in gaol between 1662 and 1679; Bunyan was imprisoned between 1660 and 1672, but was released for a time in 1666, when he travelled and preached. Nonconformists were subject to the legislation of Elizabeth I and James I, as well as that of the 1660s, and the penalties of the Church of England: the results could be both cruel and contradictory. Oliver Heywood, a Yorkshire Presbyterian, was told by the churchwarden that he would be fined for non-attendance at the parish church and ejected as an excommunicate if he did attend: 'for the law must be executed, both to keep me away and to punish my absence'.[6]

Religious policy took a sudden turn in 1672 when Charles's Declaration of Indulgence suspended 'the execution of all and all manner of penal laws in matters ecclesiastical, against whatsoever sorts of nonconformists or recusants'. Nonconformists were allowed freedom of public worship if their ministers and meeting places were licensed, and Roman Catholics were allowed to worship in private: meanwhile the Church of England was to be preserved as 'the basis, rule and standard of the general and public worship of God'. Many Dissenters were perturbed that this was freedom at a royal whim and that it seemed to condone and possibly perpetuate religious division; nevertheless, around 1500 licences were issued and Dissenters began to build their own meeting houses. Observers were convinced that the Dissenters would never again be brought to heel. The Indulgence was 'to the extreme weakening [of] the Church of England'. It 'hath made the church empty,' wailed the Rector of Somerford Magna, 'I warn communion and none appears and often time [I] read prayers to the walls'.[7]

The Declaration had been a wartime measure: ''twas because of a war with Holland that 'twas granted; and as the King said, it kept peace at home'. But when the war went badly and the money ran out, Charles was forced to face Parliament. In March 1673 the King cancelled the Declaration after a frosty exchange of messages with his MPs. It was its unconstitutional nature which most upset them, and so 'to let him see that we did not dislike the matter of his declaration but the manner, and did not doubt the prudence, but only the legality of it', MPs drew up a Bill 'for the ease of dissenters' which 'passed with little opposition, and as little approbation' before running aground in the Lords.[8]

The country had reached a watershed in 1672. Fear of Popery, France and arbitrary government was beginning to replace fear of Dissent and sedition as the ruling anxiety of the gentlemen who ran the counties and crowded on to the backbenches of the Commons. Anti-Popery was one of the era's most powerful religious and political sentiments; indeed, it exemplified the contemporary inability to distinguish political and religious questions. The paradox of this 'anti-Popery' was that the English Roman Catholic community was introspective, gentry dominated, and politically loyal, its numbers were small and stable at about 60 000, and the clergy who served it were far from aggressive. Yet, in the popular imagination, 'Popery' conjured up lurid visions of invasions, bloody risings and the massacre of Protestants, and was often only dimly associated with the local recusant family: 'Treason in papists is like original sin in mankind; they all have it in their natures, though many of them may deny it, or not know it'. None of the occasional proposals to make a legal distinction between loyal and dangerous Catholic recusants could overcome such deep-rooted prejudices. The Popish plots, real and imagined, which punctuated the seventeenth century, were based on the Jesuit 'statecraft' that in the name of religion permitted cities to be fired, monarchs deposed and murdered, and subjects absolved of their allegiance. The religion of the Church of Rome was 'written in blood, advanced by policy, and propagated by violence'. Protestant preaching must bear much of the responsibility for fuelling such hysteria about Popery. Not only did the preachers dwell upon the political dangers of Popery, but they also denounced its heresy and superstition: Popery is 'a religion (such a one as it is) that all loose and licentious people are already prepared for: 'tis the most pleasant and easy, the most gay and pompous religion in the world; 'tis such a one as they would devise, were they to make a religion for themselves'.[9] Catholics had surrendered their intellectual and moral autonomy to the church and had espoused a blind implicit faith in a supposedly infallible institution.

Although the fear of Popery and its 'damned Inquisitions, and massacring knives' may now seem ridiculous, it was real. After the Fire of London, Clarendon was taken aback at the 'sharpness and animosity against the Roman Catholics... amongst persons of quality';[10] throughout the 1670s the fear grew steadily, as Popish 'tyranny' abroad, personified by Louis XIV, was matched by developments at home. In 1673 Parliament forced Charles to agree to a Test Act designed to exclude Roman Catholics from office. To general astonishment one of the Act's first victims was James, Duke of York, soon followed by Lord Clifford. By 1674 Charles had moved into a closer alliance with the Earl of Danby, whose policy was 'to keep up Parliament, to raise the old Cavaliers and the Church party and to sacrifice Papists and Presbyterians'.[11] The church demonstrated that the Anglican interest was indeed the strongest in the nation and should be maintained by organizing the so-called Compton Census of religious allegiance in 1676. This survey showed that the Nonconformists were usually less than 5 per cent of the population of each diocese, and the Roman Catholics less than 1 per cent.[12]

The opposition to Danby's Anglican regime portrayed the 'high episcopal men and cavaliers' as engaged in a deep-laid plot to establish absolute government, a standing army, and immutable divine right episcopacy. The bishops 'neither are nor can be otherwise than creatures to prerogative, for all their promotions, dignities, and domination depends upon it,' claimed Shaftesbury.[13] Andrew Marvell's *An Account of the Growth of Popery and Arbitrary Government* (1678) supplied chapter and verse for the alleged plot to convert the lawful government into 'absolute tyranny' and the established religion into 'downright Popery'. The crisis provoked by the 'Popish Plot' helped to ruin Danby and threatened to bring down the bishops if not the church. The King could not risk losing the bishops' vote in Danby's trial, and 'told the bishops that they must stick to him, and to his prerogative ... by this means they were exposed to the popular fury'. Bishop Morley observed 'with what an evil eye those of our order and all their actions (especially such as are of public concernment) are now looked upon'. The church was in danger, too, from the 'threat' of Protestant union; by 1680 it seemed to many that 'union and moderation were coming into fashion' and that some accommodation would have to be made with Dissent. As the Exclusion

Crisis deepened, the printing presses produced an avalanche of polemic – all of it legal now that the 1662 Licensing Act had expired and most of it 'very licentious, both against the court and the clergy'. 'The bishops and the clergy, apprehending that a rebellion and with it the pulling the church to pieces were designed, set themselves ... to draw a parallel between the present time and' the Civil War.[14]

The crisis seems to have allowed a more strident generation of lay and clerical Anglicans to gain a political ascendancy, just as it may have driven some Dissenters into the arms of the radicals. 'We were mad with loyalty', observed one clergyman of the early 1680s, when Tories and Anglicans ruthlessly pursued a campaign against Whigs and Dissenters at every level of society. A newly created Ecclesiastical Commission restricted clerical preferment to men of known zeal for church and crown, while corporations were purged of Dissenters, and conventicles were harried and suppressed in the worst persecution of the century. At the same time those Anglicans whose conformity was half-hearted or partial found themselves subject to pressure. Even ordinary Anglican clergy found themselves caught between those who protested at the persecution and those 'who profess great loyalty and zeal for the church, as loud complaining because we do not proceed violently beyond the rule of law'.[15]

The Tory reaction ensured that the Catholic James II succeeded to the throne with the acclamation of the Church of England, but the honeymoon was short-lived. Despite his undertakings to protect the church, James interfered with ecclesiastical appointments, suspended preachers and set up another Ecclesiastical Commission. After failing in his attempt to browbeat MPs into a repeal of the penal laws, James began to dispense individual Catholics and Dissenters from the penalties of those laws and the requirements of the Test Acts. In 1687 he issued his own Declaration of Indulgence which suspended 'the execution of all and all manner of penal laws in matters ecclesiastical' and the operation of the Test Acts. Catholics rejoiced at this religious and civil emancipation, Anglicans were dismayed, and Dissenters faced a dilemma: many were unhappy with a liberty which also embraced Catholics and they took to heart Halifax's warning that they were being used as a stepping stone to the revival of an intolerant Popery. Meanwhile, William of Orange was making it plain that he supported liberty of conscience for Papists and 'an entire liberty for the full exercise' of the Dissenters' religion, but 'cannot agree to the repeal of the Test, or of those other penal laws ... that tend to the security of the Protestant religion'.[16] In 1688 the Church of England squared up to James, and won a convincing public relations victory in the Trial of the Seven Bishops. The church worked on several contradictory fronts at once: there was some wooing of Dissenters and even the preparation of a revised liturgy in case there should be need to 'bring in the honest, and moderate Dissenters to the church'; and simultaneously the bishops cajoled James to return to the policies of the Tory reaction.[17] William's intervention, however, transformed the political scene and when the dust settled in 1689 a new religious settlement was in place.

The 1689 Toleration Act did not repeal the laws against nonconformity, but exempted from their penalties those who took the Oath of Allegiance and the declarations in the 1678 Test Act. Roman Catholics and non-Christians, such as Jews, gained nothing from the Act. Dissenting clergy were free to exercise their ministry if they additionally subscribed to thirty-six of the Thirty-nine Articles. Dissenters were free to worship in public provided that their meeting place was registered with the authorities. The Act took some account of Baptist and Quaker scruples. Protestant Dissenters, however, did not gain full civil rights. For the Church of England, the Glorious Revolution was a disaster on several counts. Six bishops and over four hundred clergy refused to compromise their previous oath of loyalty to James with a new one to William and Mary. William therefore ejected them in a naked display of the reality of royal power over the church. The new bishops of the 1690s repeatedly found themselves at odds with the parish clergy. The Act of Toleration removed the church's legal monopoly, if not its privileges. Henceforth the Church of England was the established or state church, but had lost all right to see itself as a truly *national* church.

II

There is a widespread impression that during the Restoration a single monolith, the Church of England, enjoyed inordinate power and privileges and that 'the pivotal concern of the Anglican establishment was to preserve its political monopoly by preventing religious toleration'.[18] It is implied that the church was responsible for suppressing the civil rights of another equally homogeneous group, Dissent, and for holding back the advent of an inevitable religious toleration. Although there is much to be said for such a neat reading of Restoration politics, it is open to qualification. It is a reading which takes its cue from the views of the opponents and critics of the restored church, from Shaftesbury, Marvell, Locke and other 'radicals'. These are valid sources for one perspective on the religion of Restoration England, but there were other perspectives. As we have seen, religious politics were a roller-coaster and, as we shall see, the dominance of the Church of England was at best precarious and at worst an illusion.

Whether by accident or design, the Church of England had been restored to something very like its pre-1640 position. Ostensibly, all members of the community were also members of the Church of England. They were obliged to attend their parish church and to suffer the penalties laid down in various Elizabethan statutes if they failed to attend. The entire population was also liable to pay tithes to the local incumbent and any other fees for baptisms, marriages and funerals. The church was the only place in which people could legally be baptized, married or buried. These obligations were upheld by the state and its laws, but the most effective way of enforcing them had traditionally been through the church's own courts. The ecclesiastical courts had been restored, with a few exceptions such as the prerogative High Commission, in 1661 and continued to exercise their authority throughout the period. Their penalties culminated in excommunication, which denied culprits the sacraments and worship of the church, prevented them from pleading at law or acting as executor of a will, excluded them from all offices of authority, and supposedly cut them off from all converse with their neighbours. The ecclesiastical and secular courts tended to reinforce each other's efforts to enforce religious observance and uniformity. The tentacles of the church's power also reached into the world of education. The clergy were charged with the duty of catechizing, while schoolmasters were licensed by bishops, and the two universities were an Anglican monopoly. The Licensing Act imposed on the church and the universities the job of licensing publications on 'divinity, physic, philosophy or whatsoever science or art'.

These legal privileges were matched by the church's political influence. The bishops had regained their right to sit in the House of Lords and formed a block of government votes. Archbishops Sheldon and Sancroft extended the church's influence into the Commons through a small clique of Anglican MPs in the Commons, who tended to dominate the House by their political and administrative effectiveness and by their rhetorical ability to play upon backbench anxieties about security and stability.[19] Sheldon bound the church's fortunes to Parliament by surrendering the clergy's right to self-taxation in return for a clerical vote in parliamentary elections. Informal influence could also be brought to bear by the church as a corporate landowner and a major patron. The governing class of Restoration England were all conforming members of the church; even critics such as Shaftesbury and Marvell were outward conformists. Many, of course, were far more than mere conformists. They were enthusiastic proponents of the church, constantly reminding their tenants and neighbours of the importance of the church: in one homely simile, Peniston Whalley told the Nottingham Grand Jury that the discipline and ceremonies of the church were as necessary to preserve religion in its purity as the skin of an apple was to preserve its fruit.[20]

Most of all, the church's influence depended on its close association with the monarchy and the Stuart dynasty. The church's assumptions were patriarchal and a reverence for kingship was part of her scriptural heritage; thanks to the cult of Charles the Martyr, whose memory was kept green by 30 January, the annual day of national humiliation for the regicide, this reverence verged on idolatry. Incongruously, the notion of a sacred monarchy even seemed to apply to Charles II, who was an assiduous 'toucher for the king's evil'. The identification of church and monarchy was inescapable. Churches were adorned with the royal coat of arms; churchwardens could report that 'our minister doth yearly, if not weekly, declare the sole interest of authority in all cases ecclesiastical and civil to be in the king'.[21] The Anglican liturgy kept the anniversaries of 5 November, 30 January and 29 May (the restoration of Charles II), when sermons were preached on the role of divine providence in chastising a wicked nation. These sermons are a repository of the church's political teaching: God punished the disobedient, sometimes directly and sometimes by removing the king and giving the unruly a taste of anarchy; divine providence was the people's guarantee against royal misrule and they had no right to resist royal authority, other than by passive disobedience and then they must bear the penalties incurred. Such preaching was frequently and explicitly political, lambasting the seditious Nonconformists, castigating Popery, and denouncing

Exclusion as a 'black bill' and a 'design full of ingratitude and irreligion'.[22]

Despite all this privilege – legal, political and ideological – the Restoration Church of England felt persecuted and vulnerable. As their diaries, letters, sermons and speeches all reveal, the clergy were a prey to anxiety on a grand scale. It was an age in which Sheldon had 'met with more than ordinary discouragement'. The Archbishop himself told an Ipswich correspondent that 'the misfortunes of the church which you complain of are not peculiar to your town, but too universal throughout the whole kingdom'. The clergy saw the church as Christ crucified between two thieves, usually Popery and Dissent; despite the Restoration the Church of England 'is not yet triumphant (God knows) but too plainly militant still, and under persecution from the tongues and pens of perverse men, her adversaries on either side'. It was a commonplace 'that the Church of England hath [a] store of enemies, we are too sure; the papist, the heretic, the sectary, the atheist, all these are professed enemies of our church'. And some of these enemies were within the walls: 'church-papists and church-puritans do undermine the church, while other profess an open hostility against it'.[23]

Such anxieties were in part a product of what the church had experienced in the 1640s and 1650s, but dangers still loomed on all sides. In 1663 Pepys had no doubts 'that the present clergy will never heartily go down with the generality of the commons of England'; and five years later there was still talk 'about the bad state of the church, and how the clergy are come to be men of no worth – and, as the world doth now generally discourse, they must be reformed'. 'The common cry is, that the Church of England must go down', lamented one clergyman in 1677, and by 1679 churchmen of different outlooks shared 'the dismal apprehensions we generally had of our approaching ruin'. The canons of Gloucester Cathedral were alarmed by 'the very bad face of affairs which looked with a dismal aspect towards the church'. The church had to consider ways, in Archbishop Sancroft's words, 'for preserving itself independent of the state'; 'the more we are cramped in our temporal, the more stress should be laid in the exercise of that spiritual power by which the church subsisted so many ages before Constantine', advised Bishop Turner.[24] The truth is that 'Anglican political dominance was surprisingly shaky, nowhere more so than at court, and churchmen, lay and clerical, had to fight hard and long ... to defend it and the integrity of the Church of England'.[25]

The political history of the church under Charles II and James II revolves around its relationship with the monarchy and with parliament. Each in turn sought to undermine the church's status as the only legal religion. Charles had reservations about the Act of Uniformity from the start. His residual sympathy for Papists and his distaste for persecution helped raise the Cavalier nightmare of an alliance between the Crown and the Presbyterians. Charles made his feelings plain in 1662, when he asked Parliament to consider ways in which he might exercise his 'inherent' power of dispensing with the Uniformity Act, and in 1672. On both occasions Parliament rushed to the church's defence, but its motive was fear of Popery; as MPs told Charles in 1663, if religious liberty is permitted 'in time, some prevalent sect will, at last, contend for an establishment; which, for aught can be foreseen, will end in Popery'. One defence against Popery was to increase Protestant unity, especially by widening the terms of clerical membership of the church and effecting a 'comprehension' or reunion of moderate Dissenters with the church. In 1673 Parliament sought to deal Popery a double blow with the Test Act and the bill to help Dissenters, which would have lifted the penal laws from them and offered concessions to win over ministers who differed form the church 'only in some circumstance or ceremonial point'. This might have created a broader Protestant alliance against Popery, but no one pretended that it was in the *church's* interest. Both Charles and James were prepared to listen to 'alternative' advisers, such as the Presbyterians Manton and Baber, the Quaker Penn and the Catholics Coleman and Brent, all of whom sought to overturn the church's privileged position. Even as Duke of York, James 'made it his business to court the sectaries and the fanatics, hoping thereby to strengthen the papist interest', and as King, he created an opportunistic alliance of Catholics, Dissenters and Whigs against the Anglicans.[26] The church was, in short, threatened by royal indulgences in 1662, 1672 and 1687, and by parliamentary comprehension schemes in the later 1660s, 1673 and 1680–1. There is little wonder, then, that the dispirited churchmen were ready even in the 1670s to consider ways of preserving the church at the expense of undermining the royal supremacy, and eventually to lead an 'Anglican revolution' against James II.[27]

The church's shaky position was apparent in the provinces too. Although there had been many gentry ready to welcome returning bishops to their dioceses in 1660, there were far fewer willing to enforce the harsh penal laws on their neighbours. Sheldon lamented that 'there wants power and zeal in the magistrates and justices to do their duty' in prosecuting conventicles; while other bishops complained of living 'under a slack magistracy'. The enforcement of the Conventicle Acts in many counties rested on just a very few individual JPs, Sir Daniel Fleming in Westmorland and Cumberland, Thoroton and Whalley in Nottinghamshire in the later 1670s, or the 'lone campaigner' Sir Roger Bradshaigh in Lancashire. The majority of the country gentry did not seem eager to persecute Nonconformists. In towns such as Newcastle, Coventry and Bristol, mayors were known to 'wink' at conventicles, while Yarmouth was a notorious safe haven for Independents in the 1660s. Since the lack of prosecutions under the 1664 Conventicle Act was blamed on the unwillingness of JPs and constables to prosecute their neighbours, the next Conventicle Act transferred the initiative for prosecution to informers who, for their efforts, collected part of the fines imposed on those convicted. There is abundant evidence of popular hostility to these informers and of lay reluctance to inform: in 1668 there was 'not a man' in the county of Cheshire who had reported these preachers or their meetings 'though there be hundreds that knew it'.[28]

The suggestion that there was an Anglican hegemony in Restoration England does not withstand scrutiny. The supposedly Anglican magistrates of English towns and cities were constantly opposing the church over questions of precedence and jurisdiction.[29] Many of those in local and even national office were in fact not even conforming Anglicans. Dissenters were numerous in the government of London and many west country boroughs, and represented over a quarter of those elected to office in Coventry. They even filled parish offices such as those of constable and churchwarden: one out of every three of the churchwardens of the village of Terling had been investigated for non-conformity.[30] The church's control of ideas and education was less effective than it appeared. The notoriously ineffective censorship only operated after publication; Nonconformists did attend the universities, even if they did not take a degree there, and the Dissenters' own academies and foreign universities frequently produced a much better education than was available at Oxford and Cambridge.

The Church of England could not ensure that its own clergy conformed to their obligations. Many of them were at best semi-conformists; they might have reluctantly continued or begun their ministry at the Restoration and then evaded full conformity thereafter. These were men such as Richard Crossing, an ejected minister from Hampshire, who obtained ordination in Exeter in 1662 and served as vicar of Otterton, before being hauled up in the Consistory Court in 1681 where he confessed 'that he had sometimes omitted to read all the divine service in his said parish church as is enjoined by law. More particularly that he had sometimes omitted to read the Litany and second service at such time as the law hath enjoined ... forborne to wear the surplice during the time of executing his office ... and usually suffered the parish clerk to read the second lesson'.[31] Often such clergymen were adapting their services to the demands of their congregations or patrons. And they got away with their semi-conformity thanks to lay protection and to the church's poor administrative control. Isaac Archer, for instance, recorded that at one visitation 'God ordered it so that, though I was before the archdeacon, and was questioned about some things yet nothing was done against me, and the [archdeacon] knew not that I had not read service'.[32]

The church's control over the laity was equally weak. Even nominal Anglicans were reluctant to attend both Sunday services or to sit through the whole service: when they went, they resented the time they spent there, 'an hour spent at a sermon, yea and upon God's day too, is thought too long, when a play of three or four hours is done too soon'. Wiltshire parishioners hardly ever went to holy day services, and one can only guess at attendances on days such as 30 January or 29 May. Other voluntary duties such as catechism class or frequent communions were neglected.[33] The church courts seem to have lost their ability to terrify. Although the Lancashire apprentice Roger Lowe was frightened by a false report that he had been summoned, many seem to have laughed off the courts. Attendance rates were poor even among the clergy and in some dioceses they may have been running at 60 per cent for the laity. On the other hand, the courts were deeply unpopular: 'great clamours' were made against their delay and expense, and many felt that the church's spiritual powers of excommunication were being misused by the courts' lay officials; as Sheldon warned one official, you cannot 'be ignorant what a shock the church is at this time likely to undergo upon that account, if you mend not your ways'.[34] The desire for church reform seems to have been strong among the clergy, but as so often it lacked the political support of the King or Parliament. Only during the Danby years were serious proposals put to Parliament designed to strengthen the church by reforming glaring abuses and providing the machinery to curb atheism, profanity and vice among the laity.

The more one analyses the 'Anglican establishment', the weaker it looks. The outward conformity of the political and social élite was precisely that, external adherence which might disguise reluctance, apathy or even resentment. Well known gentry sympathizers with Dissent were also conformists to the Church of England: Sir Edward Harley 'was a favourer of such as dissented from the church for conscience's sake ... yet he constantly attended the church'.[35] More importantly, even those gentry who were unequivocal supporters of the church were not necessarily pursuing the same goals as the clergy. Gentry enthusiasm for the Prayer Book, episcopal government and uniformity was not necessarily *religious*; they were no doubt as interested in the church as a proprietor, a prop of the old order and a bulwark against sectarianism.

III

The Act of Uniformity created two artificial legal categories, Anglican and Dissenter, which referred primarily to clergymen. But the Act did not create two religious denominations to match these categories. As we shall see, neither of these labels adequately or exhaustively describes the religious beliefs and practices of those to whom they were applied. The Act established the terms of clerical communion with the church. These were designed to extract outward conformity from the clergy of the established church *or* to exclude those ministers who would not conform. Anglican clergy were those who could accept these terms, while Dissenters were those who could not. This was not necessarily a theological distinction. The decision about conformity often turned on an individual's personal scruple or difficulty rather than an issue of general principle.

Philip Henry's reasons for non-conformity were that 'I scruple to be reordained ... to declare my assent and consent to the liturgy, to renounce the covenant as an oath in itself unlawful, which are the common stumbling stones to me with others'.[36] For those clergy with Presbyterian orders who had exercised a ministry during the 1640s and 1650s, the demand that they should submit to an ordination by a bishop was tantamount to 'reordination'. It cast doubt on the validity and efficacy of all they had done as ministers during the past twenty years. Some Nonconformist ministers would have been prepared to pursue their vocations under an episcopal church government, but not to repudiate their own ordinations and past ministries. Nonconformists also objected to declaring their 'unfeigned assent and consent' to the Book of Common Prayer as if they believed the liturgy was both true and lawful, when many found things in it 'which I deem scarce right and true, much less good and expedient to be done'.[37] Renouncing the Solemn League and Covenant involved two difficulties. Many simply held that, as a solemn oath before God, the Covenant was inviolable and Nonconformists were notoriously scrupulous about oaths. But the conformist was also required to forswear 'to endeavour any change or alteration of government either in church or state'. 'Here they stick', Bishop Morley told the House of Lords: 'They will not say they will renounce the last war, and they will forestall another'.[38] A further stumbling block was subscription to the Thirty-nine Articles, three of which concerned church government. The Dissenters claimed that an Elizabethan statute allowed a minister to subscribe to the thirty-six articles dealing with doctrine alone. Again and again, personal scruples rather than issues of principle were at stake. But in this case personal decisions had wider repercussions, since many of their flocks simply followed the clergy's example or advice. The Uniformity Act had nothing to do with lay Dissenters, and although the subsequent legislation of the Clarendon Code began to impinge on the laity, its main thrust was always to control and restrain the ejected clergy and those in 'pretended orders'.

As well as those ministers who could not accept the terms of 1662, the category of 'Dissent' also covered the separatists who had no interest in membership of any national church. Sectaries, Quakers, Baptists, Independents and Presbyterians now all fell into the same legal category, but they had little else in common. Learned, university-educated and conservative Presbyterian ministers shared nothing with Baptist ex-soldiers or wandering Quaker preachers – except perhaps for resentment at the category: 'it is a palpable injury to burden us with the various parties with whom we are now herded by our ejection in the general state of dissenters'.[39] Many of the sects did not even have a clergy in the Presbyterian or Episcopalian sense of the term. The congregation simply chose the pastor on the grounds of the gifts of the Spirit rather than formal qualifications, and many were laymen, who continued to follow their trade or calling while exercising their pastoral duties. These pastors exercised no power beyond the church meeting, and the congregation retained full authority over their own affairs.

One of the most important sections of clerical Dissent – and certainly one of the most difficult to describe – is the large middle ground of mainly Presbyterian, and some Independent, ministers who retained a sympathy for the national church. Many of the clergy excluded from the ministry of the Church of England by the Uniformity Act had much in common with those who, thanks to chance, accident of birth or lack of scruple, could serve as clergy of the restored church. An arbitrary line drawn across the spectrum of English religious life had severed a broad-based Protestantism, leaving half of the ministers and their followers within the restored church and half outside. Friendships and co-operation continued to exist across the denominational boundaries; the ideal of an inclusive, truly national church continued to cast its spell. Thus the ejected Presbyterian Thomas Manton went to St Paul's Covent Garden to hear the sermons of his successor, Simon Patrick. John Corbet 'joined in all the worship with the public assembly and had no sinful separating principles', according to his friend Richard Baxter, who described himself as a 'half-conformist'. Philip Henry, another ejected minister, refused 'to overthrow our parish-order, which God hath owned' and attended Anglican services in Whitewell chapel for nearly thirty years. In order 'that I may bear my testimony against prelacy', Henry would not conform as a minister and read the liturgy to a congregation, but he would conform as a private individual and hear the liturgy in church 'to bear my testimony against Independency – looking upon both of them as bypaths, the one on the left hand, the other on the right, and the truth between them'.[40] The position taken by these divines was that although *as clergy* they were personally excluded from the ministry by the unacceptable requirements of the Act of Uniformity, there was nothing to bar them or their lay followers from attending the worship of the Church of England or the sermons of the best Anglican preachers. These moderate Dissenters feared the dangers of division and separation, and still believed that the Church of England and her parishes were fundamentally sound. Their aim was to re-unite with the church on broader terms of conformity than those of 1662; it was not to establish separate churches.

Anglicans were those clergy who could accept the terms of the Act of Uniformity. It did not matter whether they embraced them enthusiastically or accepted them reluctantly – they were all Anglicans. As a consequence the clergy of the restored church came from a variety of backgrounds. There were, of course, self-styled 'sufferers' – loyal, royalist clergy who had been sequestered from their livings in the 1640s and had spent much of the Interregnum in retirement or exile. These were enthusiastic defenders of the rights of the church and her bishops, of the liturgy and of the Stuarts, and many of them leaned towards an elevated view of episcopacy and an elaborate ritualism. Many of these divines were already middle-aged in 1660, however, and the next generation was tainted by collaboration with the regimes of the 1640s and 1650s. Some of these younger men were reluctant conformists who, in time, came to pronounce themselves 'more satisfied in the Church of England than ever'; while others, such as John Tillotson, Edward Fowler, Simon Patrick and Richard Kidder, were more enthusiastic converts to the church and, despite being suspected by some as time-servers or 'latitudinarians', eventually rose to bishoprics.[41] Also to be found among the conformists were thorough-going puritans, such as Ralph Josselin or John Angier, who by evasion, connivance and sheer good luck managed to retain their livings without using the surplice or Prayer Book. In due course another generation of Anglican clergy emerged; the high-flying divines of the later 1670s and 1680s were a new breed of highly politicized and aggressive churchmen, educated in the Restoration universities, and all too ready to wield their pen in support of the royal prerogative and the indefeasible divine right of hereditary monarchy. Tensions existed not only between the generations, but on issues of principle such as the nature of episcopacy, or the wisdom of persecuting Dissent, or the necessity of performing the Prayer Book liturgy to the letter. Those Anglican ministers who, out of scruple or in deference to the tastes of their congregations, 'omit words, and phrases, and whole prayers constantly, can come under no other notion but partial conformists'. Such partial or semi-conformist clergy were often left undisturbed until the 1680s, when the political circumstances of the Tory reaction led to a campaign against those who bent the church's rules to placate Dissenters, against 'ambiguous men, that are listed under our banner, and receive the church's pay, but serve our dangerous enemy, the fanatic and Dissenter'.[42] Although tensions occasionally boiled over in this way, they were

soon damped down by the church's leaders, who were at pains to
maintain a façade of clerical unity.

IV

Artificially categorized by the law, often with unwelcome partners
and separated from natural allies, Anglican and Dissenting clergy
nevertheless set about breathing life into their denominational
labels. In part the effort was dictated by the logic of the political
situation and its accompanying polemic. Those who had been
excluded from the church and denied their religious liberty naturally protested. Inevitably, those who had conformed felt that
their moderate Nonconformist brethren were somehow claiming
to be the more discerning or spiritually sensitive. Anglicans were
exasperated that Dissenters were seen as 'the only sober, godly
party of the nation, merely because they have the modesty to call
themselves so'. Relations were even more strained between the
sects and the church. The Baptists, for example, denounced the
Anglicans' 'superstitious and idolatrous worship, that with force
and cruelty is maintained in opposition to the true worship and
worshippers of God'. In return, Anglicans were dismissive of 'the
peddling   sectarists   of   the   nation   (those   mushrooms   of
Christianity, that so suddenly sprang up in the late night of confusion)'.[43] While Dissenters unleashed charges of persecution,
bigotry, crypto-Popery and formalism against the church, the
Anglicans replied with accusations of sedition, fanaticism, enthusiasm and hypocrisy. The superheated vocabulary of controversy
inevitably deepened animosities.

It has been argued that the shared experience of proscription
and persecution during the reigns of Charles and James helped to
create a single Dissenting identity.[44] Of course Dissenters shared
a basic supposition that they were the godly, or in the
Independents' words, 'saints by calling, visibly manifesting and
evidencing ... their obedience unto that call of Christ', and
'known to each other by their confession of the faith'. Not all of
them were prepared to join a congregation of visible saints, or
even to claim that all the godly could be known in this life but,
despite theological differences, they recognized in each other a
Puritan spirituality and a moral earnestness which was lacking in
the profane world and the 'formalism' of much of the national
church. Dissenters wanted to live, work and worship with

like-minded men and women. That a spiritual experience, rather than a doctrinal creed, was at the heart of the matter can be seen, for instance, in the way that membership of many churches depended on giving an account of one's conversion before the congregation; it is visible too in the Bristol Baptists' decisions to leave adult baptism as an 'open question' for members and to 'promote that blessed principle of union among the saints, as saints, though of different persuasions'.[45]

These, then, were the foundations upon which Dissenters could build a corporate identity. There is, however, no doubt that persecution honed their zeal and helped them shed the half-hearted. Dissenters embraced the biblical language of suffering and martyrdom with relish, and some eagerly embraced the persecution itself, refusing to meet in secret or to protect themselves, since it was their duty to witness to the Lord, and present trials were 'a manifestation of our predestination to the ease and peace of another world'. Such attitudes of self-sacrifice did not preclude organizing and co-operating so as to be able to withstand persecution. Even the sects began to create hierarchies: the Quakers set up their Monthly Meetings and began to log the tribulations of members in the 'Book of Sufferings', which remains the most detailed account of the effects of Restoration persecution; the Baptists appointed 'messengers' to superintend groups of congregations and held General Assemblies. The various congregations in Bristol co-operated in law suits and eventually met together for prayer; in London the Presbyterians and Independents set up joint lectures, and by the later 1670s there were plans afoot for an 'accommodation' or union between the two denominations. Yet we should not paint too rosy a picture of Dissenting unity. It was part of the nature of Dissent to encourage individuals to examine their consciences and to question ecclesiastical authority. Few of the congregational churches avoided internal divisions; and they quarrelled both about weighty issues such as predestination and adult baptism, and about whether singing was permissible during worship, or whether Sunday or Saturday was the sabbath. Presbyterianism was a numerically stronger tradition than the sects and was held together by the moral leadership of its ministers. But even these ministers began to disagree among themselves over questions of policy and theology. While the younger generation of Presbyterian clergy were ready to accept that they would never be part of the national church, and shared the Calvinist theology of their Independent allies, many of the older

Presbyterian clergy refused to embrace sectarianism and had become suspicious of traditional Calvinism.

The Church of England had more success in papering over its cracks. The church contained a wide range of views on the question of episcopacy, from those who thought that bishops were established by Christ and were essential to the existence of a true church to others who regarded them as a useful human institution for the government of the church. This was an important issue, not least because of the rival claim of the monarch to be the foundation of the national church. If the Church of England was the territorial church of a godly prince, this left it vulnerable to princely changes of heart – as happened in 1672 and 1687 – but if the church was constituted by the bishops, then it had a separate political and spiritual existence and might even defend itself against the prince. What is striking about the Restoration church is its ability to fudge the issue and to allow a range of views on episcopacy to co-exist among its clergy and laity.[46]

The Restoration church's self-appointed mission was to remedy the spiritual and moral errors of the Puritan past. Anglicans, for instance, were exhorted to take up holy living in conjunction with a lively faith, to add the power of godliness to its form in fulfilling 'the whole duty of man'. This insistence on 'a practical and operative faith' and on constant striving was aimed at Nonconformist teachings which seemed to encourage a presumptuous assurance of personal salvation. Anglican preachers discouraged unnecessary speculation and stressed the theological agnosticism of their church. The 'settled doctrine' of the Church of England allowed for a variety of views on speculative subtleties: when Anglicans were asked how it was that God worked on the heart of an individual who enjoyed free will, they answered 'I do not know that we are obliged to trouble ourselves with those nice inquiries'.[47] What was needed was 'plain, practical preaching' on the need for God's assistance *and* our own efforts. With the theology of men such as George Bull, the church was breaking with the traditional theological emphasis of English Protestantism and of Puritanism in particular. Bull and his colleagues were denounced as 'moralists', teaching that faith is little more than doing good, and as 'rationalists', teaching that faith is an assent to beliefs rather than an emotional trust in the Lord. They certainly did teach that a saving faith was reasonable, that it involved understanding, repentance and obedience, but their message has been grievously misrepresented as 'moralism' when in fact they required of the Christian a life of constant effort. The new theology of the Restoration church did not persuade all Anglicans, but it did win the sympathy of Dissenters such as Richard Baxter. As a result, theological alignments increasingly crossed denominational allegiances in the Restoration.[48]

Anglican pastors worked for the repentance of sinners; they admonished them to 'enter into their closets' and get on their knees. Anglican piety was a regime of introspective, almost morbid, self-examination, penitence and thanksgiving, of private and household devotion, and it was the necessary foundation of 'holy living'. Moral reformation might follow in the wake of personal piety, but its primary purpose was to prepare the individual for the public worship of the church and, above all, for a worthy reception of the Lord's Supper. The Anglican model of holy living was promoted through a large and diverse literature, which embraced works of moral exhortation and guidance such as *The Whole Duty of Man* and far more specific manuals such as *A Weeks Preparation towards a Worthy Receiving of the Lords Supper*. While the devotional writers stoked the fires of piety, the church struggled to provide a public outlet for the consequent devotion. Provision of daily prayers and of monthly communions was increased in the capital and in the cathedrals, but the parish churches of the countryside lagged far behind.[49]

The Anglican and Dissenting clergy forged parties to match the legal categories of conformist and Nonconformist, but their definitions were always at the mercy of the laity's interpretation. In a Lancashire alehouse one day in 1664, Roger Lowe, a Dissenter, began to discuss with John Potter 'the manner of God's worship. He was for episcopacy and I for Presbytery. The contention had like to have been hot, but the Lord prevented. It was two or three days ere we spoke, and I was afraid lest he should do me some hurt'.[50] This alehouse quarrel between a lay Anglican and a lay Dissenter is instructive, not simply as a reminder of how passionately people felt about religion, but in its confusion of two forms of church government with two forms of worship. As any teacher knows, people understand at their own pace and in their own way, and the Restoration laity, although well versed in their bibles, did not always respond predictably or along prescribed denominational lines to what the clergy put before them. We will learn something more about the period's religious divisions if we look at Restoration religion from the point of view of its lay 'consumers'.

V

The English had a taste for sermons: they 'generally place their religion in the pulpit, as the papists do theirs upon the altar'; 'we make the pulpit our ark and chain all religion to it'.[51] Some parishes preferred a second sermon on a Sunday, even if it meant that the minister omitted parts of the service. City men such as Pepys made a habit of 'going from one church to another hearing a bit here and a bit there'; they casually dropped in to taste a sermon or made a point of hearing a new preacher, and they were keen judges of performance, substance and style. John Evelyn commended the new plain, rational style of preaching; he disliked sermons which were too abstruse and noticed if it was a 'court sermon' or a 'theologo-political sermon'.[52] Hearing sermons was less passive than we might imagine: congregations followed them in their bibles; they discussed or repeated them after church; and, although it was becoming less common, they took notes in church. It is also apparent that many would go to hear sober Nonconformist and moderate Anglican preachers indiscriminately. In their weekly sermons both clergies concentrated on the central duties of repentance and Christian living. In 1670, Evelyn's vicar preached on successive Sundays on 'how we are justified by Christ's rising again', 'how justification has reference to works as well as faith' and 'how faith was more than a firm belief or strong persuasion'. Philip Henry pressed second table duties, and it was derided as 'good moral preaching; but let them call it as they will, I am sure it is necessary, and as much now as ever'. There was, however, a drawback to this sermon addiction in some eyes: it was 'a huge decay of Christian piety, to place all or most of our religion in hearing a sermon'; 'sermons ... are extolled to the skies, sacraments and prayers are neglected'.[53]

The popular neglect of prayers and sacraments was undeniable. The clergy frequently remarked on 'the common insensibility of most part of country people' of the duty of public prayers. The JPs complained of the 'people disaffected to the Book of Common Prayer, which frequently stand without the churches, till the common service be read; and then at the singing of the psalm, when the minister goes into the pulpit, then they come into the church and not before'. 'I find', reported one minister, 'many of the people have, at the bottom, an ill affection for the prayers and governors of the church, really judging the worship tainted with Popery'.[54] The Prayer Book certainly suffered from associations with Popery. Pepys thought that the degree of ceremony approached that in the Roman Church and Sir Edward Harley thought the surplice 'a proper massing garment'. When Lowe was chastised by the vicar in church for not standing at the gospel, he roundly denounced standing 'with other ceremonies now in use' as 'mere Romish foppery' and stormed off to a conventicle.[55] According to Heywood, Anglican worship was full of 'vain inventions' which 'mangle and trifle with the holy things of God's worship'; while Anglican clergy were alleged to be 'so formal and superstitious that if one word was displaced they could not go forward but begin again'. There were frequent complaints of 'the ineffectualness' of the liturgy: the Prayer Book was 'dry stuff'; 'I have no hope of good by it, as having been bred up under its plenty, and tired with its emptiness, and yet surfeited of it'.[56] Anglican worship simply failed to move or to satisfy. Dissenters expected to be 'edified', to be confirmed and strengthened in their Christian graces, but in their eyes, the church had signally failed to order the indifferent matters of worship 'unto edifying'. The problem may have been with prescribed, written, prayers, rather than extempore prayer and preaching: 'I am sure', wrote Bunyan, 'that it is impossible that all the prayer-books that men have made in the world should lift up or prepare the heart'. Visiting Bristol diocese in 1683, Bishop Trelawney complained of 'the confused and irregular way of reading the prayers in some ministers, either through their own dissatisfaction with them, or fear of others [being] dissatisfied with them'. Too often, the services were conducted as a series of prayers by the minister and responses by the parish clerk, who supposedly led the congregation, while parishioners mumbled their responses or looked on in silence.[57]

The sacrament of the Lord's Supper assumed an even less central role in the average persons' spiritual life than common prayer. Although communions were available, and increasingly so, many parishioners remained 'strangely averse' or 'awkward to the sacrament'; the compilers of the Compton Census observed that many who attended church did not receive the sacrament. Even those who took the church's message seriously, and prepared themselves elaborately for a 'worthy reception' of the sacrament, only received communion perhaps two or three times each year. It seems likely that many parishioners received only once a year, probably at Easter, and many of them insisted on receiving the sacrament on their own terms. At St Helen's, Bishopsgate, some

of Richard Kidder's parishioners would not kneel to receive the
sacrament. Considering 'the mischief of dismissing such a number
of communicants and sending them to the Nonconformists', Kidder
gave them the bread and wine in their seats and subsequently
gained his bishop's approval for his action. When a Puritan gentleman such as Sir Edward Harley came to receive the sacrament,
as was required under the Test Act, he chose to do so at
St Helen's.[58] Dissenters had a much richer sacramental life than
Anglicans since their churches often celebrated a monthly communion. Of course, Dissenting congregations were voluntary associations of like-minded people, who saw themselves as the godly,
and who lived under the threat of persecution, and so it was only
natural for them to strengthen their resolve by participation in
the corporate, communal act of the sacrament. Anglican parishioners, on the other hand, were simply residents of a particular
area.[59]

Consideration of the laity's preferences in worship helps to
explain the surprising fluidity of religious allegiances. It has long
been appreciated that individual Nonconformists moved from
one congregation to another, from Independency to Baptism and
then to the Quakers, but such movement also occurred across the
border between Anglicanism and Dissent. Francis Turner pointed
out in 1675 that:

> Dissenters properly so called are not in some dioceses above
> one in twenty. Many absent themselves from our churches out
> of pure indevotion and laziness. Many frequent the meeting-
> houses out of curiosity, and many for want of room in their
> churches and tabernacles at London, or because of their dis-
> tance from their own parish churches in the country. The stiff
> and irreconcilable Dissenters appear to be a handful of men in
> comparison.

The very next year, the returns to Bishop Compton's census
confirmed that large numbers of parishioners attended both
church and conventicle. In Maidstone the local Presbyterians
'usually come to church, and to divine service, one part of the
day, and go to a conventicle the other, having a Nonconformist
teacher in the town, whom they maintain'. Bishop Fell's inquiries
in his Oxford diocese in the early 1680s revealed a situation of
similar fluidity, where parishioners 'seem to be like the borderers
betwixt two kingdoms, one can't well tell what prince they are
subject to'. Nor was such indecision limited to the common

people: a gentlemen such as Sir John Gell would attend 'divine service and sermon constantly' despite also holding Dissenting conventicles at his family home. Those who went to both church and chapel in this way were aptly described by one Anglican cleric as 'neutralists between Presbyterians and conformists'.[60] This neutralism can be explained in a variety of ways. It may be a manifestation of that well-established tendency to go 'gadding' after sermons, to seek out edifying preaching wherever it was available. It could also be a result of the legal constraints on parishioners to attend church. Several commentators suggest that when these obligations were lifted in 1672 and 1687, the congregations at parish churches became very thin; conversely, when they were re-imposed the clergy reported good flocks.

VI

The laity were not only voting with their feet – staying away from prayers and the sacrament – they were also taking an active role in shaping English religion. 'Many of the gentry of late are grown more inquisitive in religious things', it was claimed in 1661, and they would no longer be constrained in what they thought by the clergy; divinity had become 'the frequentest table-talk in England'.[61] This new curiosity can be seen in the works of a host of lay writers on religion, many of whom were devout supporters of the church; such as Sir Philip Warwick, who planned a large work of Protestant apologetics, Sir Henry Yelverton, who edited the works of Bishop Morton, John Evelyn, who wrote *A History of Religion*, Sir Roger Twysden, author of a work on schism, and Sir Peter Leicester, whose work on creation and the immortality of the soul was dutifully submitted to the bishop but never published. Other authors were more lukewarm towards the church, or even hostile, but remained keen proponents of Christianity. All of this writing displays the contemporary fascination with 'reason' and wit, and at its best this fascination produced a new tone to religious debate: religion was now being discussed with 'gentlemanly candour' and 'that moderate temper that men use in debating natural experiments' rather than 'passion and loudness'.[62] But wit was often also an excuse for scoffing, especially at the clergy. 'People are taken with fooleries, plays, poems, buffooning and drolling books', observed Wood, and gave as examples John Eachard's *Contempt of the Clergy*, Marvell's *Rehearsall*

Transpros'd and Butler's *Hudibras*: the first two are attacks on the Church of England, and the third a satire on Puritan excess and all religiosity.[63] The laity's irreligious attitudes covered a spectrum: at one end lay witty gibes at the expense of the clergy and at the other lay the spectres of atheism and deism.

Suspicion of the clergy began from lay resentment. 'Generally men are become so good judges of what they hear', observed Halifax, 'that the clergy ought to be very wary before they go about to impose upon their understandings, which are grown less humble than they were in former times'. Pepys was told by a Nonconformist acquaintance that the present clergy were so haughty 'that they are hated and laughed at by everybody' and received 'affronts' from 'the gentlemen and ordinary persons of the parish'. Suspicious of the 'black coats' himself, Pepys agreed that the people 'have been so used to liberty and freedom' under the Puritan regimes that they would never stomach these proud clergy. Was this, then, the clergy's reward for standing in the breach against the tide of atheism and Popery, to be 'exposed as the ancient Christians were, amongst the beasts in the amphitheatre'? Some said that it was just deserts for the clergy's own hypocrisy, their readiness to turn coat, and their internecine quarrels, which had simply revealed 'the vanity of all their pretendings to divine right' and convinced the gentry not to tolerate 'immoderate and high behaviours in any one party of them'. One perceptive churchman believed that the gentry, especially those who were influenced by Hobbes, feared that the clergy would 'overtop' them.[64]

The charge of 'priestcraft' gave a sharper edge to all the jokes at the expense of the clergy. The term exploited the age-old suspicion that a self-interested and domineering clergy had made religion into a mystery or trade. Francis Osborne warned that the curious questions of scholastic divinity had been 'devised to puzzle the laity, and render the clergy no less necessary than honourable'. Priestcraft was a political design to keep the clergy in the saddle and the laity in tutelage, a spell which could be cast over princes to subordinate them to nefarious clerical ambitions. The Roman Catholic clergy were obvious practitioners of the art, but some Restoration Englishmen saw evidence of its practice in the English church, and especially by the bishops. It became a witty commonplace that the world contains mainly 'fools and knaves', and that the clerical knaves had usurped power 'over the folly and ignorance of the others'.[65]

'Who is so blind', asked the clergy in reply, 'as not to see that irreverence and disrespect for the Lord's clergy hath been accompanied with a manifest decay of piety, and a notorious contempt of the most essential parts of religion?'. Reverence for religion was ebbing away on all sides. Wherever they looked in society the clergy saw a rising tide of irreligion, from 'that indifferency and coldness in religion, and that worldly mindedness, which possesses the generality' in the Oxfordshire parish of Adderbury, to 'the general looseness in the manners of men' complained of by Bishop Lucy of St David's, and the 'foolish proud conceit of my own wit' which led the Cambridge don Daniel Scargill into atheism. 'Atheism and profaneness daily abound more and more', the bishops told Charles II when he sought their advice in 1675, 'and defections are frequently made on the one side to the superstitious and idolatrous practices and usurpations of Rome, on the other to the pernicious and destructive novelties of the various sects raised in the worst of times'. Atheism was 'esteemed a piece of gallantry, and an effect of that extraordinary wit in which we pretend to excel our ancestors'. Where once only the fool had denied God, now the wit rushed to follow him.[66]

Congregations and readers were repeatedly told that theirs was the most atheistical generation since the Creation, or that 'we are fallen into the dregs of time, sensuality runs everywhere into atheism'.[67] The term 'atheist' was used so often by the orthodox, both Anglican and Nonconformist, of Restoration England that it is tempting to dismiss it as a catch-all term of abuse. Profesor Hunter has shown that the atheist figure held a ragbag of inconsistent views about the natural world, the soul and the veracity of the bible, that he was a scoffer, immoral and overconfident of his own intellectual abilities, in short that he was a stereotype of Restoration deviance, a projection of the worst possible outcome of current intellectual, social and moral trends.[68] This is presumably why tireless apologists devoted so much energy to proving the existence of God, divine providences, an immortal soul and rewards and punishment after death, while simultaneously professing their utter disbelief 'that there ever was such a monster as a thorough-paced, speculative atheist in the world.'[69] Intellectual or 'speculative' atheism, where it existed, was merely a mask or justification for the vice of those who lived as if there were no God, the 'practical' atheists. By rehearsing the arguments for the existence of God, the apologists were chastising the profane and strengthening the resolve and convictions of the orthodox.

Deists did exist in Restoration England, albeit in tiny numbers. These free-thinkers pleaded 'only for a natural religion in opposition to any particular mode or way of divine revelation'. They accepted the existence of a God, a life after death, and rewards and punishments in that next life, but not that God had revealed his religion in the scriptures or that he had sent his son Christ. They believed that the natural religion which we all know in our hearts contains two cardinal articles, that men should practice virtue and should revere the deity or, in brief, 'the morality in religion is above the mystery in it'; all the doctrines, offices and worship particular to any revealed religion were 'only of human and politic institution'.[70] The publicity now accorded to such views (which were not in themselves novel) owed much to lay antagonism towards the clergy and the Anglican church.

Close reading of the pamphlet debates between the clerical profession and the witty, rational, even sceptical, writers of the Restoration, suggests that the clergy could no longer dictate the terrain on which they fought. The clergy were certainly no match for the wits and anticlericals; nor could they win the arguments about the rationality of revealed religion. Perplexed, they asked why atheism persisted 'notwithstanding so many popular discourses everywhere made about the reasonableness of religion' and concluded that the answer lay in the definition of reason. 'The bottom of the great veneration some have paid to reason', wrote one Anglican divine, is that they mean by it 'not reason in general, the common excellency of our nature ... but every man's own private and individual'.[71] The clergy sensed that, slowly but surely, they were losing the battle to define the values of English society.

VII

The drive for religious unity by means of uniformity not only failed, it perpetuated religious division in the shape of an entrenched Nonconformity. Was there more chance of harmony if the state embraced these differences, and permitted diversity? Contemporaries contemplated a range of possibilities. Some, perhaps many, wanted to see an end to the persecution of fellow Protestants; others would go a step further and rescind the laws under which the Dissenters suffered; the next step would be to permit a freedom of worship; and this could be supplemented by the restoration of full civil rights to religious dissidents. A parallel policy would be to widen the terms of communion of the national church. Few considered the far more radical step of disestablishing the church and giving all churches and, possibly, all beliefs equality before the law. These were theoretical possibilities, in practice things were much less clear cut. To judge from their language, contemporaries were often confused about terminology: they accepted 'liberty of conscience' or freedom of thought as a general principle, while shying away from 'toleration' as 'a spot on any government' and a threat to Protestantism. 'Toleration of all religions will soon destroy the right religion, it is more reasonable to subdue these parties already begun, and to bring them to conformity by severe laws'. Toleration 'is the very thing which the Romish emissaries have always aimed at; and seems to be one of the subtlest parts of the Popish plot'. So subtle were the Papists, who 'take all shapes upon them, and all disguises, of Agitator, Ranters, Levellers and Quakers', that they had made the Protestant sects their Trojan horse. After the failed Puritan revolution, they hoped to win freedom for themselves through the toleration of Dissent. These fears were used by churchmen to explain their hostility towards Dissent. Bishop Seth Ward supported the Conventicle Act because without it the country would need a standing army or a general toleration and both would end in Popery. Bishop Fell told a partisan of the 1680 comprehension that 'we both aim at ... the preservation of the Protestant religion, and established government ... you imagine the nation can only be preserved by letting in all dissenters into your church; and on the other side, we are most firmly persuaded that your proceedings must draw after them the alteration of government, and popery: toleration being certainly destructive of our reformed religion, whether procured by a Lord Clifford, or a popular pretence to the uniting of Protestants'.[72]

There were limits to tolerance even among the persecuted. Many Dissenters recoiled from the 1672 Declaration of Indulgence because 'papists and atheists enjoy so much liberty' under it. When the Indulgence was withdrawn, Oliver Heywood, who had taken out a licence, proclaimed this a 'rich mercy' because it meant that Papists would now be prosecuted once more. The demise of the Indulgence 'made many rejoice', observed Isaac Archer, and although it had had no effect in his own parish, 'if 'twas dangerous as to the growth of Popery, I am glad 'tis at end, though I could wish indulgence to sober, and peaceable, men.'[73] For others the means were as important as the ends: a royal declaration arbitrarily setting aside the penalties of laws passed by parliament was unconstitutional. Most paradoxical to modern eyes is the use of toleration as negotiating partner to comprehension. A comprehension would lift various requirements for clerical subscription, so that many of the 'moderate' Nonconformist clergy would return to the church as ministers and bring their followers with them. An indulgence or toleration would then be extended to the sects who remained resolutely outside the enlarged national church. In other words, far from being a human right, toleration was a poor second designed to cover the recalcitrant minority.

Few of the parties concerned with comprehension and toleration could agree on what they wanted. 'All that I have heard of who desire comprehension, desire indulgence also for others', noted Roger Morrice, the Presbyterian, in 1680, 'though multitudes desire indulgence that most fervently oppose comprehension'. Those who could not be comprehended feared that once 'the most considerable' Nonconformist ministers had been absorbed into the church, 'their own exclusion and suppression would be unavoidable'. Comprehension's chief advocates were the Presbyterians, who even attempted to give a gloss of comprehension to such acts as seeking a licence under the Indulgence of 1672. It is true that they were setting up congregations, but 'it is not our intention to set up any distant or separate churches in opposition to those already established, but, as members of one and the same church and preachers of the same doctrine therein declared, to be, what in us lies, helpful to the established ministers in carrying on the same general ends of piety, loyalty and charity, by instructing their people in matters of religion and duty to God and King'. Although it has often been asserted that Presbyterianism was moving towards sectarianism, the evidence of this is far from conclusive: and as late as 1689, there were Dissenters who advocated 'being made one body with the Church of England'.[74]

The Church of England, on the other hand, was always wary of comprehension. In public and in private, the Anglican clergy were consistent opponents of a scheme which would create two standards of entry for ministers of the church. Even those on the liberal wing of the church, such as Stillingfleet or Patrick, refused to countenance what would in effect 'establish a schism in the church by law, and so bring a plague into the very bowels of it'. This did not mean that liberals would not be generous once the former Nonconformists had entered the church's ministry. 'Variety of opinions and unity of opiners are not inconsistent'; the church embraced many theological outlooks and its latitude of liturgical practice was undeniable.[75]

Given that expectations were so diverse, it is not surprising that so few credible politicians took up the cause of toleration.[76] There was no single tolerationist campaign in Restoration England, but rather a series of feints and gestures. The references to liberty of conscience in 1659–61 by Anglicans such as Stillingfleet and Pett were simply bargaining chips in the efforts to re-establish episcopacy. The 1667 proposal was 'once faintly offered' to the House, but its proposer sat down 'despairing of success'; and the 1668 negotiations were a response to hints from Charles, but never came to Parliament. What response they would have received is difficult to gauge. Although opposed to 'a general toleration', Sir John Holland thought it 'very prudent to grant a relaxation of some things the law in force at present exacts and some indulgence to truly tender consciences'. These he defined as 'those that are of sober principles and agree with us clearly and entirely in fundamentals[;] that will cheerfully submit to the government established and use the liturgy, that differ with us only in things that are indifferent in their own nature and which we so hold though possibly they do not and from thence scruple their conformity in the use of them'. Certainly Pepys had heard that 'most of the sober party be for some kind of allowance to be given to them', although the Presbyterians 'will hardly trust the King or Parliament where to yield to them'. Out in the provinces, loyal gentlemen were less enthusiastic: Sir Peter Leicester told a Cheshire Grand Jury that the Nonconformist clergy 'were the main occasion and drawers on of the late rebellion ... so that if these men receive a toleration again, every man may easily guess what will follow'.[77]

The subsequent stabs at toleration and comprehension appear equally opportunistic or confused. The 1672 Indulgence was a wartime concession designed to neutralize Nonconformity as a potential ally of the Dutch enemy. During the campaign against Danby the toleration issue was caught up in the looking-glass world of polemical accusations about who provided the best defence of the Protestant religion against Popery. The Church of England believed that its alliance with Danby guaranteed the safety of Protestantism against sectarian subversion and royal interference. The church even demonstrated its credentials by proposing a Bill in 1677 which would have tied the hands of a Popish monarch in ecclesiastical matters – this was, as Dr Goldie has observed, a far more constitutionally innovative policy than Exclusion. The opposition of MPs to the church's 1677 proposal was framed in terms of the defence of monarchical powers and resistance to episcopal pretensions. The arguments about a bigoted and persecuting church and 'proud prelates', and even the abusive vocabulary of the 'priests of Baal' and 'Moses and Aaron', can be traced back to fears of the spread of clerical influence in government under Charles I.[78] There was nothing new about a conspiracy theory which suggested that the church was soft on Popery, and Shaftesbury and his allies deliberately raised the spectre of Archbishop Laud. In the eyes of its opponents, then, the church's steps to defend Protestantism were playing into the hands of Popery. Of course, in this rhetorical context 'Popery' meant any stance which diminished the civil magistrate's ecclesiastical power by emancipating the church and establishing its independent authority. Popery could emanate directly from Rome or from ambitious Anglican bishops seeking to seduce gullible princes into absolutism and to claim a status for the church independent of the monarchy.

The role of religious issues in the Exclusion Crisis awaits proper analysis. Most Dissenters were Whig sympathizers and most Tories were Anglicans; but it is not true that all Whigs were Dissenters, nor that all Anglicans were Tories. It has been shown that Whig propaganda was designed to play on Dissenters' grievances, because the Whigs needed their political support.[79] What is less easily demonstrated is the contention that the religious issue, specifically some easing of the plight of Dissenters, is what united the Whigs, rather than the constitutional issue of Exclusion. Meanwhile, every side claimed to be the champions of anti-Popery: the Whigs saw future Popery in the Duke of York and present Popery in the church; the church saw the real threat of Popery coming from another Puritan revolution, since everyone knew that 'the Pope would come in on the Puritan's back'.[80] When Popery did arrive, courtesy of James II, English Protestants were predictably divided in their response. Rumours of a toleration in July 1686 were greeted eagerly by the 'Anabaptists', but Presbyterians and Independents were inclined to stick by the Church of England.[81] When the chips were down in 1688, a significant proportion of Dissent did side resolutely with the Protestant church that had persecuted them for so long.

Perhaps the lack of any general theory of the right to religious toleration explains the absence of a concerted and coherent political campaign. Discussions of religious liberty would jumble up arguments of principle with arguments from scripture and secondary considerations, such as the likelihood of emigration or the need for a standing army to enforce a toleration. A typical appeal for religious liberty would assert that 'the mind and conscience of man, with respect to divine truths, ought not to be compelled by outward violence, and therefore ... it is unreasonable and unseasonable to prosecute so many of his majesty's Protestant subjects, merely for their nonconformity' and then go on to stress both the loyalty and trading strength of the Nonconformists.[82] The case for toleration was not much advanced by Nonconformists, who were trapped by sterile appeals to scripture and by the brute fact that competing claims based on 'conscience' are fundamentally irreconcilable. It was men such as Sir Charles Wolseley, who self-consciously applied 'reason' to the question, or the more cynical Hobbist Martin Clifford, who made progress. Appalled by religious dogmatism and its attendant cruelties and deeply suspicious of the clergy, these lay writers asserted that religious belief was a result of upbringing and environment. Since the individual had a duty to seek the truth for him or herself, God would punish no-one for 'honest' error, for error stumbled into while searching by the light of human reason for religious truth: sincerity rather than being right was what mattered. Coercion cannot compel conscience; it is impossible to believe something simply out of fear and against one's conscience.[83] The church was adamant, however, that it was prosecuting, not persecuting, its opponents. And it prosecuted for a purpose, to rescue the Nonconformists' reason from 'prejudice, wilfulness, or interest, that like so many surly door-keepers, forbid all access to right reason'.[84] The penal laws, it was claimed, helped people to think again, to ensure that they were fully informed and properly convinced.

In 1689, religious unity seemed further away than it had in 1660. The Toleration Act was a no more rational or planned piece of legislation than the Act of Uniformity. The 1680 Bills for comprehension and indulgence had been dusted off, but political jockeying and mistakes led to the shelving of the Comprehension Bill and the legislation of a toleration which covered far more non-Anglican Protestants than had been envisaged. Giving ease to the Dissenters, indulging them from various penalties, had become politically more attractive as comprehension had become increasingly less practicable. There was no sudden leap forward in English thinking about the principle of toleration; the Act's prosaic nature is well caught in John Evelyn's description of it as an 'Act of Indulgence for the dissenters, but not exempting them from paying dues to the Church of England Clergy, or serving in offices &c. according to law'.[85] The reigns of Charles II and James II had not fostered unity: religious choice had remained a reality; indeed, the rival denominations had acquired more substance, and the laity had grown bolder. It was certainly felt in 1689 that the laity intended to have the last word on religious 'liberty'. The Toleration Act will 'turn half the nation into downright atheism', complained one churchman, 'the mischief is, a liberty now being granted, more lay hold of it to separate from all manner of worship [and] to perfect irreligion' than to go to conventicles, 'and, although the Act allows no such liberty, the people will understand it so, and, say what the judges can at the assizes, or the Justices of the Peace at their sessions, or we at our visitations, no churchwarden or constable will present any for not going to church, though they go nowhere else but the alehouse, for this liberty they will have'.[86]

6. The Parties and the People: the Press, the Crowd and Politics 'Out-of-doors' in Restoration England

TIM HARRIS

The part played by the crowd in the political struggles of the Restoration period – the 'intervention of the mob' in politics, to adapt Max Beloff's phrase – has long been recognized.[1] There were riots and petitions against the republican regime in the winter of 1659–60, and Charles II's restoration in the spring of 1660 was greeted with popular demonstrations of support in many parts of the country. By the time of the Exclusion Crisis (1679–81), however, so the traditional argument runs, this enthusiasm for the Stuarts seems largely to have evaporated. Anxieties provoked by the revelations of the Popish Plot in 1678 enabled the Whigs, through their use of the popular press, to exploit the deeply embedded anti-Catholic prejudices of the English populace and rally public opinion behind them in their campaign to seek the exclusion of the Catholic heir, James, Duke of York, from the succession. There were pope-burnings and other demonstrations on behalf of the Whig cause not just in London, but in many parts of the country, while Whig mobilization of the masses is further evidenced by the monster petitions that they were able to promote in support of their position. Popular agitation against the Stuart monarchy can be seen again at the time of the Revolution of 1688, as angry crowds attacked the residences of leading Catholics and tore down Catholic meeting places in the capital and elsewhere, in protest against the policies of James II.

So much is familiar. Exactly what meaning and significance we should attach to such collective agitation, however, has been less clear. The study of crowd activity and popular petitions appears attractive as a way of shedding light on the political concerns and aspirations of the lower orders, of those who were otherwise excluded from the political process. Yet traditionally, political historians have been sceptical about the degree of political consciousness that we can ascribe to those below the level of the élite. The fact that the masses seemed to shift their political sympathies so quickly has encouraged the view that the crowd was fickle, and prone to oppose any government that was in power.[2] There has been a tendency to see crowds as being manipulated from above rather than as giving authentic expression to their own political feelings, because members of the élite often sought to promote or sponsor popular agitation; even Christopher Hill has written of 'manipulated crowds' at this time.[3] The time when the lower orders were most likely to be susceptible to such manipulation, it has been suggested, was when they were suffering economically. As J. R. Jones put it in his study of the Glorious Revolution: 'the periods during which radicals were able to mobilize popular support were ones in which there was a good deal of dislocation of trade, resulting in a shortage of employment and high prices for food and fuel'.[4]

Research carried out in recent years now allows for a more sophisticated understanding of crowd politics in Restoration England. In this chapter I propose to examine the meaning and significance of political agitation out-of-doors at this time, focusing in particular on the years of the Exclusion Crisis. I shall begin by investigating the Whig appeal to the people following the revelations of the Popish Plot, exploring not only *how* they sought to do this (through their use of the press) but also *why*. I shall then look at popular agitation on behalf of the Whigs, focusing on crowd activity and petitioning, where it will be argued that although the Whigs clearly did seek to mobilize the masses, it is wrong to talk of manipulated mobs. People could not easily be persuaded to take action on behalf of a cause for which they did not have sympathy; moreover, there is plenty of evidence to suggest that those out-of-doors were capable of coordinating political activity for themselves. Rather than manipulation from above, it is better to talk of convergence between the ideals of the Whig élite and the political concerns of their supporters amongst the masses. Finally, it will be shown that, contrary to what was once thought, the Whigs did not monopolize the sympathies of the lower orders. The Tories orchestrated their own propaganda campaign in which they deliberately sought to appeal to the masses, and there is plenty of evidence of loyalist and anti-Whig crowds in many parts of England in the years 1681–2. What we see in England in the early 1680s is a bitterly divided society, a division that was in part related to the impact which the fierce propaganda war between the Whigs and Tories had in heightening and encouraging the political awareness of those out-of-doors, but one which was also rooted in the deep political and religious tensions that already existed in Restoration English society.

I

The revelations of an alleged Popish Plot in the late summer of 1678, to kill the King, burn London to the ground and massacre thousands of Protestants, brought a heightened intensity to Restoration politics. Although questions have been raised in recent years as to whether we can talk about the emergence of parties at this time, what we can say with confidence is that a fairly well-organized opposition group, who came to be known as the Whigs, skilfully exploited the situation to offer a serious challenge to the Restoration regime. Amongst other things, the Whigs came to demand the exclusion of the Catholic heir – James, Duke of York – from the succession, and three Bills to this end were pursued in Parliament between 1679 and 1681 (this is why this period has come to be known as the 'Exclusion Crisis'). Yet, more generally, the Whigs also raised concerns about what they perceived to be a drift towards Popery and arbitrary government under Charles II. Such issues were debated not only in Parliament, but were also carried into the public domain by an aggressive press campaign. Pre-publication censorship broke down following the lapsing of the Licensing Act in 1679, and floods of pamphlets, newspapers, broadsides and other cheap printed materials – attacking both the Duke of York and the policies of the court – hit the streets.

The Whigs clearly sought to appeal to the people. Let us begin, then, by considering how they tried to do this. Not all of the Whig propaganda was officially coordinated by a 'party machine'; many of those who wrote or published on behalf of the Whig cause worked independently (whether motivated by commitment to principle or the desire to make a profit being not always easy to tell). Yet we certainly do see some orchestration from above. The Earl of Shaftesbury, one of the leading Whig spokesmen in the House of Lords, employed a small group of opposition stationers to produce and distribute Whig tracts, while some of the Whig propaganda efforts appear to have been coordinated by the various clubs which met in London – such as the Salutation Tavern Club in Lombard Street, the Sun Tavern Club behind the Royal Exchange, and the famous Green Ribbon Club, which met at the King's Head Tavern in Chancery Lane. Care was taken to ensure that the output of the press had as wide a distribution as possible, not just in London, but throughout the country. The Whigs used the national postal service to get pamphlets out into the countryside, and there was also an underground network for the circulation of opposition literature. During the parliamentary sessions of 1680 and 1681, Stafford apothecary Thomas Gyles was busy dispersing Whig tracts in his neighbourhood, which came to him through the post. We have a report from Tunbridge Wells in 1682 of how Lord Russell (the Earl of Shaftesbury's right-hand man in the House of Commons), various Nonconformist ministers and several citizens of London were active in the area 'in suggesting to the people fears and jealousies of popery and arbitrary government, printed papers being daily sent them, which speak evil of our present governors'. One such tract was even 'read on the walks' by one of Lord Russell's servants, who had brought it with him from London along with many other pamphlets. Much of the output of the press circulated in coffee houses, which were springing up in many parts of the country in the Restoration period, and where one could go to read tracts without having to purchase them. Some pamphlets were given away in the streets, while political ephemera could be affixed to public buildings so that they could be read by passers-by.[5]

Exactly what types of people might have been influenced by the Whig propaganda campaign is difficult to say. Using the test of the ability to sign one's name, it appears that only about 30 per cent of adult males were literate in mid-seventeenth-century England (with literacy rates being even lower for women). However, literacy did become more widespread in the later seventeenth century (with close to 50 per cent of adult males being able to sign by the time of George I's accession in 1714), while literacy rates were much higher in the towns (70 per cent amongst adult males in Restoration London), where much of this printed material was circulated. Moreover, it has now become apparent that the signature test seriously underestimates the ability of people to read (perhaps by as much as one and a half times for men, even more for women), since people typically learnt to read before they learnt to write.[6] Much of the material which came from the press was rather short and written in colloquial prose, and could easily be read aloud to those who could not read. Prints and woodcuts were produced, so that those who could not read could see the message in visual form; there were even illustrated playing cards which carried political messages. And in addition to the output from the press, we have what might be called the performance media – sermons, ballads and plays – which did not require literacy amongst their intended audience. Although there were few Whig clergymen, there were a number of sermons to give thanks for deliverance from the Popish Plot; the Popish Plot informer, Titus Oates, was active giving sermons at this time; and Nonconformist preachers were widely believed by Tories to be spreading the Whig message amongst their congregations. We can find professional ballad-singers performing specially composed songs with blatantly political messages, while political plays, such as the virulently anti-Catholic *The Coronation of Queen Elizabeth* (which was put on at Bartholomew and Southwark fairs in 1680), similarly conveyed their message to quite large numbers of people who might not have been able to understand the Whig tracts. The great pope-burning processions of 5 November and 17 November, discussed more fully on pp. 131–2 below, should also be included in this category of performance media.[7] On the whole, it seems that Whig propaganda probably did reach a fairly wide audience, particularly in London and in provincial towns, but even (arguably) in more remote parts of the country.

Space does not permit a full discussion of the nature and range of the arguments reflected in Whig propaganda. As an oversimplified generalization it might be suggested, however, that whereas in parliamentary speeches and in more sophisticated tracts the Whigs often developed carefully reasoned positions and specific positive proposals, cheaper and more obviously popular forms of propaganda tended to concentrate on negative factors, exploiting fears about what might happen should the drift towards Popery and arbitrary government go unchecked. The risks that the nation ran if it allowed a Catholic to succeed to the throne were repeatedly emphasized. Several authors drew attention to the alleged atrocities that had been committed against Protestants under England's last Catholic monarch, Mary Tudor (1553–58). 'The last time popery reigned amongst us', ran one typical piece, 'our divines were butchered by the name of heretic dogs, our houses plundered, our wives and daughters ravished ... nay, many of our laity were torn to pieces, and tied to a stake in the midst of flames at Smithfield, and other places'.[8] A more recent point of reference was the Thirty Years War in Germany. One illustrated broadside, ominously entitled *England's Calamity, Foreshewn in Germanie's Miserie*, was packed with horrific tales of purported Catholic barbarities. During the 1630s, it claimed, German Protestants had been slain, burnt, raped, tortured and even 'forced to eat their own dung'. In Pomerania, it continued, the Catholics 'tied burning matches to the tongue, noses, eyes, cheeks, breasts and legs: Yea! and the privy parts of women they stuffed with gunpowder and fired!'. The two accompanying wood-cuts showed 'Protestants burning for the true religion' and 'Your wives and daughters ravished ... together with little children's brains dashed against the walls'.[9] And if arguments from history were not enough, there was always the contemporary example of Louis XIV's absolutism in Catholic France, and the cruel persecu-tion of the Huguenots there.[10] The warnings were clear. If a Catholic were to succeed to the throne of England, he would not only consider himself duty-bound 'to destroy Protestantism', but would also (like Louis XIV) rule in a despotic and arbitrary way, abandoning parliament, and seeking to impose his will on the nation through a standing army supported by heavy and illegal taxation – thus posing a serious threat to the lives, liberties and properties of English Protestants.[11]

Yet the Whigs were not just concerned about what might happen in the future; they were equally alarmed by the drift towards arbitrary government under Charles II. Of concern here were the various attempts made by the government during the 1660s and 1670s to establish a standing army and the leanings of the court towards a pro-French foreign policy. The Whigs were also very critical of the religious policies of the restored regime, especially the persecution of Protestant Nonconformists under the harsh penal laws which had been enacted in the 1660s, at the time of the re-establishment of the Church of England. They urged the need for Protestant unity in the face of the Catholic threat, argued for the repeal of some of the more savage laws, and were particularly critical of the high-Anglican clergy – partly because the high-Anglican clergy were amongst the staunchest opponents of Exclusion, and partly because these clergy (in their political and religious outlooks) appeared to many Whigs to be more sympathetic to Popery than the true reformed religion.[12] Some of these themes of the double threat in the future and in the present are well-brought out in a print of 1681 called *A*

Prospect of a Popish Successor. In centre-left is a figure called 'Mack', who is half devil and half Duke of York. He is burning Protestant martyrs at the stake, while blowing flames from a cruciform which set fire to the city of London. Next to him is a figure who is half pope and half Anglican bishop, standing on the 'word of God'. The bishop is driving Protestant Dissenters out of the Church of England. On top of the church, seated as if riding backwards towards the devil, are a Jesuit, an Anglican bishop and four Protestant clergy. The Jesuit shouts: 'Room for the church; for Rome boys'.[13]

The Whigs not only endeavoured to appeal to the masses through their propaganda, but they also sought to encourage popular activism in support of their cause. Most famous in this respect are the great pope-burning processions staged in London on 17 November between 1679 and 1681. An effigy of the Pope was paraded through the streets of London, preceded by a long train of people dressed up as various Catholic clergy (cardinals, bishops, monks, friars, nuns and Jesuits) and who acted out a series of pageants. Huge numbers of people witnessed these events – one report put the figure as high as 200 000 for 1679. The processions served various functions. One was to satirize the Catholic faith. For example, in 1680 the sixth pageant showed one of the Pope's officers distributing 'pardons and indulgences, and crying aloud, here you may have heaven for money', while the eighth pageant shows the Pope's 'courtesans' – four deluded nuns and the Empress Donna Olympia. Another was to remind spectators of the horrors that would befall them should a Catholic become king: 17 November was chosen because it was the anniversary of the accession of Queen Elizabeth in 1558, the day of deliverance from the last Catholic monarch to rule England, Mary Tudor. In 1680 the ninth pageant showed the Pope, flanked by agents of the Inquisition, presiding over the burning of a Protestant martyr at the stake, who had been condemned merely 'for reading the scriptures'. In 1679 and 1680 the processions ended up at Temple Bar, where the effigy of the Pope was burnt in a huge bonfire before the statue of Queen Elizabeth, which had a shield placed in her hand, inscribed with the motto 'The Protestant Religion and Magna Carta'. In 1681 the Pope was burnt in effigy at Smithfield, the location of the burning of a number of Protestant heretics in Queen Mary's reign.[14]

Similar pope-burnings, though on a less grand scale, also took place on 5 November, the anniversary of the deliverance from the

Gunpowder Plot of 1605. On 5 November 1679 'several of the Pope's effigies were burnt in and about the City [of London] with great acclamations of the people', as they were again each year through to 1682.[15] Such rituals had their counterparts in the localities. Many places throughout the country reportedly staged pope-burnings on 5 November 1679. In Lewes in Sussex there was a long procession in which 'several pictures were carried upon long poles'. One was a Jesuit, 'represented with a bloody sword and a pistol' with the inscription 'our religion is murder, rapine and rebellion'. Another showed 'a friar and a Jesuit wantonly dallying with a nun', with the devil looking on and saying 'I will spoil no sport my dear children'. Next came a procession of Catholic clergy, headed by an effigy of the Pope, which was paraded around the town before being burnt at a bonfire.[16] Further pope-burnings were staged at Chatham, Oxford, Salisbury and Taunton on 5 November 1681.[17]

In addition to such highly ritualized affairs, there were a number of what appear to have been more spontaneous demonstrations on behalf of the Whig cause. James, Duke of Monmouth, the illegitimate but Protestant son of Charles II (seen by many as the logical alternative successor to the Duke of York), was greeted by enthusiastic crowds of supporters virtually whenever he made a public appearance. For example, when he returned to London on 27 November 1679 after a brief stay in Holland (where he had been ordered into exile by his father), the news of his arrival was welcomed the following day by numerous bonfires throughout the city; Charles Hatton counted more than sixty along the Strand alone, between Temple Bar and Charing Cross, and concluded that there were 'more bonfires ... than ever was since those for the restoration of his majesty'.[18] Whether dining with a number of leading Whigs at a London tavern, or simply going to his local church at St Martin-in-the-Fields, hundreds of well-wishers would come out to greet him, shouting 'God Bless the Protestant Duke'.[19] Monmouth also made a number of quasi-royal progresses in the years 1680–2 to test support for his position. On his progress to the north-west in the autumn of 1682, for example, he was greeted with popular demonstrations in most of the towns that he passed through, including Coventry, Macclesfield, Newcastle-under-Lyme, Nantwich, Chester and Stafford.[20] There were also popular demonstrations on behalf of other leading Whigs. Thus Shaftesbury's release from the Tower in late November 1681, after an unsuccessful attempt by the government

to indict him for high treason, occasioned numerous bonfire celebrations, not only in London but also in Bristol, Dorchester,
Salisbury, Woodbridge and several other provincial towns, to give
thanks for this 'deliverance'.[21]

Mass activism on behalf of the Whigs took other forms in addition to demonstrations. Numerous petitions came in from various
parts of the country in the years 1679–81, in response to Charles's
attempts to frustrate the opposition movement by using his prerogative power either to prorogue or dissolve Parliament. Some of
the London petitions boasted in the region of 20 000 signatures;
and one from Wiltshire an alleged 30 000.[22] We also see instructions and addresses of thanks issued to Whig MPs by their con-
stituents at the time of the Oxford Parliament, as well as
demonstrations on behalf of Whig candidates at the polls in a
number of the elections of 1679–81.[23]

In short, not only did the Whigs deliberately seek to appeal to
the masses through their propaganda, but there was also considerable mass agitation on behalf of the Whig cause. What was
going on here? Some of this activity out-of-doors was undoubtedly
encouraged from above. The great London pope-burnings of
17 November were carefully orchestrated events, sponsored in
large part by the Green Ribbon Club.[24] Other demonstrations
appear to have had élite encouragement. Thus, when news
reached the town of Walsall that Parliament was pressing on with
the Exclusion Bill, the magistrates 'caused bonfires to be made
and bells to ring, with several other demonstrations of joy'.[25] The
petitioning campaigns of 1679–80 show signs of some central
coordination, with printed sheets being carried down to the localities by party activists in order to collect subscriptions.[26] Those
who demonstrated on behalf of the Whigs or who signed Whig
petitions were often rewarded with lavish feasts. On 22 April 1682
the Duke of Monmouth himself presided over a special dinner
held at Lord Colchester's London home for the benefit of the
Whig apprentices, and presented one of the apprentices with a
large ring.[27]

Yet we have to be careful before we talk about 'manipulated
mobs'. Crowds were not particularly easy to control, and were normally reluctant to take to the streets on behalf of a cause that they
did not strongly identify with. In September 1686 the Spanish
ambassador caused bonfires to be made outside his London residence in celebration of the Spanish capture of Buda, and
'brought out wine for the mob', yet instead of welcoming this

opportunity for a free party, 'the rabble overthrew the bonfires, broke the cask of wine and broke the windows and pulled down some of the brick wall' of the ambassador's house.[28] When the Duke of York arrived back at Whitehall on the evening of 2 September 1679, a great bonfire was made in the Strand near Somerset House, but 'the young men before the fire was well kindled, taking it for granted that it was made only for joy of the Duke of York's safe coming into England, immediately kicked it about the street and would not suffer it to burn'.[29] Nor was it easy to get people to sign a petition on behalf of a cause that they did not support. When signatures were being collected in the Strand in December 1679 for a petition in favour of calling Parliament, three men feigned an interest in signing the petition only to tear it to pieces once they had got it into their possession, later claiming that they saw themselves as acting 'as loyal and dutiful subjects to his Majesty'.[30] It is, of course, possible (as Tories claimed) that some people may have been bullied or tricked into signing petitions, or that names could have been invented or fraudulently affixed, but the work of Mark Knights on those petitions for which signatures survive suggests that such practices were rare; indeed, the evidence of deleted signatures on London's monster petition of 1680 shows that it was possible to remove one's name if one so wished.[31]

Even when there is evidence of organization from above, therefore, there must have been some congruence between the aims of the organizers and the political sympathies of the masses for the attempt at mobilization to have been successful. Another factor that we have to recognize is that organization, when it is in evidence, did not always come from the political élite at the centre. Many of the Whig demonstrations and petitions of the Exclusion period were coordinated by local activists or political leaders, working on their own initiative and independent of the parliamentary Whig leaders.[32] It was also possible for the lower orders to coordinate their own political agitation. On 5 November 1679 groups of young men from the City of London can be found carrying their effigies of the Pope about with them 'to the houses of several eminent persons', soliciting contributions for their bonfires.[33] The crowds that gathered at bonfires on 28 November 1679 to celebrate Monmouth's return from Holland stopped several coaches (including that of the Lord Chancellor), and forced their passengers to give them money with which to buy alcohol to toast the Protestant Duke's health.[34] In London in

1681–2, local apprentices can be found organizing their own pope-burnings and petition campaigns.[35] The pope-burning procession at Salisbury on 5 November 1681 was put on 'at the charge of the young-men of the city'.[36] What we see here, therefore, is not so much manipulation from above but rather a convergence of interests, between the central élite, the local activists and the Whigs' supporters amongst the masses.

Why should the Whig political leaders not only welcome but go out of their way to encourage mass agitation on behalf of their cause? The opposition knew that the King held all the trump cards; the Exclusion Bill could never get through the House of Lords, where the bishops and the majority of the lay peers remained staunch in their defence of the hereditary succession; and whenever things looked like getting out of hand in the Commons, the King could always (as he did) prorogue or dissolve Parliament. But Charles had been known to yield to pressure in the past; and, given the fact that the King was widely known to be determined not to 'go on his travels again', the parliamentary Whigs thought that he would give way in the face of the sort of popular agitation that had faced his father on the eve of the outbreak of the Civil War. In this they proved disastrously mistaken, since Charles dug in his heels.[37] Yet the Whig encouragement of mass agitation also tells us something about their philosophy of government. To be legitimate, they felt, government had to rule in accordance with the wishes of its subjects. Whenever subjects felt their livelihoods threatened, they had the right to let their feelings be known, through demonstrating, or to seek redress of their grievances by petitioning the Crown. In other words, encapsulated in the Whig encouragement of mass agitation out-of-doors was a populist vision of government which placed ultimate authority – as the Tories repeatedly complained – 'radically in the people'.[38]

A further point needs to be stressed in this context. Historians often like to make a distinction between high and low politics, between the politics of the élite and that of the masses. Crowd action can tell us (it is therefore assumed) about the politics of those below the level of the élite, about popular or even plebeian political culture. On closer examination, however, this simple dichotomy breaks down. It is questionable whether the majority of those who joined in Whig agitation out-of-doors can really be described as plebeian. People from all social classes signed (or left their mark to) petitions, including the affluent and politically powerful. Many of those who participated in Whig crowds belonged to the 'middling sort', and on occasion even members of the political élite took part in crowd action. For example, Edward Norton, MP for Westbury (Wiltshire) in the second Exclusion Parliament and a member of the Green Ribbon Club, led a crowd of Londoners in celebration of Shaftesbury's release from the Tower in late November 1681, when he ran down St Paul's churchyard with his sword drawn, shouting: 'No Popish Successor, No York, a Monmouth'.[39] In other words, rather than seeing the various forms of collective agitation that we have examined as evidence of popular as distinct from élite politics, it is better to see them as a continuation and an extension of the political struggles that were being conducted in the formal institutions of central government (the court and Parliament) through unofficial and extra-institutional means (embracing in the process a much wider segment of the population).

Finally, let us consider why those out-of-doors chose to rally in support of the Whig cause, and why there appears to have been such a significant swing in public opinion since the restoration of the Stuarts a mere two decades earlier. First, we have to recognize that there was a generational shift. Many of those who demonstrated in support of the Whigs were young men and apprentices, who had not been alive in 1660; people had not necessarily changed their minds, since we are often dealing with different people. Nevertheless, we also have a changed political context, and some of those who had been around in 1660 had undoubtedly become disillusioned after twenty years of Stuart rule. Whig propaganda certainly had a powerful effect, and many people were alarmed simply by the prospect of a Popish successor. Cases of seditious words bear this out. In the spring of 1682, for example, John Whitcombe of Canterbury condemned the Duke of York as 'a Papist rogue', affirming 'they were Papist rogues that took his part', while a little over a year later a man from Roecliffe in Yorkshire was accused of saying 'that he hoped the Duke of York would never inherit the crown' and that he 'wished him in heaven'.[40] Many supported Monmouth as an alternative successor to York. On his trip to the north-west in the autumn of 1682, for example, he was greeted in several places with cries of 'Let Monmouth reign'. Stafford apothecary Thomas Gyles allegedly said on 20 September that year: 'I hope to see the duke of Monmouth King, and further that he thought him the King's lawful son'.[41]

It is clear that people were concerned not just about the prospect of a Popish successor, however; they were also very much alarmed about what their present King was doing. There were some people who had never made their peace with the restored monarchy, and we can certainly talk about the survival of a republican underground tradition since 1660. In the autumn of 1682 John Troude, a Baptist from Devon and an 'old Oliverian', was accused of saying 'that he would fight against the King for the Parliament that voted the exclusion bill, as willingly as ever he fought for the old Parliament against Charles I'.[42] But we also see evidence of people who had become critical of Charles II because of recent political developments. Charles's handling of the Popish Plot caused concern in many quarters. Londoner William Lewis thought the King was 'an absolute papist' who was endeavouring 'to stifle the Popish Plot by discharging the witnesses that gave evidence thereof' and that 'the King daily endeavours to enslave the nation with popery and superstition'.[43] Others did not like Charles's pro-French leanings. In December 1679, Francis Tranchard of Badgworth in Somerset returned from a trip to London with reports that 'there was a peace concluded between our King and the French ... and that the Parliament shall not sit these five years and the French King will give our King two hundred thousand pounds to keep the Parliament from sitting'.[44] In the same month an anonymous letter addressed to the Mayor of Bristol complained that

> our popish and treacherous King has sold the kingdoms of England, Scotland, and Ireland, together with all his dominions, to the King of France, and we are all bought as slaves, and designed as innocent sheep for the slaughter, to be butchered and sacrificed to the fury of the papists, to be murdered, burnt, and inhumanely destroyed by the most exquisite torments, and barbarous usage, that the hellish Inquisition can invent.[45]

Hostility towards the French was also reinforced by economic considerations. A slump in the cloth trade, which came to be blamed on unfair competition from the French, coupled with the fact that many of the Huguenot refugees who settled in England were engaged in cloth production and were willing to work for lower pay than their English counterparts, caused intense anti-French hatred. It came to be widely believed, amongst English weavers, that the French, in various ways, were 'robbing them as they conceive of their trade and livelihood'. There were anti-French riots in London in 1675, in Exeter and Topsham that same year, and also in Norwich in 1683.[46] Significantly, Mark Knights found that those involved in the production and finishing of cloth were prominent amongst the signatories to Whig petitions.[47]

The main reason for the growth of disillusionment after 1660 had to do with the religious policies pursued by the Restoration regime. Most Presbyterians, and many Independents and separatists, had supported the return of the monarchy, yet they had hoped for the establishment of a comprehensive church and/or some degree of religious toleration. Indeed, Charles II had promised in his Declaration of Breda of April 1660, as a condition for his restoration, that he would give liberty of conscience. The re-establishment of a narrow and intolerant Anglican church after 1662, and the consequent enactment of a severe penal code against Protestant non-conformity, inevitably alienated Dissenters. Although persecution was intermittent, when the penal laws were enforced – as they were in the first half of the 1660s, in 1670–1, in the mid-1670s and after 1681 (during the years of the Tory reaction) – the sufferings of Dissenters could be immense. Many faced heavy fines and the distraint of their goods in lieu of payment of fines, many were imprisoned, some had their livelihoods totally destroyed, and several hundreds even died in the pitiful conditions in Restoration jails. Nonconformists came to feel, quite justifiably, that their lives, liberties and properties were at threat under the Restoration regime.[48] Given the fact that the Whigs were fiercely critical of the penal laws and the intolerance of the Anglican establishment, while most of the Anglican clergy (and in particular, the bishops) remained staunch in their defence of the hereditary succession and in opposition to the Whig platform, it is hardly surprising that Protestant Dissenters strongly supported the Whig position during the Exclusion Crisis. Cases of seditious words show that many people's opposition to the government at this time was shaped by religious considerations. Occasionally the King himself was blamed. During the Christmas holidays of 1682, Thomas Ames of Batcombe in Somerset allegedly complained that 'the King (upon his coming in) at Breda did promise the liberty of conscience, and that now he found he was worse than his word'.[49] More typically, popular scorn was reserved for the Anglican clergy. In February 1682 a Shrewsbury man, who had been foreman of the Shropshire grand jury when it had returned a vote of thanks to Parliament for promoting the Exclusion Bill, was accused of saying that 'the bishops

are a pack of rascals, obstructed a happy reformation, have coun-
tenanced and encouraged popery, and have almost undone the
kingdom'.[50] Anti-Episcopalian sentiment can be detected in
demonstrations. Cries of 'no clergy' and 'no bishops' greeted the
Whig candidates at the polls at the Essex election of August 1679
and the Oxford election of 1681.[51] Recent research has confirmed
the view that Dissenters were very prominent in the Whig movement out-of-doors, as electoral agents, as local activists, as signatories to petitions and as participants in demonstrations.[52]

II

It has been shown by the foregoing analysis not only how and why
the Whigs sought to appeal to those out-of-doors, but also why
certain sorts of people were inclined to support the Whig position. Faced with the aggressive Whig challenge, the Tories conducted their own counter-propaganda campaign, with the
deliberate aim, as one Tory propagandist put it, of reducing 'the
deluded multitude to their just allegiance'.[53] Many of the Whig
techniques were mimicked: streams of pamphlets, broadsides,
newspapers, ballads, prints and playing cards were produced,
while high Anglicans preached up the duties of loyalty and obedience from the pulpit. As with the Whigs, much loyalist propaganda was produced by individuals working on their own
initiative, but there is also evidence of a coordinated campaign.
Prominent Tory publicist Roger L'Estrange was rumoured to have
been financed in part by a pension from the King, while Lord
Chief Justice Francis North appears to have had some role in
coordinating Tory propaganda. There were also Tory clubs;
L'Estrange, for example, frequented one at Sam's Coffee-House
in Ludgate.[54]

Tory propaganda worked on a number of different levels. Many
works defended the principle of indefeasible hereditary right, and
even argued that the King was absolute and could not be challenged in any way by his subjects.[55] How effective such arguments
might have been by themselves, however, is questionable. It was
obviously not a particularly strong way of dealing with the Whig
challenge simply to say: 'there is no alternative to a Popish successor, he will be absolute, and there is nothing you can do about it'.
In particular, Tory propagandists realized that they had to neutralize the opposition's claim that only by supporting the Whigs

could one avoid the drift towards Popery and arbitrary government. They therefore sought to turn this argument against their adversaries, by suggesting that the real threat of Popery and arbitrary government came from the Whigs themselves.

This was done by pointing out the similarities between the tactics of the Whigs during the Exclusion Crisis and the Puritan parliamentary opposition to Charles I in the early 1640s. As history had shown, on the earlier occasion these tactics had resulted in civil war, the overthrow of the monarchy, and the establishment of a tyrannical regime and rule through a standing army under Oliver Cromwell: the rule of law had been overturned, heavy taxes had been imposed, people had lost their lives in battle, and the Puritan leaders of the 1650s had sought to suppress traditional popular recreations and pastimes. Such arguments were made repeatedly. As Roger L'Estrange put it, the republican spirits 'trampled under foot all laws both divine and human ... They eased us of our laws, lives, liberties and estates'. The message was clear: if the Whigs were successful, arbitrary government would follow.[56]

Tory propagandists also sought to turn the charge of Popery against the Whigs. Here it is important to recognize the difference between anti-Popery and anti-Catholicism. The latter was simply a fear of the Roman Catholic faith and its adherents; the former was much broader, and was associated with hostility towards the kind of things that the Pope stood for. What did the Pope want, Tories asked, if not to overthrow the Protestant Church of England and the Protestant monarchy? This is what the Armada of 1588 and the Gunpowder Plot of 1605 had been about. But whereas Catholic conspiracies had always failed in the past, the parliamentary Puritans in the 1640s had succeeded in overthrowing the monarchy and the established church. In this way it was possible to accuse all enemies of King and Church of Popery, even if they were not Roman Catholics. And it was a charge which was easily turned against the Whigs during the Exclusion Crisis, given their close association with Protestant Dissent and their overt criticism of the high-Anglican establishment. As John Nalson put it in 1681:

> Consider who they are that made all this noise [i.e. the Whigs] ... These are the persons that fill both city and country with ... fears and dangers of popery and arbitrary government, who yet when they were got into the throne of usurpation, acted by

popish principles ... and the very worst of the very worst of
papists the Jesuits ... putting in execution their doctrines of
murdering and deposing lawful princes.[57]

The Tories even suggested that the Papists and Dissenters were
working in alliance to undermine the established church, an
observation which carried a certain amount of credibility, since
during the administration of the Cabal (1668–73) and again in
the mid-1670s, Catholics and dissenting politicians had worked in
alliance to pursue plans for religious toleration.[58] One tract, set as
a dialogue between the Pope and a fanatic, recalled how the two
had worked together to bring down Charles I and claimed that
they were now working together to overthrow Charles II. The
fanatic asserts that he and the Pope have a 'common enemy',
namely the Church of England, and that they are both 'equal
enemies to the divine right of Kings and bishops'.[59] The Tories
also played on the fear of France in this context, suggesting that
by promoting divisions at home the Whigs were actually making
things easier for the French King. As the Tory periodical
Heraclitus Ridens asked: was 'the most prudent method to secure
the nation against the formidable power of France ... to embroil
us among ourselves'; 'for this is a maxim, that the discords of
England are the great interest of France and Rome'.[60]

Many of these themes were illustrated in a print of 1680 by
Roger L'Estrange called *The Committee; Or, Popery in Masquerade*,
a powerful satirical attack on political developments in the
1640s and 1650s. A committee representing nine different
Nonconformist factions is seated around a table, presiding over
the nation. On the table are papers inscribed 'Church and Crown
Lands', 'Sequestrations', 'Remonstrances', 'Petitions', 'Court of
Justice' and 'Humiliation'. To the left is a mob who lead in chains
Charles I, the Earl of Strafford and Archbishop Laud. One of the
mob parades a bishop's mitre on a pike; another carries the
crown; others bear banners with the mottoes 'a thorough reformation', 'liberty', 'property' and 'religion'. Before their feet are
the sceptre, orb and bust of Charles I. To the right are reminders
of the sufferings that this alliance of mob and schismatics had
brought: sequestrated livings, excise, army accounts, widows' tears
and the blood of orphans. On the floor in the centre, amongst
the things discarded by the committee are 'Magna Carta' and the
Holy Bible. In the top right-hand corner is Alderman Isaac
Pennington, the man who had delivered London's root and

branch petition against episcopacy in December 1640, and standing next to him the Pope, who cries out to the committee (in
French, significantly) 'courage mes enfants'.

On the positive side, the Tories had to try to build up support
for the Duke of York, the Catholic heir to the throne. They did
this in part by appealing to patriotic sentiments, maintaining that
York was a 'great Hero' who had 'oft for haughty England
fought', and who in particular had been a very successful naval
commander in the wars against the Dutch in the 1660s and
1670s.[61] Yet they also sought to convince people that the Church
of England would be safe under a Catholic successor, since the
established church was 'sufficiently guarded by several Acts of
Parliament', which a Popish king would not be able to repeal.[62]
Indeed, the best way to protect the Church of England, and avert
the Whig and Nonconformist challenge, was through a strict
adherence to the rule of law, and especially the enforcement of
those penal laws which had been designed to extirpate Dissent.
One of the most effective pieces of propaganda was a *Declaration*
issued in April 1681 in Charles II's name, explaining why it had
been necessary to dissolve the last two Parliaments, and which was
ordered to be read in all parish churches. Here Charles sought to
reassure his subjects that he would protect the established church
and respect the rule of law; he also made clear his determination
to support his brother's right to the succession, criticized the
tactics of the Whig-dominated Exclusion Parliaments (although
promising at the same time, somewhat disingenuously, that he
would continue to hold frequent parliaments), and argued for
the need to take strict legal reprisals against Dissenters and
Nonconformist conventicles, 'the seed-places where factions are
nursed up till they may be strong enough to grapple with and
overturn the government of church and state'.[63]

In short, Tory propaganda took a stance in defence of the
church and state as by law established, against what was represented as being a threat of Popery and arbitrary government from
the Whigs and their Nonconformist allies. It was a position that
proved to have considerable appeal. The Whigs, it should be
stressed, had never totally monopolized the sentiments of the
people, and the evidence of election results (both parliamentary
and local), loyal addresses and even some street agitation points
to the existence of some support out-of-doors for the Tories or
those loyal to the court in the years of the parliamentary
Exclusion Crisis.[64] Nevertheless, there was a surge of loyalist

activism in the years following the dissolution of the Oxford Parliament in March 1681. Hundreds of loyal addresses were presented to the crown in the years 1681–3 – from JPs, grand juries, militia officers and borough corporations, and also from humbler groups, such as apprentices, the Thames watermen, the cooks and chandlers of Salisbury, and the tinners of Cornwall – in support of the King, the church, the rule of law, the hereditary succession and of the need to take action against Protestant Dissenters.[65] Some of these addresses boasted large numbers of signatories: 'above 16 000' persons allegedly signed the Devon address of 1681; a purported 18 000 apprentices put their hands to a loyal address delivered to the King at Hampton Court in June of that year; and some 12 000 young freemen and apprentices of the City presented another loyal address to the King the following year.[66]

There were also Tory demonstrations: 29 May, the anniversary of the Restoration and Charles II's birthday, became the most important day in the Tory calendar upon which loyalist crowds would burn effigies of Jack Presbyter and/or leading Whigs, as a counter to (one might even say inversion of) the Whig popeburnings of November. London, Derby, Durham, Lynn, Norwich, Portsmouth, Taunton and Windsor all witnessed such displays between 1681 and 1683. That held in Norwich on 29 May 1682 provides a typical illustration. An effigy of Jack Presbyter was burnt at 'a very great bonfire' in the centre of the city, to the 'loud acclamations of God save the King and His Royal Highness', after which several 'seditious and rebellious papers' were committed to the flames, amongst them the Presbyterian Solemn League and Covenant, the Nineteen Propositions made by the Long Parliament to King Charles I, the Bill of Comprehension and the Exclusion Bill. Then effigies of several Whig publicists, including Henry Care and Francis Smith, were burnt, all of which was performed, we are told, 'with all the expressions of joy and loyalty imaginable'.[67]

The Queen's birthday, which fell on 15 November, was another occasion for loyalist demonstrations. The Tories even sought to appropriate gunpowder treason day for their purposes, with both London and Derby seeing Presbyter-burning rituals on 5 November 1681.[68] Moreover, there were also a number of demonstrations in support of the Duke of York. York's return to England in the spring of 1682, after a period of eighteen months' 'exile' in Scotland, prompted bonfire celebrations in many parts of the country, including London, Norwich, Great Yarmouth,

Shaftesbury and Dover. On subsequent public appearances in London, the Duke of York could normally be guaranteed an enthusiastic reception. When he went to attend the Artillery Company's feast on 20 April 1682, for example, numerous spectators cheered him on his way. The evening saw several bonfires, the largest being in Ludgate Street, where crowds gathered to shout 'God bless the King, and His Royal Highness; no bill of exclusion'.[69] There were also bonfire celebrations in 'divers places' (amongst them Oxford, Plymouth, Portsmouth, Reading and Wells) on 9 September 1683, the day of official thanksgiving for deliverance from the Rye House Plot, the alleged conspiracy of radical Whigs and Nonconformists to assassinate the King and the Duke of York. At Wells an effigy of Jack Presbyter was marched through the town in a solemn procession before being committed to the flames. At Oxford, where there were numerous bonfires, Jack Presbyter was set in a tub outside the Star Inn, and 'the smart lads of the city marched down the streets with cudgels in their hands, crying for the King and the Duke of York'.[70]

As with the Whigs, much of this Tory agitation out-of-doors shows signs of being encouraged from above. The King himself had a role in planning the enthusiastic reception that the Duke of York received in London on 8 April 1682 following York's return from Scotland: Charles had written in advance to the Lord Mayor and 'willed him to give him [York] such reception as became him', dropping strong hints when he said that he 'doubted not but his loyal apprentices in London would make a body for his reception', and ordering the Lord Mayor 'to acquaint the whole city and them [the apprentices] therewith'.[71] There were 'several persons of quality' present at the pro-York demonstrations in Ludgate on 20 April 1682, who pledged the loyal toasts to the assembled crowd.[72] The Presbyter-burning at Derby on Restoration Day 1681 (which was held on the 30th, because the 29th that year fell on a Sunday) was organized by 'some eminent persons' of the town.[73] The loyal demonstration at Taunton on 29 May 1683 was sponsored by the Tory mayor, Stephen Timewell, while that at Reading on 9 September was planned in advance by the members of the corporation, who ordered the construction of a bonfire at the marketplace and made provision for beer and wine.[74] Loyal supporters were rewarded with lavish feasts. The King provided a brace of bucks for a loyal feast for the Tory apprentices of London in August 1681 and again the following year; on the latter occasion, the dinner was presided over by the

Duke of Ormonde, the Duke of Albemarle, the Earl (later
Marquis) of Halifax and the Earl of Sunderland.[75] But again, as
with the Whigs, we do not have to assume that encouragement
from above meant manipulated mobs. Not only is there evidence
of more spontaneous outbursts of Tory enthusiasm, but the Tory
platform in defence of the Anglican Church against the threat
posed by the Dissenters had a strong appeal. There is much evidence of genuine popular hostility towards Dissent in Restoration
England; the Restoration itself had been greeted with crowd
attacks on Nonconformist meeting-places, and local studies have
pointed to the existence of severe tensions between Anglicans and
Dissenters in several areas, and in particular the corporate
towns.[76]

Why should the Tories have paid so much attention to trying to
court public opinion? It might seem that such efforts were
counter-productive. The Tories liked to accuse the Whigs of being
rabble-rousers who were threatening the peace of the realm by
stirring up the masses; yet by promoting grass-roots loyalist activity, the Tories were not only rabble-rousing themselves but also
perhaps helping to create greater problems of order. I would
suggest, however, that the Tory appeal to those out-of-doors was
essential to their purpose. The opponents of the Whigs appear to
have recognized that they could not afford to abandon 'the
crowd' to the opposition. The lessons of 1640–2 were there to be
learnt, when Charles I eventually had to leave London having lost
control of the streets of his capital. Charles II and his supporters
realized the need to try to regain the hearts and minds of the
people, to prevent the situation from perhaps becoming volatile
enough to lead to the outbreak of another civil war. As L'Estrange
put it in his *Observator*: in 1641 'the people were fooled and
inflamed into a rebellion', by a group of men claiming to assert
'the Protestant cause against popery. The same pretence is now
set afoot again, and it concerns us to beware that it lead us not
into the same condition'.[77]

It also became important for Tories to be able to show that many
people did not support the Whig cause, in order to de-legitimize
the Whig claim to be representing the voice of the people. This
explains why the King and his Tory allies were so keen to encourage public manifestations of support for their position – and not
just petitions and addresses, a tamer and perhaps more easily controlled medium, but even crowd agitation. As Colin Lucas has
argued in the context of eighteenth-century France, 'the crowd

usually claimed and frequently achieved a representative status',
articulating 'what the members of the community had in
common'.[78] The intent of the Tory crowds, therefore, was to try to
lay claim to this representative status – to show what the members
of the community really thought. Furthermore, once such activity
had been encouraged and promoted, it was important to publi-
cize it as widely as possible in the media (especially in the newspapers and gazettes), in order to 'demonstrate' to the widest
possible audience what community attitudes in various localities
actually were. Tory writers were soon able to claim that the
Exclusion Bill was not widely supported by the people, since 'the
generality have for the most part protested against it'.[79]

This is not to imply that the Tory crowds invariably were representative of the collective attitudes of the community; we shall
shortly show that in many cases they were not. But here we might
suggest a further function fulfilled by Tory collective agitation.
The sociologist Leo Bogart has argued that crowd demonstrations
should be seen not so much as a manifestation of public opinion
but as 'critical events whose principal importance is their
influence on public opinion': by perhaps persuading bystanders
of the merits of one's cause, by publicizing a particular political
cause and putting it on the agenda for discussion, or by heating
up 'the atmosphere of discussion on a subject, so that conventional established opinions become volatile and vulnerable to
change'.[80] Tory crowd activity, in other words, also served as a
form of propaganda – an attempt to show that the Whigs did not
monopolize public sentiment, to advertise the position of the loy-
alists, to persuade the uncommitted or the cowardly that loyalism
was a credible and defensible position, to rally the silent and inactive into some form of positive support, and even to promote
political activism in defence of Charles II and the Duke of York.

These insights help us to understand the nature of the Whig
response to this Tory collective behaviour. It has recently been
argued that the Tory propaganda campaign was so successful in
winning back public opinion that in the years after the Oxford
Parliament we see the re-establishment of a political consensus, as
all but a few hardliners abandoned their former Whiggery and
rallied to the defence of the crown.[81] This is going too far.
Although the Tories clearly did pick up public support as the
Exclusion Crisis progressed, the result was that in the final years
of Charles II's reign England became a deeply divided society,
sharply polarized between two mutually antagonistic groups. If

anything, Whiggery became more self-assertive out-of-doors in the two years following the Oxford Parliament, as Whig groups in the localities found it necessary to define themselves in opposition to an increasing Tory presence in the streets. In other words, it became important for Whig activists to challenge the Tory crowds' pretensions to be the representatives of the community. What we see going on in 1681–3 is a contestation for that public space – or, at least, for dominance within the public arena – that would allow one crowd to lay claim to be the representative of public opinion. In Norwich on 29 May 1682, for example, rather than surrender Restoration Day to the Tories, the local Whigs decided to hold their own pope-burning 'on the other side of the water'.[82] Not only did many places see competing Whig and Tory demonstrations in the years 1681–2, but on occasion rival partisan groups came into violent conflict. In London on 5 November 1681, a group of Tories ambushed a pope-burning procession as it was making its way down Aldersgate Street, seizing the effigies of the Pope and the devil.[83] There were violent clashes in the capital on the following gunpowder treason day, between rival crowds shouting 'a York, a York' and 'no York, a Monmouth, a Monmouth'.[84] The Presbyter-burning at Derby on 30 May 1681 was disrupted by some local Whigs, while there was a violent confrontation in Oxford on 11 April 1683 between some townsmen, who had been drinking the Duke of Monmouth's health in a local tavern, and some scholars, who had been there at the same time toasting the Duke of York.[85]

It is difficult to say much about the sociology of support for the different parties. For the most part, the members of the various crowds that we have examined retain their anonymity; unless participants were arrested for riotous behaviour (and most of the demonstrations were fairly peaceful), they do not leave a trace in the historical record. Likewise with petitions; rarely do the actual sheets with subscribers' names survive – when they do, all we have to go on is the names, and it is not easy to identify who these people were or what they did for a living. The evidence that we do have suggests that, although certain groups might have been more prone to support one side or the other (the weavers the Whigs, for example), on the whole the divisions cut vertically through society, not horizontally (on the basis of class). Rich, middling sort and poor alike can be found on both sides of the divide, as can both people from the countryside and from the towns. The most striking predictor of political allegiance appears to be religious affiliation; Dissenters were overwhelmingly Whig, and hardline Anglicans Tory, although it has to be remembered that there were many moderate Anglicans who sympathized with Dissent and who therefore also tended to side with the Whigs.[86]

III

A number of general conclusions emerge from this examination of politics out-of-doors during the Exclusion Crisis; some conceptual, others empirical. The first is that we need a more sophisticated reading of the significance of crowd action and collective agitation than that which is often offered. Some of the alleged dichotomies that are frequently employed – popular versus élite politics, manipulated versus spontaneous mobs – have been shown to be inappropriate. We must examine more closely what sorts of people chose to engage in political agitation out-of-doors, why they did this, how their political attitudes came to be formed (both through exposure to the media and through direct personal experience), and how their political activity was coordinated. In this way we see that politics was not the exclusive concern of the élite, but often embraced those types who are normally regarded as the sub-political classes. We should also abandon the view that the lower orders were simply manipulated from above: the political élite certainly did try to manipulate them, both directly (by orchestrating demonstrations and petition campaigns) and indirectly (through their use of propaganda); yet those out-of-doors were clearly capable of coordinating political activity for themselves, and their support had to be won (it could not just be bought). We further need to think about why members of the élite should choose to take their political struggles out into the streets – why Tories, as well as Whigs, took the task of trying to win the hearts and minds of the people seriously. Taking such an approach we discover that it is more helpful to think in terms of convergence, with politics out-of-doors being an arena in which all classes might choose to participate, rather than in terms of a simple juxtaposition between the élite and the crowd, or high and low politics.

On the empirical level, this chapter has shown that there was a politically divided society in England during the period normally labelled the Exclusion Crisis, and it has argued against the older view, that 'the mob' was overwhelmingly Whig in sympathy at this time. Although it would be going too far to argue that a popular, loyalist consensus was restored by 1681–2, there undoubtedly was a resurgence of loyalist opinion in the early 1680s, and the significance of this should not be underestimated. The Tories were able to rally many people behind the Crown, turning latent sympathy into active support, winning over many waverers and even a number of moderates. The numerous Tory demonstrations and addresses – encouraged from above and often carefully orchestrated though many of them were – nevertheless served to show that public opinion was not overwhelmingly behind the Whigs, thus providing a vital boost to morale, both for the court and for the many people who had never been sympathetic to the Whigs, Exclusion or the Dissenters in the first place. One might go further and suggest that in an age in which local administrative and law-enforcing responsibilities devolved so far down the social scale, and when the government was so dependent not only on the tacit acquiescence but often active support of unpaid, local officers to see its policies effectively carried out, the successful Tory appeal to those out-of-doors was a crucial element in re-establishing political stability and enhancing the authority of the Crown in the early 1680s. The policies of the Tory reaction could not have been enforced as ruthlessly or as successfully as they were had the Crown not been confident that substantial numbers of people not only supported the drive against the Whigs and Dissent, but were prepared actively to help to see it carried out.[87]

Soliciting the 'crowd' – or, perhaps better, 'public opinion' – in this way was a dangerous game to play. Support clearly came with conditions attached, and the support might well be withdrawn if those in authority failed to live up to their side of the bargain.[88] This is what happened under James II. James's accession to the throne in 1685 was unquestionably welcome to many groups. There were celebrations throughout England when he was pro-claimed King in February: Chester was typical in seeing 'bonfires, ringing of bells, and repeated acclamations of joy'.[89] Some 346 loyal addresses came in from all over England and Wales, in which people pledged their allegiance to their new King, acknowl-edged his just and rightful succession, professed their abhorrence of the attempt at Exclusion, and promised to elect loyal men to the forthcoming Parliament.[90] Although undoubtedly an authen-tic expression of the genuine popularity of James II at the begin-ning of his reign, it was also the case that those in authority were keen to encourage such manifestations of loyalty. Thus local

Tories often laid on alcoholic refreshment to encourage the crowds when the new King was proclaimed,[91] and the numerous demonstrations and addresses were given maximum publicity in the official government organ, the *London Gazette*. So we are in part dealing with a propaganda exercise here: an attempt by those in authority to demonstrate that the majority of the population accepted and supported James's accession, and perhaps even to warn against the wisdom of trying something as ill-fated as the Monmouth rebellion of that summer proved to be.

Yet a political message was also being sent back to the King by his subjects. We see this in particular with the loyal addresses. Immediately upon his accession, James II had thought it prudent to issue a declaration promising to protect the church and state as by law established – clearly to defuse any notion that he might be in favour of Popery and arbitrary government. Nearly all of the loyal addresses specifically thank him for this promise. The loyal address from the lords, gentlemen, clergy and freeholders of Huntingdonshire is both typical and highly revealing. After acknowledging James's 'true and undoubted right' to the crown, the address goes on to offer thanks for his declaration

> which as it has given entire satisfaction to those who always believed your majesty would never govern otherwise then is therein mentioned; so we hope all others have now received such ample assurance by your royal word for the preservation of this government both in church and state as it is now by law established, that they will unanimously join with us in our hearty and utmost endeavours to choose such loyal representatives to serve in the next parliament, as shall truly answer the design of their meeting, and promote the ends of the said declaration.[92]

In other words, in 1685 James's subjects were pledging their loyalty to a regime which protected the church and state as by law established. When James threatened that establishment, and used his prerogative and extra-legal powers to undermine the established church, many of his former Tory allies deserted him. The power of public opinion in this political culture – the necessity of having public support for what the government was trying to do – is most clearly illustrated by what happened when James II alienated it. From 1686 we have evidence of areas which had formerly been staunchly loyalist, and had even in the past demonstrated in support of the Duke of York, now protesting against the Catholic King's attempts to undermine the Anglican monopoly of worship in an effort to help his co-religionists. By the late summer and fall of 1688 his regime had essentially already collapsed from within. James II was brought down not primarily by a foreign invasion, as some scholars would now try to convince us;[93] indeed, William of Orange would never have risked the venture had it not been clear that James's regime was falling apart. James fell because he failed to realize where his strength really lay, because he did not know how to play the game of power politics that was necessary in this political culture, and because he alienated those people whose former loyalty had been a key bulwark of the monarchy's strength in the final years of Charles II's reign.[94]

7. Landownership, the Aristocracy and the Country Gentry

JAMES M. ROSENHEIM

In the three decades following the Restoration, a reshaping of landed society began that would be completed in the eighteenth century, when a truly national, metropolitan ruling order emerged in England. Despite the hopes some had in 1660 to restore landed society to its prewar state, the contours of landed life had been so altered by the Interregnum as to preclude that return. In broad terms, these disrupted patterns included significant geographical localism, engagement with traditional cultural activities, personal involvement in provincial administration and a virtual monopoly over political discourse. None of these features had disappeared by the time William III arrived on English shores, but none retained its prewar strength. Although the kingdom's 'natural rulers' resumed dominant roles in the county society and government from which many had previously withdrawn or been excluded, they also began to rethink what was entailed in the life of a landowner and to alter the courses in which that life ran. Fearful memory of recent disorders, economic insecurity generated by a decline in rents, and uncertainty about the nature of politics in an era of rampant partisanship – these considerations shaped the new ethos of an élite gripped less by provincial affairs and more imbued with a sense of common bonds.

The disruption of prewar patterns after 1660 stemmed in part from a very real, physical dislocation of landed life in the preceding twenty years. The impact of war and fighting, politically prudent relocation and outright exile cumulatively stripped counties of many prominent families from 1642 to 1660. Their absence opened spaces in the social, cultural and political geography of the provinces in which others could participate. Absence also deprived landed families of local influence and had a psychological effect on immediate neighbourhoods, county social life and aristocratic identity that endured even after absentees returned. The exclusion from local affairs of many gentry gave others in the provinces both a novel sense of responsibility and the opportunity to participate in governance and administration.

The legacy and memory of this dislocation and its accompanying tumult shook the confidence of Restoration gentry about the preordained acceptability of their rule. Moreover, the infusion of specifically national issues and forms into even the lowest levels of county life had politicized and made partisan (rather than personal) the conflicts of provincial communities – parish, town and county.[1] In this polarized context, the landed classes tried to rebuild their confidence in the 1660s by a variety of means, using everything from legislation to intimidation in efforts to reconcile with or outlaw their enemies. Yet they could not re-knit the fabric of county life, both because revolutionary partisanship had left communities polarized and because other developments of the era began to distance landowners from their local bases.

Principal among these features was a continued absenteeism from the provinces by the gentry, which 'became a permanent part of their way of life' after 1660.[2] Landowners had, of course, never been rooted in a single place, however much their lives focused on a specific country house. Yet during the Restoration era new distractions entered their field of vision, and when they placed the country house and country living at the centre of their lives they did so more self-consciously than previously and as a matter of careful choice. Strong centrifugal forces impinged on any ideal of static country life. Those landlords who wanted personally to oversee their dispersed properties left their principal seats when doing so, and where social pursuits combined with business, their absences were extended. Although a trend toward consolidation of landholding by greater gentry is discernible after 1660, an increasingly national marriage market, linking partners across the kingdom, may have made it more common for the well-to-do to hold widely distributed lands.[3] Attractive opportunities for socializing were also more frequently available now in provincial urban centres, especially in county towns where political, legal and administrative business had long lured country society for brief stays. The length of visits had ample reason to expand after mid-century, however, when the slow accretion of new facilities (coffee houses, town halls and public walks) and of leisure activities in these settings (concerts, horse races and assize balls) began to surpass the traditional call of duty.[4]

Simple visits to friends and neighbours additionally drew the landed away from their country houses and the rhythms of the surrounding neighbourhood. A landowner's identity still rested in part on the social transactions of lord and neighbours and of host and guest; yet the personalized round of visits common in earlier times was being replaced after the Restoration by an impersonal pattern of visiting in emergent leisure towns and spas. Rural life, with its Arcadian attractions, had formerly been at the heart of gentry identity; yet by the middle of the century what one scholar calls 'the spread of Renaissance values among the élite' ensured that the pursuit of pleasure would take place in towns, because new concepts of gentility associated rustic life with coarseness and boorishness. Provincial towns, as outlets of national cultural accomplishments and taste, increasingly served to enlighten, civilize and socialize the landed gentry.[5] The social round in 1672–3 of the Ishams of Lamport, Northamptonshire, who sojourned more in places than with people, illustrates the change. In addition to Sir Justinian's trips to London and to quarter sessions, the family's travels included a tour of Althorp House, a visit to the Spencer family tombs at Brington, attendance at two sets of races and at Northampton's mayoral feasts, conveyance of a son to Oxford, and a two-week summertime circuit that took in Gloucester, Worcester and Coventry.[6]

Despite expanding opportunities for diversion, the countryside could appear dull, its lack of lustre often the result of the shadows that London threw. Travel to the capital did not merely yield an enlarged version of a visit to country friends or to the assize town. In a fundamental sense, life in London and in the provinces moved along different trajectories; their values often appeared in conflict, even mutually exclusive. Especially as portrayed in Restoration drama, the country lacked entertainment or sophistication; whereas, by contrast, London appeared as the hub of English aristocratic life. On stage, country wives naturally joined husbands on business in the metropolis and daughters weighed unattractive marriage prospects if doing so allowed them to visit the capital. Off stage, we find cases such as Humphrey Prideaux, who gauged his cultural position from a metropolitan perspective and, although a resident in the kingdom's second city, Norwich, thought himself 'remote from the centre of affairs and in a great deal of quiet'.[7]

To some extent, London was a newly potent attraction. Although nobles had for many years spent considerable time there, before 1640 gentry were far less likely to go, nor did they go for so long. London's role as the centre of consumption and as the site of marriage, financial and land markets had origins in the sixteenth century but developed markedly and continuously after the mid-seventeenth, and with the Restoration the royal court revived as well.[8] London thus understandably attracted gentlefolk from all parts of the kingdom and at all times, but particularly during the months of the social season, from mid-autumn until the spring. New developments in transport facilitated travel to enjoy this season, which itself was energized by the re-opening of the theatres and the emergence of coffee-house culture. These constituted just a few of the capital's potent lures. The power of fashion, for example, was nearly irresistible: Lady Anne Burgoyne, a rich Puritan supposedly indifferent to the material vanities of metropolitan life, none the less bought her clothes in London and 'in modesty and civility ... complied' with the 'fashions of her Age and Quality'.[9]

Business as well as pleasure reached its height in the metropolis and attracted landed families from the countryside. The most crucial legal matters were transacted in London, the vast bulk of trade ran through it, and the money market – although it had provincial outlets – principally operated there, especially where large sums, government securities and reliable mortgages were concerned. Including the Convention of 1660, Parliament met for twenty-two different sessions in the capital down to the end of James II's reign, tempting prominent county families to Westminster for unpredictable and sometimes protracted stays. The conurbation afforded the kingdom's greatest concentration of medical expertise, and many élite women preferred to give birth there. The presence of marriage opportunity in London – the centre of the national market – was universally acknowledged. A landowner helped to a bride by the banker Robert Clayton in the 1670s assumed that 'all the money and women [were] at London', an opinion shared by immediate contemporaries, such as Sir Ralph Verney's godson, who pursued a match of £6000 in the capital, or the Lowther patriarch who awaited London marital news at his seat in Westmorland.[10]

Whatever gains it brought to landowners in terms of much-sought office or much-needed loan, entertainment or luxury commodities or attractive spouse, metropolitan life also had its

sobering cost for country gentry. Some gentlemen extravagantly
damned the expense. On others it had an economizing but more
rarely a deterrent effect: many of the landed who came to London
left their families behind or lived with them less splendidly in the
metropolis, or just complained of the 'continual charge as well as
disorder it must be ... to be in towne.'[11] Yet live in town they did,
absorbing the charge and accommodating to the disorder. *The
Gentlemans Monitor* argued in the mid-1660s that one could 'live as
handsomely and cheap' in London as anywhere else, a claim that
probably held true only for those of strongest will. Yet the landed
embraced such a rationalization to justify regular visits, and of the
five groups whose presence stimulated new construction in the
West End in these years, four were temporary residents from
the landed classes – great magnates and county élite who came
regularly, lesser gentry on occasional visits, and young gentlemen
seeking metropolitan experience. However specious, the argument from economy carried more weight after the Restoration,
too, because the gentry's sense of paternalist obligation to govern
and provide hospitality in the country was being undercut by the
growth of a commercializing and cosmopolitan culture centred
on London.[12]

Landowners' absenteeism, whether in London or elsewhere,
had a mixed potential for estate management and the economic
development of the countryside. The disadvantages perhaps
appear most obvious today: decay of farms and delay of improvements through lack of an owner's oversight; opportunity afforded
to employees to cheat their absent masters; the drain of money
and loss of local employment when the landed pursued leisure
and pleasure elsewhere. On the other hand, landlords' prolonged
absences did not necessarily signal indifference or entail neglect
of estates, which, as primary capital assets, they had a strong
incentive to maintain. Resident landowners were not demonstra-
bly superior managers to steward surrogates, so that the Duke of
Buckingham, separated from his estates by massive debts, had
trustees whose entrepreneurial management and 'metropolitan
control' made him a successful *rentier*.[13] Correspondence with
those on the ground kept some owners exceedingly well
informed. Sir John Lowther visited his Cumbrian lands only eight
times between 1666 and 1698, but his curiosity about them never
flagged, and he played as much a part in increasing ground rents,
exploiting his collieries and developing the port of Whitehaven
as if he had been on the scene.[14] In the end, moreover, the

benefits or disadvantages that absent landlords bestowed on estate development may matter less in explaining the nature of Restoration landed life than does the fact that absenteeism was a product of the 'nationalization' of country society. It was a force promoting shared attitudes towards the countryside and land, that gave landowners both a new and a common outlook as a group.

A major set of consequences of the new and common outlook was cultural. Although difficult to pin to the Restoration era, the cultural and physical withdrawal of landed families into socially restricted networks has been attested by the research of historians of architecture, landscape, the grand household, the Grand Tour and the Grand Tradition. The questioning of vulgar beliefs that culminated in their condemnation by the 'enlightened' began in the mid-seventeenth century and comprised one element of a wider cultural divergence taking place between the popular and the polite. The closure of public ways, the construction of walls, extensive hedge- and tree-planting to mark distant boundaries – all began in this era and physically separated country-house owners and country houses from their plebeian environment, although this separation grew more evident in the next century.[15] New patterns of socialization and of hospitality also began to emerge, as the élite eschewed activities and spaces where social mixing was indiscriminate. Legislation passed in 1671 notably narrowed the ranks of those allowed to shoot or pursue game, by excluding those without substantial landholdings. While keeping others out of their world, the landed voluntarily withdrew from other venues. The rakish Dorimant observed in *The Man of Mode* that 'gentlemen do not of late frequent the taverns' and, when it came to gambling, the 'deep play [was] now in private houses'. The public bestowal of charity depicted in a painting such as 'The Tichborne Dole' (1670), in which Sir Henry Tichborne, lieutenant of the New Forest, prepares to distribute bread to tenants and villagers, was becoming a rare image, as the personal touch was replaced by an employer's surrogate gesture.[16]

Admittedly, even prolonged residence away from one's country home (whether or not in the metropolis) did not necessarily herald an end to all country hospitality, nor did it signal the complete abandonment of other forms of traditional involvement in rural cultural life. None the less, charity took on new forms – less personal and more institutional – as with the county feasts held in London beginning in the mid-1650s. Gentry infrequently attended these novel gatherings and their accompanying sermons, but landowners were expected to support financially their charitable ends, the apprenticing of country youth to London trades. Moreover, in the same way in which a landed family's brief or prolonged stays in the countryside had different effects on the neighbourhood economy, so too hospitality rendered with the family present had a different meaning from that supplied in its absence. The élite provision of feasts or celebratory bonfires withered in the later seventeenth century, partly because their meaning and utility were diminished when the resident paternalist and his family were present only by surrogate.[17]

The realm of hospitality was not alone in seeing a partial redefinition of élite responsibility after the Restoration, and a similar development can be seen more broadly in the gentry's behaviour as local governors. Here, a combination of absenteeism, the Interregnum's legacy of overtly partisan local politics and a shift in civic values all influenced landed men's conduct in provincial office. After Charles II's arrival, as more claimants than could be accommodated clamoured for local positions, the majority of office-holders was changed in most places. Yet because the composition of local institutions was subject to myriad influences, the turnover was not complete, and there mingled in provincial administration a combination of first-time claimants from prominent families, representatives of prewar magisterial lines and officials from revolutionary times.[18] Partly due to this diversity of personnel, gentry participation in local government took on a new profile. Neither suddenly nor universally, many of the magisterial élite all the same paid decreasing attention to the details of governance in the decades after 1660, as the importance of administrative activism in the provinces declined in the balance of their lives.

The increasing size of local institutions surely accounted for part of the reduced role accorded by gentry to participation in local government. Tax commissions expanded, the average county lieutenancy doubled compared with the prewar era and the number of militia officers also grew. The commissions of the peace, while prone to fluctuations, swelled with the appointment of claimants who could not be denied.[19] As a consequence of numerical expansion, the prestige attached to membership and to active service began the process of dilution that led to the need for clergyman and 'trading' justices in the eighteenth century. None the less, many county magistrates served conscientiously in

the critical early years of the Restoration, showing self-confidence
and energy in response to the new regime's unique vulnerability.
County quarter sessions barely missed a beat with the end of the
republic, and the performance of lieutenancies and militias from
1660 through the second Dutch war was generally effective and
enthusiastic. Both real and perceived threats from radical plotters
underscored this precariousness; which may appear in retrospect
to have been a paradoxical source of the regime's strength, since
its weakness encouraged the support of those who feared a return
of republican rule.[20]

Yet it proved difficult to sustain energy born out of anxiety, and
the spirit that stimulated revenge (not a widespread urge) waned
quickly for most. Even in the earliest extraordinary and insecure
times of the Stuart Restoration, self-interest rather than county
identity guided some gentry governors and led them away from
the arenas that once drew them. The Devon magistrates diligently
holding neighbourhood petty sessions did not do so for
efficiency's sake but to avoid the burden of attending general sessions, which inconveniently met at more distant locations, on
fixed dates and for a set number of days. Numerous West Country
deputy lieutenants in the early 1660s actually abandoned their
county responsibilities for London, where they solicited reward
for prior service to the new monarch.[21] Moreover, beyond the first
years of the regime's greatest vulnerability, the Restoration
country magistracy often exhibited modest inclination to perform
its offices and turned out only in moderate numbers to do so,
whether as a result of absenteeism, indifference or the pressure of
other business. Crisis could galvanize the magistracy. Deputy lieutenants acted with energy against Nonconformists in the early
1660s, and the striking mobilization of militias during the second
Dutch war reveals the successful vitalization of the lieutenancy
under Charles II.[22] To perform the tasks of magistracy thoroughly
and effectively none the less meant devoting significant time on
a regular basis, and this most justices and many deputies
were clearly unwilling to do. Inactivity and even abandonment
of voluntary and unpaid local service was far more common
than enthusiastic participation on the part of most county
figures.[23]

Even where zeal was perhaps of greatest local consequence – in
the prosecution of transgressors against religious statutes –
governors in few counties undertook sustained campaigns against
Dissent without central government prodding. Many factors

influenced the extent and pace of enforcement after 1660, but most justices neither aggressively nor regularly pursued Catholic or Protestant Nonconformists as part of their magisterial duties. The fact that government prodding was sporadic did nothing to make justices more dutiful. An awareness that avid prosecution would be locally unpopular, as well as many justices' own ambivalence, discouraged county benches from conducting repressive campaigns. Several studies show regional variation in the degree of enforcement, but together they indicate that there was no continuous effort 'to wipe non-conformity off the face of the English landscape in the 1660s and 1670s.'[24] The reluctance to prosecute does not reflect gentry indifference to local matters, but rather a desire on the part of some to avoid controversy, and on the part of others to ease the lot of Nonconformists. The *lack* of continuous effort to suppress non-conformity could cause its own controversy. Public disputes (at times on the bench) over refusals to prosecute and complaints about magisterial indifference made these politico-religious quarrels audible to a broad, public audience. Yet the absence of effort, the small turnouts at sessions and the silence that must have existed in many places conveyed their own message, that at least some of the countryside's governing élite was disengaged from these issues.

The history of the lieutenancy seems at first sight to contrast with that of the bench and to reflect more continuous and heartfelt local service. With the creation in the early 1660s of new machinery to assess and collect the militia levy, deputy lieutenants actively pursued rate-delinquents; in some counties they had the most important role in pursuing Dissenters during the 1660s. From the Restoration, the lieutenancy played political roles – through the patriotic rituals of musters or by an intimidating presence at elections – that in some ways overshadowed military ones. Generally, the lieutenancy was most visible in the early years of Charles II's reign and during wartime. Enthusiasm waned in peacetime and administration could become lax, a further sign that local service was becoming a less essential component of gentry life than under the early Stuarts. The militia's performance in western counties for example, was hampered by absenteeism and indifference throughout the 1660s and 1670s. During his reign James II diminished the stature of the institution itself, first by slighting his Lord-Lieutenants when he remodelled the commissions of the peace in 1686 without their advice. Then he replaced Lieutenants in twenty-one counties and purged deputies

nation-wide in 1687–8, drastically weakening the lieutenancy by
the appointment of Catholic and Nonconformist replacements.
Thus, staffed by inexperienced and disillusioned deputies, the
lieutenancy effectively ceased to function in many places. In 1687
Norfolk's Lord-Lieutenant, at his deputies' request, dispensed
with their grand review, desiring only that companies muster
briefly, as their captains saw fit, with the result that no county-
wide muster was held for two years.[25]

The passage of the militia acts of 1661–2 none the less logically
entailed a closer relationship to central government for deputies
actively involved in their implementation. The existence of
authorizing legislation encouraged the deputies to refer
specifically to statute in the course of fulfilling their duties, which
emphasized the supra-local character of the lieutenancy itself.
Statutory provisions also now clearly subordinated the lieutenancy
to royal control, especially by requiring royal approval of deputies,
which was no mere formality under Charles II and James II.[26] As a
member of an institution increasingly used by the monarch to
implement policy, a Restoration deputy lieutenant thus had to be
more dedicated to the desires of central government than had
been his prewar counterpart. The same stricture applied even
more clearly to the Lord-Lieutenants, who lost a good deal of
their traditional local freedom of action and who courted dismissal if they objected to this circumscription of their power.[27]
Conversely, the lieutenancy ceased to be the kind of buffer it had
been between central authority and county community in the
earlier era, acting instead as a 'self-conscious and ... ideologically
limited representation of a gentry-dominated society'.[28] Now
resting firmly on statute, the lieutenancy as an institution (regardless of its actions) testified to the gentry's social hegemony, and
the creation of socially exclusive troops of select militia in the
1660s further asserted the solidarity and dominance of the landed
order.[29] The political hegemony that the lieutenancy exercised,
which derived from connection to central government, 'now conveyed social dominance rather than the reverse'.[30] For deputy
lieutenants, then, the conduct of local government may have
been attractive not because it testified to one's provincial standing
but because it set them apart as members of an élite cadre that
spread across the kingdom and was directly connected to the
metropolis.

This association was less clear in service on the commission of
the peace, which explains part of the reduced enthusiasm for

magisterial duty shown by justices who accepted membership but eschewed participation in local administration. Other reasons can be adduced for this turning from the activities that had once lain near the heart of a landowner's identity. In part, new agents of authority (such as excise officers, or special appointees such as commissioners under the Corporation Act) diminished the bench's place as the principal representative of government in the county, perhaps rendering magisterial service a less attractive activity to the landowner.[31] In addition, the growing size and social heterogeneity of the bench signalled the end of the institution's exclusivity and probably contributed to the greater gentry's declining participation. Tax and peace commissions of the 1660s and 1670s both flowed with much new blood, and gained another influx of it during James II's reign. The failure to purge holdovers from the Interregnum further reduced the social value of provincial office and diminished the allure of active participation. The psychological discomfort caused by the republican legacy was evident, for example, among Restoration Devon's justices, who adopted their predecessors' administrative methods and yet condemned those predecessors for their confused and improper conduct of business.[32]

County institutions that once bestowed sought-after status for gentry of all levels of prominence were less able to do so after the Restoration. Yet as a time-tested site of public competition within the landed élite, the bench might still be expected to attract the active participation of gentry justices in the later seventeenth century, especially in the light of the polarized political culture that had been generated in the provinces during the Civil War and revolution.[33] Surprisingly, however, the provincial power struggles of the Civil War and Interregnum did not unfailingly politicize local institutions, and where they did so it was in ways that directed attention on to the national plane as the site of contest.

It does not do to exaggerate the politicization of Restoration landed society from the outset of Charles II's reign. In county after county, polarities dating from the 1640s and 1650s persisted into the next decade but paradoxically coexisted with moderation, compromise and concession. Complete purges of local office did not occur after May 1660, and men possessing parliamentarian pasts, office-holders and committee-men under the Commonwealth, were continued in many positions. The less-than-comprehensive purges, the joint service of former opponents in county administration and their frequent efforts to create or restore élite consensus all show that the politicization of local society was neither comprehensive nor uncontested. Even in years of more intense political feeling, extending through the mid-1670s, friendships persisted, connections were maintained and accommodations were sought within landed society.[34] This solidarity among the élite did not spare the socially vulnerable (especially Quakers) from persecution under religious statutes, nor did it prevent particular enthusiasts from zealously pursuing partisan courses within local government. But many electoral and magisterial contests during the Cavalier Parliament's lifetime seem to have been factional battles, and provincial religious contentions of these years have also been described as 'localized battles between particular groups'.[35] Members of the magisterial class could see both their common interests and the dangers of internal conflict, curtailing partisanship rather than engage in an unchecked conflict of proto-party and party. Although justices might resolve problematic cases by voting on the bench, perhaps both cause and consequence of polarization, such behaviour (if commonly indulged) would perilously elevate political argument over legal reasoning and so remained rare.[36] To suggest that gentry understood their common interests is not to suggest that they lived their lives along strictly consensual lines, nor to deny the existence of profound divisions within landed society, but it is to remind ourselves that the landed élite was not wholly comprised of partisans.

When politicization led to overt confrontation, especially after the late 1670s, those traditional sites of contest such as the commission of the peace were riven less by personal and factional rivalries among the landed than by ideological fractures along fault lines generated by issues and pressures that arose at the kingdom's centre rather than at its periphery. The intrusion into county affairs of a matter such as Exclusion 'forced provincial communities to divide over an issue of national importance'.[37] Dismissals of local governors – whether the widescale displacement of municipal officials under the Corporation Act or the occasional removal of troublesome justices – were most frequently occasioned by imperatives formed on the national plane and not in the local crucible of faction. Where more extensive purges during and after the later 1670s denied substantial numbers of 'natural rulers' their traditional roles in the county, these dismissals also gave them less reason to think in or live on provincial terms. The purge of Whigs in the latter years of Charles II's reign discouraged them from seeing themselves as governors of the countryside, and the multiple reshapings of lieutenancy and commissions of the peace under James II had a similar effect. The advent of Catholics in large numbers and of Dissenters in smaller ones convincingly demonstrated that the magistracy was not what it had once been.[38] That demonstration surely helped turn away from active local service – even after 1689 – the higher status gentry who had once participated willingly in it.

Several issues that had been the focus of prewar partisanship in the localities had been laid to rest: the legality of tax burdens and lines of authority governing the lieutenancy and militia had been defined legislatively. Provincial quarrels focused less on the local consequences of government policy and more on its national implications.[39] After the Restoration, many public issues generated both debate and anxiety in the localities – the effect of war, the consequences of a French alliance, the length between parliamentary sessions, Danby's efforts to build a Court party, the meaning of Exclusion, the packing of Parliament, and the rule of a Catholic King. Yet the probable *local* impact of these developments was not at stake in these debates so much as their import for the nation as a whole. In addition, the arena in which to alter or undo these policies was manifestly not at the periphery of the nation but in London. The fact that there was a session of Parliament held every year during the 1660s began to shape habits of mind, even in personal affairs. Between 1660 and 1671 some 225 private Acts were made law (compared with thirty-two from 1625 to 1642), an indication of a turning to the centre and to Parliament for effective relief of personal and local problems.[40]

A mixture of forces drew the gentry's political energies and attention from the countryside, but the transformation of landed identity that began during the Restoration did not straightforwardly replace a rural outlook with a cosmopolitan one. Gentry remained wedded to the rural life in myriad ways – economically, socially, culturally, politically and psychologically – and the Restoration may have heralded a significant increase in construction and renovation of country houses.[41] Still, landowners' relationships with the countryside and its inhabitants became less comfortable and less self-evidently comprehensible. Although metropolitan sights and sounds, fashions and fads might be disorienting, rural life posed its own problems. Much of the gentry may have seen reason to congratulate themselves on the

Restoration's constitutional or religious settlements, but in the economic sphere landed prosperity seemed under siege. Economic anxieties heightened insecurities fostered by past and current social and political developments, and the economic solidity of the landed élite in the next century contrasts with its self-perception at the Restoration that a way of life was in danger.

The expansion of the world of high finance was advantageous to the gentry in so far as it offered them new opportunities both to invest and borrow, and the appearance of a reliable means of long-term borrowing on mortgage assisted the landed through times of financial stringency. Yet other developments contributed to a sense that traditional landed life was in jeopardy. The close connection between government finance and private banking disquieted some gentry and persuaded them that, where the interests of City and country clashed, a government in thrall to bankers for a regular flow of money would favour the moneyed interest at the expense of the land.[42] The insecurity of the landed order was fuelled by fears of the landed economy's vulnerability in the face of the potentially malign influence of the City and the 'moneyed interest'. Men of business made the gentry uneasy, and although they were not objects of universal condemnation (as once was thought), they garnered praise for their genteel attributes and not for their business achievements, which remained in some ways suspect. The well-known criticisms directed at the moneyed interest of bankers and stock-jobbers for profiting from paper transactions rather than the production and sale of goods were first voiced in the years after about 1670.[43]

Whatever their uneasiness, landowners were caught up in the changes occurring in financial life; for example, when they required supplies of money away from home, a need that both encouraged and was met by new practices of money transfer and banking, most of which centred on London. Reluctant to invest large sums with private metropolitan bankers or even to lodge much money with them for current use, landowners most commonly employed the 'return', which transferred from one party to another a claim to funds payable in London. Through this mechanism, which depended on personal contacts and local markets, parties avoided the danger and inconvenience of conveying cash, and they received their money where most required. In operation, the return was a financial instrument conditioned by a provincial, face-to-face world, but it innovatively made income earned in the countryside 'more flexible in place and time', readily allowing aristocrats to spend not only time but also money away from their home estates.[44]

Restoration landowners may have found the new men, methods and institutions who appeared on the financial horizon to be challenging and confusing, in the manner of the innovations of the late-twentieth-century computer age. Yet at the heart of the aristocracy's anxiety about its economic world lay their concern that land rents – their principal source of income – were in decline. Modern observation confirms that the upward movement of the 1640s and 1650s came to a halt and then reversed course in the following three decades. Agricultural prices formerly sustained by population growth and inflation began to stagnate, and rents with them. For the first time in generations, landlords had serious difficulty profiting from their estates, as their correspondence and accounts reveal. The second Dutch war played an initial role in depressing prices by discouraging exports, but oversupply was the principal downward force, the result of increased production for a declining population.[45] The low prices that tenants got for their grain (and the weak market for animal products in the 1670s and 1680s) made it difficult for them to pay rent. Even rents on estates carefully managed by the professional employees of the London scriveners Clayton and Morris went unpaid in the 1670s. Their accumulating arrears pushed some landowners actually to lower rents, the last tactic that they normally entertained.[46]

Because élite landowning usually took the culturally acceptable form of landlordship, gentry engaged in little direct farming in this era, which meant that the inability to collect rent quickly pushed landed incomes into decline. Declining rent meant to one contemporary that 'the Nobility & Gentry who have noe other support then that of ther [landed] Revenewes ... must be undone ... must bee ruyned'. The expense incurred when the dearth of tenants forced landlords to manage estates directly only worsened the situation, and in 1669 a committee of the House of Lords was appointed to investigate the decay of rents.[47] Any diminution of gentry income potentially threatened social position too, and contemporary explanations for the economic crisis betrayed worry on the latter score.

Sir William Coventry believed that the predicament arose from a 'misapplication' of people and especially 'the nobility and gentry's living so much in London', a habit which impoverished the countryside and discouraged potential tenants from farming. This behaviour on the part of the élite, another commentator believed, had given rise to new social perceptions and expectations among lesser folk, which explained the lack of tenants, since it changed the 'very humour of ... the Yeomandry'. Successful farmers failed to raise their children to pursue husbandry and instead put them to trades, sent them to university or tried to make them gentlemen. Extending the argument full circle, a worried magistrate concluded that the yeoman's disinclination to agriculture was made even more damaging because justices of the peace (absent in London?) failed to bind apprentices in husbandry under the Poor Law. The decay of rents, caused by changing values as well as economic forces, threatened the traditional structure of rural society as well as the prosperity of the landed order.[48]

Prosperity in the form of estate income was subject to erosion by more than decaying rents, since tax payments, repairs, capital outlays on new building, and agricultural improvements also reduced net income. But even where income was stable or rose, expenses could easily outbalance it, and for those urging aristocratic economy the cost of life in London provided an easy and increasingly disturbing target. The baneful influence of London was thought to create problems for the national economy: maldistribution of domestic consumption and starving of country markets, the decay of traditional forms of rural hospitality and the flow of capital from the countryside.[49]

After mid-century, faced with novel challenges, the gentry élite thus had to work harder at *being* landowners in order to prosper. The dearth of tenants that brought lands 'in hand', to be farmed directly by estate employees, temporarily led some aristocrats to take personal direction of affairs. Here the evidence of intimate engagement with estates survives in forms such as the imprimatur ('Perused, Townshend') that the first Viscount Townshend put on estate accounts along with marginal comments and computations checking his accountants' arithmetic. Such close attention to the details of management was only one of several strategies that landowners embraced both to compensate for falling rents and to regain lost control over their agricultural lives. Ironically, however, this urgent effort was more and more carried out vicariously, through the correspondence generated by the long-distance and indirect control of absentee landlords.[50]

While many of the steps taken by Restoration landowners to control their estates are familiar facets of agricultural improvement aiming at financial benefit, we may also interpret them as elements of an effort to re-secure dominance in rural society. The creation of consolidated estates, for example, bespeaks a desire for greater control over the local environment. Similarly, the increasingly common employment of written leases with covenants that merely codified local usages, and were often unenforced or waived, indicates a practice intended more to assert than impose the landlord's privileged position in his contract with tenants. Landowners also demanded from their employees new and more detailed information, and they adopted a more rigid financial calculus by having auditors drop unrecoverable arrears from their books.[51] A more calculating approach to finances could also lead to reduction in personnel: in 1660 Sir Horatio Townshend employed an auditor, a receiver, two household stewards, three manorial bailiffs, a bailiff of husbandry and a sheep reeve on his Norfolk estates. He reduced these by the 1680s to three employees (auditor, household steward and estate steward), who were now guided by written instructions. A work such as Stephen Monteage's *Instructions for Rent-Gatherers Accompts* similarly provided both masters and managers of land with a 'plain Method' to take accounts.[52]

Such directives and publications, however, allowed absentee landlords to manage their lands from afar only if implemented by effective deputies, above all the estate steward, whose weighty influence (even on the very psychology of landownership) we are just beginning to appreciate. David Hainsworth, who has called estate management 'England's largest collective business', has shown how the reliance on increasingly professional stewards made the enterprise more homogenous from county to county, standardizing estate practices in the long run.[53] The economic problems of owners placed a premium on stewards' expertise, and even while farming, management and accounting systems varied across the kingdom, landlords had a common need for trained stewards who based their practices on studied and recognized principles. When Stephen Monteage offered twenty-three pages of model accounts in his *Instructions*, he was presuming that the methods he promoted had universal application. Although not a professional in the manner of the eighteenth-century land agent, the steward was nothing like a mere rent collector, and he made decisions about virtually all aspects of a landlord's country interests. In Monteage's eyes he would preferably not be a local man ('though versed in Country-Affairs') but rather 'a sober Citizen, who is a good Accomptant'. The employment of outsiders symbolized the conversion of the steward from a household servant into a salaried employee, an illustration that the essence of landlordship was becoming impersonal and calculating.[54]

With the steward filling an array of roles, his employment had wide-ranging effects. Some seemingly trivial practices, such as numbering and docketing letters or writing out sums both in words and numbers to prevent fraud, attest to a desire for accountability and to a rational administrative approach stressing profit and loss. The steward more visibly influenced estate affairs through the reorganization of farms, recruitment of tenants, and enforcement of methods and courses of husbandry. He also very critically preserved a landlord's local interests, whether the agrarian ones he defended against encroachment and loss or the political ones advanced by electioneering on an employer's behalf. In short, stewards performed the functions of attentive management that more and more gentry found boring and demeaning. The employment of professionals made gentry oversight vicarious rather than direct, and that very indirection must have made it harder for gentry to view landownership as they traditionally had, as an obligation or trust entailing 'patriarchal responsibilities to their tenantry'.[55]

The history of Restoration landowners in part charts a slow drift away from traditional roles, such as patriarchal landlord, and towards new identities as absentee or 'man of mode' or party politician. For gentry grounded in the countryside one of these identities was the 'patrician' magistrate, whose authority derived from law, not morality, and who performed tasks and responded to the desires of specific individuals, rather than caring for the welfare of organic local communities. Acting as a member of a putatively disinterested institution, the patrician justice distanced himself from particular localities and found fellowship among his magisterial colleagues rather than in his own rural neighbourhood.[56] For landowners less caught up in county governance, and also for the many local governors who led significant portions of their lives beyond the provincial sphere, a cosmopolitan identity offered itself. In this guise, landowners appeared as participants in a common culture being constructed around metropolitan affairs – activities and interests, connections and conceptualizations that transcended the personal and factional and provincial. This metropolitan life, although springing from London originally, was in fact not confined to the capital and was beginning to flourish in provincial towns and country seats as well. It came into being and drew its strength from various commonalities, those of social pre-eminence, geographical proximity and interaction, economic interest and partisan political identity, all of which were starting to weld the landowners of disparate regions into a national ruling order. In retrospect, analysis would reveal that the alloy of the weld included a substantial non-landed element as well, and that England's rulers were not confined to a single stratum. But during the Restoration it was the kingdom's landed élite who most clearly signalled the changes that were impelling English society towards an uncertain but transformed future.

8. The Restoration Town

PETER BORSAY

Recent decades have witnessed a research boom into the history of the early modern English town. A subject which in many respects was uncharted territory in the early 1970s, before the publication in 1972 of the path-breaking *Crisis and Order in English Towns 1500–1700*,[1] now has the character of a map the broad contours of which have been sketched in, although in which there are still obvious lacunae, and there is much scope for detailed infilling. The volume of research, and an early focus on synthesis – on viewing towns generically rather than individually[2] – has ensured that the town has emerged as a distinct (if not independent) variable in the period's history as a whole. This chapter will survey the findings of this new work as it relates to the Restoration town (1660–*c.* 1688).

Three central themes will inform the discussion. First, there is the chronology and nature of change. Early modern (1500–1800) urban historians, who have focused generally on economic or social matters, have tended to think in fairly broad time-spans. In this context, the short period 1660–88 has acquired no obvious significance, in the way it would for a political historian. Initially attention was directed towards the years 1500–1700, and in particular to what was perceived as their Tudor and early Stuart core. The Restoration town, therefore, had a peripheral status, on the edge rather than at the heart of the subject and period under review. None the less, its character was coloured by what proved to be the dominant theme of historical debate, the notion of an urban crisis. The validity and applicability of this concept has been keenly contested.[3] One challenge has come from later early modernists, eager to broaden the chronology of the discussion, who see during the long eighteenth century a decisive and – with the future in mind – highly significant upturn in urban fortunes.[4] This positive view of the final phase of the early modern era has now been widely accepted,[5] and several commentators have

171

suggested that the years after 1660 were the turning-point. However, it is true to say that their gaze has been very much on the eighteenth century, so that the position of the Restoration town still remains equivocal. This is especially so if the impact of the Civil War is considered, which applied a major shock to parts of the urban system, checking developments under way and leaving a legacy of problems to be dealt with. The debate on urban crisis appears now to have run its course, but the issues of chronology, and of the balance between continuity and change at any point in time, remain as relevant as ever. In this connection the place of the Restoration town, with its potentially transitional character, is of particular interest.

In exploring the timing and nature of urban change, the contribution of London is crucial. The impact of the metropolis is our second theme. During the sixteenth and seventeenth centuries the capital experienced explosive growth, the consequences of which reverberated throughout the urban system. London's development in the later seventeenth century, and the way in which it interacted and contrasted with provincial centres, was to play an important part in shaping the character of the Restoration town. However, the metropolis was in many respects – not least its extraordinary size – a quite atypical urban settlement. A third theme, therefore, will be to establish what made a town a town in the period, and to determine to what extent a sharp line can be drawn between the urban and rural spheres. To investigate these three themes, and to sketch a broad picture of the later Stuart town, the following areas of experience will be examined: demography, economy, society, environment, politics, religion and culture.

In the late seventeenth century there were around 800 towns, which in 1700 contained just under one-third (30.3 per cent) of the nation's population.[6] Historians have emphasized that these settlements were not isolated entities but part of a system, a 'graduated network of large and small towns', which might stretch beyond national boundaries, and in which the constituent parts displayed an increasing complexity of function the further up the urban hierarchy they were situated.[7] The proportion of town to village dwellers was not static. For much of the early modern period the country experienced some measure of urbanization. Corfield has suggested that the proportion of the English and Welsh population living in centres of over 5000 people quadrupled from about 4 per cent in the 1520s to 16 per cent by 1700, and Patten that the share of the East Anglian population living in towns as a whole rose from under a quarter in the 1520s to nearly a third in the 1670s.[8] There is little sign that the period 1660–88 deviated from the long-term trend towards urbanization. What is significant is that the marked deceleration in population growth experienced by the nation in the seventeenth century – by the 1650s absolute growth had come to a halt – does not seem to have inhibited the continuing capacity of towns to acquire a growing slice of the country's demographic cake.[9] Moreover, the position in England contrasts sharply with that in Europe, where from the early seventeenth century the urban system in general (the great cities excepted) was entering a phase of stagnation and decline which lasted until about 1750.[10]

By modern standards, the vast majority of towns were very tiny. In 1700 about 90 per cent had populations of 2500 inhabitants or under, and some possessed only 400–500 souls.[11] Some historians have doubted whether, given their size, such settlements can be described as genuinely urban.[12] There were only seven towns of 10 000 people or over.[13] However, one of these, London, was truly extraordinary. From a city of 50 000–60 000 people in the 1520s, containing some 2 per cent of the nation's inhabitants, its population rocketed to 200 000 by 1600, 375 000 by 1650 and 490 000 by 1700. By this last date it was sixteen times the size of its nearest provincial rival, Norwich, and was the largest city in Western Europe. The growth of the capital may have slackened a little after 1650, but with the now static position of the national population the metropolis continued to expand its share of the country's inhabitants, so that by the end of the century it was home to a remarkable one in ten of the peoples of England and Wales.[14]

Given the extent of London's growth it is tempting to view the process of early modern urbanization as largely a metropolitan phenomenon. However, the one-in-ten mark that the capital reached by 1700 proved to be something of a ceiling not to be surpassed in the eighteenth century. A major reason for this was vigorous growth within the provincial sector of the urban system. This was mostly to post-date 1700, but the signs of it were already visible by the late seventeenth century as, in Penelope Corfield's words, a 'more complex and polycentric urban society' began to emerge.[15] It has been argued that small towns played little part in this process, their numbers reduced by competition and rationalization.[16] However, the pioneering work of the Small Towns project at Leicester suggests that these settlements experienced

growth in the early seventeenth century, a recession in the 1640s
and 1650s associated with the Civil War, and then a revival in
demographic fortunes over the last decades of the century.[17]
Although this represents an important correction to what has
been a rather pessimistic view of the smaller centres, it remains
true that the really significant signs of change were to be found
among the middling and larger towns. The stimulus came partly
from some – although by no means all – of the traditional centres:
Norwich grew from about 20 000 inhabitants in mid-century to
30 000 by 1700, and Bristol from around 16 000 people in the
1670s to 20 000 by the end of the century.[18] More momentous in
respect of the future were the slight but indubitable signs that the
future urban giants of the Industrial Revolution were stirring:
Manchester and Birmingham increased from around 5000 people
in the 1670s to 8000 by 1700, and Liverpool from 1500 to 5000.[19]
Not too much should be made of these changes. A number of
towns may have stagnated or even declined,[20] and the real surge
of provincial growth lay in the future. But the early portents of
that shake-up in the English urban system, which was to lead to a
re-ordering of the established hierarchy, was evident from the
mid-seventeenth century, and long before such a process was
visible on the continent.

What were the characteristics of the urban demographic
regime? High levels of mortality had been a feature of the Tudor
and early Stuart period, and there is little to suggest that the
Restoration town deviated from this pattern. Plague was the most
dramatic – if not necessarily the most destructive overall – of the
epidemic diseases, and its impact was particularly severe in towns.
The major visitation of 1665–6 was focused on London, East
Anglia and southern towns in close contact with the metropolis;
over 80 000 people, or 18 per cent of the capital's population,
died (1665), as did 15 per cent of Norwich's inhabitants, at least
one in eight of Portsmouth's citizens, and perhaps half of
Colchester's.[21] In towns which were affected, many of the well-off
packed their bags and fled. The hardest hit were the poor, as
economic activity was severely disrupted and welfare provisions
were put under intense pressure. Although 1665–6 saw the last
serious outbreak of plague – perhaps as a consequence of
improved quarantine procedures[22] – there is little sign that this
reduced the level of urban mortality. A range of other killer diseases – smallpox, measles, typhus and gastric illnesses – simply
moved in to fill the vacuum.[23] The prevalence of steep mortality

rates has led demographers to play down the role of natural increase in urban growth. This conclusion may be premature, and more needs to be known about the experiences of different types of towns, especially the smaller centres.[24] However, the late seventeenth century was not a period which saw the nation's population as a whole increasing, and it is clear that London had a substantial surplus of burials over baptisms, and was quite unable even to replenish its own numbers. The considerable urban growth of the period, therefore, seems to have depended heavily upon migrants. Pre-industrial England was a surprisingly mobile society, and many of those on the move made their way to towns. Net immigration into London around 1700 is claimed to have been about 8000 people per annum. In towns as a whole between a half and two-thirds of urban residents were probably migrants.[25] Most newcomers travelled relatively short distances – 63–70 per cent of outsider-apprentices in Bristol in the late seventeenth century came from Gloucestershire and Somerset – and the volume of long-distance migration was declining after the Restoration.[26] That towns depended so heavily upon migrants had many implications for how they operated, and several of these points will be touched on later in this essay. However, in purely demographic terms the impact may have been contradictory; migrants tended to be young and therefore to raise the level of fertility, but they were also more vulnerable to disease and consequently their presence – as in the case of London – may have increased the mortality rate.[27]

In the later Stuart period urban migration became more purposeful and positive, less a question of push and more a matter of pull.[28] What drew the vast majority of newcomers to urban centres was the prospect of work, and what made Restoration towns so attractive in this respect was their general economic buoyancy. Some commentators have argued for the underlying soundness of urban economies for much of the early modern period, especially from the late sixteenth century.[29] However, this view is a controversial one. There is evidence that many traditional textile centres faced serious problems in the early seventeenth century, and that the Civil War severely disrupted the pattern of commercial life.[30] From the mid-seventeenth century the picture is much clearer. It has been maintained that for the English economy as a whole these were the years of the 'turning tide', as it entered a 'new context' of growth and prosperity in which it diverged from the general European experience.[31] Towns, as integral parts of the national economy, fully benefited from and contributed to this new context. Growth in agricultural specialization, productivity and output enhanced the demand for marketing services, which were concentrated in towns and constituted the bedrock of virtually all urban economies. The acquisition and servicing of specific trades was especially advantageous. Maidstone, for example, flourished on the handling of huge quantities of oats, hops and fruit from mid-Kent. Uttoxeter, which enjoyed a 'golden age' in the seventeenth century, prospered on its trade in dairy produce, and during the period was the major cheese market in the North Midlands.[32] Uttoxeter's fortunes also rested on its heavy involvement in leather crafts. This was indicative of the important role that towns played in processing agricultural products, and of the inextricable links between the urban and rural sectors. Such close ties may seem to blur the distinction between town and country, yet studies of even small urban settlements suggest that they possessed a distinctive economic profile distinguished, when compared to villages, by a concentration of crafts and services.[33]

Since the nineteenth century one litmus test of a place's 'urbanness' has been the presence of industry. This was not the case in the early modern period, when so much manufacture was located in the countryside. The industrial growth of the post-Restoration decades was not, therefore, necessarily synonymous with urbanization. However, rural industrial regions usually depended heavily upon an urban centre for the importation of raw materials and foodstuffs, the marketing and export of the manufactured product, and a host of other essential services. The rapid expansion under the later Stuarts of textile regional centres such as Norwich and Manchester, or metallurgical ones such as Birmingham and Sheffield, points to the close – and perhaps strengthening – links between industrialization and urbanization. This again raises the issue of to what extent it makes sense to separate town and rural region when their economies, peoples and cultures were so tightly bound together. In his study of Sheffield between 1660 and 1740, David Hey makes a strong case for examining the town and the surrounding 'distinctive local society' of which it was a part – Hallamshire – as *one* unit, 'united by a sense of common inheritance and fortune'.[34] There is much to be said for this approach. Yet the economies of town and country within such regions, although complementary, were not usually homogenous. A textile centre would concentrate typically on a marketing and service role, and on specific aspects of the manufacturing process (especially finishing), leaving basic production (spinning and weaving) to the country districts.

A number of established textile towns, which had suffered industrial decline in the early seventeenth century, reduced their dependence on the cloth trade; in certain cases – such as Winchester and Bath – virtually abandoning it altogether.[35] They did so partly because competing centres were better placed regionally to exploit the industry; but also because, with the growing diversity and prosperity of the later Stuart economy, they – and other important traditional towns – were able to develop a new role, and one that could furnish a road to recovery. Marketing remained a core aspect of activities. On to this was built sophisticated craft, consumer and service sectors which catered for the growing number of those in post-Restoration society able to command a substantial disposable income. It was a role these towns were well suited to fill, since many as county and diocesan capitals naturally attracted the gentry and better-off.[36] Associated with this trend was the proliferation of spas offering specialized medical and, to a lesser extent at this stage, recreational services. The leading centres were Bath and Tunbridge Wells, both undergoing significant development before the turn of the century.[37]

Rising levels of internal and overseas trade under the later Stuarts enhanced the demand for the communication and transport facilities provided by the urban sector.[38] The effect of this was felt in the thoroughfare towns that straddled major highways such as the Great North Road, river towns such as those on the Severn, and seaports engaged in coastal and overseas trade.[39] Britain's peripheral location on the far edge of Europe had historically restricted the commercial potential of its ports, particularly those on its western seaboard. However, with the rise of the dynamic trades with North America and the West Indies, Britain acquired a new global centrality, servicing the economies of the Americas and mediating between the Old World and the New. Although the full realization of this role lay in the future, its impact was already being felt by England's Atlantic ports before 1700, notably in the later-seventeenth-century expansion of Bristol and Liverpool.[40]

Despite the involvement of provincial ports in overseas trade, it remains true that London dominated this field. In 1700, 80 per cent of imports, 69 per cent of exports, and 86 per cent of re-exports (largely colonial goods such as tobacco, sugar, calicoes, spices and silks for which Britain was the European entrepot, and which enjoyed particularly vigorous growth) were handled by the metropolis.[41] This was indicative of the fact that Restoration London – although historians may debate the relative size of the various sectors – was by far the most important commercial, manufacturing, administrative and social centre in the nation.[42] It achieved this position because its huge population ensured that it constituted beyond comparison the largest and most concentrated market in the country; and also because the hinterland which it serviced and interacted with was a national, international and increasingly intercontinental one. The impact of the metropolis's growth on the development of the domestic economy was, as Wrigley has demonstrated, to be profound, stimulating far-reaching changes in agriculture, industry and transport, and invigorating the commercial life of a host of 'feeder' towns engaged in satisfying the capital's gargantuan appetite for foodstuffs, fuel and raw materials.[43] London's expansion and the buoyancy of the urban sector in general should not obscure the reality that towns could still experience stagnation and decline; but this was largely due to natural forces or competition between centres rather than structural faults in the national economy as a whole.[44]

Economic changes usually have social consequences. One of the most debilitating and escalating problems facing Tudor and early Stuart towns was that of poverty. The Restoration did not see an end to this malaise. Although it is misleading to quantify crude levels of indigence,[45] it is clear that a substantial proportion of town dwellers suffered a degree of poverty at some stage in their lives. However, during the later seventeenth century the problem appears to have stabilized and even reduced in its scale and seriousness. The end of plague in the 1660s removed one trigger capable of initiating a severe short-term social crisis. Growing economic prosperity reduced the risk of widespread economic dislocation and unemployment. Also, in alliance with falling grain prices, it raised the level of real incomes, improving the capacity of the poor to meet their own needs, and of potential benefactors to give. The institutionalized system of public relief pioneered in the sixteenth and early seventeenth centuries now became firmly established, and demonstrated itself capable of raising increasing sums of money. At the same time new forms of private philanthropy emerged.[46] Need still stalked the town. It was this rather than choice which compelled most women to take what was often, when compared to their male counterparts, unrewarding and poorly paid work.[47] Yet if life remained hard for the majority of town dwellers, it no longer plumbed quite the depths, or placed urban society under quite the stress it had before the Restoration.

One further reason why the sharp edge of poverty was blunted a little was the changing pattern of migration. Vagrancy – which simply imported destitution into the town – declined; whereas purposeful, short-distance and controlled mobility, which helped assure a job at the end of the road, increased.[48] Although the nature of migration was altering, its contribution to town growth remained as important as ever. What impact did this have on the unity and continuity of the urban community? An answer to this question might stress the contrast between the stability and integrity of village society and the shifting and fragmented character of the town, populated as the latter was by regular waves of immigrants. Yet such comparisons can be very misleading. Rural society was itself highly mobile, reducing the capacity of villages to sustain elaborate kinship networks.[49] Household structure in village and town appears to have been relatively similar, with nuclear family households the dominant form, and very little co-residence of kin – although evidence from Shrewsbury suggests that there was a marked tendency for parents and adult children to live close to each other.[50] Two towns in which immigration played an important part in their expansion were Southwark and Sheffield; yet both possessed a core of settled families which gave their communities a certain structure and permanence.[51]

One way to impart identity to expanding, fluid and potentially anonymous urban populations was to establish sub-communities, small enough in scale to provide a meaningful social network for their members. Concentrations of certain occupations in particular neighbourhoods and streets was a fairly common feature. Work on river or sea might provide the basis for one such grouping: 71 per cent of a batch of those whose employment can be identified in the London hamlet of Shadwell in 1650, and 75 per cent of the male inhabitants of Fryers Lane and Underhill Street listed in the 1689 Poll Tax for Bridgnorth, were engaged in jobs associated with the water. In such occupational districts the common culture of work may have provided the foundations for a closely knit world of shared interests and beliefs.[52] Another socialization strategy was to develop institutions which acted as the focal points of micro-communities, and helped incorporate migrants and residents into the urban body. The proliferation of coffee-houses, clubs and societies in post-Restoration London, and the

maturing of the alehouse as an urban institution, was a foretaste
of this type of development, which Peter Clark sees as the basis for
a 'new, dynamic, secular vision of the urban community'.[53] But we
should not become too intoxicated by the concept of community.
The late-seventeenth-century town, as will be shown, was riven by
political and religious divisions which make cosy notions of unity
and harmony difficult to sustain.

It is likely that those town dwellers who had a particular
propensity to stay put, and contributed most to the leadership
and membership of clubs and societies, were drawn from the middling sort.[54] This social stratum is now attracting particular attention from historians, who see it as an especially influential and
dynamic element in urban and national society from the
Restoration onwards. The rapid growth in the professions, allied
to increasing numbers of merchants, financiers, 'manufacturers',
and well-off innkeepers, shopkeepers, tradesmen and craftsmen,
was leading to a thickening out of the town's social structure, in
the process sharpening the contrast between urban and rural
society.[55] The middling groups emerge from recent research as
being heavily involved in town politics and administration, committed to the idea of the civic community and to urban ways of
living, disinclined to migrate to the countryside even if wealthy
enough to do so, and are portrayed overall as the critical element
in shaping a town's destiny.[56] This begs the question as to the contribution of the gentry and 'popular' society to urban development. It also raises the problem as to how homogeneous a group
were the middling sort. Did they constitute a class? Had they a
shared culture? Two historians who feel there was a common
value system have very different views as to what this might have
been. Peter Earle characterizes it as individualistic and secular,
dynamic and forward looking; for Jonathan Barry collectivism and
religion are the key elements, with the emphasis very much on
continuity with the past.[57]

One expression of social class would be for the better off to
congregate in certain areas of the town. Broadly speaking, this was
the case, with the wealthier tending to occupy the urban centre
and the poor the periphery. But crude schematization should be
avoided, as should notions of class ghettoes. Occupational group-
ings and local topography added considerable complexity to the
pattern, and even in the most exclusive areas there would always
be a miscellany of more lowly residents, often inhabiting courts
and yards to the rear of the prestigious street fronts. It must also

be said that London, with its east–west axis of poverty and wealth, hardly conformed to the archetypal concentric layout, but then the presence of the monied City in the east makes this axis itself too simplistic a description of residential patterns in the metropolis.[58]

Analysis of *where* people lived prompts examination of *what* they lived in. The Civil War had dealt a heavy blow to the built environment, especially the suburban fabric, of many towns located in the conflict zones. Gloucester, for example, lost 241 properties during the siege of 1643, and that at Taunton in 1645 destroyed two-thirds of the town. With devastation of this order postwar recovery could be very slow, soaking up building capital that might otherwise have been directed towards improving the housing stock.[59] One of the main causes of destruction during the war was fire, whether initiated by accident or intention. With the highly inflammable nature of vernacular building materials, large-scale fire damage was a spectre that haunted early modern town dwellers. There is little to suggest that the problem diminished in the later seventeenth century, with some huge conflagrations occurring, such as those at Northampton (1675), Southwark (1676) and Warwick (1694), in which hundreds of properties were damaged.[60] The most serious disaster was of course the Great Fire of London (1666) in which around 13 000 houses were burnt, not to mention the destruction of churches, public buildings, commercial stock and domestic goods. Pepys graphically captured the scale of the catastrophe when he recorded in his diary how 'we saw the fire as only one entire arch of fire from this to the other side of the bridge, and in a bow up the hill, for an arch of above a mile long. It made me weep to see it. The churches, houses, and all on fire and flaming at once, and a horrid noise the flames made, and the cracking of houses at their ruine.'[61]

Despite the scale of loss in London, and for that matter in Northampton and Warwick, it is difficult to argue that in the long- or even medium-term fire normally retarded urban development. The underlying economic strength of many towns in the late seventeenth century meant that such disasters could be weathered, and even used as a springboard for progress. The capital's rebuilding legislation of 1667 embodied simple but critical requirements of design and materials that pointed the way to what was to prove a revolution in urban building, with the adoption of classical in place of vernacular architecture, and brick, ashlar and tile instead of traditional materials such as timber (for framing), wattle and daub (for infilling), rubble stone and thatch.[62] The failure to impose an overall plan on the post-fire reconstruction of the City, despite the existence of several bold designs, might seem a wasted opportunity. Yet given the practical realities of the situation, and the absence of any operative English town planning tradition, the rebuilding acts were an important step forward towards the development of a more ordered and integrated landscape. The trend in this direction was most evident in London's burgeoning West End, where uniform streets and squares began to multiply in the later seventeenth century.[63] The rebuilding of the City and the expansion of the fashionable quarters of the metropolis set a powerful example to provincial towns. Gentry and wealthy citizens visiting the capital brought back the alluring new tastes to their home communities, and London-trained craftsmen carried their skills to places outside the capital. It is likely that the classical phase in Ludlow's building history was initiated by the construction in the 1680s of the handsome residence of Sir Job Charlton – a gentleman who moved in court circles and was a frequent visitor to London – and the two local magnates behind the earliest examples of post-medieval provincial town planning, Sir John Lowther at Whitehaven from the 1680s and Lord Brooke in Warwick after its fire of 1694, were men well acquainted with developments in the metropolis.[64]

The adoption of classical architecture and of a more uniform and planned approach to town building was to accentuate the differences between the urban and rural landscape. However, we should be wary about exaggerating the changes that were under way. The new fashions were only just beginning to make an impact in provincial towns, and were concentrated in the more prosperous and expanding centres and among their wealthier inhabitants and districts.[65] The bulk of housing stock would have continued to be of a vernacular type. As late as 1698, Celia Fiennes could discover in expanding Norwich no dwellings 'of brick except some few beyond the river which are built of some of the rich factors like the London buildings'.[66] She did, none the less, observe subtle changes, such as the use of external plasterwork to simulate ashlar and hide unfashionable timber framing. The late seventeenth century was a transitional phase in the exterior design of urban houses, with elements of past and future styles mixing freely together.[67] Throughout the early modern period the internal structure of the house had been in a process of evolution. The Tudor and early Stuart era had seen a shift away from the medieval open hall house, towards a greater subdivision, differentiation and privatization of space. This trend continued after the Restoration, but now with a greater emphasis on vertical extension – for example, in the use of garrets – and in London the growing significance among the middling groups of the parlour as an area of domestic space.[68]

In the late seventeenth century a number of urban centres were investing in substantial, and sometimes impressive civic buildings, intended to accommodate the town's ruling body.[69] Quite apart from the practical functions fulfilled by a town hall, it also played a symbolic role. To the local populace it signified and reinforced the authority of those who occupied it; to the outside world it was a statement about the independence and prestige of the civic community, and an indubitable mark of its urban character. Potentially one of the most striking differences between town and village was the sophistication of the former's political structure. In the traditional cities, with their corporations and multiple administrative bodies, this was certainly the case. But in the smaller and 'newer' towns, particularly those which were unincorporated and were governed by institutions similar to those in villages, the distinction was much less clear. It has been argued, although largely in the context of corporate communities, that the early modern period witnessed a shift towards a more élitist and oligarchic form of urban government, based upon a core of wealthy citizens; and that this trend continued and even intensified in the Restoration decades.[70] Power was concentrated in the hands of the corporation and, more particularly, its inner 'cabinet' of mayor, aldermen and administrative officers. Such bodies were subject to declining – and often largely perfunctory – wider selection and control, and were in practice self-perpetuating. However, this view has been challenged in the case of several towns. In Sheffield, which was not incorporated and may be more typical of the 'newer' rapidly expanding centres, it is argued that 'society was not dominated by an élite group of long-resident families with restricted entry', and that opportunities to govern were open to successful natives and newcomers alike. At London and Norwich it is contended that there was a trend away from oligarchy, and although at Great Yarmouth the corporation was a co-optive body, it is claimed that the town's leaders were sensitive to the needs of the wider community and governed on the basis of common economic interests.[71]

Notions of civic consensus must have been placed under the utmost strain by the bitter political tensions that racked towns in the late seventeenth century, permeating surprisingly deep into society. These differences originated in the struggles of the Civil War years, and the Restoration appears to have done little or nothing to mitigate the impact of this poisoned inheritance. By the late 1670s and early 1680s, under pressure of national events, the divisions in town society acquired formal Tory and Whig party identities ushering in an intensified level of conflict.[72] Why were townsmen – there remains a silence about the position of women, presumably because of their exclusion from the political system – so torn apart? Certain commentators identify social and even class tensions – expressed often in religious terms, and particularly reflecting pressure from middling and petty bourgeois elements – as a source of conflict; and Michael Mullett has argued for a distinctively popular political agenda and language, although this could be highly conservative in its nature.[73] Other historians maintain that political fissures cut vertically rather than horizontally through society, and that the principal factor that divided people was religion itself. The 1640s and 1650s had seen an efflorescence of non-Anglican forms of worship. These did not wither away after the Restoration, but continued to display considerable strength and resilience, especially in urban centres.[74] The key issue facing towns after 1660 was, therefore, whether to tolerate and accommodate Dissent or persecute and attempt to extirpate it. It was this problem, it is contended, which split urban communities.[75] However, it could be argued that what lay behind conflict was not so much doctrinal divisions *per se*, but – given the inextricable links between religious and political experience – a deeper struggle over the nature of authority,[76] and between unitary and pluralist views of local (and indeed national) government. Despite the intensity of the conflict, it must be added that in many towns moderate forms of Dissent went relatively unpersecuted, except in the early 1680s.[77] Moreover, there is little evidence of a fundamental breakdown in the operation of civic administration.

It could be argued that one of the reasons for instability in the town body politic was the growing interaction between the urban and national political systems, and with this the importation of conflict from outside.[78] The Civil War had proved that it was impossible for towns to isolate themselves from the storm raging around them, but there were also pressing reasons after the

Restoration why external power-mongers should interest themselves in urban affairs. Four-fifths of seats in the House of
Commons were situated in boroughs, so that the struggle for
control of parliament, an issue of mounting significance in seventeenth-century politics, was in part a battle for mastery over the
towns and their electorates. For this reason, and to assert their
regional power in general, aristocrats and gentry attempted to
intervene more and more in the business of towns, deploying
various tactics to meet the needs of widely varying franchises. A
sign of this involvement was the gentry's increasing enrolment as
burgesses and freemen, presence on corporations and engagement with the social life of the town.[79] This trend, however,
should not convey the impression either that a gentry takeover of
urban life was under way, or that towns were passive or reluctant
parties in this process. There were powerful economic, social and
political benefits for towns, and especially their élites, in courting
and catering to the local squirearchy. Moreover, towns were quite
willing to pursue their own interests, even where these clashed
with those of the neighbouring rural hierarchy; and were perfectly capable of generating internal factional and party conflict
without gentry encouragement.[80]

One potentially destabilizing factor in urban politics after the
Restoration was the interplay between crown and town. It was a
relationship that neither party could afford to ignore, and one in
which civic authorities – given the power of the monarchy and its
centrality to urban interests – were generally inclined to display
compliance and loyalty. At various points in their reigns, Charles
II and his brother were to intervene directly in town politics, especially through the device of *quo warranto* proceedings, by which
charters – the formal bases of authority in incorporated towns –
were called in and re-issued in a new form which empowered the
crown to remodel the ruling body's membership. In the 1680s
this could lead to a version of musical chairs, as first under
Charles Dissenters were ruthlessly purged and replaced by loyal
Tory Anglicans, before in the final years of James's reign the latter
were themselves booted out in favour of Nonconformists.[81] Not
too much should be made of the impact of royal policy. By a
mixture of pragmatism and local obstruction it was possible to
avoid, delay or mitigate the disruptive effects of central intervention.[82] One reason for this is that it does not now appear, despite
the earlier arguments of historians such as Sacret and Western,
that the monarchy – at least under Charles – was engaged in a

concerted policy of extending its control over urban government along the lines of an absolutist state. By and large, it was accepted that local administration was the responsibility of local men. The crown's principal concern was to ensure that towns remained politically reliable and did not become seed-beds of rebellion. Hence the King focused his attention on cities of prime strategic importance, particularly London, and only intervened extensively during moments of acute political crisis.[83] Moreover, it seems that when royal 'interference' occurred it did so invariably with a measure of local support, a faction within the town encouraging and sometimes pressurizing the government to take action.[84]

One of the hallmarks of urban politics in this period was the continuity in the underlying agenda between the 1640s and 1650s, and the late seventeenth century. Persistence was also a feature of cultural life in the Restoration town. There is a natural tendency to portray post-Reformation England, and particularly the years after 1660 when the Scientific Revolution fully matured, as an increasingly rational and de-ritualized society. Yet in exploring the late Stuart town one is struck by the extent to which ceremony, and what may be broadly categorized as symbolic behaviour and artefacts, filled the streets and public spaces.[85] Civic life relied heavily upon such forms, as can be seen in the elaborate mayor-making ceremonies mounted by cities such as London and Norwich,[86] the erection – and dismantling as the monarchy's fortunes fluctuated – of statuary, the welcoming of dignitaries to towns and the celebration of national events. Street politics was permeated by rituals of dress, language, association, action and timing, which might manifest themselves in 'riots' or processions – such as the pope-burning processions staged by the Whigs in London during the Exclusion crisis.[87] Urban popular recreations would also have been suffused with ritualized features, and although by the later seventeenth century educated and fashionable society was withdrawing from the world of magic and witchcraft, it would be dangerous to assume that this was also the case for ordinary townspeople.[88]

Cultural continuity there certainly was, but the Restoration town also displayed plenty of evidence of change. Levels of literacy were rising throughout the country in the seventeenth century and urban rates seem to have been particularly high. Around two-thirds of adult males in later Stuart Bristol were able to sign their names, and probably a similar proportion in Gloucester. For women the rates were significantly lower, although in London the proportion (amongst court witnesses) rose from 34 per cent before 1640 to over 60 per cent by 1680 and after. The capacity to read, if this is what the presence of signatures indicates, gave those who possessed it access to the expanding world of printed literature, shaping and structuring attitudes, for example, to politics and religion, which may have encouraged a greater consciousness of national issues.[89] Civic culture was not, and never had been, a static phenomenon.[90] The Midsummer Show at Chester, which had lapsed during the Civil War period, was revived in 1662 and was again abandoned in 1678; and there may have been a general trend away from a public ritual based upon the traditional seasonal and Christian calendars, towards less integrative, more privatized and politicized modes of celebration.[91] In London, popular pastimes were also evolving continuously, becoming more commercialized, professionalized, urbanized, literate and politically orientated.[92] Transformation was even more evident in the sphere of fashionable leisure, where a new world of polite urban culture was being forged to service the social and aesthetic aspirations of the upper and middling groups. The capital and its West End pioneered developments, with a re-invigorated Restoration theatre, novel forms of music making, and proliferating walks, pleasure gardens, coffee-houses, taverns, clubs and societies – all reflecting a more public, sociable and commercialized approach to the provision of élite pastimes.[93] The growth of polite leisure raised the attractiveness and prestige of the town, which had been badly damaged by the physical and cultural losses of the Reformation. However, it probably had only a limited impact on provincial centres by the late 1680s.[94] The golden age of the fashionable spa and county town was only just beginning to dawn. Moreover, despite the appeal of metropolitan and cosmopolitan taste, provincial towns retained a powerful sense of their own civic identity, traditions and history.[95]

What impact did the growth of fashionable leisure in towns have upon urban *mentalités*? Two possible consequences deserve to be explored. First, it has been argued that a long-term effect was to accelerate the evolution of separate élite and popular cultures. As polite pastimes developed in towns, so well-to-do citizens withdrew – for reasons of status and snobbery – from traditional customs and recreations which had been participated in by all, leaving these activities to become the sole preserve of ordinary townspeople.[96] However, it is also contended that rising literacy rates and the commercialization of leisure *widened* access to

fashionable taste and undermined its exclusivity; that townspeople
continued to be united by a common sense of civic identity; and
that where communities were divided in their beliefs it was along
religious not socio-economic lines.[97] A second possible outcome
of the town's increasing cultural sophistication was the enhance-
ment of its *urban* identity. Classical terraces, squares and public
buildings were forms of architecture specific to the town, and the
emphasis in the new polite pastimes upon their cosmopolitan,
commercialized and sociable character was more in tune with
urban than rural values. The development of public walks and
gardens might seem to undermine this process by intruding
nature into the town. But these facilities embodied very much a
townsman's view of the rural milieu, a carefully manicured and
idealized interpretation of nature, free from the muck and smells
of agriculture. Reinforcing this trend towards more urbanized
idioms were alterations in popular ceremonies, such as reducing
the vegetational features in the capital's May Day celebrations in
favour of household symbols;[98] and the development of printed
imagery – in the form of maps, views and prospects – which
encouraged a more abstract and conceptualized perception of the
town.[99] Yet it must be acknowledged that before the turn of the
century the changes discussed here were focused on London, and
were only just beginning to affect the cultural character of provincial towns.

   The introduction to this essay identified three key themes for
investigation: the chronology and nature of change, the impact
of London, and urban identity. What conclusions on these issues
can be drawn from our survey of demography, economy, society,
environment, politics, religion and culture? A strong impression
emerges of the Restoration town being at a point of transition
between different urban regimes; still looking backwards to the
mixed years of the Tudor and early Stuart era, but also forwards
to the buoyant eighteenth century. On the one hand, the trends
towards urbanization and rapid metropolitan growth, discernible
since the sixteenth century, continued to be evident; high mortality levels and fire remained endemic problems; the economic and
physical effects of the Civil War were not easily shaken off and its
political and religious legacy was to dominate and embitter relations within the community; and ritual and ceremony maintained
their central role in cultural life. On the other hand, urban demographic growth now took on a new significance amidst a stagnat-
ing national population and the general demise of urbanization

in Europe; a number of provincial towns were displaying dynamic growth that foreshadowed the shake-up in the urban system associated with the Industrial Revolution; a new economic prosperity brought with it some amelioration of the perennial problem of poverty, as well as stimulating the numerical growth, prosperity and influence of middling townspeople; and the first signs of an urban building revolution were discernible, as was the emergence of a new fashionable urban culture.

The elements of change were most marked in London. Its dramatic early modern expansion scarcely slackened in the later seventeenth century, so that it came to occupy a remarkable position of primacy within the urban system and nation as a whole. Servicing its needs provided business for many towns, as well as imparting a powerful stimulus to the development of the country's economy. The size of the metropolis, and the nature of its market, ensured that it was also the principal centre of innovation – such as in the fields of architecture and leisure – pioneering ideas and fashions that would later be widely disseminated. In a sense the capital reached the zenith of its ascendancy in the later Stuart years, as its share of the national population continued to grow, and the quantitative and qualitative gap between it and other towns seemed to widen further. London's pre-eminence at this time gave a very particular character to the Restoration urban world. During the eighteenth century – and the origins of this process, as we have seen, are clearly discernible before 1700 – provincial towns reasserted themselves and restored a certain balance and shape to the urban system.

No one can doubt London's credentials as an urban entity. But it could be argued that the capital was by modern standards the only true city in England, and that its very urban character highlighted the weak claims of provincial centres to be considered genuine towns. Most were very tiny settlements and operated economies – and perhaps social systems – that dovetailed closely with their surrounding rural region. Industry was no marker of a town, as became the case in the nineteenth century, but was distributed widely throughout the countryside. However, the economies of village and town (even the smallest) were different; complementary certainly, but not the same. The urban political structure was generally a little and in some cases a lot more sophisticated, and urban politics more dynamic. The social structure was more varied in towns and was characterized by an increasingly prosperous and confident middling stratum. With

high degrees of personal mobility there would be regular fertilization between urban and rural culture. But there are signs, especially with the development of fashionable architecture and
leisure, of an enhanced urban consciousness, as the town developed an increasingly positive and prestigious profile.

9. Consumption and Wealth

J. M. ELLIS

In recent decades the phenomenon of consumerism has generated an impressive amount of historical discussion and research, much of it stimulated initially by academic interest in the Industrial Revolution of the eighteenth century. As this work has continued, however, the origins of the so-called 'consumer revolution' which, some historians claim, played a vital part in stimulating industrial change have been pushed ever further back into the early modern period. There is thus a plausible connection between the rise of consumerism and the beginnings of the decisive upward movement in economic activity which occurred in Restoration England. Research appears to have vindicated the views of contemporary writers such as Defoe, who looked back on the 1670s and 1680s in particular as a period of both economic and social transformation, certainly as a period during which England's merchants and manufacturers first seized the commercial leadership of the world. However, the question of whether and to what extent this economic upsurge was reflected in rising purchasing power and rising consumer expectations among the English people as a whole has remained controversial. A 'consumer revolution' in the later seventeenth century would require not only a vast expansion in the range and quality of goods available even to those in modest circumstances but also a profound change in traditional attitudes and values. The aim of this chapter is to examine whether such a transformation actually took place in the decades between 1660 and 1688.

I

Few would dispute that overseas trade played a vital role in the expansion of both wealth and consumption in Restoration England; although the idea of a 'consumer revolution' remains controversial, it is generally accepted that the 1670s and 1680s were key decades in a 'commercial revolution' which prepared the way for England's subsequent domination of international trade. It should be stressed, however, that this revolution rested for the most part on well-established foundations. The marked revival of trade in the later 1660s, a revival which was to last, with occasional setbacks, until the 1690s, owed a great deal to the resumption of trends which were already evident before the Restoration but which had been impeded by decades of internal and external strife. The sluggish growth of traditional overseas markets for English exports, which were overwhelmingly dependent on sales of woollen cloth, and consequent anxieties about the economy's ability to sustain a growing population had led, in the sixteenth and early seventeenth centuries, to determined attempts to open up new markets and diversify into new products. The stronger presence of English merchants in the Baltic in the Restoration era and their increased penetration of the Mediterranean thus represented the logical outcome of a long period of unobtrusive endeavour on the part of both individual traders and trading companies; although successful, it could not really be described as revolutionary.

To some extent the same might be said of the growth of English trade in North America and the Indies, since there too the successful expansion of the 1670s and 1680s was the culmination of more than a century of overseas exploration. Colonies had been urgently promoted in the early years of the seventeenth century as a means both of relieving population pressure at home and of improving the prospects of those left behind by providing a new outlet for English goods. These aspirations were brought nearer to fulfilment by the fresh burst of colonization that was initiated by the acquisition of the Carolinas in 1663 and by the accompanying rapid economic development of existing colonies, but they depended ultimately on England's ability to keep the benefits of the colonial trade to itself. In this respect the Navigation Acts, first introduced in 1651 and re-enacted after the Restoration, made a crucial contribution. In their most developed form they specified that all significant colonial exports and most of their imports had to be shipped through English or colonial ports, and carried in English or colonial ships manned by mainly English or colonial crews. When combined with further provisions restricting the import of European goods into England to English ships or those of the exporting country, the regulations struck a devastating blow against the Dutch carrying trade and gave English merchants a powerful incentive to exploit their near-monopoly of these lucrative markets by investing in larger ships and more valuable cargoes. The impact of these developments was direct and immediate. By 1685 England had acquired the largest merchant fleet in Europe and the produce of the whole world – of northern and southern Europe, of the Levant, of the Americas and of the East and West Indies – now poured into English ports, above all into the port of London. It was in these decades that London emerged not simply as the fourth largest city in the world but as 'a kind of *Emporium* for the whole Earth'.[1] By the end of the century it is estimated that just over a third of English imports came from Asia, the West Indies or North America, while the value of the re-export trade in these goods to other European ports had risen to nearly £3 million, representing 31 per cent of all exports. The scale of this commercial revolution can be measured by the fact that shipments of woollen cloth, England's traditional staple, now constituted less than half of total exports, even though the value and quantity of woollen exports had continued to grow. An astonishing transformation had taken place in the nature of both the import and the export trade, a change that was largely accomplished between 1660 and 1689.

One of the most significant results of the expansion and extension of England's trade was a vast increase in its international power and reputation: by the early eighteenth century it had become almost a commonplace that '*It is Trade* has made you Great, Strong, [and] Terrible Abroad'.[2] Concurrently, and not coincidentally, this general acceptance that trade – particularly overseas trade – was vital for the nation's prosperity began to enhance the image and status of the merchants on whose capital and enterprise this prosperity ultimately rested. The hostile stereotypes of Restoration comedy never disappeared completely, but they gradually gave way to more favourable portrayals that emphasized the merchants' positive qualities as 'a species of gentry that ... are as honourable and almost as useful as you landed folk, that have always thought yourselves so much above us'. One commentator in 1700 went even further, asserting that 'The merit of the Merchant is above all other Subjects'.[3] This novel perception of the value of the commercial world must have been strengthened by the dramatic impact of the foreign and colonial trades on the domestic market, an impact that was marked by the introduction of new ranges of imported foodstuffs, raw materials and manufactured goods, often at greatly reduced prices since vigorous demand tended to stimulate equally vigorous efforts by overseas producers to expand production. Tobacco imports, for instance, rose from 50 000 lb a year in 1615 to nearly 34 000 000 lb in 1700, while domestic consumption is estimated to have risen by the 1690s to 2 lb per person per year. The price had slumped, as it had to a lesser extent for sugar; the retail price of sugar halved between 1630 and 1680, contributing to a four-fold increase in per capita consumption. Imports of lightweight and gaily coloured East India Company calicoes and chintzes, to take another example, rose from a very low base of less than 10 000 pieces a year in the 1630s to a peak of 1 250 000 pieces in the 1680s, representing nearly 14 yards of cloth for every man, woman and child in the country.[4] Coffee from Arabia, tea from China, spices and exotic pain-killers from the Orient, madeira wine from Portugal, raisins, figs and oranges from Spain, olive oil from Italy, dyestuffs, mohair, raw silk and cotton from Asia Minor, linens from Holland and Germany, manufactured silks from France, Italy and later India – the flow of imports was beginning to transform the appearance, diet and even the health of large sections of the English population.

The novelty of many of these imported goods and the sheer romance of their far-flung origins should not, however, obscure the substantial contribution made by home-produced goods and services to the transformation of English life. The inland trade was certainly a much less spectacular agent of change and did not occupy as much of the attention of contemporary commentators as overseas trade but, together with agriculture, it remained the bedrock of the national economy. Although the Restoration era is not generally recognized as a period of significant progress in industrial enterprise and expansion, the achievements of these decades, in terms of the growth of output, the increased range and variety of goods produced and a significant shift in the techniques used in production, in fact appear all the more remarkable in the light of the political and economic dislocation of the 1640s and the effects of a serious trade depression between 1658 and 1663. The result brought England closer to the ultimate goal of industrial self-sufficiency. Whereas at the beginning of the seventeenth century there was a wide range of manufactures which were obtained almost exclusively from abroad, if only in small quantities, by the 1690s English manufacturers had squeezed most foreign competition out of the home market. This admirably mercantilist agenda in itself depended partly on imports of both raw materials and expertise; a steep rise in the volume of industrial raw materials was a notable feature of England's import trade in the last thirty or forty years of the century, while the influx of over 50 000 Continental immigrants made a significant contribution to industrial growth by launching new manufactures and assisting established industries to increase the diversity of their products. Huguenot refugees, for instance, were instrumental in promoting the manufacture of porcelain and fine glass, of precision instruments, clocks and watches, and of white paper, fine silk, high-quality linen and printed calicoes.

It would be a mistake, however, to exaggerate the role of immigrant craftsmen and entrepreneurs and to overlook the many wholly or largely indigenous innovations that contributed to the industrial expansion of Restoration England. English manufacturers responded to the challenge of imported goods with ingenuity and inventiveness, qualities particularly evident among Norwich weavers, whose light worsted cloth was made and marketed in an ever-expanding range of patterns and styles: contemporary sources list a bewildering variety of cloths, including (among many others) castillianoes, cheynes, calamancoes, crapes, camlets, curlderoys, damasks, druggets, ferrandines, jollyboys, grograins, piccadillies, prunellas, russells, satins, says and tammies, all except the crape representing local variations on well-established fabrics.[5] Imported raw materials sometimes played a part in this continuing process of diversification, as in the case of the Lancashire fustian manufacturers, who began to blend eastern Mediterranean or West Indian cotton with their original Irish or German linen yarns. Imported dyestuffs were equally valuable: the keen interest taken by the Royal Society in developing new cloth dyes was a recognition of their potential benefit to what was still England's staple industry. In some of its branches technical advances in the manufacturing process itself were also instrumental. The introduction of Dutch engine looms in the 1660s, for instance, and their grouping into workshops added greatly to the cheapness and popularity of Manchester tapes and ribbons, and proved crucial at much the same time in increasing the output of silk-throwing workers of Spitalfields and Canterbury. Meanwhile, in the north and east Midlands the rapid spread of the new stocking frame meant that knitted worsted stockings could be produced in large quantities, and hence cheaply, for the first time. In other sectors of industry, too, considerable progress was made through technical advances, such as the successful development of the reverberatory furnace which permitted the use of coal to smelt lead, tin, copper and brass, though not as yet iron. The subsequent expansion of the metal industries, as well as that of the glass and salt industries which had already adapted to coal, led in turn to additional demand for the new fuel and thus to investment in the complex and expensive technology that was necessary to win coal from deeper seams and from pits that lay at ever-increasing distances from navigable water. Local pride in the achievements of the north-eastern coalfield in particular was soon to lead its inhabitants to claim that the spreading waggonway networks 'a small part of the whole Coal Works, may Vie with some of the great Works of the Roman Empire'.[6] But it would be a mistake to read the priorities of the Industrial Revolution back into Restoration England. Much more characteristic of industrial developments in this period were the apparently minor but significant innovations in the operations of the new sugar refineries or 'houses' of Liverpool, Bristol and Glasgow, of the great new breweries in Southwark, of the tobacco-processing works in Bristol, London and Liverpool, and of the saw mills in London and the other east coast ports handling imported Norwegian softwoods for use in the expanding construction industry.

Contemporary improvements in agricultural production, on the other hand, are today generally accepted as part of the 'agricultural revolution', a long-term process beginning in the 1650s and continuing well into the eighteenth century. Restoration England benefitted first and foremost from the sheer luck of a succession of good harvests in 1667–72, acknowledged as a period of 'a bounty perhaps unprecedented in English history', and especially in 1683–90.[7] Dramatic increases in the yields of wheat and scarcely less marked improvements in those of rye, oats and barley filled the barns of the eastern counties to bursting point and added to the prosperity of the ports of King's Lynn and Great Yarmouth as they flowed out not simply to Britain's expanding urban markets but also, from the 1670s, to new sources of demand in Germany and the Netherlands. Such bounty, of course, presented arable farmers with a new set of problems, since high yields led inexorably to low prices, but in the expansive climate of Restoration England enterprising farmers with ready access to buoyant markets had little difficulty in responding to the pressure. Increased specialization, for instance, was encouraged by the scale and variety of London's demand for foodstuffs: Gloucestershire, Warwickshire, Wiltshire and Cheshire provided its cheese and Suffolk, Yorkshire and Essex its butter; its livestock markets were supplied by graziers based in the Essex and Kent marshes, while its fruit and vegetable markets drew on orchards and market gardens all over the southern counties. Similar developments, although on a smaller scale, were observed around the major provincial towns, particularly Norwich and Bristol. Agricultural specialization on this scale, however successful, depended in its turn on the widespread application of new farming techniques, a process that was encouraged not only by the Royal Society's agricultural and horticultural committee but also by a host of enthusiastic pamphleteers. Arable farmers relied mainly on better fertilization: lime, seaweed, ashes, soot and human dung were all pressed into service, but the most effective method of all was for farmers to raise and maintain more livestock to increase the amount of manure that they could plough back into the soil. Floating watermeadows and improved rotations involving clover, sainfoin and new root crops – above all, turnips – made a major contribution here, encouraging the move to mixed farming which, for many farmers, proved to be the key to continued prosperity in an age of low prices. It was also the key to the central role played by meat and butter in English cooking in this period: by the 1690s the astonishment expressed by European visitors at the sheer quantities involved was already becoming a commonplace.[8]

Essential for the growth of regional specialization in both agricultural and industrial production was an equally marked improvement in transport and communications. Such changes were a necessary condition of the emergence of a national market that would increase the effective supply of goods to potential purchasers by bringing them within their reach, and it was therefore crucial to the growth of consumption that internal as well as overseas commerce flourished in the later seventeenth century. Without an upsurge in inland trade, London's continued expansion would have been brought to a shuddering halt and, as has been implied in the discussion of agricultural change, London's apparently insatiable appetite for food, fuel and manufactured goods played a key role in extending and deepening trading links throughout the country. Moreover, in the later seventeenth century the growing markets of the larger provincial towns also began to exercise a significant influence, helping to cover the country with a web of wholesale and retail networks that was sufficiently coherent and flexible to supply customers with growing quantities of an expanding range of both imported and home-produced goods. Coastal shipping continued to play a vital role in these networks, particularly in its capacity to move bulky goods such as coal, timber and grain at relatively low cost. It was also instrumental in distributing mixed cargoes of imported groceries, wine and cloth from the major ports of entry: William Stout, for instance, shipped goods to the value of £200 all the way round the coast from London to Lancaster in 1688 to stock his new shop.[9] From the coastal towns the goods then entered England's extensive river network, the contribution of which to the prosperity of inland regions was so evident that the Restoration era witnessed a proliferation of schemes designed to extend and improve river navigation. The financial and legal difficulties faced by such projects meant that many remained purely theoretical, but sufficient progress was made by 1700 to double the 500 miles or so of naturally navigable waterways that had been in use a century earlier. Improved roads and better bridges also had their parts to play. The dynamism of the Restoration economy led to a large upturn in the volume of traffic using the often primitive roads and tracks which had been sufficient in earlier periods. More and more farmers acquired heavy waggons to transport their produce to market, more and more carriers established regular services linking London and the larger provincial centres with the smaller market towns, and more and more packhorses trotted precariously over wooden bridges that were often little more than single planks laid across the stream. The maintenance of roads was the responsibility of the parish, and local resentment at the mounting cost of repairing the wear and tear caused by long-distance travellers meant that in 1663 provision was made for tolls to be levied on a very heavily used stretch of the Great North Road, setting a precedent which was to result after 1696 in a steady expansion of similar 'turnpike' schemes. The most effective improvements before this date resulted mainly from the steady accretion of minor local initiatives: increasing numbers of waymarkers, causeways and stone bridges helped to facilitate the flow of goods through even the roughest and most desolate parts of the country.[10]

The greater volume of traffic carried by road, river and coastal transport in the later seventeenth century serviced an increasingly sophisticated system of inland trade. Although old-style open markets and fairs continued to play an important role in the supply of goods to consumers in all parts of the country, their activities were now complemented by those of a multitude of middlemen, factors and wholesalers of all kinds, who were themselves seconded by thousands of respectable chapmen, traders and carriers – both short- and long-distance – and by hosts of hawkers, pedlars and petty chapmen. Such chapmen, even those who travelled on foot carrying a pack, could offer their customers a surprisingly large quantity and wide variety of goods: Spufford suggests that they may have been moving about £100 000 worth of goods about the country at any one time. They certainly attracted a great deal of hostile comment from more established traders, who were equally alarmed by the spread of permanent specialized retail shops into the smallest provincial market towns. Their anguished complaints that 'in every country village where is (it may be) not above ten houses, there is a shopkeeper' almost certainly overstated the case but the basic point that retail outlets were multiplying at a bewildering rate is substantiated by a growing body of detailed local studies.[11] Such shopkeepers had little difficulty in filling their shelves: they could obtain their stocks indirectly through wholesalers in London and the major provincial centres, they could place their orders directly with the manufacturers (as William Stout did by calling in at Sheffield on his way home from London), or they could buy in small quantities from travelling dealers, such as the 'Manchester men' who specialized in the wide range of cotton goods for which Manchester was already renowned. Their customers could also choose between a surprisingly wide range of potential suppliers when they wished to make a purchase, depending basically on how far they were able or willing to travel to get what they wanted.

II

By the end of the century, therefore, it does indeed seem that Defoe was justified in claiming that 'all the manufactures of *England*, and most of them also of foreign countries, ... are to be bought, as it were, at every body's door'.[12] What is more, every piece of direct evidence which has survived from the later seventeenth century suggests that these goods were indeed being bought in ever larger quantities: paintings and engravings, plays, poems and pamphlets, inventories and accounts, and surviving examples of the goods themselves, all indicate the arrival and gradual extension of a richer and more varied consumer culture. Diets changed as people gained access to a wider range of food-stuffs. The scale of English demand for meat and butter has already been noted, but the rapid increase in per capita consumption of sugar and fruit is equally indicative of the long-term trend to greater variety and rising quality which was established in these decades. Vast quantities of prunes, figs, currants, raisins, lemons and oranges were imported every year and dispatched to grocers' shops up and down the country: William Stout reckoned that one such shop in Lancaster sold a hundredweight of prunes a week during the summer months.[13] Imports were also instrumental in extending the range of drinks available to the consumer. Even expensive novelties such as tea, coffee and chocolate were becoming increasingly popular in the later years of the century, especially in London, and by the 1690s were beginning to move out of specialized coffee houses into consumers' own homes.

These homes themselves were changing markedly in the later seventeenth century, both outwardly in terms of design and construction and inwardly in terms of layout, furnishings and fittings. It is now recognized that this was the period in which more permanent housing in the form of sturdy, three-roomed cottages spread to the lower levels of society, so that husbandmen and labourers had at least some expectation that their houses would outlast the winter storms without crumbling or blowing away. At higher social levels too, the built environment was being transformed by the use of more expensive, more durable building materials, which were now more widely available through the domestic market, and by the fashion for classical architecture and design. Very few houses in this period needed to be rebuilt completely to achieve the desired effect: Nottingham, for example, was being reconstructed as a model of contemporary good taste by what a contemporary described as 'this Dance of building new Fronts' on to existing properties.[14] Within such houses the accommodation itself was being gradually remodelled and refurnished to meet rising standards of privacy and comfort. The use of lighter and more colourful fabrics in wall-hangings, bed-clothes, curtains and upholstery, for instance, could transform the appearance of a room, as Pepys found in 1663 when he accompanied his wife to a shop in Cornhill 'and after many tryalls bought ... a Chinke [i.e. chintz]; that is, a paynted Indian Callico for to line her new Study, which is very pretty'.[15] Mirrors and larger-paned sash windows helped to create an impression of light and space within the home, while the new amenities of domestic life were often as decorative as they were practical. Changes in eating habits, for example, filled shelves and cupboards with growing quantities of pewter, copper, tin, glass, silver and earthenware utensils and, in London at least, imported blue and white china was becoming more readily available. Furniture, which was more durable and less easily replaced, perhaps changed less dramatically, but it too was becoming lighter and more varied as well as more plentiful: cane chairs and oval tables, produced by specialist cabinet-makers, represented new standards of domestic comfort and elegance.

It was also in the Restoration period that the quality and variety of English clothing began to attract favourable comment from foreign observers. In the first place people seem to have bought more clothes: Londoners of the 'middling sort' would typically own at least three complete outfits at any one time and would renew them regularly, along with the vast array of buckles, buttons, hats, wigs, ribbons, lace and other accessories that went with them. Moreover, the clothes themselves had become more diverse and colourful with the growing popularity of lighter, brightly coloured fabrics, often in floral or geometrical patterns. What was much less visible but equally important to people's comfort and general sense of well-being was the availability of simple shirts, shifts and underclothes on a scale never seen before. This 'great reclothing' may not have been very spectacular, but its cumulative impact on both society and the economy should not be underestimated.

Explanations of these changes have in the past tended to rely on a fairly simple association between the increased availability of goods and rising incomes among potential purchasers. In the upper levels of society, growing consumption has thus been linked in general terms to the buoyancy of the Restoration economy and in particular to the profits generated by overseas trade and agricultural improvement; it has been taken for granted that these profits would stimulate increased consumer demand. Further down the social scale the emphasis has been more on rising real incomes as a result of the higher money wages paid during these decades of demographic recession, combined with the fact that the prices of many commodities, especially those of basic foodstuffs, had fallen to the lowest levels in living memory. Real wage indices point to the 1680s as the best whole decade of the seventeenth century, and even better conditions were experienced, albeit briefly, in the early 1690s, allowing the bulk of the population to raise their standards of living.[16]

However, this uncomplicated and optimistic scenario has been challenged by sceptics who question whether the apparent prosperity of Restoration England was in fact sufficient to support a significant increase in consumer demand. The profits of overseas trade, for instance, may have enriched a relatively small group of mainly London-based merchants at the expense of other sectors of the domestic economy which were starved of capital by the vast sums tied up in shipping luxury goods from distant lands and promptly re-exporting them. It can indeed be argued that the scale of the re-export trade in itself bears witness to the relative weakness of the domestic market for prime consumer goods. Nine-tenths of the pepper, two-thirds of the tobacco and most of the coffee imported into England in the decades after the Restoration went straight into the re-export trade, while in 1678 imports of less than 5000 lb of tea were said to have completely glutted the London market. The connection between overseas trade and rising consumption should not, therefore, be taken for granted. Nor should it be assumed without question that years of falling farm prices would automatically feed through into increased demand. On the contrary, farmers trying to earn a living in regions without ready access to expanding urban markets were bound to struggle, as were those who simply lacked the capital, expertise or initiative to adapt to changing conditions. Far from increasing their own levels of consumption, farmers were thus more likely to weaken the overall growth of demand, impoverishing their landlords by failing to pay their rents and doing their best to reduce labour costs to an absolute minimum. Farm labourers, even though they benefitted from cheap grain, may well have had to pay a high price in terms of under-employment and resistance to demands for higher wages.

Pessimists who doubt the existence of anything remotely resembling a mass market for consumer goods in this period point out that the improvement in real wages outlined above was not only very modest but also fell a long way short of winning back the massive erosion experienced in the 'long sixteenth century' when price inflation reduced wage-earners' spending power to less than half of its fifteenth-century level.[17] Given the conventional assumption that as much as 80 per cent of an average budget was devoted to basic foodstuffs, mostly bread, while fuel took up nearly half of the remainder, it seems very unlikely that even those few labouring families in regular work could have had much surplus spending power. And below these fortunate few came the vast numbers of unemployed and under-employed cottagers and paupers who constituted a rapidly increasing burden on both public and private charity in this period. Can a 'consumer society' really be said to exist when between a quarter and a half of the entire population were chronically below what contemporaries regarded as the official poverty line? It is important, therefore, to treat with caution contemporary reports that 'the mean Mechanics and Husband-men, want not Silver Spoons, and some Silver Cups in their Houses' or that 'the master cannot [now-adays] be known from the servant except it be because the servant wears better clothes than his master'.[18] Grossly exaggerated state-ments of this kind have served throughout the ages to express the anxieties of social conservatives rather than to represent reality, and they should be set against other, apparently contradictory, claims that workers paid unusually high wages were more likely to translate their gains into increased leisure than to purchase silver cups or an extensive wardrobe. Complaints that 'when the frame-work knitters or makers of silk stockings had a great price for their work, they have been observed seldom to work on Mondays and Tuesdays but to spend most of their time at the ale-house or nine-pins' are often accepted at face value by otherwise sceptical historians because the 'leisure preference' that they describe seems to represent a natural and indeed rational reaction to pre-vailing economic conditions.[19] In the grim world presented by the pessimists, in which the bulk of the population had no realistic chance of achieving a permanent improvement in their standards of domestic comfort, there would be little incentive to maximize their earnings once they had satisfied their minimum needs. To paraphrase Adam Smith, it was better to play for nothing than to work for nothing.

This gloomy vision of a world perched perilously close to the barest margins of subsistence serves a valuable purpose in warning us not to exaggerate either the depth or the extent of the con-sumer market in Restoration England. Recent studies of material culture have drawn attention to the relatively slow diffusion of some goods after their introduction into fashionable society and to significant regional differences in the pace of this diffusion. Tea, for example, had been available in London since the 1650s but was only gaining wider acceptance among the middling ranks of metropolitan society in the 1690s. Tea- and coffee-making equipment did not start to appear in their homes on a regular basis until the reign of Queen Anne. China, pictures, clocks and easy chairs were also rare outside aristocratic households in the late seventeenth century, and here again it was the years between 1705 and 1710 which have been identified by both Earle and Weatherill as the turning-point in their infiltration into middle-class homes. The process of diffusion was also noticeably faster in London and in regions with close economic links with the capital than it was elsewhere. The pattern which emerges is to some extent predictable, in that substantial regional differences might be expected in a country with such a complex pattern of distinctive economic and social landscapes. It is not therefore surprising that the diffusion of consumer goods tended to be slower in areas of the country which experienced relatively little agricultural change and were furthest from the most buoyant markets; Cumbria and the north-west Midlands are two such examples. In other cases, however, it is by no means obvious that the slow take-up of china, cutlery and curtains was simply the result of economic isolation. Weatherill found that the middling orders in Hampshire, for instance, showed a marked reluctance to buy decorative goods and yet spent quite freely on expensive furniture and on lavish entertainment of their families and friends. Their 'failure' to conform to the new patterns of consumption probably reflects the survival of more traditional attitudes and values in their local society rather than any lack of purchasing power.

Historians should not, therefore, be too ready to accept that rising consumption follows automatically from rising wealth and thus to assume that the relatively slow growth of the market for novel consumer goods in Restoration England necessarily reflected the relative poverty of potential consumers. Despite the capital demands of overseas trade and the patchy implementation of agricultural improvements, there is overwhelming evidence that the disposable incomes of practically every sector of society were in fact noticeably higher than they had been in the earlier years of the century. The incomes of the great nobility were protected from the effects of lower agricultural prices by a combination of vigorous estate management and astute exploitation of their favoured position at court and in the lucrative marriage market. Lesser landowners had fewer alternative sources of income and may well have suffered more from the rent famine of these years, but the gentry as a whole remained wealthy and influential: Gregory King estimated that in 1688 the baronets and gentry had a collective income of £5 million.[20] Below the ranks of the gentry came the broad middling bands of urban and rural society, who were manifestly more prosperous in 1688 than they had been in 1660 and, in the towns in particular, had also grown more numerous. The 'middling sort' are notoriously difficult to define. At the highest level they mingled imperceptibly with the lower ranks of the landed gentry or even, in the case of the great London merchants, with the nobility itself. Earle's study of the capital's 'middle class', for example, identifies a number of merchant princes worth £10 000 or more and, while the average wealth of his sample varied between £500 and £5000, its median value was £2000. On that basis he calculates that the average disposable income of a middle-class household in London would have been £300 a year, while smaller shopkeepers and traders survived on incomes of between £50 and £100. Weatherill's much broader definition of the middling sort incorporates many of these less wealthy social and occupational groups: in fact, she argues that about half the households in the country should be included within this category. Given that she also argues that an income of at least £40 a year was needed to support a 'middling' lifestyle, her conclusions seem to confirm the pessimistic view so often taken about the lower orders' ability to participate in the consumer economy. The incomes of both rural and urban labourers fell far below this threshold and would surely not stretch beyond the immediate necessities of life. Nevertheless, both Thirsk and Spufford have demonstrated the existence of a substantial new market among the labouring classes in the later seventeenth century for a whole range of consumer goods, from earthenware dishes and brass cooking pots to knitted stockings and linen sheets. They may not have been buying looking glasses or expensive tableware, but this did not mean that they were wholly excluded from the new world of material comfort.

This apparent paradox can be explained partly by the fact that many consumer goods were becoming significantly cheaper in this period. Some of this reduction can be attributed to the impact of changing fashions. To give one example, the lighter materials that were gradually replacing heavier woollen fabrics in both clothing and furnishings were much less expensive as well as much more fashionable. However, this was clearly only part of the story, since the prices of practically all textiles, including high-quality woollens, were falling simultaneously, as were the prices

of a wide range of other manufactured goods. If this reduction
had occurred at the expense of the workforce their purchasing
power would have suffered accordingly, but it is equally possible
that it resulted from the improvements in industrial organization
and production methods outlined earlier in this chapter. John
Cary, a Bristol merchant, was certainly convinced that a virtuous
circle had been created whereby 'New projections are every day
set on foot to render the making our Manufactures easie, which
are made cheap by the Heads of the Manufacturers, not by falling
the Price of poor Peoples Labour'.[21] The manufacturers' ingenuity benefitted poorer consumers in other ways as well. If we look
again at the example of textiles, it is very noticeable that potential
purchasers could choose not merely between an immense range
of fabrics but also between many different qualities of the same
fabric. Woollen broadcloth could cost as much as 10s. 6d. a yard
or as little as 5s.; the range in silk was even wider, from 50s. a yard
for gold or silver brocade to 1s. 6d. for the cheapest Indian satin.
The price of clothing in particular was further reduced by the
rapid development in this period of the ready-made clothes industry. Richer consumers continued to buy their own fabrics and
have them made up to their own specifications, a much more
expensive option, but ready-made clothing allowed a substantial
deepening of the market for manufactured goods. Clothing and
household linens also spread down the social scale through the
operations of an equally vigorous trade in second-hand goods.
This was a society in which possessions were never taken for
granted and very little was wasted: consumer goods were simply
too valuable to throw away when they could be repaired, remodelled, handed down the generations and finally, if all else failed,
sold to help pay for their replacement. Reconstructions of household economies convey a strong impression of careful management rather than extravagant spending, even among the
prosperous middle classes.

A combination of thrift and shrewd purchasing could thus
explain many of the consumer goods which Thirsk and Spufford
found within the homes of 'the poorer sort' in Restoration
England. This hypothesis, of course, still challenges the conventional assumption that wage-labourers lived in a state of chronic
poverty and deprivation, because it presumes that their incomes
could stretch beyond the basic necessities of food and shelter.
However, it is by no means certain that this conventional assumption can stand up to rigorous examination. Shammas and De

Vries both argue that the percentage of labourers' incomes that
was spent on bread has been grossly exaggerated; it may have
rarely exceeded 20 per cent. The extent of the 'great impoverish-
ment' of the sixteenth century has also been questioned, as has
the percentage of the population who were dependent on some
form of relief: one recent study suggests that the rate of 'poverty'
defined on this basis was nearer 15 than 50 per cent.[22] But whatever the outcome of this debate, it may prove surprisingly irrel-
evant to the question of how far the lower orders of Restoration
England were able to contribute to the growing demand for consumer goods. Evidence is accumulating that the links between
consumption and wealth were not as obvious and straightforward
as might be assumed, and that absolute levels of wealth were not
the main determinant of the propensity to consume. Both Earle
and Weatherill, for example, demonstrate that many shopkeepers
and traders spent more on fashionable consumer goods than
their wealthier neighbours, while De Vries points to the seemingly
irrational behaviour of Friesian peasants, whose rate of consumption increased in the later seventeenth century despite a sharp
reduction in their incomes. He argues that what underlay these
apparent anomalies was a profound change in social attitudes and
values, a change which induced growing numbers of people to
devote an increasing proportion of their resources to purchasing
material goods. Where this change affected the lower orders, they
responded by attempting to maximize their purchasing power in
a number of ways, principally by working harder for longer
periods of time in activities producing a money income. This
'industrious revolution' therefore led not only to increased consumption but also to increased production, as men, women and
children exploited themselves to satisfy their newly acquired consumer tastes. Although 'idleness' continued to dominate the
works of political economists, many of the labouring poor were
working harder than they had ever done before.

But what lay behind this change in social attitudes? Why were
material goods now valued so much more highly that people were
prepared to make considerable sacrifices to purchase them? At
the lower levels of society the sheer utility of inexpensive sheets,
underclothes and cooking pots seems to provide an obvious
answer. However, the consumer impulse becomes much more
difficult to explain once these basic standards of comfort
have been satisfied. Clever marketing on the part of merchants
and manufacturers clearly played some part in stimulating a

continued demand: Norwich weavers, for instance, deliberately varied the patterns, styles and names of their fabrics to 'comply with the buyers' fancy' and East India merchants advised their suppliers in Surat and Madras to do the same.[23] But these tactics presupposed that their customers were already highly sophisticated consumers, more sensitive to fashion than to quality or value for money, and they do not in themselves explain how this sensitivity arose. Historians are understandably inclined to gloss over this complex issue and to take refuge in the all-embracing concept of emulation. The new standards of domestic comfort and of taste thus tend to be ascribed to the influence of France on the Restoration court, from whence they are assumed to have trickled down the social order, helped on their way by the pervasive influence of London. This model of diffusion through social emulation can be abundantly documented from contemporary sources. Most commentators seem to have assumed without question that the bulk of the population, from aspiring London merchants to presumptuous domestic servants, was consumed not only with a fierce competitive desire to outshine their neighbours but also with a burning ambition to be assimilated into the world of their social superiors. The nobility and gentry, faced with this constant pressure from below, were forced to raise their own levels of consumption to keep ahead of the chase and thus to assert their continued superiority. This model of the creation and diffusion of consumer demand to some extent matches the actual distribution of goods revealed by the analysis of probate inventories and household accounts. Weatherill, however, is not at all convinced that the prevailing emphasis on emulation and public display can account for the full complexity of consumer behaviour in this or any other period. Moreover, it should be remembered that contemporary commentators were rarely disinterested social observers and that their emphasis on emulation probably reveals more about their own sense of insecurity than about the motives and desires of ordinary consumers.

Contemporary prejudices also have to be taken into account when considering the suggestion that women played a key role in both initiating and sustaining the growing market for consumer goods. The identification of women with consumption may well represent nothing more than a reworking of the traditional misogynist stereotype of female vanity, frivolity and extravagance, but it is surely significant that the identification remained so strong. Restoration comedy relentlessly satirized the 'naughty town-woman' whose insatiable pursuit of fashion was all too often accompanied by an equally insatiable appetite for adultery: Lady Fidget's assertion in Wycherley's infamous china scene that 'we women of quality never think we have china enough' encapsulates this conventional association between sex and shopping.[24] Virtuous women remained busy in their own homes rather than gadding about spending their husband's money, and when they did go shopping they were expected to put their husband's wishes before their own. On the other hand, given that so much consumer spending was directed towards foodstuffs, furnishings and household equipment generally, matters which were central to women's traditional domestic responsibilities, it seems logical to suppose that they exerted considerable influence on purchasing decisions. In the case of families caught up in the 'industrious revolution', their influence may have been even greater, since without their labour and that of their children the family would not have been able to consume at all.

It is hard to avoid the conclusion that many contemporary commentators would have looked upon the collapse of the consumer market as an unalloyed blessing. The growth of consumption was profoundly unsettling to the prevailing social, moral and economic order. At best, it represented hedonistic extravagance in a form that threatened both the health and wealth of large sections of the population, and at worst it posed a fundamental threat to the nation's moral integrity. Thus even conspicuous consumption by the aristocracy could arouse anxiety, particularly since so much of their expenditure was directed towards the purchase of 'superfluous' imported foodstuffs and clothing. Economic writers, with only a few exceptions, roundly condemned the export of bullion to the East Indies to pay for flimsy silks and cottons, and from the 1670s they drew particular attention to the adverse balance of trade with France. It was the improvident consumption of the lower orders, however, that drew their fiercest fire. Defoe inveighed against these 'fatal excesses', this 'general vice of the times' which threatened not only social disintegration but economic ruin, as honest labourers and upright tradesmen abandoned the habits of industry and frugality which defined their place in the social order and ruined themselves in a vain attempt to ape their betters.[25] This conflation of practical and moral anxieties lay at the heart of contemporary writing on consumerism, and was central to the concept of 'luxury' as a vice which threatened both the individual and the nation as a whole. The new consumer

goods were thought to be intrinsically less valuable, less worth-
while, than those that they replaced, because they were, on the
whole, so much less robust. Their association with exotic heathen
or hostile Popish countries was also held against them. They were
even blamed by medical writers for the worrying spread of wasting
diseases and nervous disorders in the later seventeenth century,
diseases that were significantly termed 'consumptions'. To many
contemporary observers it seemed that only the rapid introduction and strict enforcement of sumptuary legislation designed to
curb this excessive consumption could preserve England's new-
found prosperity and power.

III

Yet it is clear that these critics had an uneasy feeling that their
strictures came too late, and that the growth of the consumer
market had passed the point at which it could be reined in by
legislation. Bishop Berkeley, for example, complained that 'ever
since the luxurious Reign of King *Charles* the second, we have
been doing Violence to our Natures, and are by this Time so
much altered for the worse, that it is to be feared, the very same
Dispositions that make [sumptuary laws] necessary, will for ever
hinder them from being enacted or put in Execution'.[26] Modern
researchers have reached much the same conclusion, although
without the sense of moral outrage. Certainly, the term 'consumer
revolution' is inappropriate for the years between 1660 and 1688:
the extension of the market to a point at which the bulk of the
population could be said to be active and regular consumers of a
wide range of non-essential goods was a protracted and broadly
based process which still had a long way to go at the turn of the
century. What can be said, however, is that the economic and
social changes taking place in Restoration England had created
the conditions in which such an extension could take place.

10. International Relations, War and the Armed Forces

J. D. DAVIES

I Influences on policy

European statesmen of the second half of the seventeenth century conducted their relationships with one another in an ever-changing and uncertain environment. The 'turning points' and 'trends' so often identified by modern historians were often difficult or impossible to detect at the time. Rumours based on inadequate or obsolete information could alter perceptions of other states' actions; unexpected births, marriages, deaths or political upheavals could transform a state's attitudes towards the European scene, or other states' attitudes towards it. In these circumstances, it was difficult for any state or monarch to construct a long-term foreign policy based on fixed principles. These considerations affected Restoration Britain to a particularly marked extent. The Restoration itself, so rapid and unexpected from the viewpoints of almost all the courts of Europe, seemed to be further proof of the chronic political instability which had blighted the British kingdoms since 1640, and it immediately raised the question of the nature of the foreign policy which the new regime might pursue. The record of successive governments since the 1620s seemed to offer few clues. Over those four decades, British involvement in European politics had alternated between essentially isolationist (intentionally so in the 1630s, enforced in the 1640s) and erratically interventionist – disastrously so in the 1620s under James I and the Duke of Buckingham, but with dramatic effect in the 1650s, when the governments of the Commonwealth and Protectorate had aggressively deployed naval and land forces in a manner which both scared and impressed many European governments. Spanish treasure fleets and Caribbean islands had been captured,

Mediterranean corsair strongholds destroyed, and Dunkirk acquired after a successful campaign in alliance with France.[1] For the first time in well over a century, Britain seemed to have become indisputably a European power of the first rank.

Viewed from the perspective of the restored court at Whitehall, Britain's main concerns inevitably would focus on her nearest and most powerful neighbours, France, Spain and the United Provinces of the Netherlands. In 1661, at the age of twenty-three, Louis XIV took on the government of France himself following the death of Cardinal Mazarin; in the same year, an appallingly sickly heir was finally born to the prematurely aged Philip IV of Spain. The ramifications of these two events were to affect many of the foreign policies of Charles and James over three decades. Louis's determination to strengthen France after the internal upheavals of the Frondes (1648–53) and the strains imposed by many years of warfare manifested itself in many aspects of his rule – for example, in the mercantilist economic policies of his *surintendant des finances* Jean-Baptiste Colbert – and, above all, in a quest to give France more naturally defensible borders in the north and east, achieving the King's ambition for '*la gloire*' in the process. The terminal failure of the Spanish Habsburg dynasty had a direct bearing on Louis's actions: Spain's inability to pay the dowry for his bride, the Infanta Maria Theresa, invalidated her renunciation of her claim to the Spanish throne in the marriage treaty (or so Louis's lawyers claimed), and provided the pretext both for the French attempt to annex parts of the Spanish Netherlands in the so-called 'war of devolution' (1667–8) and for subsequent claims to the Spanish inheritance on behalf of Louis's children and grandchildren. In fact, following his accession in 1665, Carlos II of Spain confounded medical and diplomatic opinion by surviving for another 35 years, but his constant ill-health ensured that the Spanish succession was an ever-present preoccupation of European statesmen. So, too, was the increasingly apparent weakness of the state that he ruled. The structural weaknesses of the Spanish economy had been apparent even in the 'golden age' under Philip II (1556–98), and these were exacerbated by the fact that Spain had been at war constantly since 1621. As a result, by the 1660s she no longer possessed the resources even to reconquer her rebellious province of Portugal, at a time when she had abandoned her long-running wars against France and the United Provinces. Although historians have debated the extent and nature of the 'decline of Spain', some phenomenon of this sort was perceived by many contemporaries: in 1664, for example, the new British ambassador to Spain, Sir Richard Fanshawe, was instructed to remind his hosts 'that the monarchy of Spain is fallen to a great declination, more especially in all maritime strength'.[2]

The restored British monarchy did not have a straightforward choice between alignment with France or Spain. Although Charles and James personally admired Louis, French strength and French culture, an admiration born both of personal contact when they had been in exile in the 1650s and of their perception of the impressive qualities of the French state after 1661, other considerations could pull them in other directions. For all its political weakness, Spain was a far more lucrative trading partner for Britain, both in its own right and in conjunction with its American colonies.[3] Indeed, concern for trade was always one of the main themes underpinning the foreign policies of Charles and James, or so they said – the first article of Fanshawe's instructions concerned freedom of trade for British merchants, and similar sentiments can be found in many other instructions to diplomats and naval commanders. On the other hand, relations with France in the early years were imperilled by Louis's alliance with the Dutch and by disputes over protocol, such as Charles's insistence on the title 'King of France' and on the right of salute supposedly due from foreign vessels to his warships: from the mid-1660s onwards France's rapid creation of a powerful navy posed a direct threat to one of Britain's most obvious sensibilities, while the prospect of a French takeover of the Spanish Netherlands raised some worrying strategic questions.[4] Complicating the matter was the question of relations with the United Provinces. Long-standing commercial antagonisms and other disputes had already caused one war between the British and the Dutch in 1652–4, and Charles II brought with him the additional dimension of a sense of injured family pride. The sudden death of his brother-in-law, William II of Orange, in 1650 had brought on a republican coup, and the new regime of urban oligarchs, drawn largely from Amsterdam and led by the Pensionary of Holland, Johan de Witt, had subsequently excluded Charles's nephew William III from the offices which had traditionally devolved upon the House of Orange since the early days of the Dutch struggle for independence from Spain. A restoration of William as a client of Britain, concurrent with the elimination of the Dutch as a trading rival, offered Charles the best of both worlds, and was to help shape his attitude towards the United Provinces for at least the first half of his reign.

The attitudes, actions and perceived status of other European states formed one set of constraints on the freedom of action of Charles and James in their foreign policies; but so, too, did the perception of those policies in the 'political nation'. Ultimately, the implementation of any major policy initiative – especially paying for a war – would depend on money being voted by Parliament, and the question of how informed or ignorant Englishmen (and especially English MPs) were of international affairs vexed both some contemporaries and many later historians. In 1676 the French envoy claimed that most Englishmen 'know nothing of general affairs', but this claim runs counter to the sheer quantity of information which was available to the educated Englishman.[5] (Admittedly, availability of information in itself is no guarantee that every 'educated Englishman' took any notice of it.) Official publications, such as the *London Gazette*, were full of foreign news, often disproportionately so in relation to their 'domestic' content. In the first half of September 1667, for instance, about three-quarters of the content of the four issues of the *Gazette* consisted of news from abroad, including items from Rome, Naples, Malaga, Venice, Vienna, Paris, Genoa, Antwerp, Hamburg, The Hague, Bruges, Leghorn and Danzig.[6] The *Gazette* was often sent into the provinces as an enclosure with newsletters or ordinary correspondence, which might sometimes pick up on the more interesting items and add further comment: in May 1673, Ralph Verney, of Claydon, Buckinghamshire, speculated at length on the prospects of the French dauphin succeeding to the Holy Roman Empire as a result of the Elector of Brandenburg's decision to ally with Louis XIV and the circulation of a rumour that the dauphin would marry the Elector of Bavaria's daughter.[7]

How far this mixture of information and speculation shaped popular British perceptions of European states remains an open question. The 'traditional' interpretation of an abiding popular hostility to the nation's 'natural enemies' of Catholic Spain and France has been modified by the work of Stephen Pincus, who has argued persuasively that the consistent element in popular ideology (and the attitudes of many politicians) was opposition to whichever state seemed closest to achieving a 'universal monarchy' entailing political, economic and military domination of the European continent and the wider world. Until the 1630s at least, it was easiest to cast Spain, with its global empire and apparent strategy to destroy European Protestantism, in this role; from the 1650s into the 1660s, it seemed as though the mantle was settling on the Dutch, with their seemingly blatant ambition to control world trade; whereas from the mid-1660s onwards, following Louis XIV's spectacular successes in his early campaigns, the charge of seeking 'universal monarchy' could be pinned most readily on France. This change also restored the religious dimension which had been less prominent in the Dutch wars, especially when Louis embarked on a ferocious persecution of his Protestant subjects; indeed, J. F. Bosher has claimed that fear of Louis's expansionism and aggressive Catholicism was well-founded, rather than a product of unjustified paranoia.[8] For Charles and James to embark on policies which ran counter to these deep-rooted popular perceptions would be a dangerous course to take, a fact which they certainly recognized: when planning the secret alliance with France in 1670, which was to lead to their joint attack on the United Provinces in 1672, Charles showed himself acutely conscious of Parliament's likely hostility to such a project, believing it would vote money only if and when it thought the war was won.[9]

II The making of policy

Foreign policy was an undoubted preserve of kings. Like their cousin, Louis XIV, Charles and James exercised personal control in this sphere, although their involvement was less consistent and committed than the French King's – neither corresponded as regularly with their diplomats abroad as Louis did, for example.[10] Even though it has been argued that Charles was inexperienced in the early years of his reign, making several diplomatic errors, and that he retained what Professor Haley has called an 'incurable naïvety in dealing with European affairs' until the end of his life, it is also the case that his years of exile gave the King a sense of self-confidence born of his direct personal knowledge of foreign states and foreign languages.[11] Thereafter, Charles regularly had long, private conversations with foreign diplomats, and the French ambassador in particular was often used as a covert channel of communication to Louis when subsidies were being sought or initiatives proposed. Charles's informal methods are the crux of the problem which confronts any student of his foreign policy. His penchant for making policy personally and secretly,

often following several strategies simultaneously and lying (or at
least being 'economical with the truth') to ministers or ambassadors, makes it difficult to fathom his real attitudes. At best, such
methods made Charles appear inconsistent and unpredictable, to
both contemporaries and historians alike; at worst, he could seem
to be duplicitous and entirely untrustworthy.[12]

At a ministerial level, the key figures involved in giving advice,
corresponding with diplomats abroad, and implementing royal
policy decisions, were the two Secretaries of State. One handled
the Northern Department, which included responsibility for relations with the United Provinces, the Holy Roman Empire and
Scandinavia; and the other the more prestigious Southern
Department, which covered France, Spain and Portugal. The
exact role of the Secretaries of State depended heavily on the
political importance of the holders of the office. Henry Bennet,
later Earl of Arlington, established himself as one of the most
important ministers of the 1660s and early 1670s, but others, such
as Sir Leoline Jenkins or Lords Conway and Preston in the 1680s,
lacked an independent political power base.[13] Even so, the period
1660–88 as a whole saw a succession of Secretaries of State whose
actual diplomatic experience was significantly greater than that of
their predecessors and even of their eighteenth-century succes-
sors.[14] Other ministers, and some courtiers, were drawn into the
realm of foreign policy on an *ad hoc* basis. Holders of other great
offices of state could play a significant part in the making of
policy, depending on their personal inclinations and the King's
willingness: this was the case with Lord Chancellor Clarendon in
the early 1660s and Lord Treasurer Danby in the 1670s. The
formal body for the discussion of international issues was the Privy
Council's Committee for Foreign Affairs, although in practice its
remit also extended to aspects of domestic policy and it was soon
being termed the 'Cabinet Council'. At a meeting on 22 October
1668, for example, the committee was attended by the Duke of
York, Prince Rupert, the Lord Keeper (Sir Orlando Bridgeman),
the Duke of Ormonde, and the two Secretaries of State. They discussed several aspects of Spanish and Portuguese affairs, relations
with Sweden and the despatch of the Earl of Carlisle as ambassador to that kingdom, and the Venetian ambassador's request for
British assistance in their Candian campaign; the instructions for
Gabriel Silvius, going on a diplomatic mission to various German
courts, were read and approved, as were several letters from
Sir William Temple, ambassador in the Netherlands.[15]

Ultimately, Britain's relations with other powers were conducted by her diplomats, who were supposed to provide the King and his ministers with the intelligence that they needed for effective decision-making. In practice, Britain's diplomatic corps compared unfavourably with those of her European rivals, especially France. Permanent embassies were maintained only in France, Spain, Portugal and the United Provinces, and at Hamburg and Constantinople. The sheer expense of sustaining a resident ambassador ensured that only the last of these, which was paid for by the Turkey Company rather than by the state, was manned permanently by a diplomat of that rank – even the vital French embassy was often left in the hands of a lowly *chargé d'affaires*, and a period of retrenchment, such as the early 1680s, saw a general downgrading of ranks, with less costly envoys and agents replacing more expensive ambassadors.[16] Many states only saw British diplomats occasionally, when shifts of policy gave them a higher priority from the perspective of Whitehall. Only two missions were sent to Poland, no British diplomat went to Russia after 1669, and representation in the Italian states and even in Sweden was provided only on an infrequent basis.[17] Although the King and the Secretaries of State had other sources of information (notably consuls, who technically served merchant interests rather than those of the state), the variable nature of the representation at foreign courts inevitably led to variable intelligence being received. Diplomats relied too often on second-hand 'news', or else on unreliable informers, and their other task of propagating the British perspective in their country of residence could be blighted by communication problems. In August and September 1673, the only news that the British diplomats at Paris and the French public at large had received of the controversial naval battle off the Texel came from Dutch letters, some of them routed via Strasbourg, partly because the mail from London had been inexplicably delayed.[18]

Conversely, of course, European diplomats at the courts of Charles and James helped to shape their masters' perceptions of British policy. Their easy access to the monarch ensured that the despatches of, for example, the French and Venetian ambassadors were generally full and well-informed. In addition to the embassies that were resident in the capital, London also witnessed the occasional arrival of more exotic delegations, which provided rare points of contact with the wider world: in the first half of 1682 alone, extraordinary embassies came to England from Savoy,

Russia, Morocco and Bantam in the East Indies, becoming the focus of much public interest.[19] However, several foreign diplomats had a more influential role than that dictated by protocol and their formal duties. The prevalence of faction at court, and the peculiar importance of parliament, gave foreign diplomats opportunities for direct intervention in domestic politics. Policies which ran counter to the interests of their state could be undermined by cultivating a particular faction, by distributing judicious bribes among MPs, or even by covertly encouraging violent rebellion (as the Spanish attempted to do with republican plots in the 1660s). During 1672–4, the Dutch had particular success in building up a bloc of parliamentary opposition to the Anglo-French alliance; thereafter, William of Orange (who had been appointed to his family's traditional offices in 1672) maintained a more-or-less constant interest among certain British ministers and parliamentarians. Similarly, French diplomats strove to build up friendly parties at court and in the House of Commons, particularly from 1674 onwards, when both the chief minister, Danby, and a majority of MPs, seemed hostile to French interests. The objectives and activities of these interventions have been discussed by several historians,[20] but the very fact that they took place at all reveals something of Britain's true position among the European powers. With the exception of the United Provinces, which displayed similar characteristics of political instability and also had a volatile representative institution (the States-General), British political life seemed to be uniquely factious and unstable, particularly when the inconstant and untrustworthy nature of King Charles II was also taken into account. Adopting a consistent policy towards the British kingdoms, or expecting Britain to adopt a consistent foreign policy in return, was wishful thinking for European statesmen.

III   The armed forces

Given its all-too-apparent weaknesses, Britain could bring few potential 'trump cards' into play in its relations with other states: it was even sadly deficient in the traditional bargaining ploy of the weaker state, lacking a plentiful supply of readily marriageable princes and princesses. Alliance with Britain might possibly bring some trading benefits, but the comparatively limited financial resources of the British crown (which were largely dependent, in

any case, on the vagaries of parliamentary supply) militated
against the sorts of level of subsidy which Louis XIV's France
could provide to any of its allies. In fact, Britain's great strength in
international relations was a façade of military and above all naval
might, stemming from the formidable reputation acquired by the
republic's armed forces before 1660. When Charles was restored,
he inherited an army of about 40 000 men, with a large garrison
ensconced on the continent in the newly acquired fortress of
Dunkirk, and a navy of over 130 warships, larger in tonnage than
the two fleets of France and the United Provinces put together.
Both armed forces had grown in size during the 1640s and 1650s
to guard the insecure, illegitimate regimes of those years against
domestic and foreign enemies, but their very size and nature presented Charles with immediate problems in 1660.[21] The sheer
expense of the armed forces had effectively bankrupted the governments of the late 1650s, and had been one of the key factors in
bringing about their downfall and the return of the monarchy.
This fact, and the questionable political loyalty of a large part of
the army in particular, ensured that an early priority of the
restored monarchy was a massive demobilization. By 1661 the professional army had been reduced to 3500 men, and a substantial
part of the navy had been laid up.[22]

For much of Charles II's reign, the army was not a particularly
significant factor in domestic or international politics, although
perceptions and misperceptions of it often were. Even by 1685, it
comprised only about 9000 men in England, largely in garrisons
such as Charles's new Royal Citadel at Plymouth or else in the
Guards regiments, with another 7500 men in the Irish army and a
mere 2000 in the Scots (this at a time when Louis XIV had about
100 000 troops and even Denmark-Norway had 30 000).[23] Wars
and emergencies led to an expansion, as in the second (1664–7)
and third (1672–4) Anglo-Dutch wars and in 1677–9, but even in
these circumstances, any expansion of the army, no matter how
short-lived, brought forth a torrent of parliamentary and popular
criticism, which centred on the belief that a standing army was a
sure sign of a trend towards absolute monarchy.[24] Britons seeking
a military career were often forced to serve in foreign armies: in
the 1670s many, including the future Duke of Marlborough,
joined the French service, to the extent that almost a third of the
French infantry at the battle of Entzheim (1674) consisted of
British troops. Other opportunities for service existed in the
1660s in the British regiments fighting with the Portuguese

against Spain, and in the 1670s and 1680s in particular in the 'Anglo-Dutch brigade', a curious legacy of Elizabeth I's original alliance of 1585 with the United Provinces. Technically, the three English and three Scots regiments which formed the brigade were part of the Dutch army, but they could be recalled to Britain in an emergency, as happened during the Duke of Monmouth's rebellion in 1685; in this way, they provided the crown with a useful reserve of about 3000 veterans.[25] James VII & II's reign saw a transformation of the size and nature of the army. Ostensibly as a result of the woeful inadequacy of the traditional reserve force, the militia, during the Monmouth rebellion, James steadily increased the size of the standing army to a strength of over 30 000 men by 1688. This unprecedented expansion, together with the obvious favour which the King displayed towards his Catholic co-religionists in appointments to commands, was one of the major causes of growing opposition to James within the 'political nation'; but ironically, it was a conspiracy in the army itself, among officers politically committed to William of Orange (some of them former officers of the Anglo-Dutch brigade, which James had again recalled), which did more to topple the King in 1688.[26]

If the army was always politically contentious, the navy was more commonly seen as the truly 'British' defence of the nation – indeed, it was in Charles II's reign that the image of 'Britannia' first came to the fore. In peacetime, the operational navy usually consisted of about thirty to forty vessels deployed primarily to protect trade in home waters, the Atlantic and the Mediterranean, with larger fleets only going to sea during times of crisis. Despite its political credibility relative to the army, the nature of the navy was not an entirely uncontroversial issue. It was comfortably the largest spending department of the state (as well as being the country's largest industry, centred on the dockyards along the Thames, the Medway and at Portsmouth), so that parliamentary or Treasury-inspired pressure on public spending inevitably targeted the navy at an early stage. Moreover, the direct personal interest which Charles and James took in the service, an interest ranging across all aspects from ship design to the appointment of officers, made the navy suspect in the eyes of those who believed that the royal brothers were surreptitiously trying to create an absolute monarchy.[27] One consequence of these misgivings, and perhaps also of a complacency born of the massive scale of naval building under the Commonwealth and Protectorate, was that the navy rapidly lost the European

pre-eminence that it had possessed in 1660. During the 1660s
Britain was comprehensively out-built by the Dutch and French,
the latter building 83 vessels of *c.* 85 000 tons in the second half
of the decade alone; in all, between 1660 and 1675 Britain built
50 warships, the Dutch 98 and the French 150, an imbalance that
relegated Charles's navy firmly to third place in Europe.[28] Only a
huge programme of new construction in the 1670s, albeit one
voted through only reluctantly by a suspicious Parliament, helped
to redress the situation, putting the navy on a par with France
and well ahead of the Dutch by 1680.[29]

Despite its relative decline in the 1660s, then, the navy
remained an impressive fighting force. Its veteran officer corps, a
legacy of the Commonwealth, was purged less drastically than that
of the army, although a substantial proportion of royalist 'gentlemen officers' was introduced immediately and grew progressively
larger in the 1670s and 1680s as the older generation died out. At
the commissioned officer level, at least, naval service was made
more popular by the significant royal patronage of the service. A
series of reforms, largely directed at the officers and often introduced under the auspices of the leading naval administrator
Samuel Pepys, attempted to improve the efficiency of the
service.[30] Following precedents established in the 1650s, the navy
in peacetime maintained a permanent and effective system of
convoys and Mediterranean squadrons, the latter attempting to
prevent attacks on British merchant shipping from the Barbary
regencies of North Africa.[31] Despite all of these positive achievements, however, the Restoration navy carried with it a great deal
of historical baggage. Folk-memories of the Spanish Armada,
together with more recent recollections of Robert Blake's tri-
umphs in the 1650s and the victories over the Dutch in 1652–4,
led both British and European monarchs and statesmen to believe
that Charles II's navy was a potential war-winning machine.
Unfortunately for Charles, his naval commanders, and admiring
potential allies, the world had changed. Most significantly, according to the research of Brian Tunstall and Jan Glete, the new naval
tactic of fighting in a single line ahead, rather than in a free-for-all
(which the British had introduced with dramatic effect in the first
Anglo-Dutch war) would only work decisively if the other side did
not also organize itself into a line. In fact, by the mid-1660s the
Dutch in particular had adopted the line-of-battle as a tactic themselves: 'when everyone had learned the trick, a century of largely
indecisive naval conflicts followed'.[32]

IV   Policy in practice

1660–7

Charles II's early diplomatic moves reflected uncertainty in his dealings with both Spain and France. Although Cromwell's war against Spain was quickly brought to an end, relations remained strained (no formal treaty was agreed, and Britain refused to return conquered Spanish territory) and sporadic fighting continued in the colonies throughout the 1660s. Attempts to obtain an alliance with France foundered on matters of protocol and on Louis XIV's refusal to abandon the Dutch, although the expensive Cromwellian acquisition, Dunkirk, was successfully sold to the French in 1662. Seemingly the most significant early move was an alliance with Portugal in 1661, an alignment which brought with it a royal bride for Charles – Catherine of Braganza – and a dowry which included Bombay and Tangier. Although Louis XIV approved of the alliance as a means of keeping Spain occupied, it turned out to be less advantageous to Britain than had been hoped. It entailed a financial and military commitment to Portugal which lasted until the end of her war of independence in 1668, while on purely commercial grounds (despite some benefit for British merchants at Lisbon) it made little sense, serving only to damage Britain's far more lucrative trades with Spain.[33] The acquisition of Tangier, much vaunted at the time as a means of creating a massive entrepot and naval base to dominate the Mediterranean, turned out to be a drain on resources – it required constant defence against its Moroccan neighbours, and despite substantial investment its harbour proved completely inadequate for the tasks intended for it.[34] To add insult to injury, Charles's marriage to Catherine proved to be childless.

During the early 1660s, tension between Britain and the United Provinces increased markedly. Many long-standing commercial disputes, centred largely on the East Indies, had not been resolved by the war of 1652–4, and new ones now emerged – notably the restored monarchy's re-enactment of the Commonwealth's Navigation Act, which barred Dutch shipping from British trade, and the activities of the newly established Royal Africa Company, which sought forcibly to challenge Dutch dominance of the Guinea trade. Significantly, the new company's membership included several leading ministers, courtiers, and merchants, along with the heir to the throne and Lord High Admiral, James,

Duke of York. By 1664 pressure from these quarters for war with the Dutch was reaching fever-pitch, although it is possible to take the view that some sought only to scare the Dutch into making concessions without actually resorting to open warfare and that, in any case, different groups and individuals had very different reasons for adopting an aggressive line. Some ministers, notably Secretary of State Bennet, saw a war policy as a means of undermining the chief minister, Clarendon, who was reluctant for conflict; James and many courtiers saw a war as a means of gaining active employment and establishing their martial reputations; veterans of the first war, such as the Lord General, the Duke of Albemarle, were convinced that they had 'unfinished business' which could be concluded easily. Several different interpretations of these disparate pressures for war have evolved. The older, purely 'commercial' interpretation of the outbreak has been challenged by Paul Seaward, who has argued that the economic complaints were largely rhetoric to justify a war for honour and prestige. This view has been challenged in turn by Stephen Pincus, who perceives a strong ideological campaign by 'Anglican-Royalist' ministers and merchants, antipathetic to the Dutch system of government and religious practice, and opposed to Dutch pretensions to 'universal monarchy' as manifested in economic conflicts which were all too real. Cavalier distaste for Dutch republicanism and Calvinism was probably the sentiment which struck most of a chord with Charles II, who was otherwise reluctant to go to war, and Dutch retaliation against the Royal Africa Company on the Guinea coast proved to be the last straw. Despite a few contrary voices raised by those merchant groups whose trade would be damaged by a Dutch war, Parliament fell into line enthusiastically. In April 1664 it voted to support a war if one should break out, and followed this in November by voting an unprecedented subsidy of £2 500 000 for the conduct of hostilities.[35]

The naval campaign of 1665 began promisingly enough, with a convincing but not decisive victory over the Dutch fleet off Lowestoft. Thereafter, Britain's military and diplomatic position deteriorated considerably. France's attitude to the conflict was ambivalent: although there were obvious advantages in the spectacle of his two main maritime rivals bleeding each other white, Louis was on relatively good terms with both of them and had treaty obligations to the Dutch. Ultimately, the latter proved to be more of a factor in Louis's diplomacy. After the failure of French mediation efforts, Louis joined the war on the Dutch side in

January 1666. So, too, did Denmark-Norway, infuriated by the disastrous British attempt to destroy the Dutch East Indies fleet in neutral Bergen harbour in August 1665. It was a measure of Charles's isolation that the only ally he could obtain during the course of the war was 'Bombing Bernard', the Prince-Bishop of Munster, whose initially successful attacks on the Dutch border did little to affect the course of events.[36] On the other hand, the French intervention indirectly affected the outcome of the first battle of the 1666 campaign. At the start of June, the British fleet was divided to counter (false) rumours of a French squadron moving into the English Channel, and Albemarle's weakened force was worsted by a larger Dutch fleet. A subsequent British victory off the North Foreland, and a successful attack on Dutch merchant shipping in the Vlie anchorage, did little to redress the overall balance of the campaign. For the second successive year, the fleet had failed to achieve its objectives of destroying the Dutch battlefleet and/or seizing the valuable Dutch merchant convoys; indeed, as I have argued elsewhere, the failure to pursue one or other of these strategic objectives consistently is one of the keys to understanding the fleet's lack of success.[37]

The failure to obtain a decisive victory over the course of two campaigns served to emphasize one of the British state's chief shortcomings in the international arena, its inability to sustain a prolonged war. Parliament believed that it had voted ample funds for the war in 1664 and was reluctant to vote more, believing that the original subsidy had been mismanaged or diverted to other ends. Whatever the truth of the matter, Charles simply did not have the money to contemplate a third full-scale naval campaign. With peace talks under way at Breda, the decision was taken to lay up the main fleet for 1667 and to rely on fortifications and defensive squadrons until the peace could be concluded. The Dutch did not respond with a similarly low-key strategy. In June, Michel de Ruyter's fleet sailed into the Thames and attacked the laid-up great ships of Charles's fleet at their moorings in the Medway, towing away one of the greatest of them all, the *Royal Charles*. This humiliation, following closely behind the great plague of 1665 and the great fire of 1666, helped to create a widespread perception of the second Anglo-Dutch war as an unmitigated disaster. The Treaty of Breda largely restored the *status quo ante bellum*, doing little or nothing to resolve the underlying causes of Anglo-Dutch tension. Moreover, the crushing of the over-confident expectations of an easy victory left a legacy which was to affect Charles's subsequent foreign policy. The failures during the war, and the mistrust engendered by the suspected mismanagement of naval operations and parliamentary subsidies, would make it difficult in future to achieve anything like the unanimity which had existed in 1664. Charles's actions in the years immediately after the war were only to exacerbate this problem.

1667–74

The years between 1667 and 1674 constitute the most controversial and complex episode in Charles II's dealings with Europe. In effect, as Jeremy Black has pointed out, the King was conducting two foreign policies simultaneously – one public, the other private.[38] The public policy was epitomized by the Triple Alliance of January 1668 between Britain, the United Provinces and Sweden, an alignment which sought ostensibly to put pressure on Louis XIV to accept a moderate settlement of the 'war of devolution' (in which his forces had gained spectacularly easy victories over the weak Spanish armies in Flanders and Franche-Comté). Although considerable doubt has been cast on Charles's sincerity in entering into this alliance, which has been presented more as a consequence of pressure from ministers anxious to placate Parliament and rebuild Britain's battered reputation abroad, there did undoubtedly remain a lingering ambivalence in the King's attitude to France at this point: the prospect of an outright French conquest of the Spanish Netherlands was genuinely alarming, especially in the light of the aggressive commercial policies and rapid naval expansion which France was undertaking by 1667–8.[39] Within months of signing the Triple Alliance, however, Charles had embarked on a series of secret negotiations with Louis, relying on Arlington, on middle-ranking courtiers such as Sir Richard Bellings and Lord Arundell of Wardour, and on correspondence with his sister, Henrietta, the duchesse d'Orleans and therefore sister-in-law to Louis XIV. These negotiations culminated in the secret Treaty of Dover (May 1670). Britain and France were to launch a joint attack on the United Provinces, at the successful conclusion of which Charles would gain several Dutch towns and William of Orange would be installed as puppet ruler of a tiny, rump state. Most remarkably of all, Charles agreed to announce his conversion to Catholicism and to begin the re-catholicization of Britain, for which he would receive a subsidy of two million *livres* from Louis and the assistance of 6000 French troops if required.[40] To conceal the true nature of this remarkable change of alignment, the Duke of Buckingham and others who were 'in the dark' about the secret treaty were sent to France to negotiate a public treaty identical to the private one in almost every detail save the catholicizing clause.

The extraordinary nature of the secret treaty has caused prolonged debate among historians. Nevertheless, it seems clear that several strands of policy came together in the Dover treaty, albeit by a tortuous route, and although some writers on the subject place greater or lesser emphasis on some of these, they are not really mutually exclusive.[41] Alliance with Louis, rather than opposition to him in the Triple Alliance, might have put Charles in a better position to influence those aspects of French policy which concerned him, especially the naval build-up; indeed, the treaty negotiations included a British attempt to obtain a moratorium on French naval construction, although this was eventually dropped because of 'the unfitness of the demand'. Ronald Hutton has argued that a French alliance might have made Britain more secure in an uncertain international climate and would have prevented Louis making a deal with the Dutch (something which was under serious negotiation in 1669). The attack on the Dutch might at once have obtained revenge for the humiliations of the second war, provided sufficient compensation for William to satisfy Charles's family honour, and finally destroyed the Dutch as trading rivals. As one of the papers which preceded the treaty observed, 'such is and ever will be the competition and emulation in trade between this and that nation, and their injustices thereupon, that the King of England can never want a sufficient ground for a quarrel with them whensoever his affairs shall be ready for it'. What appeared on paper to be the overwhelming might of a land attack by Louis's massive army and a naval onslaught by a combined Anglo-French fleet ought to have made the outcome a 'sure game' which would win over even a recalcitrant Parliament, putting Charles in a position of greater strength in his domestic dealings.[42] If it is accepted from all this that Charles was trying to open up as many attractive options as possible, the catholicizing clause remains problematic. Whether it was a blatantly disingenuous attempt to wring money out of Louis, a subtle 'hook' which Charles knew his cousin would find irresistible but which he had no intention of carrying through, or a true indication of Charles's most deeply felt sentiments (perhaps, as John Miller has suggested, the product of a short-lived burst of enthusiasm which soon faded), the fact remains that it could have little immediate bearing on events.[43] The war would begin without Charles or his kingdoms having returned to Rome, and all of the possible scenarios detailed in the Treaty of Dover, including that one, would have to await the outcome of the military and naval campaigns.

During 1671 Charles managed to engineer a sufficient number of pretexts for another Anglo-Dutch war, despite widespread popular misgivings about the French alliance. Having denounced the Dutch fleet for dishonourably failing to salute the single British yacht *Merlin*, the British began the naval campaign by dishonourably launching an unprovoked attack on the Dutch Smyrna convoy before war had been declared. However, as the campaigning season of 1672 progressed, neither the land nor the sea wars went according to plan. Although the French armies initially stormed through the United Provinces, causing the Dutch to term it the *rampjaar* (year of disasters) and allowing Louis XIV to restore the mass to Utrecht cathedral, they failed to overrun the province of Holland and the key to Dutch survival, Amsterdam, which both lay safe behind deliberately flooded farmland. De Witt's republican oligarchy was overthrown, and *in extremis* the Dutch turned once again to the House of Orange. Far from preparing to become a grateful and subservient client of Charles and Louis, William of Orange began to reorganize the resistance to the onslaught. At sea, the Dutch fleet launched a pre-emptive attack on the combined Anglo-French fleet in May as it took in stores off the Suffolk coast. The battle was indecisive, although British pride was dented by the burning of the great *Royal James* and the death aboard her of the Vice-Admiral of England, the Earl of Sandwich: bad weather and Dutch skill in keeping their main fleet and merchant convoys safe from allied attack prevented any further engagement before the end of 1672.

The following year brought further disappointments. On land, the Dutch under William regained ground as Louis withdrew forces to meet new threats in the Spanish Netherlands and Germany. At sea the Dutch again successfully thwarted the allied strategy, which had been made more complicated by the addition of a scheme to land an expeditionary force in Holland and Zeeland to open up a 'second front' and obtain the towns which Charles wanted. In the event, the partial Dutch success at the battle of the Texel/Kijkduin in August ensured that the invading army would be left stranded at Great Yarmouth, and helped to sow discord between the British and French allies over the belief that the French squadron had deliberately failed to engage.[44] Popular discontent against the French alliance and the expense of the war was already vocal and came to a head in the parliamentary sessions of 1673–4. With the ministers who had been most closely associated with the war policy, such as Arlington and Buckingham, irretrievably discredited, and with no prospect of funds being voted for a continuation of the war, Charles had no alternative other than to renege on the Treaty of Dover and to agree a separate peace with the Dutch in February 1674. The war had not only failed to achieve any of its objectives, but the easy way in which Charles seemed to have abandoned the Triple Alliance in order to get into it and then unilaterally abandoned his French allies in order to get out of it seemed to prove to both British parliamentarians and European statesmen that the King was wholly untrustworthy.

1674–88

Quite by accident, the withdrawal from the Dutch war presented Britain with an unexpected opportunity. With all the major maritime states of western Europe, France, Spain and the United Provinces still embroiled in conflict until 1679, British ships became the only secure neutral carriers, particularly in the Mediterranean, and trade benefitted accordingly. However, in terms of policy-making the dichotomy between public and private policy endured. Charles attempted on the one hand to act as a mediator in the European war, and on the other continued to angle secretly for subsidies from Louis, using as a bargaining counter the increasingly vociferous anti-French sentiment in the House of Commons. At the same time his new chief minister, the Earl of Danby, was equally prepared to channel that sentiment into an attempt to create a popular, patriotic, francophobe foreign policy which might heal the rift between King and Parliament. By 1677 Danby seemed to have succeeded to the extent that Parliament had voted money for a major expansion of the navy and Charles had been persuaded to agree to the marriage of the second-in-line to the throne, Princess Mary (the Duke of York's elder daughter), to William of Orange, who was keen to use the marriage as a lever to obtain British assistance against France.[45] Preparations were made for British re-entry into the European war in 1678, this time on the Dutch side; an army was despatched to Flanders and a substantial fleet put to sea. Although Charles seemed to enter seriously into the planning for war, the precise extent of his enthusiasm for a breach with Louis remains an open question.[46] In the event, the King's belligerence or otherwise did not need to be tested. The close conjunction of the arrival of a large subsidy from Louis and the successful progress of the peace talks at the Congress of Nijmegen removed any possibility of an Anglo-French war, and domestic political developments soon diminished the prospect of any new initiatives in foreign policy.[47]

The 'Popish Plot' of 1678 and the subsequent Exclusion Crisis of 1679–81 had important implications for Britain's position in Europe. The wave of anti-Catholic and anti-French hysteria was fuelled by revelations such as the presentation to Parliament by Charles's ambassador in Paris, Ralph Montagu, of correspondence which provided proof of the secret dealings over subsidies and helped to accelerate the downfall of Danby, who had been privy to them. The new ministers whom Charles brought into the Privy Council, the Treasury and the Admiralty in 1679 embarked on a policy of retrenchment, and this, together with the unlikelihood of the Exclusionist House of Commons of 1679–81 voting substantial sums to a King whom they no longer trusted, made major foreign policy initiatives an unlikely prospect. An alliance with Spain (1680) was regarded by many as a transparent cosmetic gesture to appease Parliament.[48] Conversely, and hardly surprisingly, European states were reluctant to contemplate an alliance with a kingdom which seemed to be degenerating once more into instability and perhaps even civil war, as the Earl of Middleton found when negotiating with the ministers of the Holy Roman Empire at Linz in 1680.[49] In the same year, Charles finally became an out-and-out client of Louis by agreeing to call no more parliaments in return for French subsidies, although he continued to try to maintain a publicly independent role by mediating in several crises of the early 1680s. Additionally, in 1683 Tangier was finally abandoned to the Moors to save the costs of its defence; but in reality the Mediterranean fleet had already effectively abandoned it long before, preferring instead to rely on renting the Spanish facilities at Gibraltar.[50] The last years of Charles II therefore saw Britain largely inactive and ineffective in European affairs, at a time when, for example, Louis XIV was extending his borders still further by the dubious legal process of *réunion* and the Turks were reaching the gates of Vienna.

The accession of the Duke of York as James VII & II in February 1685 restored something of the old ambivalence towards France. An avowed Catholic and in some respects as much of a francophile as his brother had been, it had been easy for James's critics in the Exclusion Crisis to portray him as a creature of Louis, and the subsequent history of James's exile at Saint-Germain after 1688 seemed only to give credence to this interpretation, both for contemporaries and many later historians. In fact, at times James had been more critical of Louis's policies than had Charles; in 1678, for example, he had been genuinely convinced of the desirability of war with France. During his reign he was openly critical of several aspects of French policy, such as the persecution of the Huguenots and France's treatment of his nephew's ancestral territory of Orange, and in 1688 he turned down an offer of French military and naval assistance.[51] On the other hand, he had several bones of contention with William, such as the status of the Anglo-Dutch brigade.[52] Moreover, James had to contend with an increasingly complex European situation. The Holy Roman Emperor Leopold's increased freedom of action after the repulse of the Turks from Vienna put him in a better position to challenge Louis, and he found allies in a Spain which had lost territory in the Netherlands to the *réunion* policy, and in German princes nervous of Louis's perceived ambitions in the Rhineland. The formation of the League of Augsburg by these powers in 1686 was at first regarded sceptically by William, but during 1687–8 he gradually developed a closer understanding with Leopold as a powerful anti-French coalition began to come together. Indeed, several historians now present a picture of the international scene in the mid-1680s which is almost diametrically opposed to the 'traditional' view of a dominant and expansionist France: this revisionist interpretation presents an insecure, defensive and diplomatically isolated France, surrounded by increasingly powerful opponents.[53]

Britain's position in relation to these realignments, and to the subsequent crisis of 1688 which led to war over a disputed succession to the Archbishopric of Cologne, hinged on the perceptions of Louis, William and (perhaps least importantly) James. Louis simply wanted British neutrality: a land war against the coalition and a sea war against the Dutch alone was more acceptable than having a sea war against Britain as well. On the other hand, neutrality, although probably acceptable as a bare minimum, was a less attractive scenario for William, who saw Britain's fleet in particular as a valuable addition to the coalition's resources. For his part, James entertained vague and rather naïve notions of acting as a mediator between the contending powers. James's expanded army, and a navy which had been refurbished from 1686 onwards, seemed to put him in a stronger position militarily, but this impression of strength was illusory. James conceivably could use it to maintain his neutrality but, given the strength of the rival European blocs, he could hardly use it to act independently, especially in the light of his growing domestic difficulties and the limited number of diplomatic options open to him.[54] Ironically, too, the new strength of Britain's armed forces made them even more attractive to William.

Ultimately, the relationship between the three western European powers was determined by one of the accidents of birth or death which affected all royal houses. The pregnancy of James's Queen, Mary of Modena, after almost fifteen years of marriage, threatened to remove William's wife Mary (and therefore William himself) from the immediate line of succession, and opened up the prospect of a Catholic, rather than a Protestant, successor on the British thrones. However, most recent studies concur that William's publicly expressed intention to safeguard the Protestant religion, as requested by the authors of the famous 'letter of invitation', was rather less important to him than his desire to safeguard the succession and to ensure British support for the coalition. Louis's move against Philipsburg in the Rhineland in September 1688, rather than against the United Provinces, freed William to launch a Dutch invasion carefully disguised as a crusade for Protestantism and liberty.[55] For Louis, Germany was simply more important than Britain at this point, but the prospect of William distracted and Britain neutralized by a prolonged civil war would hardly have been unattractive to the French King.[56] In the event, the prolonged civil war never happened. James's navy, stymied by a combination of conspiracy and adverse winds, failed to intercept William as he sailed down the Channel; James's army, afflicted by an even larger conspiracy, simply melted away. The victorious William revealed his true colours by effectively conniving in his inconvenient father-in-law's escape to France, by insisting on becoming King in his own right despite the prior claims of his wife Mary and sister-in-law Anne, and by immediately taking Britain into the general war against France which he had wanted for so long.

V   Conclusion

Britain's place in international affairs has become the focus of an increasing amount of research, and this has led to a drastic revision of some old orthodoxies. Particularly controversial issues, such as the causes of the Dutch wars, the Treaty of Dover, and the international context of the 1688 revolution, have been rigorously re-examined, partly by means of greater use of material from foreign archives. 'Anglocentric' interpretations which held sway through the nineteenth and early twentieth centuries have given way to a much more fluid picture, in which Britain's weaknesses and the difficulties inherent in constructing a consistent foreign policy have been stressed: it has become almost commonplace to talk of Restoration Britain as a second-class power, and it has even been claimed that Charles and James really had no effective foreign policy as such.[57] However, the pendulum has started to swing the other way. The view that many leading politicians (in the 1660s at least) *did* have a coherent ideological vision of Britain's place in Europe challenges the notion that Restoration foreign policy was purely a sequence of short-term expedients.[58] Moreover, categorizing states as 'first-class' or 'second-class' powers can be misleading. The relative importance of a state at any given time depended on many complex factors which could change rapidly and unpredictably (as was the case with France's comparative weakness in the 1680s, for example), and Britain's position was made more complex than most by her possession of a particularly powerful armed service which happened to be a great navy rather than a continental army – even the most similar European power, the United Provinces, needed to maintain a large army (84 000 men in 1678) as well as a navy. If Britain was 'second-class' because it could not afford to send out the fleet very often, it was undoubtedly 'first class' on the occasions when that fleet was at sea.

The scope and complexity of the subject of international relations makes it hard for historians to present definitive interpretations, and this problem is exacerbated by the centrality of the enigmatic personality of King Charles II. In this area of policy, more so even than in the domestic arena, the King's traits of dissimulation and secrecy make it just as difficult for historians to fathom his true intentions as it did for his contemporaries. Nevertheless, it does seem clear that both Charles and James wanted their nation to be regarded as a great player on the international stage, whether as a belligerent or a mediator; but ultimately, their lack of financial resources, the factious political system over which they presided and their own lack of consistency meant that such ambitions could be attained only fitfully. Only after 1688, and only after a drastic reorganization of many aspects of the state structure to cope with the strains of prolonged warfare, were their ambitions belatedly fulfilled.[59]

List of Abbreviations

Add. MSS	Additional Manuscripts
AgHR	*Agricultural History Review*
BIHR	*Bulletin of the Institute of Historical Research*
Bodl.	Bodleian Library, Oxford
BL	British Library
CJ	*Commons Journals*
CSPD	*Calendar of State Papers Domestic*
EHR	*English Historical Review*
EcHR	*Economic History Review*
HJ	*Historical Journal*
HLQ	*Huntington Library Quarterly*
HMC	Historical Manuscripts Commission
JBS	*Journal of British Studies*
JEH	*Journal of Ecclesiastical History*
JHI	*Journal of the History of Ideas*
NS	New Series
P & P	*Past & Present*
PRO	Public Record Office
Rawl.	Rawlinson Manuscripts, Bodleian Library
TRHS	*Transactions of the Royal Historical Society*
RO	Record Office
VCH	Victoria County History

Bibliography

1. INTRODUCTION   *Lionel K. J. Glassey*

The best textbook on the period from 1660 to 1689 is Geoffrey Holmes, *The Making of a Great Power: Late Stuart and early Georgian Britain, 1660–1722* (London, 1993), which is beautifully written and has informative appendices. B. Coward, *The Stuart Age: A History of England 1603–1714* (London, 1980) and J. R. Jones, *Country and Court: England 1658–1714* (London, 1978) are beginning to date, but they have served a generation of students well and they still provide an admirable guide to the outlines of later Stuart history.

Four brief but helpful introductions for the newcomer to the period are: K. H. D. Haley, *Politics in the Reign of Charles II* (Historical Association Studies, Oxford, 1985); R. M. Bliss, *Restoration England, 1660–1688* (Lancaster Pamphlets, London, 1985); J. Miller, *Restoration England: The Reign of Charles II* (Seminar Studies in History, London, 1985); and J. Miller, *The Glorious Revolution* (Seminar Studies in History, London, 1983). More recent are: J. Miller, *An English Absolutism? The Later Stuart Monarchy 1660–1688* (Historical Association, New Appreciations in History 30, London, 1993); and M. Mullett, *James II and English Politics 1678–1688* (Lancaster Pamphlets, London, 1994). All of these books are concise and clear. Patrick Morrah, *Restoration England* (London, 1979) does not go beyond 1666, but is pleasantly reflective, if not profound, on the early years of Charles's reign. An outstanding collection of essays, which to a considerable extent has set the agenda for the revisionist interpretations of the period, is Tim Harris, Paul Seaward and Mark Goldie (eds), *The Politics of Religion in Restoration England* (Oxford, 1990). An older but still useful collection of essays is J. R. Jones (ed.), *The Restored Monarchy, 1660–1688* (London, 1979).

The two monarchs whose reigns are covered by this volume have attracted several biographers. Charles's elusive personality and equivocal policies are differently interpreted by J. Miller, *Charles II* (London, 1991), which concentrates more on foreign than on domestic affairs; R. Hutton, *Charles II: King of England, Scotland and Ireland* (Oxford, 1989), in which the reverse is the case; and J. R. Jones, *Charles II: Royal Politician* (London, 1987), which is focused, as the title suggests, on Charles's relationships with ministers, politicians and parliaments. James has been best served by J. Miller, *James II: A Study in Kingship* (Hove, 1978; 2nd edn, London, 1989).

Four collections of documents and source material are all valuable in different ways. A. Browning (ed.), *English Historical Documents, 1660–1714* (London, 1953; 2nd edn, 1966) is wide-ranging, and contributes under a variety of headings a series of admirable short summaries of the then state of knowledge. J. P. Kenyon (ed.), *The Stuart Constitution* (Cambridge, 1966; 2nd edn, 1986) likewise contains a valuable commentary on the political and constitutional material that it prints. The revision for the second edition was extensive. The collection edited by William Myers, *Restoration and Revolution* (London, 1986) provides a well-chosen selection from the prose writings of the period. Joan Thirsk (ed.), *The Restoration* (Problems and Perspectives in History, London, 1976) combines extracts both from contemporary writers and from modern historians, and is especially strong on social and economic themes. Additionally, the enterprise of the publishers of the paperback edition of *The Diary of Samuel Pepys*, eds R. Latham and W. Matthews (11 vols, London, 1970–83) is to be warmly commended.

The available bibliographies for the period are in need of revision. Mary Freer Keeler, *Bibliography of British History: Stuart Period, 1603–1714* (2nd edn, Oxford, 1970) and W. L. Sachse, *Restoration England 1660–1689* (Cambridge, 1971) are both more than a quarter of a century old. John Morrill, *Seventeenth Century Britain, 1603–1714* (Folkestone, 1980) is a combination of bibliography and extended review article.

Finally, mention should be made of two authors who wrote in a now unfashionable genre: the comprehensive, multi-volume survey. D. Ogg, *England in the Reign of Charles II* (2 vols, Oxford, 1934; 2nd edn 1955), together with his *England in the Reigns of James II and William III* (Oxford, 1955; 2nd edn 1957) had a great influence in its time. There is more on Scotland and Ireland than the titles would suggest. And no student of the period should neglect Lord Macaulay, *History of England* (5 vols, London, 1849–65; numerous later edns, including a paperback abridgement in Penguin Books). Despite the title, this is essentially a study of James's reign and the Revolution. Macaulay was prejudiced and dogmatic, but he read widely in printed and manuscript sources at a time when libraries and archives were less well-catalogued than they are now, and his gusto makes it impossible to be bored by him. It became clear in 1988 during the commemoration of the tercentenary of the Revolution that there is a widespread view among non-specialists that Macaulay said the last word on the subject.

2.   RESTORATION POLITICAL THOUGHT   *Mark Goldie*

Several treatises of political theory written or published during the Restoration are available in modern editions. For Filmer, Halifax, Hobbes, Locke, Neville, Newcastle and Sidney, see notes 2, 19, 25, 40, 48, 58 and 66 to Chapter 2. Practically nothing from the works of the Tory mainstream is available, but see R. Eccleshall (ed.), *English Conservatism since the Restoration* (London, 1990).

For the background to Restoration political thought, see: Quentin Skinner, *The Foundations of Modern Political Thought* (2 vols, Cambridge, 1978); J. H. Burns and M. Goldie (eds), *The Cambridge History of Political Thought, 1450–1700* (Cambridge, 1991); J. P. Sommerville, *Politics and Ideology in England, 1603–1640* (London, 1986); J. G. A. Pocock (ed.), *The Varieties of*

British Political Thought, 1500–1800 (Cambridge, 1993); N. Phillipson and Q. Skinner, (eds), *Political Discourse in Early Modern Britain* (Cambridge, 1993).

There is no general treatment of the culture of Restoration kingship: on particular aspects see items mentioned in notes 11–18 to Chapter 2; see also C. Edie, 'The Popular Idea of Monarchy on the Eve of the Stuart Restoration', *HLQ,* 39 (1976) 343–73. On Filmer and patriarchalism, see: G. J. Schochet, *Patriarchalism in Political Thought* (Oxford, 1975, 1988); G. J. Schochet, 'Patriarchalism, Politics and Mass Attitudes in Stuart England', *HJ,* 12 (1969) 413–41; J. Daly, *Sir Robert Filmer and English Political Thought* (Toronto, 1979); M. J. M. Ezell, *The Patriarch's Wife* (Chapel Hill, N. C., 1987). More generally, see: J. Daly, 'The Idea of Absolute Monarchy in Seventeenth Century England', *HJ,* 21 (1978) 227–50. J. N. Figgis, *The Divine Right of Kings* (Cambridge, 1896; New York, 1965) remains a classic. On Tory and Whig historiography, see J. G. A. Pocock, *The Ancient Constitution and the Feudal Law* (Cambridge, 1957, 1987) and J. W. Gough, *Fundamental Law in English Constitutional History* (1955, 1961).

The literature on Locke is huge. Two recent books to single out are J. Tully, *An Approach to Political Philosophy: Locke in Contexts* (Cambridge, 1993) and J. Marshall, *John Locke: Resistance, Religion and Responsibility* (Cambridge, 1994). For the topics I have discussed, see especially J. Franklin, *John Locke and the Theory of Sovereignty* (Cambridge, 1978) and C. Condren, *George Lawson's 'Politica' and the English Revolution* (1989). See the bibliography in Locke, *Two Treatises of Government,* ed. M. Goldie (London, 1993).

For other Whigs, see: J. Scott, *Algernon Sidney and the English Republic, 1623–1677* (Cambridge, 1989) and *Algernon Sidney and the Restoration Crisis, 1677–1683* (Cambridge, 1991); A. C. Houston, *Algernon Sidney and the Republican Heritage in England and America* (Princeton, 1991); B. Worden, 'The Commonwealth Kidney of Algernon Sidney', *JBS,* 24 (1985) 1–40; J. W. Gough, 'James Tyrrell, Whig Historian and Friend of John Locke', *HJ,* 19 (1976) 581–610; C. Condren and A. D. Cousins, (eds), *The Political Identity of Andrew Marvell* (Aldershot, 1989); Z. Fink, *The Classical Republicans* (Evanston, 1945). More generally, see: B. Behrens, 'The Whig Theory of the Constitution in the Reign of Charles II', *Cambridge Historical Journal,* 7 (1941) 42–71; O. W. Furley, 'The Whig Exclusionists: Pamphlet Literature in the Exclusion Campaign', *Cambridge Historical Journal,* 13 (1957) 19–36.

Such is the importance of Charles I's Answer to the Nineteen Propositions that several books have paid substantial attention to its implications for the history of political thought: C. C. Weston, *English Constitutional Theory and the House of Lords, 1556–1832* (London, 1965); C. C. Weston and J. Greenberg, *Subjects and Sovereigns* (Cambridge, 1981); J. G. A. Pocock, *The Machiavellian Moment* (Princeton, 1975); M. Mendle, *Dangerous Positions: Mixed Government, the Estates of the Realm, and the 'Answer to the XIX Propositions'* (Alabama, 1985).

On the treatment of Hobbes during the Restoration, see: M. Goldie, 'The Reception of Hobbes' in Burns and Goldie (see above); D. E. C. Yale, 'Hobbes and Hale on Law, Legislation, and the Sovereign', *Cambridge Law Journal,* 31 (1972) 131–56; J. Bowle, *Hobbes and his Critics* (1951, 1969). I have not had space to consider 'interest' and 'reason of state' arguments. For a start here, see J. A. W. Gunn, *Politics and the Public Interest in the Seventeenth Century* (London, 1969).

3. POLITICS, FINANCE AND GOVERNMENT   *Lionel K. J. Glassey*

Two outstanding, up-to-date books, both designed as a general introduction to the political history of the Restoration period, are: Paul Seaward, *The Restoration, 1660–1688* (London, 1991); and Tim Harris, *Politics under the Later Stuarts* (London, 1993). Neither makes any concessions to over-simplification, yet both are lucid and informative. Their interpretations differ a little in detail, but both emphasize the continuing importance of religion in politics in the period. For the Restoration itself, R. Hutton, *The Restoration: A Political and Religious History of England and Wales, 1658–1667* (Oxford, 1985) deals both with the processes by which the monarchy was restored and with the working out of the Restoration Settlement, and is very strong on the local dimension to national politics. Paul Seaward, *The Cavalier Parliament and the Reconstruction of the Old Regime, 1661–1667* (Cambridge, 1989) has supplanted D. T. Witcombe, *Charles II and the Cavalier House of Commons, 1663–1674* (Manchester, 1966), although the latter is still valuable for the period after 1667, as is Maurice Lee, Jr, *The Cabal* (Urbana, Illinois, 1965). The trilogy by R. L. Greaves, *Deliver Us From Evil: The Radical Underground in Britain, 1660–1663* (Oxford, 1986), *Enemies Under His Feet: Radicals and Nonconformists in Britain, 1664–1677* (Stanford, California, 1990) and *Secrets of the Kingdom: British Radicals from the Popish Plot to the Revolution of 1688–1689* (Stanford, California, 1992), describes the conspiracies and insurrections of Restoration England, Scotland and Ireland in a convincing demonstration of the vulnerability of the reigns of Charles and James. The years of the Popish Plot and the Exclusion Crisis, more than any other subdivision of the period, have been reinterpreted by iconoclastic scholars to the point at which even the use of the conventional phrase 'Exclusion Crisis' has been questioned. In two books by Jonathan Scott, *Algernon Sidney and the English Republic, 1623–1677* (Cambridge, 1988) and *Algernon Sidney and the Restoration Crisis, 1677–1683* (Cambridge, 1991), the reader is provided both with a study of Sidney and with a sustained examination of the political milieu in which Sidney moved. In particular, the section headed 'Part One: The Restoration Crisis' in the second of these volumes is a challenging revision of traditional orthodoxy. Scott's views include a distrust of the concept of organized political parties and a reluctance to regard the Exclusion Bill as a central feature of the political crisis of the late 1670s and early 1680s, which he regards as more about the wider issues of 'Popery and arbitrary government' in the European as much as the British context. These interpretations are further elaborated by Scott in a number of essays, including an important reassessment of the Popish Plot in Tim Harris, Paul Seaward and Mark Goldie (eds), *The Politics of Religion in Restoration England* (Oxford, 1990). They are discussed under the collective title 'Order and Authority: Creating Party in Restoration England' in *Albion*, xxv[4] (1993), in which a group of historians including G. S. De

Krey, Tim Harris, James M. Rosenheim and R. L. Greaves, as well as Scott himself, analyse some of the issues that Scott has raised. G. S. De Krey, 'The London Whigs and the Exclusion Crisis Reconsidered', in A. L. Beier, David Cannadine and James M. Rosenheim (eds), *The First Modern Society: Essays in English History in Honour of Lawrence Stone* (Cambridge, 1989) is another valuable contribution to the debate. Mark Knights, *Politics and Opinion in Crisis, 1678–1681* (Cambridge, 1994) has combined an assessment of the differing interpretations of the politics of the late 1670s and early 1680s with a number of insights derived from his own research in a judicious and important study. The books on the Exclusion Crisis published before this wealth of new interpretation emerged include: J. R. Jones, *The First Whigs* (London, 1961), a fine achievement in its time, although its conclusions on the nature of the early Whig and Tory parties are the chief target of the revisionist school; the early chapters of J. H. Plumb, *The Growth of Political Stability in England 1675–1725* (London, 1967); R. Ashcraft, *Revolutionary Politics & Locke's* Two Treatises of Government (Princeton, New Jersey, 1986); and the three introductory studies on the reign of Charles II by K. H. D. Haley, R. M. Bliss and J. Miller, all published in 1985 and listed above in the Bibliography to Chapter 1. Another essential contribution to the history of the Exclusion Crisis is Tim Harris, *London Crowds in the Reign of Charles II: Propaganda and Politics from the Restoration until the Exclusion Crisis* (Cambridge, 1987). The Bibliography to Chapter 6 below is, of course, also relevant to the theme of politics.

The reign of James VII & II and the Revolution of 1688 was a focus of attention at the time of the tercentenary of the Revolution in 1988. The best single-volume studies of the Revolution in England are W. A. Speck, *Reluctant Revolutionaries: Englishmen and the Revolution of 1688* (Oxford, 1988) and (with a different emphasis) George Hilton Jones, *Convergent Forces: The Immediate Causes of the Revolution of 1688 in England* (Ames, Iowa, 1990). Robert Beddard, *A Kingdom without a King: The Journal of the Provisional Government in the Revolution of 1688* (Oxford, 1988) prints an important group of documents with an extended commentary. J. R. Jones, *The Revolution of 1688 in England* (London, 1972), J. R. Western, *Monarchy and Revolution: The English State in the 1680s* (London, 1972), John Carswell, *The Descent on England: A Study of the English Revolution of 1688 & its European Background* (London, 1969) and D. H. Hosford, *Nottingham, Nobles and the North: Aspects of the Revolution of 1688* (Hamden, Connecticut, 1976) retain much value. Two older books are not without interest: G. M. Trevelyan, *The English Revolution, 1688–9* (London, 1938) is a concise distillation of the nineteenth-century Whig interpretation popularized by Trevelyan's great uncle Macaulay; while Lucille Pinkham, *William III and the Respectable Revolution* (Cambridge, Massachusetts, 1954) sustains a debatable case for the view that William's ambition to be King in the British Isles went back much further than his acceptance of the invitation of June 1688. A number of collections of essays have added a good deal to our understanding of the Revolution. Robert Beddard (ed.), *The Revolutions of 1688* (Oxford, 1991); Jonathan I. Israel (ed.), *The Anglo-Dutch Moment: Essays on the Glorious Revolution and its World Impact* (Cambridge, 1991); Eveline Cruickshanks (ed.), *By Force or By Default? The Revolution of 1688–1689* (Edinburgh, 1989); Lois G. Schwoerer (ed.), *The Revolution of 1688–1689:*

Changing Perspectives (Cambridge, 1992); and J. R. Jones (ed.), *Liberty Secured? Britain Before and After 1688* (Stanford, California, 1992), contain between them more than sixty essays on many different aspects of the Revolution and its aftermath.

Some local studies are listed in notes 10 and 94 to this chapter; to these might be added P. J. Norrey, 'The Restoration Regime in Action: the Relationship between Central and Local Government in Dorset, Somerset and Wiltshire', *HJ* xxxi (1988); L. K. J. Glassey, 'The Origins of Political Parties in Late Seventeenth-century Lancashire', *Transactions of the Historic Society of Lancashire and Cheshire*, cxxxvi (1987 for 1986); and G. C. F. Forster, 'Government in Provincial England under the Later Stuarts', *TRHS*, 5th ser., xxxiii (1983).

Several of the more important politicians active in the Restoration period have been the subject of excellent biographies. Pride of place must go to K. H. D. Haley, *The First Earl of Shaftesbury* (Oxford, 1968), an exhaustive, subtle analysis of Shaftesbury's career. J. P. Kenyon, *Robert Spencer, Earl of Sunderland 1641–1702* (London, 1958) brilliantly exploited what was then newly discovered material. Two biographies of Clarendon by R. W. Harris, *Clarendon and the English Revolution* (London, 1983) and R. Ollard, *Clarendon and his Friends* (London, 1987) are competent studies of a politician who wrote so much, and whose career was so long, that he presents particular difficulties for a biographer. A. Browning, *Thomas Osborne, Earl of Danby and Duke of Leeds, 1632–1712* (3 vols, Glasgow, 1944–51) is still well worth reading on Danby's period in office as Lord Treasurer in the 1670s. However, Clifford, Arlington, Rochester and Halifax all await new studies. B. D. Henning (ed.), *The History of Parliament: The House of Commons, 1660–1690* (London, 1983) contains a biography of every member of the House of Commons in the period. Those of the principal figures are extended in length, and contain much esoteric information (there are also potted electoral histories of each constituency, plus a methodical and systematic introduction). The biographies of the Duke of Monmouth are better passed over in silence, but three studies of his rebellion are worth mentioning: Peter Earle, *Monmouth's Rebels: The Road to Sedgemoor* (1977); Robin Clifton, *The Last Popular Rebellion: The Western Rising of 1685* (London, 1984); and David Chandler, *Sedgemoor 1685: From Monmouth's Invasion to the Bloody Assizes* (2nd edn, Staplehurst, 1995).

Constitutional history has attracted much less attention than political history in recent years. Howard Nenner, *The Right to be King: The Succession to the Crown of England, 1603–1714* (London, 1995), the same author's *By Colour of Law: Legal Culture and Constitutional Politics in England, 1660–1689* (Chicago, 1977), Michael Landon, *The Triumph of the Lawyers: Their Role in English Politics, 1678–1689* (Alabama, 1970), Clayton Roberts, *The Growth of Responsible Government in Stuart England* (Cambridge, 1966) and – just outside our period but still containing much of relevance – Lois G. Schwoerer, *The Declaration of Rights, 1689* (Baltimore, 1981) are all admirable on their respective themes, but the best overview is still G. E. Aylmer, *The Struggle for the Constitution, 1603–1689* (London, 1963; 2nd edn 1968), while Mark A. Thomson, *A Constitutional History of England, 1642–1801* (London, 1938) is also helpful on particular points despite its age.

The best short introduction to government finance is Henry Roseveare, *The Financial Revolution 1660–1760* (Seminar Studies in History, London, 1991). C. D. Chandaman, *The English Public Revenue, 1660–1688* (Oxford, 1975) is a massive scholarly achievement, although it is not for the faint-hearted. Stephen B. Baxter, *The Development of the Treasury, 1660–1702* (London, 1957) and H. Roseveare, *The Treasury, 1660–1870: The Foundations of Control* (London, 1973) both deal more with the Treasury as an administrative institution than with finance. Christopher Clay, *Public Finance and Private Wealth: The Career of Sir Stephen Fox, 1627–1716* (Oxford, 1978) is both a biography of Fox and an analysis of the methods by which he rose to wealth through a combination of private speculation and public service.

Much important work on the political, administrative and financial history of the period has appeared in the form of articles in journals. It is impossible to give more than a selection here, but the following are all relevant and interesting in the treatment of their different subjects: J. Miller, 'Charles II and his Parliaments', *TRHS*, 5th ser., xxxii (1982); J. Miller, 'The Crown and the Borough Charters in the Reign of Charles II', *EHR*, c (1985); J. C. Sainty, 'A Reform in the Tenure of Offices during the reign of Charles II', *BIHR*, xli (1967); R. Willman, 'The Origins of "Whig" and "Tory" in English Political Language', *HJ*, xvii (1974); J. R. Jones, 'James II's Whig Collaborators', *HJ*, iii (1960); H. Horwitz, 'Protestant Reconciliation in the Exclusion Crisis', *JEH*, xv (1964); J. Miller, 'The Potential for Absolutism in Later Stuart England', *History*, lxix (1984); J. Childs, '1688', *History*, lxxiii (1988); and W. A. Speck, 'The Orangist Conspiracy against James II', *HJ*, xxx (1987).

4. THE TRIPLE-CROWNED ISLANDS   *Ronald Hutton*

There is no narrative history of the British Isles during the Restoration period to compare with that of Gardiner for the preceding age and that of Macaulay for the succeeding one. For general surveys the reader has to make do with the most recent textbooks upon the respective nations which cover these years, most notably T. W. Moody, F. X. Martin and F. J. Byrne (eds), *A New History of Ireland* (Oxford, 1976), volume 3, Rosalind Mitchison, *Lordship to Patronage: Scotland 1603–1745* (London, 1983), and Keith M. Brown, *Kingdom or Province? Scotland and the Regal Union* (London, 1992). A survey of how government policy was made for both kingdoms is found in Ronald Hutton, *Charles II: King of England, Scotland and Ireland* (Oxford, 1989). There is no exact equivalent for the reign of James VII & II, although useful material is found in John Kenyon, *Robert Spencer, Earl of Sunderland* (London, 1958) and John Miller, *James II* (Hove, 1978). John Miller has also provided a fine case-study of how royal policy evolved towards Ireland under this monarch, in 'The Earl of Tyrconnel and James II's Irish Policy 1685–1688', *HJ*, xx (1977) 803–23.

Otherwise, a student must piece together different studies made of themes in, or portions of, the period in one or other of the countries. J. G. Simms, *Jacobite Ireland 1685–91* (London, 1969) provides a useful overview of the island's experiences under James. The remodelling of its military forces is examined in John Childs, *The Army, James II and the Glorious Revolution* (Manchester, 1980), chapter 3. The same period is treated again by James McGuire, 'James II and Ireland', in W. A. Maguire (ed.), *Kings in Conflict* (Belfast, 1990), chapter 2. An aspect of the land settlement and of the interplay between Irish and court politics is well investigated in Jane H. Ohlmeyer, *Civil War and Restoration in the Three Stuart Kingdoms* (Cambridge, 1993). Other useful monographs covering different issues within the broad range of the subject are C. E. Pike, 'The Intrigue to Deprive the Earl of Essex of the Lord Lieutenancy of Ireland', *TRHS*, 3rd ser. v (1911) 95–103; J. I. McGuire, 'The Dublin Convention, the Protestant Community and the Emergence of an Ecclesiastical Settlement in 1660', in Art Cosgrove and J. I. McGuire (eds), *Parliament and Community* (Belfast, 1983), pp. 121–46; and Celestine Murphy, 'The Wexford Catholic Community in the Later Seventeenth Century', in R. V. Comerford, Mary Cullen, Jacqueline Hill and Colm Lennon (eds), *Religion, Conflict and Coexistence in Ireland: Essays Presented to Monsignor Patrick J. Corish* (Dublin, 1990), chapter 4.

In Scotland the making of ecclesiastical policy during two-thirds of the period is covered by Julia Buckroyd in her general survey *Church and State in Scotland 1660–1681* (Edinburgh, 1981), and her biography of its principal churchman, *The Life of James Sharp* (Edinburgh, 1987). The victims are portrayed in Ian B. Cowan, *The Scottish Covenanters* (London, 1976), and their ideology in I. M. Smart, 'The Political Ideas of the Scottish Covenanters 1638–88', *History of Political Thought*, i (1980) 167–93, and T. Brotherstone (ed.), *Covenant, Charter and Party* (Aberdeen, 1989), pp. 25–49. Allan I. Macinnes, 'Repression and Conciliation: The Highland Dimension 1660–1688', *Scottish Historical Review*, lxv (1986) 167–95, takes a much-needed look at the northern half of the country, while issues in its central politics are treated by John Patrick, 'The Origins of the Opposition to Lauderdale', *Scottish Historical Review*, liii (1974) 1–21, and Bruce P. Lenman, 'The Scottish Nobility and the Revolution of 1688–90', in Robert Beddard (ed.), *The Revolutions of 1688* (Oxford, 1991), chapter 3. Finally, a contribution to the economic history of the time is made by Eric J. Graham, 'In Defence of the Scottish Maritime Interest, 1681–1713', *Scottish Historical Review*, lxxi (1992) 88–109.

5. RELIGION IN RESTORATION ENGLAND *John Spurr*

The best account of the restoration of the Church of England is I. M. Green, *The Re-establishment of the Church of England, 1660–1663* (Oxford, 1978), which qualifies R. S. Bosher's *The Making of the Restoration Settlement 1649–62* (London, 1951), and for the political dimension P. Seaward, *The Cavalier Parliament and the Restoration of the Old Regime, 1661–1667* (Cambridge, 1989) is indispensable. J. Spurr, *The Restoration Church of England, 1646–1689* (New Haven and London, 1991), attempts to portray the church's view of itself and its mission and to synthesize much recent and unpublished work. Many insights into clerical life can be gained from J. H. Pruett, *The Parish Clergy under the Later Stuarts – The Leicestershire Experience* (Urbana, Illinois, 1978); *The Rector's Book, Clayworth*, ed. H. Gill and E. L. Guilford (Nottingham, 1910); *Bishop Fell and Nonconformity: Visitation Documents from the Oxford Diocese, 1682–3*, ed. M. Clapinson (Oxfordshire Record Society, lxii, 1980); and *The Diary of Ralph Josselin, 1616–83*, ed. A. Macfarlane (London, 1976). On the history of the Church of England, see: N. Sykes, *From Sheldon to Secker – Aspects of English Church History 1660–1768* (Cambridge, 1959); A. Whiteman (ed.), *The Compton Census of 1676: A Critical Edition* (London, 1986); R. A. Beddard, 'The Commission for Ecclesiastical Promotions, 1681–84: An Instrument of Tory Reaction', *HJ*, x (1967); and G. F. Nuttall and O. Chadwick (eds), *From Uniformity to Unity* (London, 1962). The laity's response to the church is discussed by D. A. Spaeth, 'Common Prayer? Popular Observance of the Anglican Liturgy in Restoration Wiltshire', in S. J. Wright (ed.), *Parish, Church and People – Local Studies in Lay Religion 1350–1750* (London, 1988); M. Spufford, *Contrasting Communities – English Villagers in the Sixteenth and Seventeenth Centuries* (Cambridge, 1974); J. D. Ramsbottom, 'Presbyterians and "Partial Conformity" in the Restoration Church of England', *JEH*, xliii (1992); E. Duffy, 'The Godly and the Multitude in Stuart England', *The Seventeenth Century*, i (1986); and some of the essays in T. Harris, P. Seaward and M. Goldie (eds), *The Politics of Religion in Restoration England* (Oxford, 1990).

The best introduction to Restoration Dissent is contained in M. R. Watts, *The Dissenters – From the Reformation to the French Revolution* (Oxford, 1978; paperback reprint 1985). C. E. Whiting, *Studies in English Puritanism from the Restoration to the Revolution, 1660–1688* (London, 1931; 2nd impression 1968) remains valuable. More specialized studies include: N. H. Keeble, *The Literary Culture of Nonconformity in Later Seventeenth-century England* (Leicester, 1987); J. T. Cliffe, *The Puritan Gentry Besieged, 1650–1700* (London, 1993); G. R. Cragg, *Puritanism in the Period of the Great Persecution 1660–1688* (Cambridge, 1957). The character of Dissent may best be appreciated in works such as John Bunyan's *Grace Abounding to the Chief of Sinners* (1666; Everyman paperback reprint, 1976); *The Diary of Roger Lowe*, ed. W. L. Sachse (London, 1938); or *The Autobiography of Richard Baxter*, abridged by J. M. Lloyd Thomas and edited by N. H. Keeble (London, 1974). N. H. Keeble and G. F. Nuttall have also edited a *Calendar of the Correspondence of Richard Baxter*, 2 vols (Oxford, 1991).

The political involvement of Dissent is the subject of D. R. Lacey, *Dissent and Parliamentary Politics in England 1661–1689* (New Brunswick, New Jersey, 1969), and R. L. Greaves' trilogy: *Deliver Us from Evil: The Radical Underground in Britain, 1660–1663* (Oxford, 1986), *Enemies Under His Feet: Radicals and Nonconformists in Britain, 1664–1677* (Stanford, California, 1990) and *Secrets of the Kingdom: British Radicals from the Popish Plot to the Revolution of 1688–89* (Stanford, California, 1992).

Roman Catholicism can be approached through J. Bossy, *The English Catholic Community 1570–1850* (London, 1975); J. Miller, *Popery and Politics in England 1660–1688* (Cambridge, 1973); J. A. Williams, 'English Catholicism under Charles II', *Recusant History*, vii (1963); and J. J. Hurwich, 'Dissent and Catholicism in English Society: A Study of Warwickshire, 1660–1720', *JBS*, xvi (1976).

On the many intellectual developments which impinged on religion, see: M. Hunter, *Science and Society in Restoration England* (Cambridge, 1981); S. I. Mintz, *The Hunting of Leviathan* (Cambridge, 1962); H. R. McAdoo, *The Spirit of Anglicanism* (London, 1965); L. I. Bredvold, *The Intellectual Milieu of John Dryden* (Chicago, 1934); G. R. Cragg, *From Puritanism to the Age of Reason* (Cambridge, 1950); G. Reedy, *The Bible and Reason* (Philadelphia, 1975); P. Harth, *Contexts of Dryden's Thought* (Chicago, 1968); I. Rivers, *Reason, Grace and Sentiment: A Study of the Language of Religion and Ethics in England, 1660–1780* (Cambridge, 1991).

The debate on toleration can be approached through the essays in O. P. Grell, J. I. Israel and N. Tyacke (eds), *From Persecution to Toleration – The Glorious Revolution and Religion in England* (Oxford, 1991) and in J. R. Jones (ed.), *Liberty Secured? Britain Before and After 1688* (Stanford, California, 1992).

6. THE PARTIES AND THE PEOPLE: THE PRESS, THE CROWD AND POLITICS 'OUT-OF-DOORS' IN RESTORATION ENGLAND   *Tim Harris*

The classic survey of crowd unrest in later-Stuart England, although now somewhat dated, is Max Beloff, *Public Order and Popular Disturbances, 1660–1714* (London, 1938). For a detailed analysis of propaganda and public opinion in London during the reign of Charles II, see Tim Harris, *London Crowds in the Reign of Charles II: Propaganda and Politics from the Restoration until the Exclusion Crisis* (Cambridge, 1987). The same author takes the account up to 1688 in his 'London Crowds and the Revolution of 1688', in Eveline Cruickshanks (ed.), *By Force or By Default? The Revolution of 1688* (Edinburgh, 1989). This should be read in conjunction with W. L. Sachse, 'The Mob and the Revolution of 1688', *JBS*, IV (1964) 23–41. The London pope-burnings have been covered in two brief articles by O. W. Furley, 'The Pope-burning Processions of the Late Seventeenth Century', *History*, XLIV (1959) 16–23; and Sheila Williams, 'The Pope-burning Processions of 1679–81', *Journal of the Warburg and Courtauld Institutes*, XXI (1958) 104–18. For London petitions, see the three articles by Mark Knights: 'London Petitions and Parliamentary Politics in 1679', *Parliamentary History*, XII (1993) 29–46; 'London's "Monster" Petition of 1680', *HJ*, XXXVI (1993) 39–67; 'Petitioning and the Political Theorists: John Locke, Algernon Sidney and London's "Monster" Petition of 1680', *P&P*, CXXXVIII (February 1993) 94–111. London radicalism has been covered in a series of excellent articles by Gary S. De Krey: 'The London Whigs and the Exclusion Crisis Reconsidered', in Lee Beier, David Cannadine and James Rosenheim (eds), *The First Modern Society: Essays in English History in Honour of Lawrence Stone* (Cambridge, 1989), pp. 457–82; 'London Radicals and Revolutionary Politics, 1675–1683', in Tim Harris, Paul Seaward and Mark Goldie (eds), *The Politics of Religion in Restoration England* (Oxford, 1990), pp. 133–62; 'Revolution *Redivivus*: 1688–1689 and the Radical Tradition in Seventeenth-century London Politics', in Lois G. Schwoerer (ed.), *The Revolution of 1688–1689: Changing Perspectives* (Cambridge, 1992), pp. 198–217. We still know too little about crowd politics and collective political agitation in the provinces for the Restoration period, although some useful snippets can be found in Tim Harris, *Politics under the Later Stuarts: Party Politics in a Divided Society 1660–1715* (London, 1993). Valuable insights into the political and religious upheavals in England's second and third cities can be gleaned from John T. Evans, *Seventeenth-century Norwich: Politics, Religion and Government, 1620–1690* (Oxford, 1979) and Jonathan Barry, 'The Politics of Religion in Restoration Bristol' in Harris *et al.* (eds), *Politics of Religion*, pp. 163–89. For 'Anti-Popery on the Welsh Marches in the Seventeenth Century', see the excellent article by Philip Jenkins of that title in *HJ*, XXIII (1980) 275–93; while pro-Catholic and anti-Presbyterian agitation in Wigan has been the subject of an intriguing study by Michael Mullett, '"A Receptacle for Papists and an Assilum": Catholicism and Disorder in late Seventeenth-century Wigan', *Catholic Historical Review*, LXXIII (1987) 391–407. Mark Knights's major new study, *Politics and Opinion in Crisis, 1678–81* (Cambridge, 1994), offers an important reassessment of the Exclusion Crisis, with much to say about the press and public opinion, both in London and the provinces, and certainly supplants J. R. Jones's earlier study of *The First Whigs: The Politics of the Exclusion Crisis, 1678–83* (Oxford, 1961). K. H. D. Haley's exhaustive biography of *The First Earl of Shaftesbury* (Oxford, 1968) contains a mine of information, not just about the Whig leader, but also about politics out-of-doors (including petitions and demonstrations). John Miller, *Popery and Politics in England, 1660–1688* (Cambridge, 1973), remains a useful survey of anti-Catholicism during this period. For the latest views about the place of party and the nature of public opinion in Restoration England, see the lively debate between Gary S. De Krey, Tim Harris, James Rosenheim, Richard L. Greaves and Jonathan Scott entitled 'Order and Authority: Creating Party in Restoration England', in *Albion*, XXV (1993) 565–651.

7. LANDOWNERSHIP, THE ARISTOCRACY AND THE COUNTRY GENTRY
    James M. Rosenheim

Of all the books published about landed life, relatively few specifically address the Restoration. The period provides the starting point for J. V. Beckett's thematic survey of élite life, *The Aristocracy in England 1660–1914* (Oxford, 1986) and for Sir John Habbakuk's *Marriage, Debt and the Estates System: English Landownership, 1650–1950* (Oxford, 1995), as well as the endpoint for F. Heal and C. Holmes, *The Gentry in England and Wales, 1500–1700* (London, 1994). C. Clay lays out the challenges to and accomplishments of landlords between 1640 and 1750 in 'Landlords and Estate Management', in J. Thirsk (ed.), *The Agrarian History of England and Wales*, V, pt II (Cambridge, 1985), chapter 14, and endorses the view of a general drift of property to larger owners after the 1650s. P. Roebuck follows in detail the economic history of four landed families through this period in *Yorkshire Baronets 1640–1760: Families, Estates and Fortunes* (Oxford, 1980). An indispensable account of estate-management practices and their non-economic consequences for landed society is D. R. Hainsworth's superb study, *Stewards, Lords and People: The Estate Steward and his World in Late Stuart England* (Cambridge, 1992). S. K. Roberts's examination of county governance in Devon, *Recovery and Restoration in an English County:*

Devon Local Administration 1646–1670 (Exeter, 1985), reveals the transformation that the Civil War wrought on provincial power relations. In his examination of Hampshire, *Central Government and the Localities: Hampshire 1649–1689* (Cambridge, 1987), A. M. Coleby shows the impact of centralization on provincial society, a theme implicit in A. Fletcher's survey of local government, *Reform in the Provinces: The Government of Stuart England* (New Haven and London, 1986). The first half of J. M. Rosenheim, *The Townshends of Raynham: Nobility in Transition in Restoration and Early Hanoverian England* (Middletown, Connecticut, 1989) lays out the competing claims of centre and locality in one nobleman's Restoration career. V. Stater describes the effective use of the lieutenancy as an instrument of central policy in *Noble Government: The Stuart Lord Lieutenancy and the Transformation of English Politics* (Athens, Georgia, 1994). Among a growing number of case studies of county interactions with central authorities, the more useful include D. P. Carter, 'The Lancashire Militia, 1660–1688', *Transactions of the Historic Society of Lancashire and Cheshire*, 132 (1982), 155–81; P. J. Challinor, 'Restoration and Exclusion in the County of Cheshire', *Bulletin of the John Rylands University Library of Manchester*, 64, (1982), 360–85; N. Key, 'Comprehension and the Breakdown of Consensus in Restoration Herefordshire', in T. Harris, P. Seaward and M. Goldie (eds), *The Politics of Religion in Restoration England* (Oxford, 1990), pp. 191–215; P. J. Norrey, 'The Restoration Regime in Action: The Relationship between Central and Local Government in Dorset, Somerset and Wiltshire, 1660–1678', *HJ*, 31 (1988) 789–812; H. S. Reinmuth, 'A Mysterious Dispute Demystified: Sir George Fletcher *vs.* the Howards', *HJ*, 27 (1984) 289–308; J. M. Rosenheim, 'County Governance and Elite Withdrawal in Norfolk, 1660–1720', in A. L. Beier, D. Cannadine and J. M. Rosenheim (eds), *The First Modern Society: Essays in English History in Honour of Lawrence Stone* (Cambridge, 1989), pp. 95–125; and V. Stater, 'Continuity and Change in English Provincial Politics: Robert Paston in Norfolk, 1676–1682', *Albion*, 25 (1993) 194–216.

8.   THE RESTORATION TOWN   *Peter Borsay*

Urban historians tend to work across broad rather than narrow chronologies, so there are no specific studies of the Restoration town. The best starting points are P. Clark and P. Slack's influential and admirably concise *English Towns in Transition 1500–1700* (London, 1976); and J. Barry (ed.), *The Tudor and Stuart Town: A Reader in English Urban History 1530–1688* (Harlow, 1990), which contains a valuable introduction, and reprints several key essays with a critical commentary. Other surveys of the early modern town can be found in J. Patten, *English Towns 1500–1700* (Folkestone, 1978); A. McInnes, *The English Town 1660–1760*, Historical Association (London, 1980); and P. J. Corfield, 'Urban Development in England and Wales in the Sixteenth and Seventeenth Centuries', reprinted in Barry above. The wider European context can be examined in J. de Vries, *European Urbanization 1500–1800* (London, 1984). Some of the most innovative research has appeared in three volumes of essays, which contain stimulating introductions: P. Clark and P. Slack (eds), *Crisis and Order in English Towns 1500–1700* (London, 1972); P. Clark (ed.), *Country Towns in Pre-industrial England* (Leicester, 1981); and P. Clark (ed.), *The Transformation of English Provincial Towns 1600–1800* (London, 1984). Two more general collections also contain important pieces which embrace the late seventeenth-century town: A. Everitt (ed.), *Perspectives in English Urban History* (London, 1973), with essays on the buildings of Burford and the urban inn; and D. Fraser and A. Sutcliffe (eds), *The Pursuit of Urban History* (London, 1983), with pieces on London popular culture and the writing of urban history in the period. A number of towns have been the subject of major studies: A. L. Beier and R. Finlay (eds), *London 1500–1700: The Making of the Metropolis* (London, 1986); P. Earle, *The Making of the English Middle Class: Business, Society and Family Life in London, 1660–1730* (London, 1989); P. Earle, *A City Full of People: London 1660–1760* (London, 1994); D. Hey, *The Fiery Blades of Hallamshire: Sheffield and its Neighbourhood, 1660–1740* (Leicester, 1991); D. H. Sacks, *The Widening Gate: Bristol and the Atlantic Economy, 1450–1700* (Berkeley and Los Angeles, 1991). On the general themes of demography and economy, and the interaction between the two, see: E. A. Wrigley, 'Urban Growth and Agricultural Change; England and the Continent in the Early Modern Period', *Journal of Interdisciplinary History*, XV (1985); E. A. Wrigley, 'A Simple Model of London's Importance in Changing English Society and Economy 1650–1750', *P & P*, XXXVII (1967); P. Clark and D. Souden (eds), *Migration and Society in Early Modern England* (London, 1987). The built environment, and its social contextualization, can be explored in J. Langton, 'Residential Patterns in Pre-industrial Cities: Some Case Studies from Seventeenth-century Britain', reprinted in Barry above; L. Stone, 'The Residential Development of the West End of London in the Seventeenth Century', in B. C. Malament (ed.), *After the Reformation* (Manchester, 1980); N. G. Brett-James, *The Growth of Stuart London* (London, 1935); S. Collier with S. Pearson, *Whitehaven 1660–1800* (London, 1991). Important studies of urban politics and religion – the two are inextricably intertwined – can be found in J. T. Evans, *Seventeenth-century Norwich: Politics, Religion, and Government, 1620–1690* (Oxford, 1979); J. Miller, 'The Crown and the Borough Charters in the Reign of Charles II', *EHR*, C (1985); C. Jones (ed.), *Britain in the First Age of Party 1680–1750* (London, 1987); T. Harris, *London Crowds in the Reign of Charles II* (Cambridge, 1987); T. Harris, P. Seaward and M. Goldie (eds), *The Politics of Religion in Restoration England* (Oxford, 1990). Differing views about the evolution of post-Restoration urban culture can be investigated in A. McInnes, 'The Emergence of a Leisure Town: Shrewsbury 1660–1760', *P & P*, CXX (1988); P. Borsay, *The English Urban Renaissance: Culture and Society in the Provincial Town 1660–1770* (Oxford, 1989); J. Barry, 'Provincial Town Culture, 1640–1780; Urbane or Civic?', in J. H. Pittock (ed.), *Interpretation and Cultural History* (London, 1991). For the development of spas, see P. Hembry, *The English Spa 1560–1815: A Social History* (London, 1990); and, for 'popular' culture, B. Reay (ed.), *Popular Culture in Seventeenth-century England* (London, 1988). Two contemporary sources, rich in urban content, are *The Diary of Samuel Pepys*, ed. R. Latham and W. Matthews, 11 vols (London, 1970–83); and *The Journeys of Celia Fiennes*, ed. C. Morris (London, 1947).

9. CONSUMPTION AND WEALTH   *J. M. Ellis*

A general introduction to economic development in this period can be found in D. C. Coleman, *The Economy of England 1450–1750* (Oxford, 1977) and C. G. A. Clay, *Economic Expansion and Social Change: England 1500–1700* (2 vols, Cambridge, 1984). K. Wrightson, *English Society, 1580–1680* (London, 1982) and J. A. Sharpe, *Early Modern England: A Social History, 1550–1750* (London, 1987) provide excellent introductions to social development. There is a useful volume of essays on overseas trade edited by W. E. Minchinton, *The Growth of English Overseas Trade in the Seventeenth and Eighteenth Centuries* (London, 1969) and an excellent summary of developments in R. Davis, *English Overseas Trade 1500–1700* (London, 1973). Agricultural change is covered in J. Thirsk (ed.), *The Agrarian History of England and Wales, v: 1640–1750* (London, 1984) and A. Kussmaul, *A General View of the Rural Economy of England, 1538–1840* (Cambridge, 1990): the continuing debate on the interaction of agricultural productivity and economic growth can be followed in E. L. Jones (ed.), *Agriculture and Economic Growth in England 1650–1815* (London, 1967) and P. K. O'Brien, 'Agriculture and the Home Market for English Industry 1660–1820', *EHR*, c (1985) 773–99. Industrial change is best served by reference to a number of regional and local studies including: J. D. Chambers, *The Vale of Trent 1670–1800: A Regional Study of Economic Change* (Cambridge, 1958); M. Rowlands, *Masters and Men in the West Midland Metalware Trades Before the Industrial Revolution* (Manchester, 1975); A. P. Wadsworth and J. de L. Mann, *The Cotton Trade and Industrial Lancashire 1600–1780* (Manchester, 1931). For inland trade and the retail network, see T. S. Willan, *The Inland Trade: Studies in English Internal Trade in the Sixteenth and Seventeenth Centuries* (London, 1976), J. A. Chartres, *Internal Trade in England 1500–1700 (London, 1977)* and M. Spufford, *The Great Reclothing of Rural England: Petty Chapmen and Their Wares in the Seventeenth Century* (London, 1984).

Spufford is also essential reading for the 'consumer revolution' itself, since it is one of a growing number of specialist works which have transformed our understanding of the issues involved. Key texts include: J. Thirsk, *Economic Policy and Projects: The Development of a Consumer Society in Early Modern England* (Oxford, 1978); L. Weatherill, *Consumer Behaviour and Material Culture in Britain, 1660–1760* (London, 1988); P. Borsay, *The English Urban Renaissance: Culture and Society in the Provincial Town, 1660–1770* (Oxford, 1989); P. Earle, *The Making of the English Middle Class: Business, Society and Family Life in London 1660–1730* (London, 1989); C. Shammas, *The Pre-industrial Consumer in England and America* (Oxford, 1990); B. Lemire, *Fashion's Favourites: The Cotton Trade and the Consumer, 1660–1800* (Oxford, 1991) and, above all, J. Brewer and R. Porter (eds), *Consumption and the World of Goods in the Seventeenth and Eighteenth Centuries* (London, 1992). The latter contains stimulating essays by many of the leading writers in the field and provides an essential springboard for further reading. Other recent specialist studies relevant to consumer spending in the later seventeenth century are: N. Harte, 'The Economics of Clothing in the Late Seventeenth Century', *Textile History*, xxii (1991) 277–96; B. Lemire, 'Consumerism in Preindustrial and Early Industrial England: The

Trade in Secondhand Clothes', *JBS*, xxvii (1988) 1–24; R. Machin, 'The Great
Rebuilding: A Reassessment', *P & P*, lxxvii (1977) 33–56; U. Priestley and
A. Fenner, *Shops and Shopkeepers in Norwich 1660–1730* (Norwich, 1985);
C. Shammas, 'Food Expenditures and Economic Well-being in Early Modern
England', *Journal of Economic History*, xxi (1984) 254–69; L. Weatherill, 'A
Possession of One's Own: Women and Consumer Behaviour in England
1660–1740', *JBS* xxv (1986) 131–56; *idem*, 'Consumer Behaviour and Social
Status in England 1660–1750', *Continuity & Change*, i (1986) 191–216;
D. Woodward, 'Wage-rates and Living Standards in Pre-industrial England',
P & P, xci (1981) 28–45; *idem*, 'Swords into Ploughshares: Recycling in
Pre-industrial England', *EcHR*, xxxviii (1985) 175–91.

10. INTERNATIONAL RELATIONS, WAR AND THE ARMED FORCES
J. D. Davies

Although any comprehensive study of Britain's relation with foreign powers
should ideally make use of primary material in foreign archives, a substantial
amount can be gleaned from holdings in British repositories. Particularly
important are the State Papers (Foreign) and the Baschet transcripts of
French ambassadors' despatches, both at the PRO, while the *Calendar of State
Papers, Venetian*, publishes the Venetian ambassadors' reports to 1675. The
papers of several Secretaries of State and leading diplomats are also accessible: these include the Clifford papers relating to the Secret Treaty of Dover
(BL Add. MSS 65 138), the papers of Henry Coventry (at Longleat House, but
on microfilm as M/882 at the British Library) and, from the 1680s, papers
relating to the careers of Lord Middleton, Sir William Trumbull and Lord
Preston (respectively, BL Add. MSS 41 803–42; BL Add. MSS 34 799; HMC,
Seventh Report, I 261–428). For the armed forces, by far the largest body of
material on the navy can be found in the Admiralty papers at the PRO (especially in Adm 1, 2, 3 and 106), and the Navy Records Society has transcribed
and published many of the sources for this period in other archives. The doc-
umentation relating to the army is less extensive, with the War Office papers
at the PRO forming the major archive.
  A great deal of new work on international relations has appeared in recent
years, much of it coming from the prolific pen of the leading authority in the
field, Jeremy Black. His *A System of Ambition? British Foreign Policy 1660–1793*
(London, 1991, paperback) covers a wide range of contexts and has a substantial bibliography which contains a particularly useful list of Professor
Black's many other works. Other useful introductory surveys have been pro-
vided by J. L. Price, 'Restoration England and Europe', in J. R. Jones (ed.),
The Restored Monarchy 1660–1688 (London, 1979), pp. 118–35, and by J. R.
Jones himself in *Britain and the World 1649–1815* (London, 1980). For the
earlier period, older authorities such as Sir Keith Feiling's brilliant *British
Foreign Policy 1660–72* (London, 1930) and Charles Wilson's study of the first
two Anglo-Dutch wars, *Profit and Power: A Study of England and the Dutch Wars*
(London, 1957) still contain much valuable material but are becoming dated,

particularly in the light of the work of Ronand Hutton (notably his 'The Making of the Secret Treaty of Dover', *HJ*, XXIX (1986) 297–318) and above all that of Steven Pincus. Dr Pincus's 'England and the World in the 1650s', in J. Morrill (ed.), *Revolution and Restoration* (London, 1992, paperback), pp. 129–47, and his 'Popery, Trade and Universal Monarchy: The Ideological Context of the Outbreak of the Second Anglo-Dutch War', *EHR*, CVII (1992) 1–29, are accessible introductions to his survey of foreign policy from 1650–68, *Protestantism and Patriotism* (Cambridge, 1996). K. H. D. Haley's *An English Diplomat in the Low Countries: Sir William Temple and John de Witt, 1665–72* (Oxford, 1986) provides an excellent survey of relations with the Netherlands and of the methods employed in diplomacy. For any study of the latter theme, it should be supplemented by G. H. Jones, *Charles Middleton: The Life and Times of a Restoration Politician* (Chicago, 1967), which also gives a good impression of the work of a Secretary of State.

The tercentenary of the Glorious Revolution of 1688 prompted a serious reassessment of Britain's place on the international stage in the 1680s. A particularly important contribution was made by Jeremy Black, 'The Revolution and the Development of English Foreign Policy' in E. Cruickshanks (ed.), *By Force or By Default? The Revolution of 1688–9* (Edinburgh, 1989); other studies in the same field are enumerated in the notes to this chapter. Given the central place of the monarchs in the making of foreign policy, the recent biographies of both Charles II and James II assume a particular importance for any study of the subject. R. Hutton, *Charles II: King of England, Scotland and Ireland* (Oxford, 1989) and J. Miller, *Charles II* (London, 1991) are both very thorough, but are more political histories than true biographies. They both devote much attention to foreign policy, making extensive use (for example) of the French ambassadors' despatches; Miller has more on foreign affairs as a whole, but Hutton is better on Anglo-Spanish relations. J. Miller, *James II: A Study in Kingship*, 2nd edn (London, 1989) gives similar treatment to the reign of James.

Both of the armed forces have received serious treatment in print. John Childs's two books, *The Army of Charles II* (London, 1976) and *The Army, James II and the Glorious Revolution* (Manchester, 1979) provide detailed coverage of most aspects of the military. For the navy, my *Gentlemen and Tarpaulins: The Officers and Men of the Restoration Navy* (Oxford, 1991) is concerned primarily with naval personnel, but also looks at administrative and operational aspects, while 'The Birth of the Imperial Navy? Aspects of English Naval Strategy c. 1650–90', in M. Duffy (ed.), *Parameters of British Naval Power 1650–1850* (Exeter, 1992), pp. 14–38, considers strategic issues. Other important treatments of naval themes are Sari Hornstein's *The Restoration Navy and English Foreign Trade 1674–88* (Aldershot, 1991), which provides an excellent survey of the navy's activities in the Mediterranean, and Jan Glete's *Navies and Nations: Warships, Navies and State Building in Europe, 1500–1860* (Stockholm, 1993), which employs an astonishing amount of data to construct a comparative analysis of the European navies in this period.

Notes and References

1. INTRODUCTION   *Lionel K. J. Glassey*

1. *Letters of Humphrey Prideaux to John Ellis, 1674–1722*, ed. E. M. Thompson (Camden Soc., NS xv, 1875), 150–1, 160–1.

2. Charles Carlton, *Going to the Wars: The Experience of the British Civil Wars, 1638–1651* (London, 1992), *passim*, esp. chs 5, 7, 14; I. Roy, 'England Turned Germany? The Aftermath of the Civil War in its European Context', *TRHS*, 5th ser., xxviii (1978) 133–44.

3. R. Hutton, *The Restoration: A Political and Religious History of England and Wales, 1658–1667* (Oxford, 1985), pp. 82–3.

4. 12 Car. II, c. 11; printed in J. P. Kenyon (ed.), *The Stuart Constitution* (2nd edn, Cambridge, 1986), pp. 339–44.

5. HMC, *Ormonde MSS*, NS iv. 488.

6. BL, Add. MSS 28 046, fos. 6–9: notes of a debate on the Disbanding Bill, 12 Dec. [1678].

7. [E. Bohun], *The History of the Desertion, or An Account of all the Publick Affairs in England …* (London, 1689), p. 58.

8. *Correspondence of the Family of Hatton, 1601–1704*, ed. E. M. Thompson (Camden Soc., NS xxii, xxiii, 1878), i. 220.

9. A. Grey, *Debates of the House of Commons, from the Year 1667 to the Year 1694* (London, 1769), vii. 395–415.

10. *CSPD 1687–9*, p. 358.

11. *The Ellis Correspondence*, ed. G. A. Ellis (London, 1829), ii. 319–20; HMC, *Le Fleming MSS*, pp. 223–4.

12. HMC, *Dartmouth MSS*, i. 210, 271–2; iii. 58, 66–7; J. D. Davies, *Gentlemen and Tarpaulins: The Officers and Men of the Restoration Navy* (Oxford, 1991), p. 216.

13. [Bohun], *History of the Desertion*, p. 18.

14. *The Correspondence of Henry Hyde, Earl of Clarendon, and of his brother Laurence Hyde, Earl of Rochester*, ed. S. W. Singer (1828), ii. 201, 202, 205; *Ellis Correspondence*, ii. 301, 308.

15. HMC, *Kenyon MSS*, pp. 208, 212.

16. *CSPD 1687–9*, p. 364.

17. *Original Letters Illustrative of English History*, ed. H. Ellis, 2nd ser. (London, 1827), iv. 166–7.

18. R. Beddard, *A Kingdom without a King: The Journal of the Provisional Government in the Revolution of 1688* (London, 1988), pp. 68, 71, 174, 178; HMC, *Dartmouth MSS*, iii. 69.

19.　J. Whittle, *An Exact Diary of the Late Expedition of His Illustrious Highness the Prince of Orange* (London, 1689), pp. 57–9, 68–9; HMC, *Seventh Report, Appendix Part I, Graham MSS*, p. 417a; *Ellis Correspondence*, ii. 326, 329–30, 346; J. Childs, *The Army, James II and the Glorious Revolution*, pp. 193–4.

20.　*An Account of the Proceedings of the Estates in Scotland, 1689–1690*, ed. E. W. M. Balfour-Melville (Scottish History Society, 3rd ser., xlvi, xlvii, 1954–5), i. 12, 15, 22, 32–3, 46, 105, 107, 110–11, 125–6; Earl of Balcarres, *Memoirs touching the Revolution in Scotland* (Bannatyne Club, Edinburgh, 1841), pp. 39–49.

21.　H. Murtagh, 'The War in Ireland, 1689–1691', in *Kings in Conflict: The Revolutionary War in Ireland and its Aftermath, 1689–1750*, ed. W. A. Maguire (Belfast, 1990), pp. 61–91, especially p. 89.

22.　*Memoirs of Sir John Reresby*, ed. A. Browning (2nd edn, London, 1991), p. 365.

23.　J. Scott, 'England's Troubles: Exhuming the Popish Plot', in T. Harris, P. Seaward and M. Goldie (eds), *The Politics of Religion in Restoration England* (Oxford, 1990), pp. 107–31, especially pp. 111–12. A similar case is argued, less persuasively, by J. F. Bosher, 'The Franco-Catholic Danger, 1660–1715', *History*, lxxix (1994) 5–30.

24.　PRO, PC 2/64, Privy Council Register, pp. 405ff: 14, 28 Apr. 1675.

25.　*The Acts of the Parliament of Scotland*, ed. T. Thomson and C. Innes (Edinburgh, 1814–1875), ix. 33–4, 38–40.

26.　Balcarres, *Memoirs touching the Revolution in Scotland*, p. 35; *Letters and State Papers chiefly addressed to George Earl of Melville … 1689–1691*, ed. W. L. Melville (Bannatyne Club, Edinburgh, 1843), p. 9.

27.　R. North, *Lives of the Norths* (London, 1826), i. 266–71; *The Autobiography of Roger North*, ed. A. Jessopp (London, 1887), pp. 131–4.

28.　Geoffrey Holmes, *Augustan England: Professions, State and Society, 1680–1730* (London, 1982), chs 3, 6.

29.　*Memoirs of Sir John Reresby*, p. 522.

2.　RESTORATION POLITICAL THOUGHT　*Mark Goldie*

1.　*The Parliamentary History of England* (London, 1808), IV, cols. 202–3.

2.　Thomas Hobbes, *Behemoth*, ed. F. Tönnies (London, 1969), epistle dedicatory. These reflections on the Civil War were first published in 1679. Hobbes's other post-Restoration work of political reflection was *A Dialogue Between a Philosopher and a Student of the Common Laws* (1681; modern edn, ed. J. Cropsey, Chicago, 1971).

3.　J. P. Kenyon (ed.), *The Stuart Constitution, 1603–1688* (Cambridge, 2nd edn, 1986), p. 292.

4.　Edward Hyde, *The Life of Edward, Earl of Clarendon* (Oxford, 1827), II, 97.

5.　*Statutes of the Realm* (London, 1819), V, 288, 308, 513; cf. pp. 232, 237, 304–5; Kenyon (ed.), *Stuart Constitution*, p. 349.

6.　*Statutes of the Realm*, V, 322, 366, 575; also in Kenyon (ed.), *Stuart Constitution*, pp. 351, 355.

7. R. Steele, *Bibliography of Royal Proclamations of the Tudor and Stuart Sovereigns* (Oxford, 1910), No. 3239; Scottish Proclamations, Nos. 2188, 2263. Milton's *Defence of the People of England* is reprinted in Milton, *Political Writings*, ed. M. Dzelzainis (Cambridge, 1991).

8. T. B. Howell (ed.), *A Complete Collection of State Trials* (London, 1811), VI, 119–202; M. A. Judson, *The Political Thought of Sir Henry Vane the Younger* (Philadelphia, 1969).

9. *Mene Tekel* (1663), p. 82; J. Hetet, 'A Literary Underground in Restoration England' (Ph.D. thesis, Cambridge, 1987), pp. 50–2.

10. Ibid., p. 115.

11. On kingship and the stage in the early Restoration, see N. K. Maguire, *Regicide and Restoration: English Tragicomedy, 1660–1671* (Cambridge, 1992).

12. HMC, *Portland MSS*, III, 394.

13. *The Poems and Fables of John Dryden*, ed. J. Kinsley (Oxford, 1958), p. 24. See H. D. Weinbrot, *Augustus Caesar in Augustan England* (Princeton, 1978).

14. John Monson, *Discourse Concerning Supreme Power* (1680), pp. 4–5. This tract was originally written in the 1640s. This style of thought is explored in A. O. Lovejoy, *The Great Chain of Being* (New York, 1936) and W. H. Greenleaf, *Order, Empiricism and Politics* (Oxford, 1964).

15. Simon Ford, *Parallela* (1660), pp. 1–2; John Dryden, *Absolom and Achitophel* (1681), pp. 2, 3, 32. See P. Harth, *Pen for a Party: Dryden's Tory Propaganda in its Contexts* (Princeton, 1993); S. N. Zwicker, *Dryden's Political Poetry: The Typology of King and Nation* (Providence, R.I., 1972).

16. H. W. Randall, 'The Rise and Fall of a Martyrology: Sermons on Charles I', *HLQ*, 10 (1946–7), pp. 135–67; D. Cressy, *Bonfires and Bells: National Memory and the Protestant Calendar in Elizabethan and Stuart England* (London, 1989), ch. 11.

17. John Browne, *Charisma Basilicon* (pt. III of *Adenochoiradelogia*, 1684), sig. d6v–d7r. See K. Thomas, *Religion and the Decline of Magic* (London, 1971), pp. 227–44; R. Crawfurd, *The King's Evil* (Oxford, 1911).

18. J. G. A. Pocock, *The Ancient Constitution and the Feudal Law* (Cambridge, 1987), p. 215.

19. *Ideology and Politics on the Eve of the Restoration: Newcastle's Advice to Charles II*, ed. T. P. Slaughter (Philadelphia, 1984), pp. 5, 21, 50, 68 and *passim*; C. Condren, 'Casuistry to Newcastle: "The Prince" in the World of the Book', in *Political Discourse in Early Modern Britain*, ed. N. Phillipson and Q. Skinner (Cambridge, 1993).

20. Henry Foulis, *History of the Wicked Plots* (2nd edn, 1674), pp. 158–9.

21. See M. Goldie, 'Danby, the Bishops, and the Whigs', in T. Harris, P. Seaward and M. Goldie (eds), *The Politics of Religion in Restoration England* (Oxford, 1990).

22. *The Autobiography of Roger North*, ed. A. Jessopp (London, 1887), pp. 61–3.

23. *A Letter from a Person of Quality* (1675), pp. 1–3, 34.

24. Earl of Shaftesbury, *Two Speeches* (1675), pp. 10–11.

25. See Robert Filmer, *Patriarcha and Other Writings*, ed. J. P. Sommerville (Cambridge, 1991); King James VI and I, *Political Writings*, ed. J. P. Sommerville (Cambridge, 1994).

26. See J. P. Sommerville, *Politics and Ideology in England, 1603–1640* (London, 1986).

27. Bodl. MS Rawl. D389. I shall cite it as 'Royal Power', abbreviating its heading.

28. Ibid., pp. 3, 12.

29. Ibid., pp. 3, 7, 12, 14.

30. We confuse ourselves today by speaking anachronistically of the Queen as the 'sovereign', a legacy of pre-1688 circumstances; we speak more accurately when pondering whether the European Union erodes the 'sovereignty of the British Parliament'.

31. 'Royal Power', pp. 1–2, 7, 51–2.

32. Ibid., pp. 49–53; Filmer, *Patriarcha and Other Writings*, pp. 3, 184.

33. 'Royal Power', pp. 1, 25–6; Robert Parsons, *A Conference about the Next Succession* (1594; reprints in 1649, 1655, 1681).

34. 'Royal Power', p. 38; Aristotle, *Nicomachean Ethics*, bk 8, ch. 10.

35. 'Royal Power', p. 7; Hobbes, *Behemoth*, p. 116; Filmer, *Patriarcha and Other Writings*, pp. 131ff.

36. Kenyon (ed.), *Stuart Constitution*, pp. 21–3.

37. 'Royal Power', fo. 2; pp. 7, 9–10.

38. Ibid., pp. 29–33. Filmer's account of parliament was available before the publication of *Patriarcha* in his *Freeholder's Grand Inquest* (1648).

39. Pocock, *Ancient Constitution*, ch. 8.

40. 'Royal Power', pp. 42ff; Algernon Sidney, *Discourses Concerning Government*, ed. T. G. West (Indianapolis, 1990), pp. 70, 370ff; *The Autobiography of Sir John Bramston*, ed. Lord Braybrooke (London, 1845), p. 189.

41. 'Royal Power', pp. 13–14.

42. Ibid., pp. 3, 10.

43. Ibid., fo. 2.

44. *The Correspondence of Henry Hyde, Earl of Clarendon*, ed. S. W. Singer, 2 vols (London, 1828), II, 479–80. See M. Goldie, 'The Political Thought of the Anglican Revolution', in R. Beddard (ed.), *The Revolutions of 1688* (Oxford, 1991).

45. 'Royal Power', pp. 5, 10–12.

46. Sir Philip Warwick, *A Discourse of Government* (1694), p. 56. Warwick's tract was written before the Revolution.

47. *The Judgement and Decree of the University of Oxford* (1683): extracts in Kenyon (ed.), *Stuart Constitution*, pp. 471–4.

48. See the editions by P. Laslett (Cambridge, 1960, 1967, 1988) or M. Goldie (London, 1993).

49. Published in Latin as *Vindiciae Contra Tyrannos* and *De Jure Regni apud Scotos*.

50. Locke, *Two Treatises*, Preface; I, paras 3, 6. See M. Goldie, 'John Locke and Anglican Royalism', *Political Studies* 31 (1983) 61–85.

51. Locke, *Two Treatises*, II, paras 4, 6, 8, 22, 54, 56, 57, 95.

52. Ibid., II, paras 19, 21, 24, 34, 74–5, 88–9, 95, 97, 100, 103, 113–14, 123–31, 137, 175.

53. Ibid., II, paras 19, 21, 109, 131, 149, 156, 168, 176, 199, 202, 205, 211, 226–7, 241–2.

54. Ibid., II, paras 155, 215–22.

55. Ibid., II, paras 7, 9, 11, 13, 20.

56. Ibid., II, paras 149, 151, 220, 243.

57. Ibid., I, paras 79, 121; II, paras 196, 203–10, 223–5, 240–3.

58. Marquis of Halifax, *Complete Works*, ed. J. P. Kenyon (London, 1969), p. 197; Pocock, *Ancient Constitution*, ch. 8.

59. John Somers, *A Brief History of the Succession* (2nd edn, 1689), pp. 4, 6 and *passim*.

60. Locke, *Two Treatises*, II, paras 213, 243; *The Correspondence of John Locke*, ed. E. S. de Beer (Oxford, 1976–89), III, 545, IV, 19; Locke, *Some Thoughts Concerning Education*, ed. J. W. and J. S. Yolton (Oxford, 1989), pp. 322–3; M. E. Parker (ed.), *North Carolina Charters and Constitutions, 1578–1698* (Raleigh, N.C., 1963), pp. 132ff.

61. Algernon Sidney, *Court Maxims*, ed. H.W. Blom, E.H. Mulier and R. Janse (Cambridge, 1996).

62. Sidney, *Discourses*, pp. 8, 31, 69, 101–7, 117, 189, 195, 313, 376, 474, 486.

63. For Sidney's trial, see J. Scott, *Algernon Sidney and the Restoration Crisis, 1677–1683* (Cambridge, 1991), pt. 3.

64. Sidney, *Discourses*, pp. 143, 226, 273, 313, 315, 347–8, 455. In republican Rome the dictator was a citizen given full executive power during a temporary emergency; Cincinnatus, summoned to the task, left his farm to do his patriotic duty; power did not tempt him, and he later returned to his farm. The American city, Cincinnati, is named after him.

65. Ibid., pp. 124–8, 209, 487–8, 527.

66. Henry Neville, *Plato Redivivus*, in C. Robbins (ed.), *Two English Republican Tracts* (Cambridge, 1969).

67. Halifax, *Works*, p. 156.

3. POLITICS, FINANCE AND GOVERNMENT   *Lionel K. J. Glassey*

1. *The Diary of John Evelyn*, ed. E. S. de Beer (Oxford, 1955), iii. 246.

2. *The Diurnal of Thomas Rugg 1659–61*, ed. W. L. Sachse (Camden Soc., 3rd ser. xci, 1961), 90.

3. *The Flemings in Oxford ... 1650–1700*, ed. J. R. Magrath (Oxford Historical Society, xliv, lxii, lxxix, 1904–24), i. 131.

4. J. Nicoll, *A Diary of Public Transactions and Other Occurrences, Chiefly in Scotland, 1650–1667*, ed. D. Laing (Bannatyne Club, Edinburgh, 1836), p. 283.

5. R. L. Greaves, *Deliver Us from Evil: The Radical Underground in Britain, 1660–1663* (Oxford, 1986); *Enemies Under His Feet: Radicals and Nonconformists in Britain, 1664–1677* (Stanford, 1990); *Secrets of the Kingdom: British Radicals from the Popish Plot to the Revolution of 1688–1689* (Stanford, 1992). For Nangle, see S. J. Connolly, *Religion, Law and Power: The Making of Protestant Ireland, 1660–1760* (Oxford, 1992), pp. 206–7.

6. C. H. Firth and G. Davies, *The Regimental History of Cromwell's Army* (Oxford, 1940), i. 75, 80.

7.   G. Burnet, *History of My Own Time*, ed. M. J. Routh (Oxford, 1833), iii. 32.

8.   Barbara Taft, 'Return of a Regicide: Edmund Ludlow and the Glorious Revolution', *History*, lxxvi (1991) 197–228.

9.   Paul Seaward, *The Cavalier Parliament and the Reconstruction of the Old Regime, 1661–1667* (Cambridge, 1989), pp. 54–5.

10.   J. S. Morrill, *Cheshire 1630–1660: County Government and Society during the 'English Revolution'* (Oxford, 1974), pp. 326–30; Andrew M. Coleby, *Central Government and the Localities: Hampshire 1649–1689* (Cambridge, 1987), pp. 90–1; Anthony Fletcher, *A County Community in Peace and War: Sussex 1600–1660* (London, 1975), p. 134; Stephen K. Roberts, *Recovery and Restoration in an English County: Devon Local Administration 1646–1670* (Exeter, 1985), pp. 146–50, 156–8; James M. Rosenheim, 'An Examination of Oligarchy: The Gentry of Restoration Norfolk, 1660–1720' (Ph.D. thesis, Princeton University, 1981), pp. 201–3; Philip Jenkins, *The Making of a Ruling Class: The Glamorgan Gentry 1640–1790* (Cambridge, 1983), pp. 121–4.

11.   Roberts, *Recovery and Restoration*, pp. 109–10, 115–16.

12.   R. Hutton, *The Restoration: A Political and Religious History of England and Wales, 1658–1667* (Oxford, 1985), pp. 158–61; for a specific example, see John T. Evans, *17th Century Norwich: Politics, Religion and Government 1620–1690* (Oxford, 1979), pp. 240–51.

13.   Hutton, *The Restoration*, pp. 125–84.

14.   Greaves, *Deliver Us from Evil*, pp. 35–40, 50–7.

15.   Basil D. Henning (ed.), *The History of Parliament: The House of Commons, 1660–1690* (London, 1983), i. 32–3; Seaward, *The Cavalier Parliament*, pp. 35–8.

16.   Richard Ollard, *Clarendon and his Friends* (London, 1987), pp. 226–7.

17.   17 Car. I, c. 14.

18.   A. Browning, *English Historical Documents, 1660–1714* (2nd edn, London, 1966), p. 58.

19.   Much of what follows is based on C. D. Chandaman, *The English Public Revenue 1660–1688* (Oxford, 1975), a book to which historians of politics and the constitution owe a debt no less than do historians of government finance.

20.   *CJ*, viii. 150: 4 Sept. 1660; *The Diaries and Papers of Sir Edward Dering, Second Baronet, 1644 to 1684*, ed. M. F. Bond (London, 1976), p. 48.

21.   T. H. Lister, *Life of Clarendon* (London, 1837–8), iii. 504–8.

22.   S. R. Gardiner, *The Constitutional Documents of the Puritan Revolution 1625–1660* (3rd edn, Oxford, 1906), pp. 431, 444–5, 452–3.

23.   *Calendar of Clarendon State Papers* (Oxford, 1869–1970), v, ed. F. J. Routledge, pp. 125–6.

24.   Chandaman, *Public Revenue*, pp. 332–3.

25.   *The Diary of John Milward*, ed. Caroline Robbins (Cambridge, 1938), pp. 40–1.

26.   Chandaman, *Public Revenue*, pp. 224–8.

27.   *The Hatton Correspondence*, ed. E. M. Thompson (Camden Soc., NS xxii, xxiii, 1878), i. 212, 214.

28.   *The Life of Edward Earl of Clarendon ... containing ... A Continuation ... of his History of the Grand Rebellion ...* (Oxford, 1760), i. 440.

29. Chandaman, *Public Revenue*, pp. 265–8.

30. Chandaman, *Public Revenue*, pp. 219, 235–6, 239, 270–3.

31. H. Forneron, *The Court of Charles II, 1649–1734, compiled from State Papers* (5th edn, London, 1897), pp. 204–5.

32. BL, Add. MSS 28 094, fos. 54–5: paper endorsed 'Money paid to the D. of Portsmouth and Mrs Gwyn between the 27th of March 1676 and the 14 of March 1678/9'. There is another list of secret service payments, mostly to mistresses, for a slightly earlier period at BL, Add. MSS 28 080, f. 14.

33. Bodl. MS Carte 70, fos. 563–4: Ormonde to Arran, 10 Jan. 1682/3 (copy).

34. H. M. Colvin (ed.), *The History of the King's Works* (London, 1963–73), v. 304–13.

35. R. North, *Lives of the Norths* (London, 1826), ii. 104. One of North's brothers was Lord Keeper from 1682, and another was a Lord of the Treasury from 1684.

36. Chandaman, *Public Revenue*, pp. 256–9; and see the same author's essay 'The Financial Settlement in the Parliament of 1685', *British Government and Administration: Studies presented to S. B. Chrimes*, ed. H. Hearder and H. R. Loyn (Cardiff, 1974), pp. 144–54.

37. Chandaman, *Public Revenue*, p. 261, n. 2.

38. Burnet, *History*, ed. Routh, iii. 9–11; Roger North, *Lives of the Norths*, ii. 110–14.

39. L. G. Schwoerer, *The Declaration of Rights, 1689* (Baltimore, 1981), pp. 68–9.

40. *The Diary of Samuel Pepys*, ed. R. Latham and W. Matthews (London, 1970–83), iv. 406.

41. Colvin (ed.), *History of the King's Works*, iv. 300–43, v. 263–304; *Diary of Samuel Pepys*, x (*Companion Volume*), 477–84; R. Hutton, *Charles the Second*, (Oxford, 1989), pp. 133–4.

42. Seaward, *The Cavalier Parliament*, pp. 120–1, 126–7, 179–80, 193–5, 252–4, 282–4, 291–2.

43. Hutton, *Charles the Second*, p. 254, and chapter 10, 'The Ministry of Arlington, 1668–1672', *passim.*

44. HMC, *Ormonde MSS* NS iv. 433–4; for Carr, see Henning (ed.), *History of Parliament 1660–1690*, ii. 21–6.

45. HMC, *Ormonde MSS* NS iv. 290–1.

46. HMC, *Ormonde MSS* NS iv. 229–30, 320–1.

47. Bodl. MS Carte 103, f. 228: newsletter, 5 Aug. 1678.

48. *Diary of the Times of Charles the Second by the Honourable Henry Sidney ... including his Correspondence ...*, ed. R. W. Blencowe (London, 1843), ii. 165. The same letter, from the Countess of Sunderland to Henry Sidney, who was then Envoy at The Hague, concludes (pp. 167–8) by asking if Sidney would like his friends to try to buy his place to enable him to return to England.

49. Bodl. MS Carte 103, f. 238: newsletter, 19 Aug. 1678.

50. HMC, *Ormonde MSS* NS v. 39.

51. HMC, *Ormonde MSS* NS iv, p. xx (the document is printed in the introduction out of chronological sequence).

52. Bodl. MS Carte 216, fos. 198–9: Israell Feilding to [Arran], 3 Oct. 1682.

53. *Hatton Correspondence*, ii. 21–2.

54. *Memoirs of Sir John Reresby*, ed. A. Browning (2nd edn, London, 1991), p. 537.

55. *Hatton Correspondence*, i. 181.

56. G. Davies, 'Council and Cabinet, 1679–1688', *EHR*, xxxvii (1922) 55–62; M. A. Thomson, *A Constitutional History of England, 1642–1801* (London, 1938), pp. 102–7, 212–15.

57. *Calendar of Treasury Books*, 1685–1689, pp. 863, 1236; PRO, DL 41/19/10: 'Reasons against the Bill for takeing away the Dutchy and County Pallatine of Lancaster', no date [after 1691], but containing the phrase 'The desire of takeing away the Dutchy was never aimed at till the late King James's time ... and it's hoped these times will take noe paterne from what was done then.'

58. J. M. Sosin, *English America and the Revolution of 1688: Royal Administration and the Structure of Provincial Government* (Nebraska, 1982), pp. 24–5, 63.

59. Andrew P. Barclay, 'The Impact of King James on the Departments of the Royal Household' (unpubl. Ph.D. thesis, University of Cambridge, 1993), pp. 59–97.

60. *Diary of Samuel Pepys*, iv. 115, 219–20, 229; viii. 342, 449, 584–5, 596–7; HMC, *Ormonde MSS* NS iv. 105–6, 110, 204, 401, 452.

61. Seaward, *The Cavalier Parliament*, pp. 71–99.

62. *The Poems and Letters of Andrew Marvell*, ed. H. M. Margoliouth (3rd edn, Oxford, 1971), i. 150, 'The last Instructions to a Painter', lines 105–14. A 'pair of tables' is a backgammon board; 'trick-track' is a form of backgammon.

63. Clarendon, *Continuation of the Life*, i. 495–506; ii. 59–64; reprinted in part in Browning, *English Historical Documents 1660–1714*, pp. 229–33.

64. Henning (ed.), *History of Parliament 1660–1690*, i. 33–4; ii. 91–4.

65. G. Burnet, *History of My Own Time*, ed. O. Airy (Oxford, 1897–1900), ii. 79.

66. Henning (ed.), *History of Parliament 1660–1690*, iii. 52.

67. A. Browning, *Thomas Osborne, Earl of Danby and Duke of Leeds, 1632–1712* (Glasgow, 1944–51), iii. 56–125, 140–51; E. S. de Beer, 'Members of the Court Party in the House of Commons, 1670–1678', *BIHR*, xi (1933–4) 1–23; J. R. Jones, 'Shaftesbury's "Worthy Men": A Whig View of the Parliament of 1679', *BIHR*, xxx (1957) 232–41; K. H. D. Haley, 'Shaftesbury's Lists of Lay Peers and Members of the Commons, 1677–8', *BIHR*, xliii (1970) 86–105.

68. HMC, *Ormonde MSS* NS iv. 177–9.

69. J. Welwood, *Memoirs of the Most Material Transactions in England for the Last Hundred Years Preceding the Revolution in 1688* (London, edition of 1710), pp. 111–12.

70. Burnet, *History*, ed. Airy, ii. 287; R. North, *Examen* (London, 1740), pp. 320–1; *Lives of the Norths*, i. 404–7.

71. Lord Campbell, *Lives of the Lord Chancellors and Keepers of the Great Seal of England* (London, 1846), iv. 421–2.

72.   C. J. Fox, *History of the Early Part of the Reign of James II* (London, 1808), pp. 41–3, 72; Lord John Russell, *The Life of William Lord Russell* (London, 1819), pp. 109–11.

73.   J. Scott, *Algernon Sidney and the Restoration Crisis, 1677–1683* (Cambridge, 1991), pp. 6–8, 17–21; M. Knights, *Politics and Opinion in Crisis, 1678–1681* (Cambridge, 1994), pp. 29–30, 348–51.

74.   T. Harris, 'Tories and the Rule of Law in the Reign of Charles II', *The Seventeenth Century*, viii (1993) 9–27.

75.   K. H. D. Haley, *The First Earl of Shaftesbury* (Oxford, 1968), pp. 353, 590, 744–5; Scott, *Algernon Sidney and the Restoration Crisis*, p. 81; Knights, *Politics and Opinion in Crisis*, p. 355.

76.   *Memoirs of Thomas, Earl of Ailesbury*, ed. W. E. Buckley (Roxburghe Club, Westminster, 1890), i. 94; H. C. Foxcroft, *Life and Letters of Sir George Savile, Bart., First Marquis of Halifax* (London, 1898), ii. 281.

77.   Scott, *Algernon Sidney and the Restoration Crisis*, pp. 22–5.

78.   T. Harris, *London Crowds in the Reign of Charles II* (Cambridge, 1987), pp. 100–1; Knights, *Politics and Opinion in Crisis*, p. 129; J. R. Jones, 'The Green Ribbon Club', *Durham University Journal*, xlix (1956), 17–20. For a contrary view, that the Green Ribbon Club was the focus of an organized party, see R. Ashcraft, *Revolutionary Politics & Locke's* Two Treatises of Government (Princeton, 1986), pp. 143–5.

79.   An issue of the journal *Albion* (xxv[4], Winter 1993) is devoted to a vigorous discussion of these themes under the collective title 'Order and Authority: Creating Party in Restoration England', with contributions by G. S. De Krey, T. Harris, J. Rosenheim, R. L. Greaves, and J. Scott.

80.   *The Works of Sir William Temple*, ed. Jonathan Swift (2nd edn, London, 1731), i. 331–59. The passages quoted are at pp. 353, 358. For Essex, see p. 348.

81.   M. Knights, 'London Petitions and Parliamentary Politics in 1679', *Parliamentary History*, xii (1993) 29–46; 'London's "Monster" Petition of 1680', *HJ*, xxxvi, no. 1 (1993) 94–111; Harris, *London Crowds in the Reign of Charles II*, pp. 98–108, 131–3.

82.   T. Harris, *Politics under the Later Stuarts: Party Conflict in a Divided Society, 1660–1715* (London, 1993), pp. 84–5.

83.   L. K. J. Glassey, *Politics and the Appointment of Justices of the Peace, 1675–1720* (Oxford, 1979), pp. 41–62.

84.   Browning, *Danby*, iii. 127–9, 148–51; R. Davis, 'The "Presbyterian" Opposition and the Emergence of Party in the House of Lords in the Reign of Charles II', in C. Jones (ed.), *Party and Management in Parliament, 1660–1784* (Leicester, 1984), pp. 27–35; A. Swatland, 'The House of Lords in the Reign of Charles II, 1660–1681' (unpubl. Ph.D. thesis, University of Birmingham, 1985). The calculations are my own.

85.   Knights, *Politics and Opinion in Crisis*, pp. 112–45.

86.   BL, Add. MSS 27 447, 27 448, *passim*. The passage quoted is at 27 447, fos. 389–90: John Gough to Viscountess Yarmouth, 1 May 1678. A draft of Yarmouth's letter to Charles II asking for an earldom is at 27 447, fos. 412–13: 17 July 1679. See also Rees [J. R.] Jones, 'The First Whig Party in Norfolk', *Durham University Journal*, NS xv (1953) 13–21; Victor L. Stater, 'Continuity

and Change in English Provincial Politics: Robert Paston in Norfolk, 1675–1683', *Albion*, xxv [2] (1993) 193–216; Evans, *17th Century Norwich*, pp. 267–96.

87. Bodl. MS Carte 79, fos. 168–9: [Lord Wharton] to 'My Dear Child', 27 Jan. 1678 [/9].

88. Bodl. MS Carte 216, fos. 67–8, 149–50, 195–6: Longford to [Arran], 3 June, 19 Aug., 3 Oct. 1682.

89. J. Levin, *The Charter Controversy in the City of London, 1660–1688, and its Consequences* (London, 1969), pp. 21–8; G. S. De Krey, *A Fractured Society: The Politics of London in the First Age of Party, 1688–1715* (Oxford, 1985), pp. 11–13.

90. Bodl MS Carte 70, fos. 563–4: Ormonde to Arran, 10 Jan. 1682/3 (copy).

91. *Memoirs of Sir John Reresby*, p. 395.

92. J. R. Jones, 'James II's Whig Collaborators', *HJ*, iii (1960) 65–73.

93. Bodl. MS Carte 69, fos. 97–100: paper endorsed 'Mem. This was given me by the Earl of Egmont. Tho. Carte', no date, containing anecdotes of Ormonde apparently supplied to Sir Robert Southwell for a projected memoir. See also T. Carte, *The Life of James Duke of Ormond* (2nd edn, Oxford, 1851), iv. 687–8.

94. L. K. J. Glassey, 'The Revolution of 1688 in the North-West of England', *Transactions of the Lancashire and Cheshire Antiquarian Society*, lxxxvi (1990) 37–43; Mary K. Geiter, 'Sir John Reresby and the Glorious Revolution', *Northern History*, xxv (1989) 174–87; W. A. Speck, 'The Revolution of 1688 in the North of England', *Northern History*, xxv (1989) 188–204.

95. Sir J. Dalrymple, *Memorials of Great Britain and Ireland* (London, 1771–3), ii, Appendix, Part II, 94.

96. T. Rowlands, 'Robert Harley's Parliamentary Apprenticeship, 1690–1695', *British Library Journal*, xv (1989) 173–86.

97. Burnet, *History*, ed. Routh, iii. 358.

98. Foxcroft, *Life and Letters of Halifax*, ii. 204.

4. THE TRIPLE-CROWNED ISLANDS   *Ronald Hutton*

1. J. G. Simms, *Jacobite Ireland 1685–91* (1969), pp. 3–4, and 'The Restoration, 1660–85', in T. W. Moody, F. X. Martin and F. J. Byrne (eds), *A New History of Ireland* (Oxford, 1976), iii. 428.

2. Trinity College, Dublin, MS 808, fos. 156–8; PRO, PC 2/54, p. 125; PRO, SP 63/304/154, p. 160; Scottish RO, CH 1/1/11, pp. 188–205; Patrick Adair, *A True Narrative of the Rise and Progress of the Presbyterian Church in Ireland*, ed. W. D. Killen (Belfast, 1866), pp. 243–7.

3. Bodl. MS Carte 31, 42, 45, 48, 49, 64, 66, 70, 185, 221, 225, *passim*; PRO, SP 63/304–5, 307, *passim*; PRO, PC 2/54–6, *passim*; PRO, SP SO 1/4, *passim*; Bodl. MS Clarendon 74, fos. 345–460, and 75, fos. 171–2, 263–4; Thomas Morrice, *A Collection of the State Letters of ... The First Earl of Orrery* (1742), pp. 23–38.

4.   National Library of Ireland, MS 13 217, fo. 2, and 13 223, fo. 6; Robert
Steele (ed.), *Tudor and Stuart Proclamations* (Oxford, 1910), ii, nos. 647, 674,
677; PRO, SP 63/307/194; Bodl. MS Carte 214, fos. 309, 315; Bodl. MS
Clarendon 76, fos. 178, 205–7; *Orrery State Letters*, pp. 47, 55–6.

5.   Scottish Record Office, CH 1/1/11, *passim*; *Mercurius Publicus*, 3 issues
30 August–27 Sept. 1660; Robert Wodrow, *The History of the Sufferings of the
Church of Scotland* (Glasgow edn, 1836–8), i. 68–130; David Laing (ed.), *The
Letters and Journals of Robert Baillie* (Edinburgh, 1842), iii. 410–11, 446–8;
Osmund Airy (ed.), *The Lauderdale Papers* (Camden Soc., 1885), i. 34, 105;
The Life of Mr Robert Blair, ed. T. McCrie (Wodrow Soc., 1848), p. 240; Gilbert
Burnet, *History of My Own Time*, ed. Osmund Airy (Oxford, 1897), i. 198–237;
Scottish Record Office, PA 11/12, *passim*; James Kirkton, *The Secret and True
History of the Church of Scotland* (Edinburgh, 1817), pp. 114–35; Sir George
Mackenzie, *Memoirs of the Affairs of Scotland* (Edinburgh, 1821), pp. 6–56;
Bodl. MS Clarendon 74, fos. 64, 67, 220, 222, 290–2, MS 75, fo. 400, and MS
77, fo. 373; National Library of Scotland, MS 2512, fos. 6, 10, and MS 3922, fo.
17; *Register of the Privy Council of Scotland*, ed. P. Hume Brown (3rd ser., 1908),
i. 28–270.

6.   Mackenzie, *Memoirs*, pp. 29–33; *Mercurius Publicus*, 3 issues 21 Feb.–14
Mar. 1661; PRO SP 63/305/22 and 63/307/179, 200, 232.

7.   Scottish RO, CH 1/1/11, *passim*; Baillie, *Letters*, iii. 443; *Lauderdale
Papers*, i. 32–163; Blair, *Life*, pp. 351–5; Kirkton, *Secret History*, pp. 68–159;
Mackenzie, *Memoirs*, pp. 8–133; BL Add. MSS 23 114, fo. 50; *The Life of
Edward, Earl of Clarendon* (Oxford, 1826), i. 365–7; Bodl. MS Clarendon 73, fo.
380; Burnet, *History*, i. 363–4; BL Add. MSS 23 119, fo. 86.

8.   The main source for all this is, of course, Lauderdale's own collection
of papers, whether those edited by Osmund Airy or those lying unedited in
National Library of Scotland, MS 2512. The official tale is told by the *Register
of the Privy Council of Scotland* and the *Acts of the Parliaments of Scotland*. Views of
allies and enemies can be found in Mackenzie, *Memoirs*; Kirkton, *Secret History*;
Burnet, *History*; Tweeddale's papers in National Library of Scotland, MSS
3136, 7023–5, 14 488, 7034 and 7005–6; and in the HMC reports upon the
Hamilton MSS, Laing MSS and Atholl MSS.

9.   Sources as at n. 8.

10.   The *Register* and *Acts of Parliament* remain as important as ever when
dealing with this period, as do the Hamilton, Laing and Atholl MSS and the
accounts by Mackenzie, Kirkton, Wodrow and Burnet. Aberdeen's papers are
published in *Letters to George, Earl of Aberdeen* (Spalding Club, 1851), and
Queensberry's in HMC *Buccleugh and Queensberry MSS (Drumlanrig)*.
Observations by Sir John Lauder, Lord Fountainhall, are printed as his
Chronological Notes (Edinburgh, 1822) and *Historical Observes* (Bannatyne Club,
1840). Other commentators are represented by Lindsay, Earl of Balcarres,
Memoirs Touching the Revolution in Scotland, ed. A. W. C. Lindsay (Bannatyne
Club, 1841); HMC, *Stuart MSS*, vol. i; BL Add. MSS 15 395; and (after a
fashion), J. S. Clarke (ed.), *Life of James II* (1816).

11.   The main collections of evidence for all the above are the Irish State
Papers in the Public Record Office (SP 63/307–33 and SO 1/4) and
Ormonde's papers gathered in Bodl. MS Carte. The Bodleian also has some

items of interest in Clarendon MSS 74–8, and Orrery's correspondence is edited in the *Orrery State Letters*. Supplementary material is found in the Privy Council Registers, 2/54–6, in the Public Record Office, and in Trinity College Dublin, MS 808.

12. The Irish State Papers (SP 63/333–40) and Carte MSS remain invaluable for this period, but are joined by the *Essex Papers*, ed. Osmund Airy (Camden Soc., 1890). Lesser information is contributed by the Coventry MSS at Longleat House and the Leconfield MSS at Petworth Park. Ranelagh's financial trickery is revealed in Sean Egan, 'Finance and the Government of Ireland, 1660–85' (Ph.D. thesis, Trinity College, Dublin, 1983).

13. For Ormonde's second viceroyalty, the Carte MSS are partly replaced by another huge collection of his papers calendared in HMC, *Ormonde MSS*, NS iv–vi. Sean Egan's thesis remains very important and is joined by James Ernest Aydelotte, 'The Duke of Ormond and the English Government of Ireland, 1677–1685' (Ph.D. thesis, University of Iowa, 1975). Also of interest is Dublin Central Library, Gilbert Collection, MS 109, some observations by Mountjoy.

14. S. W. Singer (ed.), *The Correspondence of Henry Hyde, Earl of Clarendon and of his brother Laurence Hyde, Earl of Rochester* (1828), i. 298.

15. See also James's later remarks on this in Clarke (ed.), *Life of James II*, ii. 636–8.

16. The main source for Irish affairs in James's reign is the Clarendon and Rochester correspondence edited by Singer. Some of Tyrconnel's letters survive in BL Add. MSS 32 095 and 41 805 and Bodl. MS Arch. f.c.b. An important narrative by Thomas Sheridan, printed in HMC, *Stuart MSS*, vol. i, is examined by John Miller in *Irish Historical Studies*, xx (1976) 105–28. Royal directives and discussion papers concerning Ireland are printed at intervals in the *CSPD* for 1685, 1686–7 and 1687–9. Comments on the evolution of policy by different observers are found in the HMC, *Ormonde MSS*, NS vol. vii; the HMC, *Egmont MSS*, vol. ii; Robert Parker, *Memoirs of the most Remarkable Military Transactions from the Year 1683 to 1718* (1747); 'Sir Paul Rycaut's Memoranda and Letters from Ireland, 1686–1687', *Analecta Hibernica*, xxvii (1972) 129–57; the papal envoy's despatches in BL Add. MSS 15 395–6; and those of the French ambassador in Public Record Office, PRO/31/3/161–76.

17. Simms, *Jacobite Ireland*, pp. 12–17; L. M. Cullen, 'Economic Trends, 1660–91', in Moody, Martin and Byrne (eds), *New History of Ireland*, iii. 389–402, and *idem, Anglo-Irish Trade 1660–1800* (Manchester, 1968), pp. 33–5.

18. R. Lawrence, *The Interest of Ireland in its Trade and Wealth Stated* (Dublin, 1682), p. 18.

19. Daniel Corkery, *The Hidden Ireland* (Dublin, 1924), pp. 97–111; J. C. MacErlean (ed.), *Poems of O Bruadair* (Dublin, 1917), 3 vols.

20. Rosalind Mitchison, *Lordship to Patronage* (London, 1983), pp. 94–107.

21. Allan Macinnes, 'Repression and Conciliation: The Highland Dimension 1660–1688', *Scottish Historical Review*, lxv (1986) 168–73.

22. *Poems of O Bruadair*, iii. 15.

23. BL Egerton MS 917, f. 88.

24.   T. W. Moody, 'Redmond O'Hanlon', *Proceedings of the Belfast Natural History and Philosophical Society*, 2nd ser., i (1937) 17–33; Simms, 'The Restoration', in Moody, Martin and Byrne (eds), *New History of Ireland*, iii. 448.

25.   Public Record Office, PRO/31/3/149, fos. 54, 58.

26.   According to Sir William Petty, *The Political Anatomy of Ireland* (1691), p. 16.

27.   Especially in 1663–4, 1671–3 and 1682–5.

28.   Simms, *Jacobite Ireland*, pp. 7–8.

29.   Macinnes, 'Repression and Conciliation'; Ian B. Cowan, *The Scottish Covenanters* (London, 1976).

30.   Cowan, *Scottish Covenanters*, pp. 51–132, *passim.*

31.   Macinnes, 'Repression and Conciliation'; Mitchison, *Lordship to Patronage*, pp. 113–14.

32.   Cowan, *Scottish Covenanters*, pp. 69–70, 98–101, 132.

5.   RELIGION IN RESTORATION ENGLAND   *John Spurr*

1.   J. C., *A Guide to True Religion* (1668), sig. A3.

2.   Roger L'Estrange, *Toleration Discussed* (1663), p. 86; see also Sir Philip Warwick, *A Discourse of Government* (1694), pp. 130–45; Sir Peter Leicester, *Charges to the Grand Jury at Quarter Sessions 1660–1677*, ed. E. M. Halcrow (Chetham Society, v, 1953), p. 48.

3.   [Edward Polhill], *The Samaritan* (1682), p. 49.

4.   Sir Robert Pointz quoted in P. Seaward, *The Restoration, 1660–1688* (London, 1991), p. 145.

5.   The terms 'Dissenter' and 'Nonconformist' are often used interchangeably – as they are in this essay – but see N. H. Keeble, *The Literary Culture of Nonconformity in Later Seventeenth-century England* (Leicester, 1987), pp. 41–4.

6.   *The Rev. Oliver Heywood B.A., 1630–1702; His Autobiography, Diaries, Anecdote and Event Books*, ed. J. H. Turner (Bingley, 1881–5), i. 190.

7.   Evelyn, *Diary*, iii. 328; D. A. Spaeth, 'Parsons and Parishioners: Lay–Clerical Conflict and Popular Piety in Wiltshire Villages, 1660–1740' (Ph.D. thesis, Brown University, 1985), p. 34.

8.   Cambridge University Library, Add. MSS 8499, fo. 166 (Diary of Isaac Archer); *The Parliamentary Diary of Sir Edward Dering 1670–73*, ed. B. D. Henning (New Haven, 1940), p. 145.

9.   William Payne, *The Unlawfulness of Stretching Forth the Hand to Resist or Murder Princes* (1683), sermon 2, p. 20; Henry Anderson, *A Sermon Preached in the Cathedral Church at Winchester* (1681), p. 29; Robert Hancocke, *A Sermon preached before the Lord Mayor* (1680), pp. 5–6.

10.   Quoted in P. Seaward, *The Cavalier Parliament and the Reconstruction of the Old Regime, 1660–1667* (Cambridge, 1989), p. 246.

11.   A. Browning, *Thomas Osborne, Earl of Danby* (Glasgow, 1951), ii. 63; *The Essex Correspondence*, ed. C. E. Pike (Camden Society, xxiv, 1913), 1.

12. A. Whiteman (ed.), *The Compton Census of 1676: A Critical Edition* (1986).

13. [Anthony Ashley Cooper, Earl of Shaftesbury], *A Letter from a Person of Quality* (1675), p. 34.

14. Gilbert Burnet, *History of His Own Time*, ii. 220; Bodl. MS Tanner 38, fo. 20; *Moderation a Vertue* (1683), p. 16; Bodl. MS Tanner 37, fo. 234; Burnet, *History*, ii. 221.

15. *The Life of Richard Kidder D. D. Bishop of Bath and Wells Written by Himself*, ed. A. E. Robinson (Somerset Record Society, xxxvii, 1922), p. 36; Bodl. MS Tanner 35, fo. 170.

16. *A Letter wrote by Mijn Heer Fagel* (1687).

17. J. Spurr, 'The Church of England, Comprehension and the Toleration Act of 1689', *EHR*, civ (1989) 437–8; M. A. Goldie, 'The Political Thought of the Anglican Revolution', in *The Revolutions of 1688*, ed. R. A. Beddard (Oxford, 1991), pp. 102–36.

18. M. A. Goldie, 'John Locke and Anglican Royalism', *Political Studies*, xxxi (1983) 75.

19. Seaward, *Cavalier Parliament*, pp. 62, 67, 193–5, 328; see also R. A. Beddard, 'The Character of a Restoration Prelate: Dr John Dolben', *Notes and Queries*, NS xvii (1970), 418–21.

20. Peniston Whalley, *The Civil Rights, and Convenience of Episcopacy* (1661), pp. 10–11.

21. *Episcopal Visitation Returns for Cambridgeshire*, ed. W. M. Palmer (Cambridge, 1930), p. 14.

22. Thomas Cartwright, *A Sermon Preached upon the Anniversary ... [of] ... James II* (1686), p. 34; Shadracke Cooke, *A Sermon Preached at Islington* (1685), pp. 6–7. See also J. Spurr, '"Virtue, Religion and Government": The Anglican Uses of Providence', in T. Harris, P. Seaward and M. Goldie (eds), *The Politics of Religion in Restoration England* (Oxford, 1990).

23. Bodl. Add. MSS C308, fo. 130; William Jegon, *The Damning Nature of Rebellion* (1685), p. 7; Francis Gregory, *Concio ad Clerum* (1673), p. 7; John Shaw, *No Reformation of the Established Church* (1685), sig. a.

24. Pepys, *Diary*, iv. 372, ix. 72–3; R[ichard] A[llen], *England's Distempers, Their Cause and Cure* (1677), dedication to Charles II; Kidder, *Life*, p. 36; C. Clay, '"The Greed of Whig Bishops"?: Church Landlords and their Lessees 1660–1760', *P & P*, lxxxvii (1980) 148; Bodl. Sancroft MSS 64 (of a date after 5 March 1680); Bodl. MS Tanner 30, fo. 104.

25. Seaward, *Restoration*, p. 51.

26. J. R. Jones, 'A Representative of the Alternative Society of Restoration England?', in R. S. Dunn and M. M. Dunn (eds), *The World of William Penn* (Philadelphia, 1982); *The Memoirs of Sir John Reresby*, ed. A. Browning (Glasgow, 1936), p. 121.

27. J. Spurr, *The Restoration Church of England, 1646–1689* (New Haven and London, 1991), pp. 147–8; Goldie, 'Political Thought of Anglican Revolution'.

28. Bodl. Add. MSS C308, fo. 130; *Bishop Fell and Nonconformity: Visitation Documents from the Oxford Diocese, 1682–3*, ed. M. Clapinson (Oxfordshire Record Society, lxii, 1980), p. 2; A. Fletcher, 'The Enforcement of the Conventicle Acts 1664–1679', *Studies in Church History*, xxi (1984); Leicester, *Charges*, p. 47.

29. See R. A. Beddard, 'The Privileges of Christchurch, Canterbury: Archbishop Sheldon's Enquiries of 1671', *Archaeologia Cantiana*, lxxxvii (1972) 81–100.

30. See Spurr, *Restoration Church*, pp. 55, 204; T. Harris, *Politics under the Later Stuarts* (1993), pp. 66–7; K. Wrightson and D. Levine, *Poverty and Piety* (1979), pp. 165–8; M. Goldie and J. Spurr, 'Politics and the Restoration Parish: Edward Fowler and the Struggle for St Giles Cripplegate', *EHR*, cix (1994) 572–96.

31. P. W. Jackson, 'Nonconformists and Society in Devon 1660–1689', (Ph.D. thesis, Exeter University, 1986), p. 94.

32. Cambridge University Library, Add. MSS 8499, fo. 115.

33. Matthew Bryan, *A Perswasive To the Stricter Observation of the Lord's Day* (1686), p. 20; D. A. Spaeth, 'Common Prayer? Popular Observance of the Anglican Liturgy in Restoration Wiltshire', in S. J. Wright (ed.), *Parish, Church and People* (1988); also see Spurr, *Restoration Church*, pp. 358, 201, 243; Clapinson, op. cit., pp. xxxv, 22–4.

34. *The Diary of Roger Lowe*, ed. W. L. Sachse (London, 1938), pp. 58–9; Bodl. Add. MSS C308, fo. 114; and Spurr, *Restoration Church*, pp. 188–90, 209–19.

35. J. T. Cliffe, *The Puritan Gentry Besieged, 1660–1700* (London, 1993), p. 84.

36. *Diaries and Letters of Philip Henry*, ed. M. H. Lee (London, 1882), p. 254.

37. A. B., *A Letter from a Minister to a Person of Quality, shewing some Reasons for his Non-Conformity* (1679), p. 2.

38. C. Robbins, 'The Oxford Session of the Long Parliament of Charles II', *BIHR*, xxi (1948) 223–4.

39. John Corbet, *An Account Given of the Principles and Practices of Several Nonconformists* (1680), p. 27. I discuss Dissent in 'From Puritanism to Dissent, 1660–1700', in C. Durston and J. Eales (eds), *The Culture of English Puritanism 1560–1700* (London, 1996).

40. *Diaries of Philip Henry*, p. 277.

41. Cambridge University Library, Add. MSS 8499, fo. 161; also see J. Spurr, '"Latitudinarianism" and the Restoration Church', *HJ*, xxxi (1988) 61–82.

42. Bodl. Eng. Letters MSS C210, fo. 65; *Moderation a Vertue* (1683), p. 2.

43. Richard Pearson, *Providence Brings Good Out of Evil* (1684), p. 32; H. G. Tibbutt (ed.), *The Minutes of the First Independent Church (now Bunyan Meeting) at Bedford, 1656–1776* (Bedfordshire Historical Record Society, lv, 1976), p. 62; William Gould, *Domus mea, domus orationis* (1672), ep. ded.

44. Keeble, *Literary Culture of Nonconformity*, p. 47.

45. A. G. Matthews (ed.), *The Savoy Declaration of Faith and Order 1658* (1959), p. 122; E. B. Underhill (ed.), *The Records of a Church of Christ Meeting in Broadmead Bristol* (Hanserd Knollys Society, 1847), pp. 213, 211.

46. See Spurr, *Restoration Church*, ch. 3.

47. John Wallis, *The Necessity of Regeneration* (1682), sig. Av, p. 32.

48. On Restoration theology, see Spurr, *Restoration Church*, ch. 6; N. Tyacke, 'Arminianism and the Theology of the Restoration Church', in

Britain and the Netherlands: XI, ed. S. Groenveld and M. Wintle (Zutphen, 1994), pp. 68–83.

49. See Spurr, *Restoration Church*, ch. 7.

50. *Lowe Diary*, p. 52.

51. *The Life and Letters of ... Marquis of Halifax*, ed. H. C. Foxcroft (London, 1898), i. 467; *The Sermons of the Rev. Anthony Farindon*, ed. J. Nicholls (London, 1849), i. 471.

52. Pepys, *Diary*, iii. 47; Evelyn, *Diary*, iv. 361, 381.

53. Matthew Henry, *The Life of the Rev. Philip Henry*, corrected and enlarged by J. B. Williams (1825), p. 136; *The Remains of Denis Granville*, ed. G. Ornsby (Surtees Society, xxxvii and xlvii, 1860 and 1865), ii. 73–4; *The Diary and Autobiography of Edmund Bohun*, ed. S. W. Rix (Beccles, 1852), p. 32.

54. Bodl. MS Tanner 31, fo. 296; Leicester, *Charges*, p. 47; Clapinson, op. cit., p. 22.

55. *Lowe Diary*, p. 121.

56. J. Hunter (ed.), *The Rise of the Old Dissent Exemplified in the Life of Oliver Heywood* (1842), p. 132; Wood, *Life and Times*, i. 356; *Oliver Heywood's Life of John Angier of Denton*, ed. E. Axon (Chetham Society, xcvii, 1937), p. 107; see also *The Autobiography of William Stout of Lancaster 1665–1752*, ed. J. D. Marshall (Chetham Society, 3rd ser., xiv, 1967), pp. 82–3.

57. John Bunyan, *I Will Pray With the Spirit* (1663); Bodl. MS Tanner 30, fo. 50; see also N. Temperley, *The Music of the Parish Church: I* (Cambridge, 1979).

58. Kidder, *Life*, pp. 19–20; Cliffe, op. cit., p. 88.

59. M. Spufford, 'The Importance of the Lord's Supper to Seventeenth-century Dissenters', *Journal of the United Reformed Church History Society*, v (1993) 62–80; J. Spurr, 'The Church, the Societies and the Moral Revolution of 1688', in J. Walsh, C. Haydon and S. Taylor (eds), *The Church of England c. 1689–c. 1833* (Cambridge, 1993), offers examples of Anglican voluntarism.

60. Francis Turner, *Animadversions* (1676), pp. 31–2; Whiteman, *Compton Census*, p. xxxix; Clapinson, op. cit., p. 2; Cliffe, op. cit., p. 88.

61. [Pete]R. [Pet]T., *A Discourse concerning Liberty of Conscience* (1661), pp. 47–9, 55; Obadiah Walker (1673) quoted in M. Hunter, *Science and Society in Restoration England* (Cambridge, 1981), p. 163.

62. Sir Peter Pett (1681) quoted by M. Goldie, 'Sir Peter Pett, Sceptical Toryism and the Science of Toleration in the 1680s', *Studies in Church History*, xxi (1984) 265.

63. Wood, *Life and Times*, ii. 240.

64. *Halifax – Complete Works*, ed. J. P. Kenyon (Harmondsworth, 1969), p. 73; Pepys, *Diary*, iv. 372–7; A. M., *Plain Dealing* (1675), pp. 76–7; Pett, *Discourse*, p. 55; Richard Hollingworth, *A Modest Plea for the Church of England* (1676, 2nd edn), p. 56.

65. Francis Osborne, *Advice to a Son* (Oxford, 1656), pp. 153–4; *The Genuine Works of His Grace George Villiers, Duke of Buckingham* (Edinburgh, 1754), p. 407.

66. Miles Barne, *A Sermon Preached before the King* (1675), p. 40; Clapinson, op. cit., p. 1; Bodl. MS Tanner 146, fo. 138; J. Axtell, 'The Mechanics of Opposition: Restoration Cambridge vs. Daniel Scargill', *BIHR*, xxxviii (1965);

CSPD 1673–5, p. 549; *Remarques on the Humours and Conversation of the Gallants of the Town* (2nd edn, 1673), p. 69; John Goodman, *A Serious and Compassionate Inquiry* (1675, 2nd edn), p. 225; Turner (ed.), *Heywood*, 1, 218.

67.   John Flavell, *Divine Conduct* (1678), sigs A4–A5.

68.   M. Hunter, 'Science and heterodoxy: an early modern problem reconsidered', in D. C. Lindberg and R. S. Westman (eds), *Reappraisals of the Scientific Revolution* (Cambridge, 1990).

69.   John Evelyn, *The History of Religion*, ed. R. M. Evanson (London, 1850), i. 89.

70.   George Rust, *A Discourse of the Use of Reason in Matters of Religion* (1683), preface by Henry Halywell; [Edward Wetenhall], *Two Discourses for the Furtherance of Christian Piety and Devotion* (1671), sig. A4, 236–8; I have discussed the Anglican response to the rationalist threat in '"Rational Religion" in Restoration England', *JHI*, xlix (1988).

71.   George Seignior, *Moses and Aaron* (1670), p. 30; [Richard Allestree], *The Causes of the Decay of Christian Piety* (1667), p. 327.

72.   Leicester, *Charges*, p. 78; Robert Grove, *A Perswasive to Communion* (1683), in *A Collection of Cases* (1694 edn), p. 1; George Stradling, *Sermons* (1692), pp. 383, 393; Walter Pope, *The Life of ... Seth Ward* (1697), p. 68; Warwickshire RO, CR 136, B413 (Fell to Newdigate): this transcript was very kindly supplied by Dr V. M. Larminie.

73.   Hunter, *Heywood*, p. 229; Cambridge University Library, Add. MSS 8499, fo. 161.

74.   Dr Williams's Library, Morrice Ent'ring Books P, fo. 288; *Reliquiae Baxterianae*, ed. M. Sylvester (1696), ii. 433–4; Hunter, *Heywood*, p. 229; N. N., *A Letter from a Dissenter* (1689); Spurr, 'From Puritanism to Dissent', develops this point.

75.   Spurr, 'Church, Comprehension and Toleration Act', pp. 941–2; Thomas Tanner, *A Sermon Preached Near Exeter on Canticles VI.13* (1674), p. 13.

76.   On Shaftesbury, see Burnet, *History*, i. 172; and on Buckingham, see B. Yardley, 'George Villiers, Second Duke of Buckingham, and the Politics of Toleration', *HLQ*, lv (1992) 317–37.

77.   Spurr, 'Church, Comprehension and Toleration Act', p. 933; *The Diary of John Milward MP*, ed. C. Robbins (Cambridge, 1938), p. 326; Pepys, *Diary*, ix. 30–1; Leicester, *Charges*, p. 46.

78.   M. Goldie, 'Danby, the Bishops and the Whigs', in Harris, Seaward and Goldie, op. cit., pp. 83–90; A. Foster, 'The Clerical Estate Revitalized', in K. Fincham (ed.), *The Early Stuart Church of England, 1603–1640* (1993), pp. 147, 160.

79.   T. Harris, *London Crowds in the Reign of Charles II* (Cambridge, 1987).

80.   Francis Fullwood, *Toleration Not To Be Abused* (1672), p. 34.

81.   Wood, *Life and Times*, iii. 191.

82.   T. H., *Compulsion of Conscience Condemned* (1683), pp. 1, 3.

83.   Charles Wolseley, *Liberty of Conscience* (1668), p. 17; Martin Clifford, *A Treatise of Human Reason* (1675), pp. 4, 44, 63–6.

84.   Henry Maurice, *The Antithelemite* (1685), p. 41.

85.   Evelyn, *Diary*, iv. 640.

86. *The Letters of Humphrey Prideaux*, ed. E. M. Thompson (Camden Society, xv, 1875), p. 154.

6. THE PARTIES AND THE PEOPLE: THE PRESS, THE CROWD AND POLITICS 'OUT-OF-DOORS' IN RESTORATION ENGLAND   *Tim Harris*

1. Max Beloff, *Public Order and Popular Disturbances, 1660–1714* (London, 1938), p. 34.

2. L. S. Sutherland, 'The City of London in Eighteenth-century Politics', in R. Pares and A. J. P. Taylor (eds), *Essays Presented to Sir Lewis Namier* (Oxford, 1956), p. 59.

3. Christopher Hill, *Some Intellectual Consequences of the English Revolution* (London, 1980), p. 31; Christopher Hill, *The World Turned Upside Down: Radical Ideas During the English Revolution* (Harmondsworth, 1975), pp. 41, 354.

4. J. R. Jones, *The Revolution of 1688 in England* (London, 1972), p. 306.

5. *CSPD 1682*, pp. 303, 456; Tim Harris, *London Crowds in the Reign of Charles II: Propaganda and Politics from the Restoration until the Exclusion Crisis* (Cambridge, 1987), pp. 100–1, 107–8; Mark Knights, *Politics and Opinion in Crisis, 1678–81* (Cambridge, 1994), pp. 160–4, 170–84; Steven Pincus '"Coffee Politicians Does Create": Coffee Houses and Restoration Political Culture', *Journal of Modern History*, LXVII (1995), 807–34.

6. David Cressy, *Literacy and the Social Order: Reading and Writing in Tudor and Stuart England* (Cambridge, 1980), esp. chs 6, 7, and pp. 176–7; David Cressy, 'Literacy in Context: Meaning and Measurement in Early Modern England', in John Brewer and Roy Porter (eds), *Consumption and the World of Goods* (London, 1993), pp. 305–19; Keith Thomas, 'The Meaning of Literacy in Early Modern England', in Gerd Bauman (ed.), *The Written Word: Literacy in Transition* (Oxford, 1986), pp. 100–3; Barry Reay, 'The Context and Meaning of Popular Literacy: Some Evidence from Nineteenth-century Rural England', *P & P*, CXXXI (1991) 112–14; Jonathan Barry, 'Literacy and Literature in Popular Culture: Reading and Writing in Historical Perspective', in Tim Harris (ed.), *Popular Culture in England, c. 1500–1850* (Basingstoke and London, 1995), pp. 75–9.

7. Harris, *London Crowds*, pp. 98–108.

8. J. S., *Popery Display'd in its Proper Colours* (London, 1681), p. 4.

9. *England's Calamity, Foreshewn in Germanie's Miserie. Being the Dire Consequent of the Growth of Popery* (London, 1680).

10. See, for example: *The Humble Petition of the Protestants of France* (London, 1680); *The Horrible Persecution of the French Protestants in the Province of Poitou* (London, 1681); E[dmund] E[verard], *The Great Pressures and Grievances of the Protestants in France* (London, 1681).

11. J. S., *Popery Display'd*, p. 10; *A Letter from a Gentleman in the City, to One in the Country* (London, 1680), p. 8; [Charles Blount], *An Appeal from the Country to the City* (London, 1679); *A Character of Popery and Arbitrary Government* (London, 1681).

12.   Harris, *London Crowds*, pp. 118–29; Tim Harris, *Politics under the Later Stuarts: Party Conflict in a Divided Society 1660–1715* (London, 1993), pp. 93–4.

13.   *A Prospect of a Popish Successor* (London, 1681).

14.   *The Solemn Mock Procession; Or, The Trial and Execution of the Pope* (London, 1680); *The Solemn Mock Procession of the Pope, Cardinals, Jesuits, Fryers, Nuns* (London, 1680); *The Domestick Intelligence*, no. 39, 18 Nov. 1679; ibid., no. 40, 21 Nov. 1679; O. W. Furley, 'The Pope-burning Processions of the Late Seventeenth Century', *History*, XLIV (1959) 16–23; Sheila Williams, 'The Pope-burning Processions of 1679–81', *Journal of the Warburg and Courtauld Institutes*, XXI (1958) 104–18.

15.   F[olger] S[hakespeare] L[ibrary, Washington D.C.], Newdigate newsletter Lc. 859, 8 Nov. 1679; Harris, *London Crowds*, pp. 157, 180, 186–7.

16.   *Domestick Intelligence*, no. 38, 14 Nov. 1679; ibid., no. 39, 18 Nov. 1679. For the pope-burning at Abergavenny, see *The Pope's Downfall at Abergaveny* (1679); Philip Jenkins, 'Anti-Popery on the Welsh Marches in the Seventeenth Century', *HJ*, XXIII (1980) 285.

17.   *True Protestant Mercury*, no. 89, 9–12 Nov. 1681; ibid., no. 90, 12–16 Nov. 1681; David Cressy, *Bonfires and Bells: National Memory and the Protestant Calendar in Elizabethan and Stuart England* (London, 1989), p. 179.

18.   *Correspondence of the Family of Hatton, A.D. 1601–1704*, ed. E. M. Thompson (2 vols, London, 1873), I. 203.

19.   HMC, *7th Report*, p. 478; *Protestant (Domestick) Intelligence*, no. 87, 11 Jan. 1680/1; *True Protestant Mercury*, no. 19, 26 Feb.–2 Mar. 1680/1.

20.   Robin Clifton, *The Last Popular Rebellion: The Western Rising of 1685* (London, 1984), pp. 135–6; *CSPD 1682*, pp. 383, 387–416 (*passim*).

21.   Narcissus Luttrell, *A Brief Historical Relation of State Affairs from September, 1678, to April, 1714* (6 vols. Oxford, 1857), I. 146, 148; *True Protestant Mercury*, no. 95, 30 Nov.–3 Dec. 1681; *Loyal Protestant Intelligence*, no. 85, 3 Dec. 1681; Harris, *London Crowds*, pp. 180–2.

22.   *The Address of above 20,000 of the Loyal Protestant Apprentices of London, Humbly Presented to the Right Honourable Lord Mayor, September 2nd, 1681* (London, 1681); Mark Knights, 'London Petitions and Parliamentary Politics in 1679', *Parliamentary History*, XII (1993) 29–46; Mark Knights, 'London's "Monster" Petition of 1680', *HJ*, XXXVI (1993) 39–67; Mark Knights, 'Petitioning and the Political Theorists: John Locke, Algernon Sidney and London's "Monster" Petition of 1680', *P & P*, CXXXVIII (February 1993) 94–111; Knights, *Politics and Opinion*, chs 8, 9.

23.   *Vox Patriae* (London, 1681); J. R. Jones, *The First Whigs: The Politics of the Exclusion Crisis, 1678–83* (Oxford, 1961), pp. 167–73; Harris, *Politics under the Later Stuarts*, pp. 103–4; Knights, *Politics and Opinion*, pp. 291–303.

24.   Harris, *London Crowds*, p. 101.

25.   *CSPD 1680–1*, p. 555. The report is from [Nov.?] 1681; no date is given for the demonstrations, but they probably occurred in November 1680.

26.   Edmund Bohun, *The Third and Last Part of the Address to the Free-Men and Free-Holders of the Nation* (London, 1683), p. 9; Jones, *First Whigs*, p. 117; Knights, *Politics and Opinion*, pp. 233–4, 242.

27.   L[ibrary of] C[ongress], MS 18, 124 (London Newsletters Collection, 1665–85, 9 vols), VIII, fo. 47, 22 Apr. 1682.

28. HMC, *Portland*, III. 397; BL, Add. MSS 4182, fo. 64; Luttrell, *Brief Historical Relation*, I. 385; *Middlesex County Records*, ed. J. C. Jeaffreson (4 vols, London, 1888–92), IV. 310–11.

29. FSL, Newdigate newsletter Lc. 831, 6 Sep. 1679.

30. PRO, KB 10/1, part 4, ind. of Whitfield *et al.*

31. Knights, 'London's "Monster" Petition', pp. 42–3.

32. *CSPD 1680–1*, p. 555; Knights, 'London Petitions', p. 43.

33. *Domestick Intelligence*, no. 36, 7 Nov. 1679.

34. *Hatton Correspondence*, I. 203; HMC, *7th Report*, p. 478.

35. Harris, *London Crowds*, pp. 177–8.

36. *True Protestant Mercury*, no. 89, 9–12 Nov. 1681.

37. John Miller, *Popery and Politics in England, 1660–1688* (Cambridge, 1973), pp. 169–70.

38. *A Letter to a Friend. Shewing … How False that State-Maxim is, Royal Authority is Originally and Radically in the People* (London, 1679).

39. Basil Duke Henning (ed.), *The House of Commons, 1660–1690* (3 vols, London, 1983), III. 158–9; *CSPD 1680–1*, p. 583.

40. Centre for Kentish Studies, Maidstone, Q/SB/14/64–6; West Yorkshire Archives Society, MX/R/23/54–5, informations of Mrs Ann of Frickley.

41. *CSPD 1682*, p. 452.

42. *CSPD 1682*, p. 493.

43. *CSPD 1682*, p. 479.

44. S[omerset] R[ecord] O[ffice], Q/SR/142, no. 1, information of George Wickham.

45. Longleat House, Coventry MSS, VI, fo. 199.

46. Harris, *London Crowds*, ch. 8; PRO, PC2/65, pp. 6–7; *CSPD Jul.–Sep. 1683*, p. 363.

47. Knights, 'London Petitions', pp. 41–2; Knights, 'London's "Monster" Petition', pp. 61–3.

48. Tim Harris, '"Lives, Liberties and Estates": Rhetorics of Liberty in the Reign of Charles II', in Tim Harris, Paul Seaward and Mark Goldie (eds), *The Politics of Religion in Restoration England* (Oxford, 1990), pp. 217–41.

49. SRO, Q/SR/153, no. 19.

50. Dr Williams's Library, Roger Morrice Ent'ring Book, P, p. 326.

51. *A Faithfull and Impartial Account of the Behaviour of a Party of the Essex Freeholders* (London, 1679), p. 6; *CSPD 1680–1*, p. 232; Bodl. MS Ballard 12, fol. 39; Henning, *House of Commons*, I. 229, 360; Mark Goldie, 'Danby, the Bishops and the Whigs', in Harris *et al.* (eds), *Politics of Religion*, p. 98.

52. Harris, *London Crowds*, pp. 119–21, 178–9; Harris, *Politics of Religion*, p. 93; Gary S. De Krey, 'The London Whigs and the Exclusion Crisis Reconsidered', in Lee Beier, David Cannadine and James Rosenheim (eds), *The First Modern Society: Essays in English History in Honour of Lawrence Stone* (Cambridge, 1989), pp. 462–6; Knights, 'London Petitions', pp. 38–41; Knights, 'London's "Monster" Petition', pp. 48–52.

53. Nathaniel Thompson (ed.), *A Collection of One Hundred and Eighty Loyal Songs* (3rd edn, London, 1685), preface.

54. Harris, *London Crowds*, pp. 131–3; Harris, *Politics under the Later Stuarts*, p. 95; Knights, *Politics and Opinion*, pp. 164–8.

55. Alan Craig Houston, *Algernon Sidney and the Republican Heritage in England and America* (Princeton, 1991), ch. 2, provides a useful general overview of royalist thought at this time. See also Tim Harris, 'Tories and the Rule of Law in the Reign of Charles II', *The Seventeenth Century*, VIII (1993), 9–27, for a consideration of the extent to which the Tories should be seen as royal absolutists.

56. Roger L'Estrange, *The Character of a Papist in Masquerade* (London, 1681), p. 10; Harris, 'Lives, Liberties and Estates', pp. 231–6.

57. [John Nalson], *The Character of a Rebellion and What England May Expect From One* (London, 1681), p. 4.

58. Harris, *Politics under the Later Stuarts*, pp. 55–6, 71; K. H. D. Haley, *The First Earl of Shaftesbury* (Oxford, 1968), pp. 370–402.

59. *A Dialogue Between the Pope and a Phanatic* (London, 1681), quotes on pp. 9, 10.

60. *Heraclitus Ridens*, no. 2, 8 Feb. 1681; ibid., no. 4, 22 Feb. 1681.

61. *The Charter* [ND], in Nathaniel Thompson (ed.), *A Collection of Eighty-six Loyal Poems* (London, 1685), p. 150; *A Congratulatory Poem upon the Arrival of His Royal Highness James, Duke of York, at London, April 8th, 1682* (London, 1682), in ibid., p. 251.

62. B. T[horogood], *Captain Thorogood His Opinion of the Point of Succession* (London, 1680), p. 9.

63. Charles II, *His Majesties Declaration To All His Loving Subjects, Touching the Causes and Reasons that Moved Him to Dissolve the Two Last Parliaments* (London, 1681).

64. Harris, *London Crowds*, pp. 164–8, 169–70; Henning, *House of Commons*, I. 329–31, 414–16 (Norwich and Southwark are examples of popular constituencies that returned two Tory MPs to all three Exclusion Parliaments); John T. Evans, *Seventeenth-century Norwich: Politics, Religion and Government, 1620–1690* (Oxford, 1979), pp. 269–76; Victor L. Stater, 'Continuity and Change in English Provincial Politics: Robert Paston in Norfolk, 1675–1683', *Albion*, XXV (1993) 212–13; Knights, *Politics and Opinion*, pp. 237, 259, 264–8, 273, 291, 298–300; P. J. Challinor, 'Restoration and Exclusion in the County of Cheshire', *Bulletin of the John Rylands University Library of Manchester*, LXIV (1981–2) 360–85; Newton E. Key, 'Politics beyond Parliament: Unity and Party in the Herefordshire Region during the Restoration Period' (unpubl. Ph.D. dissertation, Cornell University, 1989), p. 450; P. J. Norrey, 'The Relationship between Central Government and Local Government in Dorset, Somerset and Wiltshire 1660–1688' (unpubl. Ph.D. thesis, University of Bristol, 1988), pp. 170–89, 238–50.

65. *Vox Angliae* (London, 1682); John Oldmixon, *The History of Addresses* (2 vols, London, 1709–11), I. 27–86; Knights, *Politics and Opinion*, pp. 325–45. Knights has identified 210 loyal addresses presented in response to Charles II's *Declaration* of April 1681 alone (*Politics and Opinion*, p. 335). There were further loyal addresses the following year in abhorrence of Shaftesbury's 'Association', and in 1683 in detestation of the Rye House Plot.

66. Oldmixon, *History of Addresses*, I.47; HMC, *Ormonde*, NS VI. 91; *London Gazette*, no. 1738, 13–17 Jul. 1682; *Loyal Protestant Intelligence*, no. 181, 15 Jul. 1682.

67. For Norwich, see: *Loyal Protestant Intelligence*, no. 165, 8 Jun. 1682; *The Domestick Intelligence; Or, News both from City and Country Impartially Related*, no. 108, 1–5 Jun. 1682. For the others, see: Roger L'Estrange, *The Observator in Dialogue* (3 vols, London, 1684–7), I, no. 151, 8 Jun. 1682; Luttrell, *Brief Historical Relation*, I. 92, 193; *CSPD Jan.–Jun. 1683*, pp. 286–7; *Loyal Protestant Intelligence*, no. 30, 18 Jun. 1681; Harris, *London Crowds*, pp. 168, 179–80.

68. HMC, *10th Report*, Appendix IV, pp. 173, 174; Luttrell, *Brief Historical Relation*, I.142, 144; *CSPD 1680–1*, p. 571; LC, MS 18, 124, VII, fo. 264, 8 Nov. 1681; R. Clark, 'Anglicanism, Recusancy and Dissent in Derbyshire, 1603–1730' (unpubl. D. Phil. thesis, University of Oxford, 1979), p. 216.

69. *CSPD 1682*, pp. 124, 165; *Loyal Protestant Intelligence*, no. 143, 18 Apr. 1682; ibid., no. 145, 22 Apr. 1682; Harris, *London Crowds*, pp. 170–1.

70. Luttrell, *Brief Historical Relation*, I. 279; LC, MS 18, 124, fo. 385; *CSPD, Jul.–Sept. 1683*, p. 395; Anthony Wood, *Life and Times, 1632–1695*, ed. A. Clark (5 vols, Oxford, 1891–1900), III. 72; Berkshire RO, R/AC1/1/16, p. 19.

71. LC, MS 18, 124, VIII, fo. 27, 9 Mar. 1682.

72. *Loyal Protestant Intelligence*, no. 145, 22 Apr. 1682.

73. *Loyal Protestant Intelligence*, no. 30, 18 Jun. 1681.

74. *CSPD Jan.–Jun. 1683*, pp. 286–7; Berkshire RO, R/AC1/1/16, p. 19.

75. *Loyal Protestant Intelligence*, no. 43, 2 Aug. 1681; LC, MS 18,124, VIII, fo. 220, 10 Aug. 1682.

76. Harris, *London Crowds*, ch. 3; P. J. Norrey, 'The Restoration Regime in Action: The Relationship between Central and Local Government in Dorset, Somerset and Wiltshire', *HJ*, XXXI (1988) 789–812; Colin Lee, '"Fanatic Magistrates": Religious and Political Conflict in Three Kent Boroughs, 1680–1684', *HJ*, XXXV (1992) 43–61.

77. L'Estrange, *Observator*, I, no. 68, 5 Nov. 1681.

78. Colin Lucas, 'The Crowd and Politics between Ancien Régime and Revolution in France', *Journal of Modern History*, LX (1988) 427.

79. John Northleigh, *The Triumph of our Monarchy* (London, 1685), p. 393.

80. Leo Bogart, 'Public Opinion and Collective Behaviour', *Public Opinion Quarterly*, XLVII (1983) 487.

81. Jonathan Scott, *Algernon Sidney and the Restoration Crisis, 1677–1683* (Cambridge, 1991), esp. pp. 45–8.

82. *True Protestant Mercury*, no. 151, 14–17 Jun. 1682. The sources are not complete enough to allow us to count the number of Whig and Tory demonstrations in different parts of the country each year. Not only are there gaps and discontinuities in the coverage (thus making any attempt to assess changes in frequency over time very dangerous), but also many of the sources are imprecise when detailing exactly where demonstrations took place. Typical in this respect is Luttrell's report that 'several places in this kingdom' saw bonfire demonstrations for Charles II's birthday in 1681, 'particularly Windsor, Portsmouth, Lynn, etc.': Luttrell, *Brief Historical Relation*, I.92.

83. *True Protestant Mercury*, no. 88, 5–9 Nov. 1681.

84. *Loyal Protestant Intelligence*, no. 231, 9 Nov. 1682; *CSPD 1682*, pp. 528–30.

85. *Loyal Protestant Intelligence*, no. 30, 18 Jun. 1681; Wood, *Life and Times*, III. 42–3; Richard L. Greaves, *Secrets of the Kingdom: British Radicals from the*

Popish Plot to the Revolution of 1688–89 (Stanford, 1992), p. 51. For the survival of Whig–Tory tensions after the Oxford Parliament more generally, see the preliminary discussion in Tim Harris, 'Party Turns? Or, Whigs and Tories Get Off Scott Free', *Albion*, XXV (1993) 581–90, and 'Sobering Thoughts, But the Party is Not Yet Over: A Reply', ibid., pp. 645–7.

86.   Harris, *London Crowds*, ch. 8; Gary S. De Krey, 'Revolution *Redivivus*: 1688–1689 and the Radical Tradition in Seventeenth-century London Politics', in Lois G. Schwoerer (ed.), *The Revolution of 1688–1689: Changing Perspectives* (Cambridge, 1992), pp. 205–6; Knights, 'London Petitions', p. 41; Knights, 'London's "Monster" Petition', pp. 59–64.

87.   Tim Harris, 'Was the Tory Reaction Popular?: Attitudes of Londoners towards the Persecution of Dissent, 1681–6', *London Journal*, XIII (1988) 106–20.

88.   Cf. Lucas, 'The Crowd and Politics', p. 439.

89.   *London Gazette*, no. 2008, 12–16 Feb. 1684/5.

90.   The figure is taken from those loyal addresses cited in the *London Gazette*. Further loyal addresses came in from Ireland, Scotland, various residents abroad and colonial dependencies, making a total of 439 in all.

91.   Berkshire RO, H/FAcl, fo. 81; Dorset RO, DC/LR/N23/3, fo. 32; BL, Add. MSS 41 803, fo. 138; *London Gazette*, no. 2008, 12–16 Feb. 1684/5; ibid., no. 2012, 26 Feb.–2 Mar. 1684/5.

92.   *London Gazette*, no. 2012, 26 Feb.–2 Mar., 1684/5.

93.   Jonathan Israel (ed.), *The Anglo-Dutch Moment: Essays on the Glorious Revolution and its World Impact* (Cambridge, 1991), p. 5; Jeremy Black, *A System of Ambition? British Foreign Policy 1660–1793* (London, 1991), p. 135.

94.   Tim Harris, 'London Crowds and the Revolution of 1688', in Eveline Cruickshanks (ed.), *By Force or By Default? The Revolution of 1688* (Edinburgh, 1989), pp. 44–64, offers a preliminary investigation into this issue. The themes developed in these last few paragraphs are explored more fully in my forthcoming monograph on the British revolutions of the late 17th century.

7.   LANDOWNERSHIP, THE ARISTOCRACY AND THE COUNTRY GENTRY
James M. Rosenheim

1.   S. K. Roberts, 'Public or Private? Revenge and Recovery at the Restoration', *BIHR*, 59 (1986) 172–88.

2.   D. R. Hainsworth, *Stewards, Lords and People: The Estate Steward and his World in Late Stuart England* (Cambridge, 1992), p. 13.

3.   C. Clay, 'Landlords and estate management', in J. Thirsk (ed.), *The Agrarian History of England and Wales*, v, *1640–1750* (Cambridge, 1984), Part ii, pp. 179–84, 196–97, 208.

4.   P. Borsay, *The English Urban Renaissance: Culture and Society in the Provincial Town 1660–1770* (Oxford, 1989), Part III and appendices 2, 4–7.

5.   A. McInnes, 'The Emergence of a Leisure Town: Shrewsbury 1660–1760', *P & P* 120 (1988) 78; Borsay, op. cit., chs 5 and 10.

6.   Sir Gyles Isham (ed.), *The Diary of Thomas Isham of Lamport* (Farnborough, 1971), pp. 131, 159, 161, 167, 217–21, 225–9.

7. E. M. Thompson (ed.), *Letters of Humphrey Prideaux* (Camden Society, NS, 15, 1875), p. 146.

8. J. V. Beckett, *The Aristocracy in England 1660–1914* (Oxford, 1986), pp. 363–4; L. Stone, *The Crisis of the Aristocracy* (Oxford, 1965), pp. 385–92; F. Heal, *Hospitality in Early Modern England* (Cambridge, 1990), pp. 141–7; P. Roebuck, 'Absentee Landownership in the Late Seventeenth and Early Eighteenth Centuries: A Neglected Factor in English Agrarian History', *AgHR*, 21 (1973) 11–12; Hainsworth, *Stewards*, pp. 13-17.

9. J. T. Cliffe, *The Puritan Gentry Besieged, 1650–1700* (London, 1993), p. 172.

10. F. T. Melton, *Sir Robert Clayton and the Origins of English Deposit Banking, 1658–1685* (Cambridge, 1986), p. 48; M. Slater, *Family Life in the Seventeenth Century: The Verneys of Claydon House* (London, 1984), p. 76; D. R. Hainsworth, 'Fathers and Daughters', in L. O. Frappell (ed.), *Principalities, Powers and Estates* (Adelaide, 1980), p. 17.

11. Draft, *c.* 1664, 'First that his lordship sees', Raynham Hall, Norfolk, uncatalogued papers of first Viscount Townshend.

12. L. Stone, 'The Residential Development of the West End of London in the Seventeenth Century', in B. Malament (ed.), *After the Reformation* (Philadelphia, 1980), pp. 174–7, 181–2.

13. F. T. Melton, 'Absentee Land Management in Seventeenth-century England', *Agricultural History*, 52 (1978) 147–59; J. V. Beckett, 'Absentee Landownership in the Later Seventeenth and Early Eighteenth Centuries: The Case of Cumbria', *Northern History*, 19 (1983) 87–107; Hainsworth, *Stewards*, pp. 12–17.

14. D. R. Hainsworth (ed.), *The Correspondence of Sir John Lowther of Whitehaven 1693–1698, Records of Social and Economic History*, NS, 7 (London, 1983).

15. L. and J. C. F. Stone, *An Open Elite? England 1540–1880* (Oxford, 1984), pp. 329–49; M. Girouard, *Life in the English Country House* (New Haven, 1978), pp. 129–45; A. Everitt, *Perspectives in English Urban History* (London, 1973), pp. 110–14; P. Burke, *Popular Culture in Early Modern Europe* (New York, 1978), pp. 277–8; K. Thomas, *Religion and the Decline of Magic* (New York, 1971), ch. 22.

16. Beckett, *Aristocracy*, pp. 342–3; G. Etherege, *The Man of Mode*, act III, scene ii; G. Jackson-Stops, *The Treasure Houses of Britain* (New Haven, 1985), p. 147.

17. Heal, op. cit., p. 148; N. Key, 'The Political Culture and Political Rhetoric of County Feasts and Feast Sermons, 1654–1714', *JBS*, 33 (1994) 245. Borsay, op. cit., pp. 296–300, addresses a slightly later period.

18. A. Fletcher, *Reform in the Provinces: The Government of Stuart England* (New Haven, 1986), pp. 19–20; R. Hutton, *The Restoration: A Political and Religious History of England and Wales 1658–1667* (Oxford, 1985), p. 129. On the continuity of personnel, see P. J. Norrey, 'The Restoration Regime in Action: The Relationship between Central and Local Government in Dorset, Somerset and Wiltshire, 1660–1678', *HJ*, 31 (1988) 804; A. M. Coleby, *Central Government and the Localities: Hampshire 1649–1689* (Cambridge, 1987), p. 90; P. J. Challinor, 'Restoration and Exclusion in the County of Cheshire', *Bulletin of*

the John Rylands University Library of Manchester, 64 (1982) 361; S. K. Roberts, *Recovery and Restoration in an English County: Devon Local Administration 1646–1670* (Exeter, 1985), p. 148 and 'Revenge and Recovery', 181–2.

19.   For the tax commissions, see *Statutes of the Realm*, vol. 5; for the lieutenancy and militia, see V. Stater, *Noble Government: The Stuart Lord Lieutenancy and the Transformation of English Politics* (Athens, Georgia, 1994), pp. 82–3; for commissions of the peace, see L. K. J. Glassey, *Politics and the Appointment of Justices of the Peace 1675–1720* (Oxford, 1979), pp. 15–17 and N. Landau, *The Justices of the Peace, 1679–1760* (Berkeley, 1984), Appendix A.

20.   Roberts, *Recovery and Restoration*, p. 186; Coleby, op. cit., p. 109; Fletcher, *Reform*, pp. 19–20; Stater, op. cit., pp. 96–121; R. Greaves, *Deliver Us From Evil: The Radical Underground in Britain, 1660–1663* (New York, 1986).

21.   Roberts, *Recovery and Restoration*, p. 189; Norrey, op. cit., 790.

22.   Stater, op. cit., pp. 96–121.

23.   Fletcher, *Reform*, ch. 5, discusses the volume of work. For evidence that lesser gentry increasingly performed administrative tasks, see Glassey, op. cit., p. 24; P. Roebuck, *Yorkshire Baronets 1640–1760: Families, Estates, and Fortunes* (Hull, 1980), pp. 55–6; C. Holmes, *Seventeenth-century Lincolnshire* (Lincoln, 1980), p. 83; J. M. Rosenheim, 'County governance and elite withdrawal in Norfolk, 1660–1720', in A. L. Beier, D. Cannadine and J. M. Rosenheim (eds), *The First Modern Society: Essays in English History in Honour of Lawrence Stone* (Cambridge, 1989), pp. 106–15; G. C. F. Forster, *The East Riding Justices of the Peace in the Seventeenth Century* (York, 1973), p. 32.

24.   Norrey, op. cit., 808. See A. Fletcher, 'The Enforcement of the Conventicle Acts 1664–1679', in W. J. Shiels (ed.), *Studies in Church History*, 21 (1984) 235–46; R. Greaves, *Enemies Under his Feet: Radicals and Nonconformists in Britain, 1664–1677* (Stanford, 1990), pp. 131–4, 148–9, 160–5; P. Seaward, *The Restoration* (New York, 1991), p. 58; Hutton, op. cit., p. 210; Coleby, op. cit., pp. 138–9.

25.   Stater, op. cit., chs 4–5 and Fletcher, *Reform*, pp. 333–48; Coleby, op. cit., pp. 111–13; Norrey, op. cit., 789–96; F. Negus to Norfolk's deputies, 30 August 1687, Norfolk RO, L'Estrange P20, f. 117.

26.   For example, B. Coward, *The Stanleys, Lords Stanley and Earls of Derby, 1385–1672*, Chetham Society, 3rd ser., 30 (1983), 180–1.

27.   Fletcher, *Reform*, pp. 323–4; Stater, op. cit., pp. 77–8, 88–9, 117, 125–6, 139.

28.   A. Hughes, *Politics, Society and Civil War in Warwickshire, 1620–1660* (Cambridge, 1987), p. 334.

29.   Fletcher, *Reform*, p. 323; J. L. Malcolm, 'Charles II and the Reconstruction of Royal Power', *HJ*, 35 (1992) 311–14.

30.   Stater, op. cit., p. 6.

31.   J. S. Morrill, *Cheshire 1630–1660: County Government and Society during the English Revolution* (Oxford, 1974), pp. 225–6.

32.   Roberts, *Recovery and Restoration*, p. 190.

33.   M. Kishlansky, *Parliamentary Selection* (Cambridge, 1986), ch. 5; Hughes, *Politics*, chs 6, 8; A. Hughes, 'Parliamentary Tyranny? Indemnity Proceedings and the Impact of the Civil War', *Midlands History*, 11 (1986) 49–78.

34. Kishlansky, *Parliamentary Selection*, pp. 106–7, 124, 129–30, 139–48; P. J. Challinor, 'Restoration and Exclusion in the County of Cheshire', *Bulletin of the John Rylands University Library of Manchester*, 64 (1982) 368; N. E. Key, 'Comprehension and the Breakdown of Consensus in Restoration Herefordshire', in T. Harris, P. Seaward and M. Goldie (eds), *The Politics of Religion in Restoration England* (Oxford, 1990), pp. 191–215.

35. Fletcher, 'Enforcement of the Conventicle Acts', p. 245. A survey of parliamentary by-elections, based on B. D. Henning (ed.), *The House of Commons 1660–1690*, 3 vols (London, 1983), shows that fifteen of thirty-three contests were fought on identifiable national issues from 1662 to 1670, while the same was true of only nineteen of sixty-eight contests from 1670 to 1678.

36. Fletcher, *Reform*, p. 91; *CSPD 1682*, pp. 54–55.

37. Challinor, op. cit., 374.

38. Glassey, op. cit., chs 2 and 3; Fletcher, *Reform*, pp. 21–6; Stater, op. cit., pp. 133, 138–45, 163–8, 171–5.

39. T. Harris, *Politics under the Later Stuarts* (London, 1993), chs 3–4.

40. Coleby, op. cit., p. 145.

41. Beckett, *Aristocracy*, pp. 324–7.

42. Beckett, *Aristocracy*, pp. 295–6; Melton, *Sir Robert Clayton*, pp. 53–5, 126–34; C. Clay, *Public Finance and Private Wealth: The Career of Sir Stephen Fox, 1627–1716* (Oxford, 1978), chs III–IV.

43. N. McKendrick, '"Gentlemen and Players" revisited: the gentlemanly ideal, the business ideal and the professional ideal in English literary culture', in N. McKendrick and R. Outhwaite (eds), *Business Life and Public Policy* (Cambridge, 1986), pp. 105–6, 115–16; Stone and Stone, *Open Elite?*, pp. 21–3.

44. M. G. Davies, 'Country Gentry and Payments to London, 1650–1714', *EcHR*, 2nd ser., 24 (1971), 36 and *passim*; Hainsworth, *Stewards*, ch. 5.

45. P. J. Bowden, 'Agricultural prices, wages, farm profits, and rents', in Thirsk (ed.), *Agrarian History of England and Wales*, v. ii. 75–8, 851; M. G. Davies, 'Country Gentry and Falling Rents in the 1660s and 1670s', *Midland History*, 4 (1977) 86–96; Hainsworth, *Stewards*, pp. 54–7.

46. Melton, *Sir Robert Clayton*, pp. 192–7; Roebuck, *Yorkshire Baronets*, p. 164; J. M. Rosenheim, *The Townshends of Raynham* (Middletown, Connecticut, 1989), p. 94.

47. 'Sir John Hollands speeches', Raynham Hall box files, first Viscount Townshend – Felton; Bodl. MS Tanner 239, fos. 53v–54; J. Thirsk and J. P. Cooper (eds), *Seventeenth-century Economic Documents* (Oxford, 1972), pp. 68–9; Thirsk (ed.) *Agrarian History of England and Wales*, v, ii, p. xxvii; Davies, 'Country Gentry and Falling Rents', 91.

48. Thirsk and Cooper, op. cit., pp. 81, 86; 'Sir John Hollands speeches made in 75', Raynham Hall box files, first Viscount Townshend – Felton; J. M. Rosenheim (ed.), *The Notebook of Robert Doughty 1662–1665*, Norfolk Record Society, 54 (1989) 119.

49. Thirsk and Cooper, op. cit., pp. 81–4.

50. C. Clay, *Economic Expansion and Social Change*, vol. 1, *People, Land and Towns* (Cambridge, 1984), p. 123; Rosenheim, *Townshends*, pp. 96–104.

51. Rosenheim, *Townshends*, pp. 90–6; Clay, 'Landlords and estate management', pp. 184, 228; J. R. Wordie, *Estate Management in Eighteenth-century England: The Building of the Leveson–Gower Fortune*, (London, 1982), pp. 33–5.

52. Raynham Hall, uncatalogued estate accounts 1660–1687; Raynham Hall library, 'Directions from his Lordship to Auditor', drawer 112 and 'Direccons for Ward', drawer 66; S. Monteage, *Instructions for Rent-gatherers Accompts* (London, 1683).

53. Hainsworth, *Stewards*, p. 28. This and the next paragraph are based on Hainsworth's book.

54. *Instructions*, pp. 3, 8, 33 (pp. 10–32 for the model accounts); Hainsworth, *Stewards*, p. 261.

55. Holmes, *Lincolnshire*, p. 72.

56. Landau, op. cit., pp. 334–43, 359–62.

8. THE RESTORATION TOWN   *Peter Borsay*

1. P. Clark and P. Slack (eds), *Crisis and Order in English Towns 1500–1700* (London, 1972).

2. For early syntheses, see Clark and Slack, *Crisis and Order*, Introduction; P. Clark and P. Slack, *English Towns in Transition 1500–1700* (London, 1976); P. J. Corfield, 'Urban Development in England and Wales in the Sixteenth and Seventeenth Centuries', in D. C. Coleman and A. H. John (eds), *Trade, Government and Economy in Pre-Industrial England* (London, 1976), pp. 214–47; J. Patten, *English Towns 1500–1700* (Folkestone, 1978).

3. For a survey of the crisis debate, see A. Dyer, *Decline and Growth in English Towns 1400–1640* (London, 1991).

4. E. L. Jones and M. E. Falkus, 'Urban Improvement and the English Economy in the Seventeenth and Eighteenth Centuries', in P. J. Uselding (ed.), *Research in Economic History, Volume 4* (Greenwich, Conn., 1979), pp. 193–233; A. McInnes, *The English Town 1660–1760* (London, 1980); P. Borsay, 'The English Urban Renaissance: The Development of Provincial Urban Culture *c.* 1680–*c.* 1760', *Social History*, 2, No. 2, (1977) 581–603.

5. See, for example, the changing views of Peter Clark in the Introductions to Clark and Slack, *Crisis and Order*; P. Clark (ed.), *Country Towns in Pre-industrial England* (Leicester, 1981); and P. Clark (ed.), *The Transformation of English Provincial Towns 1600–1800* (London, 1984).

6. The figures are derived from the following. (i) Clark's estimate of *c.* 738 small towns (population 400–2500) and 44 large towns (population above 2500) in the mid-seventeenth century; P. Clark, 'Changes in Patterns of English Small Towns in the Early Modern Period', in *Gründung und Bedeutung Kleinerer Städte im Nördlichen Europa der Frühen Neuzeit* (Wolfenbüttel, 1991), pp. 68–70. (ii) Clark's estimate of *c.* 750 small towns, and of 46 per cent of English townspeople occupying settlements of less than 5000 inhabitants, in 1700; P. Clark, 'Small Towns in England 1550–1850: National and Regional Population Trends', unpublished paper presented to a conference on European Small Towns in the Early Modern Period, University of Leicester, July 1990, p. 1. (iii) Corfield's estimate of 68 towns with populations of 2500

or more people in 1700, and her estimate that settlements of 5000 or more people contained 850 000 people out of a total population for England and Wales of 5.2 million in 1700; P. Corfield, *The Impact of English Towns 1700–1800* (Oxford, 1982), p. 8.

7. E. A. Wrigley, 'City and Country in the Past: A Sharp Divide or a Continuum?', *Historical Research*, LXIV, No. 154 (1991) 110–11; and also J. de Vries, *European Urbanization 1500–1800* (London, 1984), pp. 9–10, 253–4; Patten, *English Towns*, pp. 244–96.

8. Corfield, 'Urban Development', pp. 217, 223; J. Patten, 'Population Distribution in Norfolk and Suffolk during the Sixteenth and Seventeenth Centuries', *Transactions of the Institute of British Geographers*, LXV (1975) 48–9.

9. For the national population, see E. A. Wrigley and R. S. Schofield, *The Population History of England 1541–1871* (London, 1981), pp. 208–9.

10. de Vries, *European Urbanization*, pp. 257–8; E. A. Wrigley, 'Urban Growth and Agricultural Change: England and the Continent in the Early Modern Period', in P. Borsay (ed.), *The Eighteenth-century Town: A Reader in English Urban History 1688–1820* (Harlow, 1990), esp. pp. 60–7.

11. See above, n. 6.

12. Corfield, 'Urban Development', pp. 221–2.

13. Corfield, *Impact of English Towns*, p. 8.

14. Figures for the 1520s and for Norwich from Corfield, 'Urban Development', pp. 217, 219; other figures for London from R. Finlay and B. Shearer, 'Population Growth and Suburban Expansion', in A. L. Beier and R. Finlay (eds), *London 1500–1700: The Making of the Metropolis* (London, 1986), p. 48; national population figure from Wrigley and Schofield, *Population History of England*, pp. 208–9.

15. Corfield, 'Urban Development', p. 229.

16. A. Everitt, 'Urban Growth, 1570–1770', *Local Historian*, VIII, No. 4 (1968) 120–1; Clark and Slack, *Towns in Transition*, pp. 24–5; J. Chartres, *Internal Trade in England 1500–1700* (London, 1977), p. 48; J. Chartres, 'The Marketing of Agricultural Produce', in J. Thirsk (ed.), *The Agrarian History of England and Wales*, Volume 5, *1640–1750, Part 2, Agrarian Change* (Cambridge, 1985), pp. 409–14.

17. Clark, 'Small Towns in England', p. 5; A. Wilson, 'Population Developments of Early Modern English Small Towns: The Parish Register Evidence for Four Regions', unpublished paper presented to a conference on European Small Towns in the Early Modern Period, University of Leicester, July 1990, p. 12; and also A. Dyer, 'The Market Towns of Southern England', *Southern History*, I (1979), pp. 123–34; J. D. Marshall, 'The Rise and Transformation of the Cumbrian Market Town 1660–1900', *Northern History*, XIX (1983) 133–53.

18. P. Corfield, 'A Provincial Capital in the Late Seventeenth Century: The Case of Norwich', in Clark and Slack, *Crisis and Order*, pp. 266–7; D. H. Sacks, *The Widening Gate: Bristol and the Atlantic Economy, 1450–1700* (Berkeley and Los Angeles, 1991), p. 353.

19. C. Chalklin, *The Provincial Towns of Georgian England: A Study of the Building Process 1740–1820* (London, 1974), pp. 20, 22; Corfield, 'Urban

Development', p. 220 and n. 22, p. 241. The estimates for Birmingham and Manchester vary a good deal.

	Chalklin		Corfield	
	1660s/70s	1700	1660s	1700
Birmingham	c. 4400	5000–7000		7000–8000
Manchester	c. 5000		c. 6000	8000–9000
Liverpool	c. 1500	5000+		c. 5000

20. VCH, *County of Gloucester*, Volume IV, *The City of Gloucester* (Oxford, 1988), p. 102; VCH, *County of York East Riding*, Volume VI, *The Borough and Liberties of Beverley* (Oxford, 1989), pp. 107–8; M. Laithwaite, 'Totnes Houses 1500–1800', in Clark, *Transformation of English Provincial Towns*, pp. 64, 87.

21. P. Slack, *The Impact of Plague in Tudor and Stuart England* (Oxford, 1990), pp. 133, 151; J. Taylor, 'Plague in the Towns of Hampshire: The Epidemic of 1665–6', *Southern History*, VI (1984) 111; I. G. Doolittle, 'The Effects of the Plague on a Provincial Town in the Sixteenth and Seventeenth Centuries', *Medical History*, XIX (1975) 333.

22. A. B. Appleby, 'The Disappearance of Plague: A Continuing Puzzle', *EcHR*, 2nd ser., XXXIII, No. 2 (1980) 161–73; P. Slack, 'The Disappearance of Plague: An Alternative View', *EcHR*, 2nd ser., XXXIV, No. 3 (1981) 469–76; Slack, *Impact of Plague*, pp. 311–37.

23. Finlay and Shearer, 'Population Growth and Suburban Expansion', pp. 48–9; J. Landers and A. Mouzas, 'Burial Seasonality and Causes of Death in London 1670–1819', *Population Studies*, XLII (1988) 59–83; Corfield, 'Provincial Capital', p. 269; A. Dyer, 'Epidemics of Measles in a Seventeenth-century English Town', *Local Population Studies*, XXXIV (1985) 35–45; VCH, *City of Gloucester*, p. 102; VCH, *Beverley*, p. 107.

24. Wilson, 'Population Developments of Early Modern English Towns', pp. 7–9.

25. E. A. Wrigley, 'A Simple Model of London's Importance in Changing English Society and Economy 1650–1750', *P & P*, XXXVII (1967) 46; D. Souden, 'Migrants and the Population Structure of Later Seventeenth-century Provincial Cities and Market Towns', in Clark, *Transformation of English Provincial Towns*, p. 139.

26. J. R. Holman, 'Apprenticeship as a Factor in Migration: Bristol 1675–1726', *Transactions of the Bristol and Gloucestershire Archaeological Society*, XCVII (1980) 85; M. J. Kitch, 'Capital and Kingdom: Migration to Later Stuart London', in Beier and Finlay, *London 1500–1700*, pp. 229–31; P. Earle, 'Age and Accumulation in the London Business Community, 1665–1720', in N. McKendrick and B. Outhwaite (eds), *Business Life and Public Policy* (Cambridge, 1986), p. 44; D. Hey, *The Fiery Blades of Hallamshire: Sheffield and its Neighbourhood, 1660–1740* (Leicester, 1991), pp. 74–80; Souden, 'Migrants and the Population Structure', pp. 142–9; P. Clark, 'Migration in England during the Late Seventeenth and Early Eighteenth Centuries', *P & P*, LXXXIII (1979) 66–75.

27.   J. Landers, 'Mortality, Weather and Prices in London 1675–1825: A Study of Short-term Fluctuations', *Journal of Historical Geography*, XII, No. 4 (1986) 359–61; *idem*, 'Mortality and Metropolis: The Case of London 1675–1825', *Population Studies*, XLI, No. 1 (1987) 68–76; and on urban migration in general, P. Clark and D. Souden (eds), *Migration and Society in Early Modern England* (London, 1987).

28.   Clark and Souden, *Migration and Society*, pp. 32–6.

29.   N. Goose, 'In Search of the Urban Variable: Towns and the English Economy 1500–1650', *EcHR*, 2nd ser., XXIX, No. 2 (1986) 165–85; C. Husbands, 'Regional Change in a Pre-industrial Economy: Wealth and Population in England in the Sixteenth and Seventeenth Centuries', *Journal of Historical Geography*, XIII, No. 4 (1987), esp. p. 356.

30.   Clark, *Country Towns*, pp. 11–15; N. Goose, 'Decay and Regeneration in Seventeenth-century Reading: A Study in a Changing Economy', *Southern History*, VI (1984) 57–61; A. Rosen, 'Winchester in Transition 1580–1700', in Clark, *Country Towns*, pp. 148–70; S. McIntyre, 'Bath: The Rise of a Resort Town 1660–1800', in Clark, *Country Towns*, p. 201; VCH, *City of Gloucester*, pp. 75–81, 96–7; VCH, *Beverley*, p. 93; VCH, *County of Wiltshire*, Volume VI (London, 1962), p. 129; I. Roy, 'England Turned Germany? The Aftermath of the Civil War in its European Context', *TRHS*, 5th ser., XXVIII (1978) 127–44; J. Binns, 'Scarborough and the Civil Wars, 1642–1651', *Northern History*, XXII (1986) 117–22.

31.   C. Wilson, *England's Apprenticeship 1603–1763*, 2nd edn (Harlow, 1984), Part Two; D. C. Coleman, *The Economy of England 1450–1750* (Oxford, 1977), pp. 91–110, 196–201.

32.   A. Everitt, 'The Food Market of the English Town 1660–1760', in *Third International Conference of Economic History* (Munich, 1965), pp. 59–71; C. W. Chalklin, *Seventeenth-century Kent: A Social and Economic History* (Rochester, 1978), pp. 92, 162, 165, 175, 185; A. McInnes, 'The Golden Age of Uttoxeter', in P. Morgan (ed.), *Staffordshire Studies* (Keele, 1987), pp. 118–21; A. D. Dyer, 'Warwickshire Towns under the Tudors and Stuarts', *Warwickshire History*, III, No. 4 (1976/7) 123; Goose, 'Decay and Regeneration', pp. 61–4.

33.   P. Ripley, 'Village and Town: Occupations and Wealth in the Hinterland of Gloucester, 1660–1700', AgHR, XXXII (1984) 170–8, esp. pp. 177–8; C. W. Chalklin, 'A Seventeenth-century Market Town: Tonbridge', *Archaeologia Cantiana*, LXXVI (1961) 158–61; P. Styles, 'Henley-in-Arden in the Seventeenth Century', in P. Styles, *Studies in Seventeenth Century West Midlands History* (Kineton, 1978), pp. 205–12; G. H. Kenyon, 'Petworth Town & Trades Pt. 1', *Sussex Archaeological Collections*, XCVI (1958) 35–107.

34.   Hey, *Fiery Blades of Hallamshire*, p. 3; C. Phythian-Adams, *Re-thinking English Local History* (Leicester, 1987), pp. 13–14.

35.   Rosen, 'Winchester in Transition', pp. 150, 172; McIntyre, 'Rise of a Resort Town', p. 201.

36.   A. Everitt, 'Country, County and Town: Patterns of Regional Evolution in England', *TRHS*, 5th ser., XXIX (1979) 91–108; Rosen, 'Winchester in Transition', pp. 170–84; VCH, *City of Gloucester*, pp. 101, 103–10; VCH, *Beverley*, pp. 105–7; VCH, *County of Yorkshire, The City of York* (London, 1961), pp. 166–7; VCH, *County of Warwickshire*, Volume VIII (London, 1969),

pp. 506–7; A. McInnes, 'The Emergence of a Leisure Town: Shrewsbury 1660–1760', *P & P*, CXX (1988) 55–65; G. Talbut, 'Worcester as an Industrial and Commercial Centre, 1660–1750', *Transactions of the Worcestershire Archaeological Society*, X (1986) 91–102.

37. P. Hembry, *The English Spa 1560–1815: A Social History* (London, 1990), pp. 66–110; R. Lennard, 'The Watering-Places', in *idem* (ed.), *Englishmen at Rest and Play: Some Phases of English Leisure 1558–1714* (Oxford, 1931), pp. 1–79; McIntyre, 'Rise of a Resort Town', pp. 201–4.

38. Chartres, *Internal Trade in England*, pp. 37–8, 46; Coleman, *Economy of England*, pp. 131–50; W. E. Minchinton (ed.), *The Growth of English Overseas Trade in the Seventeenth and Eighteenth Centuries* (London, 1969); G. Jackson, 'Trade and Shipping', in J. R. Jones (ed.), *The Restored Monarchy 1660–1688* (London and Basingstoke, 1979), pp. 136–54.

39. A. Everitt, 'The English Urban Inn 1560–1760', in *idem* (ed.), *Perspectives in English Urban History* (London, 1973), pp. 94–7; M. D. G. Wanklyn, 'The Severn Navigation in the Seventeenth Century: Long Distance Trade of Shrewsbury Boats', *Midland History*, XIII (1988) 34–5.

40. Sacks, *The Widening Gate*, Part 3; P. G. E. Clemens, 'The Rise of Liverpool 1665–1750', *EcHR*, 2nd ser., XXIX, No. 2 (1976) 211–25; Minchinton, *Growth of English Overseas Trade*, pp. 33–4.

41. Minchinton, *Growth of English Overseas Trade*, p. 35; R. Davis, 'English Foreign Trade, 1660–1700', in Minchinton, *Growth of English Overseas Trade*, pp. 80–2, 89–90, 92.

42. Beier and Finlay, *London 1500–1700*, pp. 11–17 and Part 2; J. Alexander, 'The Economic Structure of the City of London at the End of the Seventeenth Century', *Urban History Yearbook* (1989), esp. pp. 55, 59; P. Earle, *The Making of the English Middle Class: Business, Society and Family Life in London, 1660–1730* (London, 1989), pp. 17–81; L. Stone, 'The Residential Development of the West End of London in the Seventeenth Century', in B. C. Malament (ed.), *After the Reformation* (Manchester, 1980), pp. 167–212.

43. Wrigley, 'Simple Model of London's Importance', pp. 55–65; T. Barker, 'Business as Usual? London and the Industrial Revolution', *History Today*, XXXIX (February 1989) 45–50; J. Chartres, 'Food Consumption and Internal Trade', in Beier and Finlay, *London 1500–1700*, pp. 168–96; *idem*, 'Road Carrying in England in the Seventeenth Century: Myth and Reality', *EcHR*, 2nd ser., XXX, No. 1 (1977), esp. pp. 87–8; for criticism of Chartres, see D. Gerhold, 'The Growth of the London Carrying Trade, 1681–1838', *EcHR*, 2nd ser., XLI, No. 3 (1988) 392–410; J. H. Andrews, 'The Port of Chichester and the Grain Trade, 1650–1750', *Sussex Archaeological Collections*, XCII (1954) 100–2.

44. K. R. Adey, 'Seventeenth-century Stafford: A County Town in Decline', *Midland History*, II, No. 3 (1974) 152–67; Laithwaite, 'Totnes Houses 1500–1800', pp. 86–7; N. Alldridge, 'The Mechanics of Decline: Migration and Economy in Early Modern Chester', in M. Reed (ed.), *English Towns in Decline 1350–1800*, Centre for Urban History, University of Leicester, Working Papers No. 1 (1986), esp. p. 5.

45. T. Arkell, 'The Incidence of Poverty in England in the Later Seventeenth Century', *Social History*, XII, No. 1 (1987) 23–47.

46. P. Slack, *Poverty and Policy in Tudor and Stuart England* (London, 1988), pp. 53–5, 169–73; *idem, The English Poor Law 1531–1782* (London, 1990), pp. 26–9, 33–4, 50–3; Clark, *Transformation of English Provincial Towns,* pp. 30–1; VCH, *City of Gloucester,* pp. 111–12.

47. P. Earle, 'The Female Labour Market in London in the Late Seventeenth and Early Eighteenth Centuries', *EcHR,* 2nd ser., XLII, No. 3 (1989) 328–9, 336–44, 346; M. Prior, 'Women and the Urban Economy: Oxford 1500–1800', in *idem* (ed.), *Women in English Society 1500–1800* (London, 1985), pp. 93–117.

48. Clark and Souden, *Migration and Society,* pp. 33–6; P. Clark, 'Migrants in the City: The Process of Social Adaptation in English Towns', in Clark and Souden, *Migration and Society,* pp. 279–80.

49. Clark, 'Migration in England', pp. 65–7; for the high rates of turnover of persons in villages, see P. Laslett, *Family Life and Illicit Love in Earlier Generations* (Cambridge, 1977), p. 98.

50. N. Goose, 'Household Size and Structure in Early Stuart Cambridge', in J. Barry (ed.), *The Tudor and Stuart Town: A Reader in English Urban History* (Harlow, 1990), pp. 74–120; J. C. Hindson, 'Family, Household, Kinship and Inheritance in Shrewsbury, 1650–1750' (Ph.D. thesis, University College of Wales, Aberystwyth, 1990), pp. 98, 100–1, 172–9.

51. J. Boulton, 'Residential Mobility in Seventeenth-century Southwark', *Urban History Yearbook* (1986), pp. 1–14; Hey, *Fiery Blades of Hallamshire,* pp. 197–201.

52. M. J. Power, 'Shadwell: The Development of a London Suburban Community in the Seventeenth Century', *London Journal,* IV, No. 1 (1978) 36; Wanklyn, 'Severn Navigation in the Seventeenth Century', p. 35; and also M. J. Power, 'The East London Working Community in the Seventeenth Century', in P. J. Corfield and D. Keene (eds), *Work in Towns 850–1850* (Leicester, 1990), p. 116; M. Prior, *Fisher Row: Fishermen, Bargemen and Canal Boatmen in Oxford 1500–1900* (Oxford, 1982); M. J. Power, 'The Social Topography of Restoration London', in Beier and Finlay, *London 1500–1700,* pp. 216–18; Alexander, 'Economic Structure of the City of London', p. 57; J. Langton, 'Residential Patterns in Pre-industrial Cities: Some Case Studies from Seventeenth-century Britain', *Transactions of the Institute of British Geographers,* LXV (1975) 15–19; J. C. Hindson, 'The Marriage Duty Acts and the Social Topography of the Early Modern Town – Shrewsbury, 1695–8', *Local Population Studies,* XXXI (1983) 25–8; Patten, *English Towns,* pp. 194–6.

53. P. Clark, *Sociability and Urbanity: Clubs and Societies in the Eighteenth-Century City* (Leicester, 1986), p. 6; Clark, 'Migrants in the City', pp. 280–6; A. Ellis, *The Penny Universities: A History of the Coffee-houses* (London, 1956); B. Lillywhite, *London Coffee-houses* (London, 1963).

54. Boulton, 'Residential Mobility', pp. 6–7; Hey, *Fiery Blades of Hallamshire,* pp. 197–201; Earle, *Making of the English Middle Class,* pp. 240–2.

55. G. S. Holmes, *Augustan England: Professions, State and Society 1680–1730* (London, 1982); P. Borsay, *The English Urban Renaissance: Culture and Society in the Provincial Town 1660–1770* (Oxford, 1989), pp. 204–11.

56. Earle, *Making of the English Middle Class,* esp. Preface, and chs 1, 9, 12; *idem,* 'Age and Accumulation in the London Business Community', pp. 53–4;

J. Barry, 'Urban Identity and the Middling Sort in Early Modern England', paper delivered to the New Directions in Urban History seminar, University of Essex, September 1992; L. Stone, *An Open Elite? England 1540–1880* (Oxford, 1986), pp. 132–41, 286–8; T. Harris, 'Was the Tory Reaction Popular? Attitudes of Londoners towards the Persecution of Dissent, 1681–6', *London Journal*, XIII, No. 2 (1987–8) 107–8.

57. Earle, *Making of the English Middle Class*, pp. 335–7; Barry, 'Urban Identity and the Middling Sort'.

58. For social zoning, see Langton, 'Residential Patterns in Pre-industrial Cities', pp. 7–11; Patten, *English Towns*, pp. 36–9; Hindson, 'Marriage Duty Acts', pp. 25–8; Power, 'Social Topography of Restoration London', pp. 202–12; *idem*, 'Shadwell', pp. 33–5; L. Stone, 'Residential Development of the West End of London', pp. 186–96. For occupational zoning, see above, n. 52.

59. VCH, *City of Gloucester*, p. 121; S. Porter, 'Property Destruction in the English Civil Wars', *History Today*, XXXVI (August 1986), pp. 36–41; *idem*, 'The Fire-raid in the English Civil War', *War and Society*, II, No. 2 (1984) 27–40; *idem*, 'The Destruction of Axminster in 1644', *Devon and Cornwall Notes and Queries*, XXV (1985) 243–5; D. Lloyd, *Broad Street*, Ludlow Research Paper No. 3 (Birmingham, 1979), p. 23.

60. E. L. Jones, S. Porter and M. Turner, *A Gazetteer of English Urban Fire Disasters 1500–1900*, Historical Geography Research Ser., No. 13 (Norwich, 1984); Patten, *English Towns*, pp. 60–5; M. Turner, 'The Nature of Urban Renewal after Fire in Seven English Provincial Towns, *circa* 1675–1810' (Ph.D. thesis, Exeter University, 1985).

61. W. G. Bell, *The Great Fire of London in 1666* (London, 1951), pp. 210–29; *The Diary of Samuel Pepys*, eds R. Latham and W. Matthews, Volume VII (London, 1972), pp. 271–2.

62. 18 and 19 Car. II, c.7; T. F. Reddaway, *The Rebuilding of London after the Great Fire* (London, 1951), pp. 68–90; J. Summerson, *Georgian London* (Harmondsworth, 1962), pp. 52–4; D. Cruickshank and P. Wyld, *London: The Art of Georgian Building* (London, 1975), pp. 22–4; Borsay, *English Urban Renaissance*, ch. 2.

63. S. E. Rasmussen, *London the Unique City* (Harmondsworth, 1960), pp. 93–114, 152–8; Reddaway, *Rebuilding of London*, pp. 40–67, 311–12; Summerson, *Georgian London*, pp. 27–51; N. G. Brett-James, *The Growth of Stuart London* (London, 1935), pp. 366–404; Stone, 'Residential Development of the West End of London', pp. 189–208.

64. Lloyd, *Broad Street*, p. 48; S. Collier with S. Pearson, *Whitehaven 1660–1800* (London, 1991), pp. 27–36; Borsay, *English Urban Renaissance*, pp. 90–7.

65. See Laithwaite, 'Totnes Houses 1500–1800', pp. 87–92, for an example of a town where a 'subsidence to a lower level of prosperity' led to slowness in implementing the new building fashions.

66. *The Journeys of Celia Fiennes*, ed. C. Morris (London, 1947), p. 148.

67. E. McKellar, 'The Design and Building of Late Seventeenth Century Houses in London' (Ph.D. thesis, Royal College of Art, 1992), pp. 189–207.

68. U. Priestley and P. J. Corfield, 'Rooms and Room Use in Norwich Housing, 1580–1730', *Post-Medieval Archaeology*, XVI (1982) 93–123; A. D. Dyer, 'Urban Housing: A Documentary Study of Four Midland Towns 1530–1700', *Post-Medieval Archaeology*, XV (1981) 207–18; V. Parker, *The Making of King's Lynn* (Chichester, 1971), pp. 79–110; F. E. Brown, 'Continuity and Change in the Urban House: Developments in Domestic Space Organization in Seventeenth-century London', *Comparative Studies in Society and History*, XXVIII (1986) 558–90.

69. Borsay, *English Urban Renaissance*, pp. 101–6, 325–8; for the period before this, see R. Tittler, *Architecture and Power: The Town Hall and the English Urban Community* c. *1500–1640* (Oxford, 1991); and after this, K. Grady, *The Georgian Public Buildings of Leeds and the West Riding*, publications of the Thoresby Society, Volume LXII, No. 133 (Leeds, 1989).

70. Clark and Slack, *English Towns in Transition*, pp. 126–40; Tittler, *Architecture and Power*, pp. 98–128; P. Clark, 'The Civic Leaders of Gloucester 1580–1800', in Clark, *Transformation of English Provincial Towns*, pp. 324–5; VCH, *City of Gloucester*, pp. 116–17; VCH, *Beverley*, pp. 101–3; R. Howell, 'Newcastle and the Nation: The Seventeenth-century Experience', in Barry, *Tudor and Stuart Town*, pp. 276–8; J. W. Kirby, 'Restoration Leeds and the Aldermen of the Corporation, 1661–1700', *Northern History*, XXII (1986) 123–74; M. A. Mullett, '"Men of Knowne Loyalty": The Politics of the Lancashire Borough of Clitheroe, 1660–1689', *Northern History*, XXI (1985) 124–5.

71. Hey, *Fiery Blades of Hallamshire*, pp. 213–30, quotation from p. 225; V. Pearl, 'Social Policy in Early Modern London', in H. Lloyd-Jones, V. Pearl and B. Worden (eds), *History and Imagination: Essays in Honour of H. R. Trevor-Roper* (London, 1981), pp. 119–20; J. T. Evans, *Seventeenth-century Norwich: Politics, Religion, and Government, 1620–1690* (Oxford, 1979), p. 319; P. L. Gauci, 'The Corporation and the Country: Great Yarmouth 1660–1722' (D. Phil. thesis, University of Oxford, 1991). H. Horwitz, 'Party in a Civic Context: London from the Exclusion Crisis to the Fall of Walpole', in C. Jones (ed.), *Britain in the First Age of Party 1680–1750* (London, 1987), p. 175, writes of 'the complex mix of oligarchical and participatory elements in the corporation's "constitution"' in London.

72. G. S. De Krey, *A Fractured Society: The Politics of London in the First Age of Party 1688–1715* (Oxford, 1985), pp. 9–14; *idem*, 'London Radicals and Revolutionary Politics, 1675–1683', in T. Harris, P. Seaward and M. Goldie (eds), *The Politics of Religion in Restoration England* (Oxford, 1990), pp. 133–62; Horwitz, 'Party in a Civic Context', pp. 177–81; Harris, 'Was the Tory Reaction Popular?', pp. 106–20; VCH, *City of Gloucester*, pp. 112–15; Evans, *Seventeenth-century Norwich*, esp. pp. 318–20.

73. Earle, *Making of the English Middle Class*, pp. 260–8; Sacks, *The Widening Gate*, Part 3; D. Beaver, 'Conscience and Context: The Popish Plot and the Politics of Ritual, 1678–1682', *HJ*, XXXIV, No. 2 (1991) 297–327; M. A. Mullett,' Popular Culture and Popular Politics: Some Regional Case Studies', in Jones, *Britain in the First Age of Party*, pp. 129–50.

74. J. J. Hurwich, '"A Fanatick Town": The Political Influence of Dissenters in Coventry, 1660–1720', *Midland History*, IV (1977–78) 30–2;

C. Brent, 'The Neutering of the Fellowship and the Emergence of a Tory Party in Lewes (1663–1688)', *Sussex Archaeological Collections*, CXXI (1983) 102; VCH, *County of Warwick*, Volume VIII (London, 1969), pp. 374–6; VCH, *County of Stafford*, Volume XIV, *Lichfield* (Oxford, 1990), p. 158; VCH, *City of Gloucester*, pp. 117–18; VCH, *Beverley*, pp. 96–7.

75. T. Harris, *London Crowds in the Reign of Charles II* (Cambridge, 1987), esp. pp. 217–22; *idem*, 'The Problem of "Popular Political Culture" in Seventeenth-century London', *History of European Ideas*, X, No. 1 (1989) 51–2; *idem*, 'The Bawdy House Riots of 1668', *HJ*, XXIX, No. 3 (1986) 537–56; J. Barry, 'The Parish in Civic Life: Bristol and Its Churches 1640–1750', in S. J. Wright (ed.), *Parish, Church and People: Local Studies in Lay Religion 1350–1750* (London, 1988), pp. 167–8; J. Barry, 'The Politics of Religion in Restoration Bristol', in Harris, Seaward and Goldie, *Politics of Religion*, esp. pp. 163–89.

76. Beaver, 'Conscience and Context', pp. 321, 326; P. Seaward, 'Gilbert Sheldon, the London Vestries, and the Defence of the Church', in Harris, Seaward and Goldie, *Politics of Religion*, pp. 55–7.

77. D. Underdown, *Fire From Heaven: The Life of an English Town in the Seventeenth Century* (London, 1992), pp. 240–3, 255–6; Hurwich, '"A Fanatick Town"', pp. 16, 30–2; Brent, 'Neutering of the Fellowship', p. 102; P. Styles, 'The Corporation of Bewdley under the Later Stuarts', in *idem*, *Seventeenth-century West Midlands History*, pp. 48–9.

78. Clark, 'Civic Leaders of Gloucester', p. 327.

79. Clark, *Country Towns*, pp. 19–20; *idem*, 'Civic Leaders of Gloucester', pp. 322–8; *idem*, 'Visions of the Urban Community: Antiquarians and the English City before 1800', in D. Fraser and A. Sutcliffe (eds), *The Pursuit of Urban History* (London, 1983), pp. 115–16; VCH, *City of Gloucester*, pp. 105, 113–14; VCH, *Lichfield*, p. 79; Styles, 'Corporation of Bewdley', p. 55; M. A. Mullett, 'Conflict, Politics and Elections in Lancaster, 1660–1688', *Northern History*, XIX (1983), p. 72; *idem*, 'Popular Culture and Popular Politics', p. 137.

80. Gauci, 'The Corporation and the Country'; Hey, *Fiery Blades of Hallamshire*, pp. 54–60, 197–248; C. Lee, '"Fanatic Magistrates": Religious and Political Conflict in Three Kent Boroughs, 1680–1684', *HJ*, XXXV, No. 1 (1991) 43–61.

81. L. K. J. Glassey, 'Local Government', in Jones, *Britain in the First Age of Party*, pp. 153–6.

82. Hurwich, '"A Fanatick Town"', pp. 16, 30–2; Underdown, *Fire From Heaven*, pp. 230–59; VCH, *Lichfield*, p. 79.

83. J. H. Sacret, 'The Restoration Government and Municipal Corporations', *EHR*, XLV (1930) 232–59; J. R. Western, *Monarchy and Revolution: The English State in the 1680s* (London, 1972), pp. 69–77; R. G. Pickavance, 'The English Boroughs and the King's Government: A Study of the Tory Reaction, 1681–85' (D.Phil. thesis, University of Oxford, 1977); J. Miller, 'The Crown and the Borough Charters in the Reign of Charles II', *EHR*, C (1985), pp. 53–84; Horwitz, 'Party in a Civic Context', pp. 177–81. The crown's response to London 'radical' politics during the Exclusion Crisis can be explored in two articles by M. Knights, 'London Petitions and Parliamentary Politics in 1679', *Parliamentary History*, XII, No. 1 (1993) 29–46; 'London's "Monster" Petition of 1680', *HJ*, XXXVI, No. 1 (1993) 39–67.

84. Miller, 'Crown and the Borough Charters', pp. 73–5, 79–84; Lee, '"Fanatic Magistrates"', pp. 43–61; Mullett, 'Conflict, Politics and Elections in Lancaster', pp. 69–76.

85. P. Borsay, '"All the Town's a Stage": Urban Ritual and Ceremony 1660–1800', in Clark, *Transformation of English Provincial Towns*, pp. 228–46.

86. *Journeys of Celia Fiennes*, pp. 149, 284–7; B. Klein, '"Between the Bums and Bellies of the Multitude": Civic Pageantry and the Problem of the Audience in Late Stuart London', *London Journal*, XVII, No. 1 (1992) 18–26.

87. Harris, *London Crowds*, especially pp. 101–6; J. Brand, *History and Antiquities of the Town and County of Newcastle upon Tyne*, 2 vols (Newcastle upon Tyne, 1789), Volume II, pp. 30–1, 48; M. R. Toynbee, 'Fresh Light on William Larson's Statue of James II at Newcastle upon Tyne', *Archaeologia Aeliana*, 4th ser., XXIX (1951) 108–12; Howell, 'Newcastle and the Nation', pp. 291–2; D. Allen, 'Political Clubs in Restoration London', *HJ*, XIX, No. 3 (1976) 568–9; D. Cressy, *Bonfires and Bells: National Memory and the Protestant Calendar in Elizabethan and Stuart England* (London, 1989), pp. 64–6, 78–80, 86–92, 171–89.

88. Much of the evidence for popular recreations comes from the eighteenth century; see R. W. Malcolmson, *Popular Recreations in English Society 1700–1850* (Cambridge, 1973). On magic, see K. Thomas, *Religion and the Decline of Magic: Studies in Popular Beliefs in Sixteenth- and Seventeenth-century England* (Harmondsworth, 1973), pp. 681–98, 767–800.

89. D. Cressy, *Literacy and the Social Order: Reading and Writing in Tudor and Stuart England* (Cambridge, 1980); R. A. Houston, *Scottish Literacy and the Scottish Identity: Illiteracy and Society in Scotland and Northern England 1600–1800* (Cambridge, 1985), pp. 20–109; J. Barry, 'Popular Culture in Seventeenth-century Bristol', in B. Reay (ed.), *Popular Culture in Seventeenth-century England* (London, 1988), pp. 62–3; VCH, *City of Gloucester*, p. 119; Earle, 'Female Labour Market in London', pp. 333–6; Harris, 'The Problem of "Popular Political Culture"', pp. 50–1; P. Burke, 'Popular Culture in Seventeenth-century London', in Reay, *Popular Culture*, pp. 48–51.

90. See, for example, M. Berlin, 'Civic Ceremony in Early Modern London', *Urban History Yearbook* (1986), pp. 15–27.

91. D. Mills, 'Chester Ceremonial: Re-creation and Recreation in the English "Medieval" Town', *Urban History Yearbook*, XVIII (1991) 11–14; F. Heal, *Hospitality in Early Modern England* (Oxford, 1990), p. 349; Borsay, '"All the Town's a Stage"', pp. 231–2.

92. Burke, 'Popular Culture in Seventeenth-century London', pp. 39–54; C. Phythian-Adams, 'Milk and Soot: The Changing Vocabulary of a Popular Ritual in Stuart and Hanoverian London', in Fraser and Sutcliffe, *Pursuit of Urban History*, pp. 92–104.

93. See above, n. 53, and J. H. Plumb, *The Commercialization of Leisure in Eighteenth-century England* (Reading, 1973); Borsay, *English Urban Renaissance*; W. Wroth, *The London Pleasure Gardens of the Eighteenth Century* (Michigan and London, 1979); J. Harley, *Music in Purcell's London* (London, 1968).

94. See, for example, the apparently limited impact on Beverley, Gloucester, Lichfield and Winchester by 1690: VCH, *Beverley*, pp. 110–11;

VCH, *City of Gloucester*, pp. 107, 119; VCH, *Lichfield*, pp. 159–70; Rosen, 'Winchester in Transition', p. 180.

95.   J. Barry, 'Provincial Town Culture, 1640–1780: Urbane or Civic?', in J. H. Pittock (ed.), *Interpretation and Cultural History* (London, 1991), pp. 198–234.

96.   Borsay, *English Urban Renaissance*, pp. 284–308. For the withdrawal argument in a European context, see P. Burke, *Popular Culture in Early Modern Europe* (London, 1979), especially Part 3.

97.   Barry, 'Popular Culture in Seventeenth-century Bristol', pp. 59–90; *idem*, 'Provincial Town Culture', pp. 205–24; Harris, 'Problem of "Popular Political Culture"', pp. 43–58.

98.   Phythian-Adams, 'Milk and Soot', pp. 95–6, 104.

99.   J. Elliott, *The City in Maps: Urban Mapping to 1900* (London, 1988), pp. 47–50; P. Glanville, *London in Maps* (London, 1972); J. E. Pritchard, 'A Hitherto Unknown Original Print of the Great Plan of Bristol by Jacobus Millerd, 1673', *Transactions of the Bristol and Gloucestershire Archaeological Society*, XLIV (1922) 203–20; R. Hyde, *Gilded Scenes and Shining Prospects: Panoramic Views of British Towns 1575–1900* (New Haven, Conn., 1985), pp. 11–18, 36–61; Borsay, *English Urban Renaissance*, pp. 80–5.

9.   CONSUMPTION AND WEALTH   *J. M. Ellis*

Readers should note that economy measures have been taken to keep what would otherwise have been a huge number of references within reasonable limits; in particular, some detail which derives from specific works listed in the bibliography is not separately referenced here.

1.   Joseph Addison, *The Spectator*, no. 69 (19 May 1711); Edward Chamberlayne, *Angliae Notitia: or, the Present State of England* (London, 1670; 19th edn, 1700), p. 328. See also N. Zahedieh, 'London and the colonial consumer in the late seventeenth century', *EcHR*, xlvii (1994) 239–61.

2.   [Daniel Defoe], *A Review of the State of the British Nation*, viii. 16 (1 May 1711); *The Works of Lord Bolingbroke*, 4 vols (London, 1844), ii. 414.

3.   Richard Steele, *The Conscious Lovers* (London, 1722), act 4, scene 2; Edward Hatton, *The Merchant's Magazine, or the Tradesman's Treasury* (London, 1695; 4th edn, 1701), p. iv. See also J. McVeagh, *Tradeful Merchants: The Portrayal of the Capitalist in Literature* (London, 1981).

4.   C. Shammas, 'The decline of textile prices in England and America prior to industrialization', *EcHR*, xlvii (1994) 502.

5.   E. Kerridge, *Textile Manufactures in Early Modern England* (Manchester, 1985), pp. 83–4.

6.   Roger North, *The Lives of the Norths*, 3 vols (London, 1890), i. 173–78; Henry Bourne, *The History of Newcastle on Tyne: or, the Ancient and Present State of that Town* (Newcastle, 1736), p. 159. The main demand for coal, however, remained that from domestic consumers.

7.   W. G. Hoskins, 'Harvest fluctuations and English economic history 1620–1759', *AgHR*, xvi (1968), 21–2.

8. *M. Misson's Memoirs and Observations in his Travels over England* (London, 1719), quoted in J. Ashton, *Social Life in the Reign of Queen Anne* (London, 1897), p. 141; John Macky, *A Journey through England, in Familiar Letters*, 2 vols (London, 1714; 3rd edn, 1723), ii. 274.

9. *The Autobiography of William Stout of Lancaster 1665–1752*, ed. J. D. Marshall, (Manchester, 1967), pp. 89–90: Stout's journey to London on horseback took five days, whereas the vessel carrying his purchases made the passage in seven days.

10. See D. Hey, *Packmen, Carriers and Packhorse Roads: Trade and Communications in North Derbyshire and South Yorkshire* (Leicester, 1980).

11. *The Trade of England Revived* (1681), reprinted in *Seventeenth-century Economic Documents*, ed. J. Thirsk and J. P. Cooper (Oxford, 1972), p. 397; N. Cox, 'The distribution of retailing tradesmen in north Shropshire 1660–1750', *Journal of Regional & Local Studies*, xiii (1993) 4–22.

12. Daniel Defoe, *The Complete English Tradesman in Familiar Letters*, 2 vols (London, 1726; 2nd edn, 1727), i. 328.

13. *Autobiography of William Stout*, pp. 79–80. See also *The Diary of Samuel Pepys*, ed. R. C. Latham and W. Matthews, 11 vols (London, 1970–83), xi. 143–49, 104–8; xii. index.

14. R. Thoroton, *The Antiquities of Nottinghamshire* (1677), p. 499; HMC, *Portland MSS.*, ii (1893), 308; *The Journeys of Celia Fiennes*, ed. C. Morris (London, 1947), p. 72.

15. *Pepys's Diary*, iv. 299; Defoe, *Review*, v. 12 (31 Jan. 1708).

16. E. A. Wrigley and R. S. Schofield, *The Population History of England 1541–1871* (Cambridge, 1981), pp. 642–43.

17. E. H. Phelps Brown and S. V. Hopkins, *A Perspective of Wages and Prices* (London, 1981), pp. 13–30.

18. Chamberlayne, *Angliae Notitia*, p. 317; Worcestershire Grand Jury presentments, 23 Apr. 1661, reprinted in *English Economic History: Select Documents*, ed. A. E. Bland, P. A. Brown and R. H. Tawney (London, 1914), p. 361.

19. John Houghton, *A Collection of Letters for the Improvement of Husbandry and Trade*, 4 vols (London, 1681–83), iv. 177; Bernard Mandeville, *The Fable of the Bees: or, Private Vices, Publick Benefits*, 2 vols (London, 1714; Oxford, 1924), i. 194. See also E. S. Furniss, *The Position of the Labourer in a System of Nationalism* (New York, 1957 edn), pp. 117–25.

20. G. S. Holmes, 'Gregory King and the social structure of pre-industrial England', *TRHS*, xxvii (1977) 66.

21. John Cary, *An Essay on the State of England, in Relation to its Trade ...* (Bristol, 1695), p. 147. Shammas, 'Textile prices', 483–507, draws much less optimistic conclusions about the relationship between prices and wages.

22. S. Rappaport, *Worlds Within Worlds: Structures of Life in Sixteenth-century London* (Cambridge, 1989), pp. 123–45, 401–7; T. Arkell, 'The incidence of poverty in England in the later seventeenth century', *Social History*, xii (1987) 23–47.

23. P. Corfield, 'A provincial capital in the late seventeenth century: the case of Norwich', in P. Clark and P. Slack (eds), *Crisis and Order in English Towns 1500–1700* (London, 1972), p. 281.

24. William Wycherley, *The Country Wife* (1675), act 4, scene 3.

25. Daniel Defoe, *A Tour Thro' the Whole Island of Great Britain*, 2 vols (London, 1724–7; 1962 edn), i. 165; Defoe, *Complete Tradesman*, i. 112.

26. *The Works of George Berkeley*, ed. A. A. Luce and T. E. Jessop, 8 vols (London, 1953), vi. 76.

10. INTERNATIONAL RELATIONS, WAR AND THE ARMED FORCES
J. D. Davies

1. S. Pincus, 'England and the World in the 1650s', in J. Morrill (ed.), *Revolution and Restoration: England in the 1650s* (London, 1992), pp. 129–47.

2. PRO, S[tate] P[apers] F[oreign] 94/45, fo. 174v, instruction to Fanshawe.

3. C. G. A. Clay, *Economic Expansion and Social Change: England 1500–1700, II: Industry, Trade and Government* (Cambridge, 1984), pp. 140, 148–51, 160.

4. J. Miller, *Charles II* (London, 1991), pp. 88–93; J. D. Davies, 'The Birth of the Imperial Navy? Aspects of English Naval Strategy *c.* 1650–90', in M. Duffy (ed.), *Parameters of British Naval Power 1650–1850* (Exeter, 1992), pp. 25–6.

5. J. Black, *A System of Ambition? British Foreign Policy 1660–1793* (London, 1991), pp. 102–9, 134 (quotation from p. 102).

6. *London Gazette*, nos. 188–91, 2–16 September 1667; cf. P. Fraser, *The Intelligence of the Secretaries of State* (Cambridge, 1956), pp. 28–56.

7. BL, M636/26, Ralph Verney to Edmund Verney, 13 May 1673.

8. Pincus, 'England and the World', pp. 137–43; Pincus, 'Popery, Trade and Universal Monarchy: The Ideological Context of the Outbreak of the Second Anglo-Dutch War', *EHR*, CVII (1992) 18–22; J. F. Bosher, 'The Franco-Catholic Danger, 1660–1715', *History*, LXXIX (1994) 5–30.

9. BL, Add. MSS 65138, fo. 31, paper preceding Treaty of Dover.

10. P. S. Lachs, *The Diplomatic Corps under Charles II and James II* (New Brunswick, New Jersey, 1965), p. 17; V.-L. Tapié, 'Louis XIV's Methods in Foreign Policy', in R. Hatton (ed.), *Louis XIV and Europe* (London, 1976), pp. 3–15.

11. Miller, *Charles II*, p. 86; K. H. D. Haley, *An English Diplomat in the Low Countries: Sir William Temple and John de Witt, 1665–72* (Oxford, 1986), pp. 33–4.

12. Miller, *Charles II*, *passim*; R. Hutton, *Charles II: King of England, Scotland, and Ireland* (Oxford, 1989), *passim*.

13. Black, *System of Ambition*, pp. 68–9.

14. D. B. Horn, 'The Diplomatic Experience of Secretaries of State, 1660–1852', *History*, XLI (1956) 91–3.

15. PRO, S[tate] P[apers] D[omestic] 104/176, fo. 77, minutes of meeting, 22 Oct. 1668; cf. PRO SPD 104/176–80, *passim*.

16. Lachs, *Diplomatic Corps*, pp. 3–14.

17. G. M. Bell, *A Handlist of British Diplomatic Representatives 1509–1688* (London, 1990), pp. 166–9, 216, 226, 276–9.

18. PRO, SPF 78/138, fos. 41, 44, 54, 64, 65: William Perwich to Arlington, 30 Aug. 1673 New Style; William Lockhart to Arlington, 31 Aug.

1673 New Style; same to same, 7 Sept. 1673 New Style; Sir Peter Wyche to Arlington and Williamson, 1 Sept. 1673 New Style. Cf. Lachs, *Diplomatic Corps*, pp. 31–41.

19. N. Luttrell, *A Brief Historical Relation of State Affairs from September 1678 to April 1714* (Oxford, 1857), I. 154–209.

20. K. H. D. Haley, *William of Orange and the English Opposition 1672–4* (Oxford, 1953), *passim*; J. R. Jones, 'French Intervention in English and Dutch Politics, 1677–88', in J. Black (ed.), *Knights Errant and True Englishmen: British Foreign Policy, 1660–1800* (Edinburgh, 1989) 1–23; Jones, 'William and the English', in D. Proctor and C. Wilson (eds), *1688: The Seaborne Alliance and Diplomatic Revolution* (Greenwich, 1989), pp. 13–30; Miller, *Charles II*, p. 233.

21. J. Childs, *The Army of Charles II* (London, 1976), pp. 7–10; B. Capp, *Cromwell's Navy: The Fleet and the English Revolution 1648–60* (Oxford, 1989), pp. 1–11 and *passim*; J. Glete, *Navies and Nations: Warships, Navies and State Building in Europe and America, 1500–1860* (Stockholm, 1993), pp. 179, 184, 186.

22. Childs, *Army of Charles II*, pp. 7–10; Capp, *Cromwell's Navy*, pp. 371–5; R. Hutton, *The Restoration: A Political and Religious History of England and Wales 1658–67* (Oxford, 1985), p. 139.

23. J. Childs, *The Army, James II and the Glorious Revolution* (Manchester, 1980), pp. 1–2.

24. L. G. Schwoerer, *'No Standing Armies!': The Anti-Army Ideology in Seventeenth Century England* (Baltimore, 1974), pp. 91, 93, 96–107; Childs, *Army of Charles II*, pp. 213–32.

25. Childs, *Army [and] James II*, pp. 119–37.

26. Ibid., *passim*; W. A. Speck, 'The Orangist Conspiracy against James II', *HJ*, XXX (1987) 453–62.

27. J. D. Davies, *Gentlemen and Tarpaulins: The Officers and Men of the Restoration Navy* (Oxford, 1991), pp. 9–15; Davies, '"A Lover of the Sea, and Skilful in Shipping": King Charles II and his Navy', *Royal Stuart Papers*, XLII (1992) *passim*; Davies, 'The Navy, Parliament and Political Crisis in the Reign of Charles II', *HJ*, XXXVI (1993) 271–88.

28. Glete, *Navies and Nations*, pp. 186–92.

29. Ibid., pp. 194–5; Davies, 'Parliament and Political Crisis', 273–4.

30. Davies, *Gentlemen and Tarpaulins, passim*.

31. S. Hornstein, *The Restoration Navy and English Foreign Trade 1674–88* (Aldershot, 1991), *passim*.

32. Glete, *Navies and Nations*, p. 175. Cf. B. Tunstall, *Naval Warfare in the Age of Sail: The Evolution of Fighting Tactics 1650–1815* (London, 1990), pp. 16–41.

33. R. Stradling, *Europe and the Decline of Spain* (London, 1990), pp. 165–6; Miller, *Charles II*, pp. 88–94, 112–16; Hutton, *Charles II*, pp. 157–60.

34. Hornstein, *Restoration Navy*, pp. 155–208.

35. P. Seaward, 'The House of Commons Committee of Trade and the Origins of the Second Anglo-Dutch War, 1664', *HJ*, XXX (1987) 437–52; Pincus, 'Popery, Trade and Universal Monarchy', 1–29; Miller, *Charles II*, pp. 116–18; Hutton, *Restoration*, pp. 214–19.

36. Ibid., pp. 222–3, 240; Haley, *Sir William Temple*, pp. 53–91.

37. Davies, 'Imperial Navy', pp. 19–25.

38. Black, *System of Ambition*, p. 126.

39. Ibid., pp. 126–8; Miller, *Charles II*, pp. 142–7; Hutton, *Charles II*, pp. 254–7; Haley, *Sir William Temple*, pp. 142–82.

40. BL, Add. MSS 65138, fos. 85–109; original copy and English translation of the Treaty of Dover; R. Hutton, 'The Making of the Secret Treaty of Dover', *HJ*, XXIX (1986) 297–318.

41. The interpretations of the treaty outlined in this paragraph are drawn from Hutton, 'Secret Treaty', *passim*, and *Charles II*, pp. 263–6, 270–4; Miller, *Charles II*, pp. 143–4, 158–68, 179–80.

42. BL, Add. MSS 65138, fos. 30–2: paper preceding Treaty of Dover.

43. Miller, *Charles II*, pp. 162–3, 179–80.

44. Davies, *Gentlemen and Tarpaulins*, pp. 171–5. For the invasion plan of 1673, see Miller, *Charles II*, pp. 194–6, 206–10.

45. The best account of the complex foreign policy of the mid-1670s is provided by Miller, *Charles II*, pp. 229–34, 236–40, 252–9, 266–73, 276–8.

46. Ibid., pp. 270–3; Hutton, *Charles II*, pp. 341–8; Davies, 'Imperial Navy', pp. 27–30.

47. Miller, *Charles II*, pp. 280–1; Hutton, *Charles II*, pp. 352–6.

48. Miller, *Charles II*, pp. 326, 361–5; Black, *System of Ambition*, p. 133.

49. G. H. Jones, *Charles Middleton: The Life and Times of a Restoration Politician* (Chicago, 1967), pp. 53–7.

50. Hornstein, *Restoration Navy*, pp. 179–208.

51. J. Miller, *James II: A Study in Kingship* (1978), pp. 143–5, 159–60, 190–1; J. Black, 'The Revolution and the Development of English Foreign Policy', in E. Cruickshanks (ed.), *By Force or By Default? The Revolution of 1688–9* (Edinburgh, 1989), pp. 138–50.

52. Miller, *James II*, pp. 133–4, 138–40, 159–60; Childs, *Army [and] James II*, pp. 122–31.

53. R. Hatton, 'Louis XIV and his Fellow Monarchs', in Hatton (ed.), *Louis XIV and Europe*, pp. 16–59; J. C. Rule, 'France Caught Between Two Balances: The Dilemma of 1688', in L. G. Schwoerer (ed.), *The Revolution of 1688–9* (Cambridge, 1992), pp. 35–51.

54. Black, 'Development of Foreign Policy', pp. 142–3.

55. For the idea of 1688 as a Dutch invasion and conquest, see J. I. Israel, 'The Dutch Role in the Glorious Revolution', in Israel (ed.), *The Anglo-Dutch Moment: Essays on the Glorious Revolution and its World Impact* (Cambridge, 1991), pp. 105–62; R. Beddard, 'The Unexpected Whig Revolution of 1688', in Beddard (ed.), *The Revolutions of 1688* (Oxford, 1991), pp. 11–18, 95–101.

56. J. Stoye, 'Europe and the Revolution of 1688', in Beddard, *Revolutions*, pp. 206–12; J. Black, 'British Foreign Policy and International Affairs during Sir William Trumbull's Career', *British Library Journal*, XIX (1993) 204–6.

57. Haley, *Sir William Temple*, pp. 30–1; cf. the various works of J. Black, cited above.

58. Pincus, 'Popery, Trade and Universal Monarchy', 1–29.

59. J. Brewer, *The Sinews of Power: War, Money and the English State 1688–1783* (London, 1989), *passim*.

Notes on Contributors

PETER BORSAY is a Senior Lecturer in the History Department at the University of Wales Lampeter. He is author of *The English Urban Renaissance: Culture and Society in the Provincial Town 1660–1770* (Oxford, 1989), editor of *The Eighteenth-century Town: A Reader in English Urban History* (London, 1990), and an associate editor of the journal *Urban History*. He is also a contributor of essays to several books and learned journals, and is currently working on a study of the image of Georgian Bath.

J. D. DAVIES teaches at Bedford Modern School and is a chief examiner for A-level History. He completed his D. Phil. on the seagoing personnel of the Restoration Navy at the University of Oxford in 1986, and a revised version of this was subsequently published as *Gentlemen and Tarpaulins: The Officers and Men of the Restoration Navy* (Oxford, 1991). He won the Julian Corbett Essay Prize for Naval History (1986), and has written widely on strategic, political and administrative aspects of seventeenth-century naval history, including contributions to the centenary volume of the Navy Records Society, to S. Fisher, B. Greenhill and J. Youings (eds), *A New Maritime History of Devon* (London and Exeter, 1992–4) and to J. R. Hill (ed.), *Oxford Illustrated History of the Royal Navy* (Oxford, 1995). He is now working on a study of the Anglo-Dutch wars.

J. M. ELLIS is Senior Lecturer in History at the University of Nottingham. She studied at the University of Oxford and in 1975–77 held the Sir James Knott Fellowship at the University of Newcastle. She subsequently taught at Leicester, Oxford and Loughborough Universities, before moving to Nottingham in 1988. She has published a number of books and articles on the economic and social development of the Newcastle coalfield 1660–1760 and is currently working on the urban history of this period.

LIONEL K. J. GLASSEY is a Senior Lecturer in the Department of Modern History at the University of Glasgow. He studied at Lincoln College, Oxford, graduating in 1966. He has published *Politics and the Appointment of Justices of the Peace, 1675–1720* (Oxford, 1979) and several articles. He is currently engaged on a new edition of Gilbert Burnet's *History of His Own Time*.

MARK GOLDIE is a Lecturer in History at the University of Cambridge, and Vice-Master of Churchill College. He was formerly an undergraduate at Sussex University and a Research Fellow at Gonville and Caius College, Cambridge. He has published many articles on politics, religion and ideas in Britain in the seventeenth and eighteenth centuries. He is co-editor with Paul Seaward and Tim Harris of *The Politics of Religion in Restoration England* (Oxford, 1990), and with J. H. Burns of *The Cambridge History of Political Thought, 1450–1700* (Cambridge, 1991); and editor of *John Locke: Two Treatises of Government* (London, 1993) and *John Locke: Political Essays* (Cambridge, 1997).

TIM HARRIS, formerly a Fellow of Emmanuel College, Cambridge, is now Professor of History at Brown University, Providence, R. I. His publications include *London Crowds in the Reign of Charles II* (Cambridge, 1987), *Politics under the Later Stuarts* (London, 1993), *Popular Culture in England, c. 1500–1850* (London, 1995), and (co-edited with Paul Seaward and Mark Goldie) *The Politics of Religion in Restoration England* (Oxford, 1990). He is currently working on a history of politics, power and public opinion in England, Scotland and Ireland, 1660–1707, as well as editing a collection of essays on politics out-of-doors in early modern England, *c.* 1500–1850. He is also involved in a team project to edit the Roger Morrice 'Ent'ring Books' for publication by the Parliamentary History Records Series.

RONALD HUTTON is Professor of History at the University of Bristol. He is the author of seven books upon different aspects of British and Irish history, spanning topics from the dawn of recorded time to the present day. These include *The Restoration: A Political History of England and Wales, 1658–1667* (Oxford, 1985) and *Charles II: King of England, Scotland and Ireland* (Oxford, 1989).

JAMES M. ROSENHEIM is Associate Professor of History, Texas A & M University. He completed a doctoral thesis on the gentry of Restoration Norfolk at Princeton University in 1981, and is the author of *The Townshends of Raynham* (Middletown, Connecticut, 1989) and of several essays on Restoration political culture. He has edited *The Justice's Notebook of Robert Doughty, 1662–1665* (Norfolk Record Society, liv, 1991), and was co-editor with A. L. Beier and D. N. Cannadine of *The First Modern Society: Essays in English History in Honour of Lawrence Stone* (Cambridge, 1989). He is currently engaged on a study of landed society, 1650–1750.

JOHN SPURR was educated at St Edmund Hall, Oxford, and now teaches history at University of Wales Swansea. He is the author of *The Restoration Church of England, 1646–1689* (New Haven, 1991) and *English Puritanism 1603–1689* (forthcoming). At present, he is completing a study of English politics in the 1670s and a book on the use of oaths in early modern England.

Index

Bergen, 224
Berkeley, George, Bishop of
Cloyne, 210
Berkeley, John, 1st Lord Berkeley
of Stratton, 82
Birmingham, 174, 176, 279–80
n.19
Black, Jeremy, 225
Blake, Robert, 221
Blarney, 86
Bodin, Jean, 20
Bogart, Leo, 146
Bohun, Edmund, 19
Bombay, 222
Booth, Henry, 2nd Lord Delamer,
1st Earl of Warrington, 66, 68
Borsay, Peter, 7, 9
Bosher, J. F., 215
Bothwell Bridge, battle of, 37, 79
Boyle, Robert, 10
Boyle, Roger, Lord Broghill, 1st
Earl of Orrery, 16, 81–3
Bradshaigh, Sir Roger, 102
Brady, Robert, 24, 32
Brandenburg, Elector of, see
Frederick William
Breda, Declaration of (1660), 2,
41, 138
Breda, Treaty of (1667), 224
Brennans, the (Irish bandits),
86–7
Brent, Robert, 101
Bridgeman, Sir Orlando, 216
Bridges, Captain, 54
Bridgnorth, 179
Brington, 154
Bristol, 92–3, 102, 109, 113, 133,
137, 174, 175, 177, 186, 196,
197, 206
Bristol, Earl of, see Digby
Broghill, Lord, see Boyle
Brooke, Lord, see Greville
Browne, John, 15
Bruadair, Dáibhidh ó, 86
Bruce, Alexander, 2nd Earl of
Kincardine, 77
Bruges, 214
Brutus, 14

Buchanan, George, 13, 19, 29
Buckingham, Dukes of, see Villiers
Buda, 133
building, 180–3, 188–90, 200–1,
284 n.65
Bull, George, 110
Bunyan, John, 93, 113
Burgoyne, Lady Anne, 155
Burnet, Alexander, Archbishop of
Glasgow, 78, 88
Burnet, Gilbert, Bishop of
Salisbury, 60, 62
Butler, James, 12th Earl of
Ormond, 1st Marquis, 1st
Duke of Ormonde, 37, 47, 53,
54, 55, 63, 64, 67–8, 81–4,
86–7, 145, 216
Butler, Samuel, 116
Butler, Thomas, 1st Earl of Ossory,
61

Cabal, the, 53, 141
Cabinet, 55–6, 216
Cade, Jack, 31
Calgacus the Pict, 86
Calvin, Jean, 34
Calvinism, 12, 29, 34, 109–10
Cambridge, University of, 98, 102,
107, 117; St John's College, 19
Cameron, clan, 88
Cameronians, 88
Campbell, Archibald, 9th Earl of
Argyll, 77, 88; Rebellion of
(1685), 37, 49, 79–80, 87
Candia (Crete), 216
Canterbury, 136, 195
Capel, Arthur, 1st Earl of Essex,
55, 63–4, 82–3
Care, Henry, 143
Caribbean, 211
Carlisle, Earl of, see Howard
Carlos II, King of Spain, 212
Carolina, 33, 192
Carr, Sir Robert, 54
Cary, John, 206
Castlemaine, Lady, see Palmer
Catherine of Braganza, Queen, 7,
44, 143, 222

Marlborough, Duke of, *see*
Churchill
Marvell, Andrew, 10, 59, 95, 98,
99, 115–16
Mary of Modena, Duchess of York
and Queen, 6, 231
Mary I (Stuart), Queen of
Scotland, 8
Mary I (Tudor), Queen of
England, 8, 129, 131
Mary II (Stuart), Queen of
England and Scotland,
Princess of Orange before
1689, 97, 228, 231
Mazarin, Cardinal, 212
Mediterranean, 192, 195, 212, 220,
221, 222, 228, 229
Medway, River, 44, 220, 224
Melfort, Earl of, *see* Drummond
Meres, Sir Thomas, 60
Mhor, Iain, 86
mickelgemote, 32
Middleton, Charles, 2nd Earl of
Middleton, 229
Middleton, John, 1st Earl of
Middleton, 76–8
'middling sort', 180, 189, 205
migration, 175, 179
Mildmay, Henry, 4
militia, *see* local government
Miller, John, 226–7
Milton, John, 13, 29
Monck, Christopher, 2nd Duke of
Albemarle, 145
Monck, George, 1st Duke of
Albemarle, 38, 41, 223, 224
Monmouth, Duke of, *see* Scott
Mons, 61
Monson, Sir John, 14–15
Montagu, Ralph, 1st Duke of
Montagu, 229
Monteage, Stephen, 168
Montrose, Marquis of, *see* Graham
Moore, Sir John, Lord Mayor of
London, 144
Moray, Earl of, *see* Stewart
Morley, George, Bishop of
Winchester, 95, 105

Mornay, Philippe du, 29
Morocco, 218, 222
Morrice, Roger, 120
Morris, John, 166
Morton, Thomas, Bishop of
Durham, 115
Mountagu, Edward, 1st Earl of
Sandwich, 227
Mountrath, Earl of, *see* Coote
Muggletonians, 91
Mullett, Michael, 184
Münster, Prince-Bishop of, *see*
Galen
Murray, John, 2nd Earl, 1st
Marquis of Atholl, 77
Murray, Sir Robert, 77
Musgrave, Sir Christopher, 68

Nalson, John, 19, 140–1
Nangle, Edward, 37
Nantwich, 132
Naples, 214
Naseby, battle of, 1
navy, 5–6, 44, 50, 220–1, 231, 232;
see also wars
Nero, Emperor, 26
Netherlands, *see* Spanish
Netherlands; United
Provinces
Neville, Henry, 34
Newcastle, Duke of, *see* Cavendish
Newcastle under Lyme, 132
Newcastle upon Tyne, 102;
Propositions of (1646–7), 17
New Forest, 157
New Model Army, 1, 38, 41–3, 140,
219; *see also* army
Newton, Sir Isaac, 10
Nicoll, John, 36
Nijmegen, Treaty of, 46, 229
Nonconformity, *see* Dissent
Norfolk, 38, 66, 161, 168
Norfolk, Duke of, *see* Howard
North, Dudley, 67
North, Francis, 1st Lord Guilford,
139
North, Roger, 17, 49, 51, 62
Northampton, 154, 181

religion, 96–7
Scotland, 6, 9
Williamson, Sir Joseph, 54, 61
Wiltshire, 103, 133, 197
Wincanton (Somerset), 6
Winchester, 177; Palace, 48, 52
Windsor, 143, 273 n.82
Wiseman, Sir Richard, 61
witchcraft, 10, 89, 186
witenagemote, 32, 33
Witt, Johan de, 213, 227
Wodrow, Robert, 89
Wolseley, Sir Charles, 123
Wolsey, Cardinal Thomas, 52
Wood, Anthony, 115–16
Woodbridge, 133
Worcester, 154

Wren, Sir Christopher, 48
Wrigley, E. A., 178
Wriothesley, Thomas, 4th Earl of
        Southampton, 52
Wycherley, William (author of
        The Country Wife), 209

Yarmouth, *see* Great Yarmouth
Yarmouth, Viscount, Earl of, *see*
        Paston
Yelverton, Sir Henry, 115
York, 5–6, 68
York, Duchesses of, *see* Hyde,
        Anne; Mary of Modena
York, Duke of, *see* James VII & II
Yorkshire, 10–11, 37, 92, 93,
        197